BEYOND HIGH SCHOOL
Preparing Adolescents for Tomorrow's Challenges

Second Edition

Frank R. Rusch
Pennsylvania State University

Upper Saddle River, New Jersey
Columbus, Ohio

Library of Congress Cataloging-in-Publication Data

Beyond high school : preparing adolescents for tomorrow's challenges / [edited by] Frank R. Rusch. — 2nd ed.
  p. cm.
  Includes bibliographical references and index.
  ISBN-13: 978-0-13-238469-8
  ISBN-10: 0-13-238469-8
  1. Youth with disabilities—Education (Secondary)—United States. 2. Youth with disabilities—Vocational education—United States. 3. People with disabilities—Vocational guidance—United States. 4. School-to-work transition—United States. 5. Educational change—United States. I. Rusch, Frank R.
  LC4031.B45 2008
  371.9'0473—dc22

2007016621

Vice President and Executive Publisher: Jeffery W. Johnston
Executive Editor: Ann Castel Davis
Editorial Assistant: Penny Burleson
Senior Production Editor: Sheryl Glicker Langner
Production Coordination: Rebecca K. Giusti, GGS Book Services
Design Coordinator: Diane C. Lorenzo
Cover Designer: Kristina Holmes
Cover Image: Super Stock
Production Manager: Laura Messerly
Director of Marketing: David Gesell
Marketing Manager: Autumn Purdy
Marketing Coordinator: Brian Mounts

This book was set in Palatino by GGS Book Services. It was printed and bound by R.R. Donnelley & Sons Company. The cover was printed by R.R. Donnelley & Sons Company.

Copyright © 2008 by Pearson Education, Inc., Upper Saddle River, New Jersey 07458. Pearson Prentice Hall. All rights reserved. Printed in the United States of America. This publication is protected by Copyright and permission should be obtained from the publisher prior to any prohibited reproduction, storage in a retrieval system, or transmission in any form or by any means, electronic, mechanical, photocopying, recording, or likewise. For information regarding permission(s), write to: Rights and Permissions Department.

Pearson Prentice Hall™ is a trademark of Pearson Education, Inc.
Pearson® is a registered trademark of Pearson plc
Prentice Hall® is a registered trademark of Pearson Education, Inc.
Merrill® is a registered trademark of Pearson Education, Inc.

Pearson Education Ltd.
Pearson Education Singapore Pte. Ltd.
Pearson Education Canada, Ltd.
Pearson Education—Japan

Pearson Education Australia Pty. Limited
Pearson Education North Asia Ltd.
Pearson Educatión de Mexico, S.A. de C.V.
Pearson Education Malaysia Pte. Ltd

10 9 8 7 6 5 4 3 2 1
ISBN-10: 0-13-238469-8
ISBN-13: 978-0-13-238469-8

Teacher Preparation Classroom

See a demo at
www.prenhall.com/teacherprep/demo

Your Class. Their Careers. Our Future. Will your students be prepared?

We invite you to explore our new, innovative and engaging website and all that it has to offer you, your course, and tomorrow's educators! Preview this site today at www.prenhall.com/teacherprep/demo. Just click on "go" on the login page to begin your exploration.

Organized around the major courses pre-service teachers take, the Teacher Preparation site provides media, student/teacher artifacts, strategies, research articles, and other resources to equip your students with the quality tools needed to excel in their courses and prepare them for their first classroom.

This ultimate online education resource will provide you and your students access to:

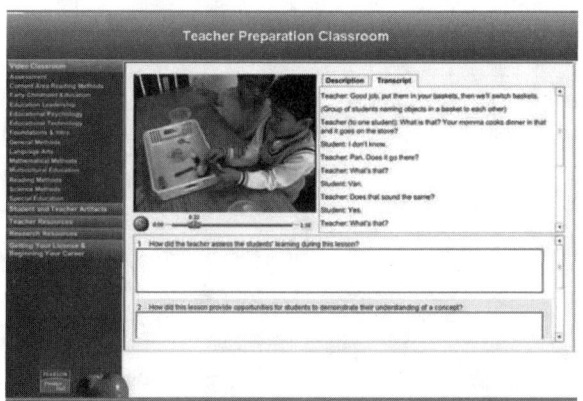

Online Video Library. More than 250 video clips—each tied to a course topic and framed by learning goals and Praxis-type questions—capture real teachers and students working in real classrooms.

Student and Teacher Artifacts. More than 200 student and teacher classroom artifacts—each tied to a course topic and framed by learning goals and application questions—provide a wealth of materials and experiences to help your students observe children's developmental learning.

Lesson Plan Builder. Step-by-step guidelines and lesson plan examples support students as they learn to build high-quality lesson plans.

Articles and Readings. Over 500 articles from ASCD's renowned journal *Educational Leadership* are available. The site also includes Research Navigator, a searchable database of additional educational journals.

Strategies and Lessons. Over 500 research-supported instructional strategies appropriate for a wide range of grade levels and content areas.

Licensure and Career Tools. Resources devoted to helping your students pass their licensure exam; learn standards, law, and public policies; plan a teaching portfolio; and succeed in their first year of teaching.

How to ORDER *Teacher Prep* for you and your students:

For students to receive a *Teacher Prep* Access Code with this text, instructors **must** provide a special value pack ISBN number on their textbook order form. To receive this special ISBN, please email Merrill.marketing@pearsoned.com and provide the following information:
- Name and Affiliation
- Author/Title/Edition of Merrill text

Upon ordering *Teacher Prep* for their students, instructors will be given a lifetime *Teacher Prep* Access Code.

This book is dedicated to
Silas, Eddie, Mark, Craig, Sharon, Molly, and
the many hundreds of people with disabilities
whom I have had the privilege to meet and
work with over the years.

ABOUT THE AUTHOR

Over the past 30 years, Professor Frank R. Rusch has studied self-instructional strategies, using coworkers as change agents, and reforming secondary education. He has also served as associate editor for numerous journals and has published more than 200 books, chapters, and articles. Professor Rusch is one of the most cited social scientists in the country, and was identified as the most productive educational researcher in the field of mental retardation worldwide (Research Developmental Disabilities, 2000). His texts, including *Beyond High School*, *Competitive Employment*, *Supported Employment*, *Transition from School to Work*, and *Rethinking Disability*, are leading-edge publications in the field today.

Professor Rusch joined the Pennsylvania State University faculty in 2004. He is currently teaching advanced seminars in single-subject research methods, grant writing, adolescent development, and general topics related to mental retardation and special education.

FOREWORD

In his masterful introduction to this timely and critically important book, Frank Rusch writes: "Most students with disabilities know little about career options, their own talents, what it is really like to work, and what preparation is needed for the kinds of jobs or further education that will lead to competitive employment and a career path. High schools are often not organized or staffed to manage the transition process for students with or without disabilities; high school counselors are often overwhelmed, with an average of over 300 students per full-time staff member." What is especially striking about this passage—aside, of course, from the staggering workload of high school counselors—is the way it portrays students with disabilities as facing the unknown, and doing so unknowingly. Often, I think, the parents of those students are in slightly more informed but potentially more psychologically painful positions, facing the unknown consciously, apprehensively. Oddly enough, some of us face that unknown apprehensively even when we talk about it. Because we don't want to know what we know: that, as Rusch writes, "students with disabilities are not being prepared like their peers without a disability for adult roles."

My second child, Jamie, has Down syndrome. He's been included in regular classrooms all his life, and by the time this book appears he will be in high school. Right now he's 15, and he's in eighth grade. Last year, in seventh grade, my wife and I insisted that he be included in the regular classrooms for science and French class. He'd always been good in math, but was having trouble with area and perimeter and (we agreed) wouldn't have much use for or understanding of the equations for the area of irregularly shaped objects. In science and French he didn't master as much material as the other kids did, although he learned a great deal about cells and species and French verbs, and so far he's retained most of what he learned. (I will want to see the ten-year followup on how many of his classmates remember mitochondria and vacuoles and cell walls.) He now has an adapted curriculum, and we anticipate that his high school experience will look like more of the same—with some surprises along the way, like the surprise we got this year when we found out how much Jamie loves learning about the major composers of the West. "Stravinsky," he will say out of nowhere, "he was another great composer. Like Debussy."

But in another five years, all Jamie's knowledge of science and music and math (and French) may not be enough for him. Because in another five years, he'll be transitioning out of school altogether, and then . . . who knows?

When Jamie was ten, I first broached the subject of what his life might be like when he grew up to be a big man. I told him that he would have a number of choices when he got older: He could live with us; he could live with us but in a separate residence where he'd be more independent; he could live in a group home with other adults with disabilities; he could live all by himself or with a wife or girlfriend. (I was not ranking these in any order of plausibility or desirability.) Jamie replied that what he really wanted, when he grew up, would be to live in "an apartment with a pool." What he meant, as I well understood, was an apartment *building* with a pool—like a hotel. It sounded fine to me, in theory; I wouldn't mind an apartment with a pool myself. But later that year, Jamie learned an important lesson about independent living, when he discovered to his shock that when you transfer pizza from the refrigerator to the microwave without removing the tinfoil, you get a lot of smoke and fire and fire alarms beeping and frantic dogs barking. I don't know whether that event was decisive for Jamie, but I do know that the next time I spoke with him about his future living arrangements, a year or two later, he had decided against the apartment with a pool. "I want to live with *you*," he said, in an almost wounded tone that seemed to suggest that any other option would be tantamount to our throwing him out of the house. "Jamie," I replied, as I tucked him into bed for the night, "you will always have a place in our house. You can always live with us. But if someday you want to be more independent and have some privacy, you can have your own place too." He nodded contently and soon drifted off to sleep.

When Jamie became a teenager, he became very self-conscious about being a teenager. And very proud. And he stopped calling me "Daddy" and began calling me "Michael."

One weekend, as we came out of the gym where he and I used to swim on the weekends (before we dropped the gym in favor of the Penn State Natatorium, where Jamie learned to go off the diving board), Jamie decided to take his own gym pass off the front counter. "You want to hold onto that?" I asked. "Yes," he said. "It's *my* card." "Cool," I replied, "but it might be easier if you put it in my wallet, so it won't get lost." Jamie likes putting things in his pockets; he likes getting a few bucks or a bunch of quarters for pinball, for example, but he usually forgets about them before too long, and our efforts to get him to treat money more carefully have not yet had any measurable effect. So he agreed, slipping his card into my wallet—and then taking my wallet from me. "Well, sweetie," I said, "I'll hold your card *for* you. That's the idea."

"I can have a wallet," Jamie replied. "I'm a teenager. I'm allowed."

I snapped to attention. "Yes, you are allowed," I said. "And that sounds like a good idea, too. But I need my wallet, you know. See, it has my credit cards."

"I *love* credit cards," Jamie shot back. "Hey," he added, finding his school ID tucked behind my AAA card, "that's my card too. Gimme my cards, Michael."

Janet bought Jamie a wallet that weekend, and he carried it to school the next day. In fact, he walked to the bus stop with his hand on his wallet pocket all the way. And he still owns that wallet today, even if he doesn't always pay attention to the things he puts in his pockets.

Foreword

So Jamie doesn't understand everything he needs to understand about independent living—although he *has* learned to use the microwave judiciously. And Jamie doesn't understand everything he needs to understand about money—although I *have* begun to teach him how much things cost, and he is capable of doing the math.

But then, Janet and I don't understand everything *we* need to understand, either. In this, we suspect that we are not alone. The American educational system is bewildering regardless of whether your child has a disability: National laws and standards are passed, but their implementation varies from state to state, and school funding varies from district to district. In one county, no child is left behind; in an adjacent county, children are not merely left behind but jettisoned. And in every county, the children most likely to be left behind—or jettisoned—are children with disabilities.

Yet this is the era of the Individuals with Disabilities Education Act; better still, this is the era in which the IDEA is, in many districts, interpreted so that the "least restrictive environment" is understood to be the "regular" classroom. We have, in other words, established—fitfully, and not completely—a society in which the classroom that integrates "normal" children with "disabled" children is *itself* understood to be "normal," and in which "inclusive education" is actually *the default position* against which advocates of separate classrooms for children with disabilities have to argue. It's an amazing thing in the history of public education, and Janet and I (and Jamie) are thankful for it every single day. But with all our sense of good fortune and our thankfulness, have we gotten complacent over the past 10 years of Jamie's life? Years ago, I would write and speak in defense of inclusive education, arguing that we don't know what "normal" is unless we try inclusion first, and that we need to be able to imagine an inclusive society in elementary and secondary school if we're going to be able to imagine it for adults. The thinking behind the latter claim, of course, is that Jamie's peers have grown up with the expectation that they will see people with disabilities in "normal" and "regular" settings and will not be surprised or dismayed to find people with disabilities in their workplaces when they are adults. But there's a profound disjunction between the first and the second halves of this claim, because, as many of the contributors to this volume note, when a child turns 21 and runs out of IEPs—or, one might say, refusing to avoid the bad pun, runs out of IDEA—he or she simply falls off a legal cliff, and the ADA does not provide a safety net. Some students, indeed, drop out—and off that cliff—long before they turn 21.

Now that Jamie is 15, Janet and I have begun to worry in earnest. Are we living in the right district for transition services? Are we living in the right state? Are we living in the right *country*? Have we, after all, been lulled into complacency by our school district's array of disability services and accommodations, lulled into thinking that there will always be something there for Jamie, some program, some initiative, some social service? Or have we lulled *ourselves* somehow, not wanting to know how little we know about what we need to know?

Foreword

Beyond High School tells me a great deal about what we as parents, and what we as a society, need to know. In that respect, it was not an easy read. But it was a necessary one.

Around the time teenager Jamie got his first wallet, he and I had one of our first conversations about what kind of job he might like to have when he gets older. We were watching TV, and I decided to tell him how good he'd been with the younger kids of some colleagues who'd been to our house recently. "You really are good with little kids," I said. "You're very gentle with them, and you play very carefully, and you always try to help them. You know, you might think about doing that when you're a big man and you have a job. You might be a good helper someplace where they work with little kids."

"*Michael*," he said with some exasperation, "I'm going to be a Marine."

My blood froze. "Excuse me? Did you say a Marine?"

"Uh-huh."

"Where did that come from? You mean a Marine like a soldier?"

"No," he said, waving me off, "a marine *biologist*." And he went right back to watching *Animal Planet*. Whew! I thought. You always have to wait for the other shoe.

Though marine biology is a tall order for someone with Down syndrome (and many people without), Jamie does know the differences between seals and sea lions, and he knows more about sharks than most of his fellow humans. Plenty of people know the differences among great white sharks and tiger sharks and hammerhead sharks; Jamie also knows about basking sharks and nurse sharks and Port Jackson sharks. He knows which marine animals are mammals and which are fish, and why; he knows that sharks are ancient animals, invertebrates, cartilaginous fish; and despite his speech delays, he says "cartilaginous fish" pretty clearly.

But in seventh grade, as Jamie tried to get a grip on biology, he began to realize how difficult the "biologist" part of "marine biologist" could be. At one point, he simply gave up and said it was *too hard*. I didn't take that at face value right away—after all, four years earlier I'd learned he could do multiplication in his head when I'd asked him *what's seven times three* and he'd replied *too hard! Twenty-one*. But I did tell him that being a marine biologist meant knowing all about everything from individual cells to organic systems: Jamie knows he has a muscular and a skeletal and a nervous and a cardiovascular system, and I reminded him that he would have to know all about those things in marine animals as well. "Except sharks," he said. "They have *cartilage*, Michael, not bones."

"That's right, Jamie," I replied. "But do you remember when you were talking about being a marine biologist, and I was talking about you working with kids?"

"Uh-huh."

"Well, this is what I was talking about, you see. It's hard to learn biology and be a marine biologist. It's not enough just to love animals and know a lot about marine life. You have to go to high school and then college and then graduate school too, and you might find that all the science is too hard for you."

Jamie nodded thoughtfully. I wondered if my words were crushing his dreams.

"So it might be a good idea," I added, "for us to think about you being a marine biologist's *helper*. Does that sound OK?"

"OK," Jamie chirped, and we got back to his homework.

Janet and I have begun to talk about what all this means. If we live in a rural area when Jamie turns 21, then maybe we can help him find work on a local farm; if we live in a city, then maybe we can help him find work at an aquarium or a zoo or a marine science facility. These are our (and his) first choices, hashed out over many discussions in which we've explained to Jamie why there are no aquariums or zoos or marine science facilities in rural areas. But every once in a while, I try to remind him of second and third choices, just in case.

One day we were grocery shopping at the local Giant when Jamie had to use the bathroom. The bathroom is located in the back of the store, and when we opened the swinging doors behind the deli section, Jamie saw piles of boxes everywhere—paper towels, canned goods, crackers, and snacks. "Wow," he exclaimed. "Yeah, it's pretty cool," I said. "When the trucks come to the store, they're filled with boxes, and this is where the boxes go before people open them up and put everything on the shelves." I noted Jamie's fascination and informed him that unloading trucks and shelving at Giant isn't a bad job, as jobs go. Ten minutes later, as we checked out, what did we see but an adult man with disabilities working as a bagger? "Hey, Jamie," the man called out. "Hi, Jason!" Jamie shot back. "You know this man?" I asked. "Yeah, from basketball," Jamie replied. They greeted each other again as we loaded our bags into our cart, and on the way out to the car I took the opportunity to mention the obvious yet again. "You see what I mean, Jamie? A man with a disability could work at Giant and bag the groceries, like Jason. Or you could work with the boxes in the back, if you like."

"*Michael*," Jamie said—and with his mildly chiding tone, that was all he needed to say. *We've had this conversation before, remember?*

"I know, I know," I singsonged. "Our first choice is that we find an aquarium or a zoo someplace."

"Right, exactly," Jamie said, strapping on his headphones and turning on his iPod.

He still wants to live with us when he gets older. "You could always live with other people too," I keep saying, "and have a little more privacy." To which his most recent reply was simply, "Michael! That's *impossible*!"—uttered, I noted, in precisely the same incredulous tone with which he batted away my question about whether he ever dreams about flying.

Now, I know these conversations don't amount to actual plans. They're not even adequate substitutes *for* actual plans. As Wendy Parent, Denise Gossage, and

Molly Jones write in "Working With Parents" (Chapter 5), "even with this knowledge of what leads to positive post-school outcomes, transition planning is often less than effective, resulting in students exiting school only to sit home, attend sheltered work and day programs, live with families or more restricted settings, be unemployed, and have their name added to long waiting lists." When I pointed out to Jamie that in a few years he would be done with school, his first reaction was "yay!" When I asked him what he would do all day, he said, "play *Harry Potter*." This, I think, is a transition plan that is less than effective.

Beyond High School speaks to families like mine. It speaks also to overworked high school counselors, to transition team members, to prospective employers, to job coaches, and, most important, to students with disabilities themselves. To all of us—to those of us who oversee transition from high school to the workplace as part of our jobs, and to those of us who hope for successful transitions from high school to the workplace for our adolescent children—*Beyond High School* offers research, resources, exhortations, and advice. And it offers a principle that should guide any child's education and any nation's educational policy: "Every student," writes Rusch, "is entitled to the belief that his or her education will result in personally meaningful outcomes." Surely everyone who reads *Beyond High School* will be persuaded to share that belief; and perhaps someday, when we all share that belief, it will have become something more than a belief. It will have become something that helps us all face the unknown world beyond high school: a principle that every student is entitled to an education that will result in personally meaningful outcomes, backed by policies and practices that change even my Jamie's—and my—sense of what is possible and impossible.

Michael Bérubé
Paterno Family Chair in Literature
Department of English
Pennsylvania State University

PREFACE

In 1975 I remember asking Professor Norris G. Haring where I could find material on secondary special education as I was preparing for my "quals" at the University of Washington. I was surprised when he answered that I would not find anything of "real use." Norrie went on to say that secondary-level special education students had not yet received the attention that children had received. He also made the comment that if someone would focus on this area of study, he or she would make a huge contribution in a very short period of time.

Norrie was right. Indeed, an entire field of study has emerged over the past 25 years. Many of the authors of this text were at the forefront of defining transition services and developing the field of study now referred to as secondary special education and transition services.

This second edition of *Beyond High School* addresses the field of transition services and the complexity of providing secondary special education services today. The complexities involved have been largely underestimated and, as you will learn by reading Chapter 1, although a lot has changed, the outcomes of our transition services have effected very little change in the lives of most students with disabilities leaving high school. Youth with disabilities remain under- and unemployed, socially isolated, and dependent on their families.

Thus, despite the best intentions, our collective efforts have not resulted in ensuring that youth realize their ambitions. To do so would involve reorganizing our high school resources to form new partnerships and expectations that extend our collective understanding of how to help adolescents adjust to adult roles. Whether this is possible is still not clear—the jury is still out. This text is about changing our conceptions about how to prepare students for adult roles. The resources are available to accomplish socially responsible goals—that is, increasing the chance that exiting students with disabilities will assume responsible and desired positions in their communities.

ORGANIZATION OF THIS BOOK

Three interrelated transition services have been shown to have a positive impact on promoting socially valued change: (a) planning and preparation, (b) placement, and (c) support. The first two services, planning and preparation, have been the most studied "best practices" over the past decade (Kohler, 1996; Kohler & Hood, 2000), and both topics have widespread appeal across disciplines.

Planning per se has probably enjoyed the most attention and growth as entire curricula have emerged focusing on teaching students to be self-determined while participating in interdisciplinary planning designed to identify their interests and preferences (Halpern, Herr, Doren, & Wolf, 1997; Martin & Marshall, 1995; Wehmeyer, 1997). Preparation has also been the topic of considerable attention, as reflected in numerous curricula in special education (Gajar, Goodman, & McAfee, 1993; Sitlington & Clark, 2006); vocational education (Phelps & Lutz, 1977); vocational rehabilitation (Szymanski & Parker, 2003); and career education (Brolin, 1995; Clark, 1979; Clark & Kolstoe, 1990).

However, high schools have not focused on the third service, placement of students with a disability after completing their education; nor have high schools typically collaborated with post–high school adult-oriented services in delivering post–high school support services, the fourth major topic of this book. Traditionally, high schools have not been thought of as agencies that assume a postsecondary curricular interest in departing students, leaving the responsibility for post–high school adjustment up to either the departing young adult and/or his or her parents, guardians, and friends.

Beyond High School has been reorganized to address placement and support in addition to planning and preparation. Chapter 10 introduces procedures for placing students in jobs in the community and the steps necessary to redesign the job and/or job site. Chapters 11 and 12 present new ways to think about supporting students in their transition from school to adult life, including using natural supports.

The final two chapters discuss procedures to consider when addressing students who drop out of school and how to evaluate a program's effectiveness in relation to its outcomes. We still have large numbers of students dropping out of school well in advance of completing their high school education. If we were to include in the totals students who drop out beginning at age 14, we would find an alarming statistic: Over one third of students with disabilities depart high school before they have learned how to cope with the world as adults.

For the past 20 years we have received conflicting information about the effectiveness of transition services. On one hand, model programs have been effective in their efforts to design and deliver transition-focused IEPs. On the other hand, the number of students who prematurely exit high school who enter employment has not changed. Chapter 14 provides guidelines for measuring program effectiveness. As we begin to associate effective practice with desired outcomes, we hope that high schools will become more effective in their delivery of an education that is relevant and that can boast of outcomes that help launch future generations of young adults with disabilities toward a fulfilling life in the community.

DEFINITION OF TRANSITION

The Individuals with Disabilities Education Improvement Act of 2004 (P.L. 108-446) represents the latest amendments to IDEA and includes language related to transition services. The federal definition of *transition service* is

> a coordinated set of activities for a child with a disability that:
>
> (A) is designed to be within a results-oriented process, that is focused on improving the academic and functional achievement of the child with a disability to facilitate the child's movement from school to post-school activities, including post-secondary education, vocational education, integrated employment (including supported employment), continuing and adult education, adult services, independent living, or community participation;
>
> (B) is based on the individual child's needs, taking into account the child's strengths, preferences, and interests; and
>
> (C) includes instruction, related services, community experiences, the development of employment and other post-school adult living objectives, and, when appropriate, acquisition of daily living skills and functional vocational evaluation. (Section 602)

The 2004 amendments to IDEA emphasize that transition planning should be a results-oriented process, focusing on both academic and functional skills of the students. Students are considered important participants in the transition planning process, and their individual needs and strengths, as well as their preferences and interests must be taken into account. As a general outcome, students have to be prepared for further education, and/or employment and independent living.

The 2004 amendments also emphasize adult roles students will eventually assume, and the scenes in community life where students should be prepared to participate and perform (i.e., holding a job, participating in postsecondary education, maintaining a home, becoming appropriately involved in the community, and experiencing satisfactory personal and social relationships). Not only is the students' participation in the transition planning process encouraged, but they are to assume maximal potential responsibility in the planning and execution of services. The age for required transition planning is 16 years, but IDEA does not preclude introducing transition services at an earlier age for students with a disability. The 2004 definition is useful. However, their definition does not emphasize the importance of our considering planning, preparation, and placement as distinct and ongoing activities that occur for all youth throughout their high school experience. Consequently, for the purposes of this text, *transition* refers to a period of time defined by planning, preparation, and placement activities that typically occur for all youth beginning at age 16, when students and their families are typically planning high school–related services (e.g., appropriate coursework and work experiences) that focus on preparation for additional, postsecondary education (e.g., 2- and 4-year college attendance, specialized vocational/trades training) and/or eventual employment in typical occupations that define communities (e.g., employment in the services industry and light industrial occupations). All planning should begin by 16 years of age, or earlier, and all students should be provided the training necessary for them to direct or coordinate their planning, make informed choices, and evaluate overall effectiveness. Finally, because the transition period may require that multiple agencies coordinate their transition services to help adolescents attain their career goals, high schools should be responsible for coordinating the placement of youth entering into postsecondary education and employment.

How to Use This Text

Beyond High School is intended to be used in upper-division undergraduate and graduate courses. The chapters contained in Part 1 are historical accounts of the emergence of secondary education and transition services in the United States. They provide a foundation for understanding why secondary special education is important. Part 2 includes three chapters on planning and assessment centered on the interests and preferences of students, including how to work with parents. Part 3 overviews how to build teams to facilitate transition services and how to collaborate with agencies apart from schools.

The final part contains seven chapters that provide more in-depth information about planning and preparation, placement, and support. Specifically, Chapter 8 outlines the assessment process and how to develop a student portfolio; Chapter 9 introduces alternative work experience approaches that, if adopted, will provide students with real-life opportunities to engage in work at several levels, from part- to full-time. Traditionally, schools have not accepted responsibility for the placement of students, nor have schools arranged for supports. Chapters 10, 11, and 12 represent a first attempt at outlining placement procedures and follow-up practices that can be used by schools to ensure that students enter into adult roles and participate in those roles for extended periods of time. The final two chapters outline procedures to prevent dropping out of high school and evaluating overall effectiveness, respectively.

References

Brolin, D. (1995). *The life centered career education curriculum.* Reston, VA: Council for Exceptional Children.

Clark, G. M. (1979). *Career education for the handicapped child in the elementary classroom.* Denver, CO: Love.

Clark, G. M., & Kolstoe, O. P. (1990). *Career development and transition education for adolescents with disabilities.* Boston: Allyn & Bacon.

Gajar, A., Goodman, L., & McAfee, J. (1993). *Secondary schools and beyond: Transition of individuals with mild disabilities.* Upper Saddle River, NJ: Merrill/Prentice Hall.

Halpern, A. S., Herr, C. M., Doren, B., & Wolf, N. K. (1997). *NEXT S.T.E.P.: Student transition and educational planning* (2nd ed.). Austin, TX: PRO-ED.

Individuals with Disabilities Education Improvement Act of 2004 (IDEA), Pub. L. No. 108-446, H.R. 1350, 108th Cong.

Kohler, P. D. (1996). *A taxonomy for transition programming: Linking research and practice.* Champaign: University of Illinois, Transition Research Institute.

Kohler, P. D., & Hood, L. K. (2000). *Improving student outcomes: Promising practices and programs for 1999–2000.* Champaign: University of Illinois, Transition Research Institute.

Martin, J. E., & Marshall, L. H. (1995). ChoiceMaker: A comprehensive self-determination transition program. *Intervention in School and Clinic, 30,* 147–156.

Phelps, L. A., & Lutz, R. J. (1977). *Career exploration and preparation for the special needs learner.* Boston: Allyn & Bacon.

Rusch, F. R. & Phelps, L. A. (1986). Principles that guide research related to the education of youth with disabilities. In R. E. Stake (Ed.) *Issues in Research on Evaluation in Transition* (p. i). Champaign, IL: Transition Research Institute at Illinois.

Sitlington, P. L., & Clark, G. M. (2006). *Transition education and services for students with disabilities* (4th ed.). Boston: Allyn & Bacon.

Szymanski, E. M., & Parker, R. M. (2003). *Work and disability: Issues and strategies in career development and job placement* (2nd ed.). Austin, TX: PRO-ED.

Wehmeyer, M. L. (1997). Self-directed learning and self-determination. In M. Agran (Ed.), *Student-directed learning: teaching self-determination skills* (pp. 28–59). Pacific Grove, CA: Brooks/Cole.

ACKNOWLEDGMENTS

First and foremost, I am most grateful to the authors of this second edition of *Beyond High School*, many of whom I have worked with for more than 20 years. Marty Agran, Jim Martin, Bruce Menchetti, Rob Cimera, John Trach, and Carolyn Hughes are former students of mine at the University of Illinois. They have contributed enormously to the field and all have been wonderful collaborators. Bob Stodden, Mike Wehmeyer, Wendy Parent, Jane Everson, Joan Guillory, David Hagner, Judy Elliott, and Martha Thurlow contributed to the first edition of *Beyond High School*. Their combined vision, then and now, continues to move this field forward. I would also like to thank the reviewers for this edition: Patricia S. Lynch, Texas A & M University; Sheila Saravanabhavan, Virginia State University; and Connie Weidenthal, George Washington University.

In addition, a number of people have influenced my work over the past 25 years; many were part of our early research related to competitive employment, supported employment, secondary special education, and transition services, and 15 years devoted to the Transition Research Institute at Illinois. They include Dianne Berkell, Bob Linn, Dennis Mithaug, Carl and Sue Suter, Ann and Rud Turnbull, Timm Vogelsberg, Bill Halloran, Paul Wehman, Gene Edgar, Pat

Gonzalez, Richard Horne, David Johnson, Margo Izzo, Tom Grayson, Del Harnisch, Laird Heal, Paula Kohler, Mike Ward, Mary Wagner, and David Test. My appreciation is extended to each and every one of them. They continue to influence my work as well as the work of so many others in the field.

The first edition of *Beyond High School* came out 10 years ago and the second edition should have been released about 5 years ago. But many obstacles and challenges fell on my path over this period, including the tragic death of one of my sisters and the passing of both my parents, after several years of personal care, nursing homes, and more. I also spent a few years in administration while associate director of the National Center for Super Computer Applications. These years were challenging in a different way. Administration has some distinct advantages, particularly if these are one's personal goals. I sought the opportunity to work with NCSA because I believed it would open new doors for the study of virtual reality and new learning opportunities for individuals with disabilities (similar to some of my earlier work with young adults with severe mental retardation who learned how to cross busy intersections). Very quickly I learned that administration is sometimes more about others' problems at work than it is about blazing new paths in uncharted territory. Gratefully, I was eventually able to resurface and find my way back to shore.

I also want to thank Cindy Reiter and Betty Taylor for their devotion to my work. Cindy helped me with the day-to-day work at the institute; Betty was always there to make sure that my work got done on time. Incredible women. I also want to thank Kirsten McBride for her editorial assistance on this text. She has really unraveled a lot of babble! And, special thanks are extended to one of my students at Penn State—Balázs Tarnai—who helped get this project out the door on time.

Finally, I want to thank my children, Alexia, Paul, and Emily, for their love and friendship, and support. My wife, Carol McCabe, deserves special recognition for slowing down long enough for me to catch her. I am fortunate to have met Carol.

F. R. R.

DISCOVER THE MERRILL RESOURCES FOR SPECIAL EDUCATION WEBSITE

Technology is a constantly growing and changing aspect of our field that is creating a need for new content and resources. To address this emerging need, Merrill Education has developed an online learning environment for students, teachers, and professors alike to complement our products—the *Merrill Resources for Special Education* Website. This content-rich website provides additional resources specific to this book's topic and will help you—professors, classrooms teachers, and students—augment your teaching, learning and professional development.

Our goal is to build on and enhance what our products already offer. For this reason, the content for our user-friendly website is organized by topic and provides teachers, professors, and students with a variety of meaningful resources all in one location. With this website, we bring together the best of what Merrill has to offer: text resources, video clips, web links, tutorials, and a wide variety of information on topics of interest to general and special educators alike. Rich content, applications, and competencies further enhance the learning process.

The *Merrill Resources for Special Education* Website includes:

- Video clips specific to each topic, with questions to help you evaluate the content and make crucial theory-to-practice connections.
- Thought-provoking critical analysis questions that students can answer and turn in for evaluation or that can serve as basis for class discussions and lectures.
- Access to wide variety of resources related to classroom strategies and methods, including lesson planning and classroom management.
- Information on all the most current relevant topics related to special and general education, including CEC and Praxis™ standards, IEPs, portfolios, and professional development.
- Extensive web resources and overviews on each topic addressed on the website.
- A search feature to help access specific information quickly.

To take advantage of these and other resources, please visit the *Merrill Resources for Special Education* Website at

http://www.prenhall.com/rusch

CONTRIBUTORS

Martin Agran, PhD, University of Wyoming

Michael Berube, PhD, Pennsylvania State University

Gaylan L. Brown, Vanderbilt University

Robert Cimera, PhD, Kent State University

Judy Elliott, PhD, Long Beach Unified School District

Jane M. Everson, PhD, University of South Carolina School of Medicine

Renee Feldman, University of Kansas

Denise Gossage, University of Kansas

Joan D. Guillory, MEd, Louisiana State University Health Sciences Center

David Hagner, University of New Hampshire

Katie E. Hildebrand, MS, Pennsylvania State University

Thomas Holub, PhD, Edgewood College

Carolyn Hughes, PhD, Vanderbilt University

Joy Ivester, MEd, University of South Carolina School of Medicine

Molly Jones, University of Kansas

Dianne Lounsbury, University of New Hampshire

James E. Martin, PhD, University of Oklahoma

Bruce M. Menchetti, PhD, Florida State University

David A. Noyes, PhD, San Diego State University

Wendy Parent, PhD, University of Kansas

Erin Reid, University of Minnesota

Kelly D. Roberts, University of Hawaii

Frank R. Rusch, PhD, Pennsylvania State University

Caren L. Sax, PhD, San Diego State University

Robert A. Stodden, PhD, University of Hawaii

Lorraine Sylvester, University of Oklahoma

Balázs Tarnai, Pennsylvania State University

Martha Thurlow, PhD, University of Minnesota

John S. Trach, PhD, University of Illinois at Urbana–Champaign

Patty Turner, University of Kansas

Chris Walker, University of Kansas

Barbara H. Washington, Vanderbilt University

Michael Wehmeyer, PhD, University of Kansas

Lee L. Woods, University of Oklahoma

BRIEF CONTENTS

Part I	*Introduction to Transition Services and Legislation 1*	
Chapter 1	Preparing Adolescents for Adult Roles 2	
Chapter 2	Transition Legislation and Policy: Past and Present 24	

Part II	*Student Involvement, Planning, and Assessment 55*	
Chapter 3	Person-Centered Career Planning 56	
Chapter 4	Building an Employment Vision: Culturally Attuning Vocational Interests, Skills, and Limits 78	
Chapter 5	Working with Parents: Using Strategies to Promote Planning and Preparation, Placement, and Support 110	

Part III	*Building Teams and Interagency Coordination 135*	
Chapter 6	Using Interagency and Interdisciplinary Teams to Enhance Transition Services 136	
Chapter 7	Interagency Collaboration: It Takes Communication to Support Transitions 160	

Part IV	*Assessment, Work Experience Opportunities, Job Placement, and Student Support 177*	
Chapter 8	Transition Assessment: Emerging Guidelines and Promising Practices 178	

Chapter 9   Work-Based Learning: Developing Work Experience Opportunities for Transitioning Students   200
Chapter 10   Job Placement and Job Redesign   224
Chapter 11   Natural Supports in the Workplace and Beyond   250
Chapter 12   Supporting Students in the Transition from School to Adult Life   266
Chapter 13   Dropout Prevention: Using Self-Determination to Achieve Desired Postschool Outcomes   288
Chapter 14   Evaluation Practices for Transition Planning   304

CONTENTS

Part I *Introduction to Transition Services and Legislation* 1

CHAPTER 1 **Preparing Adolescents for Adult Roles** 2

Frank R. Rusch *Pennsylvania State University*

What Is the Typical State of Affairs for Youth with Disabilities? 4

What Do We Know About How to Train Adolescents with Disabilities? 6

Overview of High School Attendance, Programs, and Outcomes 7

  High School Enrollments, Graduation, and Dropouts 8

  Overview of Employment-Related Participation After Age 14 10

Emerging Organizational Model-Planning and Preparation, Placement, and Support 13

Summary 16 • Case Study 1 17 • Study Questions 17 • Recommended Reading 20 • Web Resources 20 • References 21

CHAPTER 2 **Transition Legislation and Policy: Past and Present** 24

Robert A. Stodden and Kelly D. Roberts *University of Hawaii*

Early Legislation Related to Employment Training, Rehabilitation, and Education 27

  1915–1945: Support and Training for Veterans with Disabilities 28

  1946–1965: Training and Rehabilitation for Persons with Disabilities 28

  1970s: Appropriate Access and Accommodations 29

  1980s: Funds to Develop Transition Models and Practices 31

Emergence of the Transition Initiative for Youth with Disabilities 31

Expansion of Disability Policy in the 1990s and 2000s 33

  Education 35

  Employment and Training 40

  Quality of Life 42

Summary 43 • Case Study 1 45 • Study Questions 48 • Recommended Reading 50 • Web Resources 51 • References 51

Part II Student Involvement, Planning, and Assessment 55

CHAPTER 3 Person-Centered Career Planning 56

Martin Agran *University of Wyoming* **and Michael Wehmeyer** *University of Kansas*

What Is Self-Determination? 58

Active Student Involvement 60

Evidence of the Importance of Self-Determination: Student-Directed Learning 61

Person-Centered Planning 62

Recommended Practices 64

Teaching Needs 64

Teaching Skills to Promote Self-Determination 65

Summary 72 • Case Study 2 72 • Study Questions 73 • Recommended Reading 74 • Web Resources 74 • References 75

CHAPTER 4 Building an Employment Vision: Culturally Attuning Vocational Interests, Skills, and Limits 78

James E. Martin, Lee L. Woods, and Lorraine Sylvester *University of Oklahoma*

Case Studies 80

Julie—A 17-Year-Old Who Wants to Become a Chef 80

Christopher—A 17-Year-Old Who Likes to Fish 81

Summary 82

Julie's Example: Building an Employment Vision for a Student with Mild Disabilities Who Will Make Her Own Decisions with Family Support 83

Middle School Career Exploration 83

High School Exploration and Preparation 84

Christopher's Example: Building an Employment Vision for a Student with Mental Retardation from a Collectivist Decision-Making Family 93

Middle School Career Awareness 93

High School Career Exploration Year 1 98

Culturally and Linguistically Diverse Students, Their Families, and Transition   102
Individualism and Collectivism   103
Cultural Reciprocity   103
Summary 105   •   Study Questions 106   •   Recommended Reading 108   •   Web Resources 108   •   References 108

CHAPTER 5   **Working with Parents: Using Strategies to Promote Planning and Preparation, Placement, and Support   110**
Wendy Parent, Denise Gossage, and Molly Jones with Patty Turner, Chris Walker, and Renee Feldman University of Kansas

Recommended Practices   114
Student-Level Strategies   115
School-Level Strategies   119
District-Level Strategies   123
Summary 126   •   Study Questions 127   •   Recommended Reading 130   •   Web Resources 130   •   References 130

Part III   *Building Teams and Interagency Coordination   135*

CHAPTER 6   **Using Interagency and Interdisciplinary Teams to Enhance Transition Services   136**
Jane M. Everson and Joy Ivester University of South Carolina School of Medicine **and Joan D. Guillory** Louisiana State University Health Sciences Center

Overview of Community Development and Teamwork Concepts   137
Civic Engagement   138
Community Connections   138
Social Capital   139
Putting It All Together: Community Development   139
Teamwork: A Critical Component   139
Community-Level Teamwork: Recommended Practices   140
Getting Started: Are We Forming, Storming, Norming, or Performing?   143
Developing a Shared Foundation: Core Elements   143
Moving Through the Stages: Developing Work Plans   145

Case Study Overviews   146
    Community Needs and Demographics   146
    The Forming Stage: Establishing Community-Level Teams   146
    The Storming Stage: Getting Down to Work   147
    The Norming Stage: Beginning to Address Systems Changes in Communities   150

Summary 153 • Study Questions 155 • Recommended Reading 158 • Web Resources 158 • References 159

CHAPTER 7 Interagency Collaboration: It Takes Communication to Support Transitions   160
Caren L. Sax and David A. Noyes *San Diego State University*

The Need for Collaboration   161

Use of Dialogue   163
    Interagency Dialogue and Collaboration   164

Dialogue in Action   166
    Traditional Process Before Interagency Dialogue   167
    Meaningful Dialogue   167

Summary 170 • Study Questions 171 • Recommended Reading 173 • Web Resources 173 • References 174

Part IV *Assessment, Work Experience Opportunities, Job Placement, and Student Support*   177

CHAPTER 8 Transition Assessment: Emerging Guidelines and Promising Practices   178
Bruce M. Menchetti *Florida State University*

Legal Requirements Impacting Transition Assessment   179

Longitudinal Approaches to Transition Assessment   181
    Career Development Models of Assessment   182
    Person-Centered Approaches   182
    Summary of the Longitudinal Approach   184

Other Assessment Practices That Improve Student Outcomes   184
    Consensus Regarding Transition Outcome and Assessment Areas   185

Adherence to Professional Guidelines in Design and Selection of Assessment Methods 186

Transition Assessment Methods 188

Formal Methods 188

Informal Methods 189

Putting It All Together: Developing an Individualized Transition Profile 192

Summary 194 • Study Questions 194 • Recommended Reading 197 • Web Resources 197 • References 197

CHAPTER 9

Work-Based Learning: Developing Work Experience Opportunities for Transitioning Students 200

David Hagner and Dianne Lounsbury *University of New Hampshire*

Types of Work Experiences 202

Work Exposure 203

Work Experience 204

Integrating Work Experiences into the High School Curriculum 206

Adherence to Labor Regulations 207

Provision for Training and Support 209

Administrative Logistics 211

Availability of Academic Credit 212

Developing Internships in Community Businesses 212

Interagency Collaboration 214

Summary 216 • Study Questions 217 • Recommended Reading 220 • Web Resources 221 • References 221

CHAPTER 10

Job Placement and Job Redesign 224

Katie E. Hildebrand, Frank R. Rusch, and Balázs Tarnai *Pennsylvania State University*
Robert Cimera *Kent State University* **and James E. Martin** *University of Oklahoma*

Job Placement 227

Job Redesign 236

Job Site Modification 237

Job Restructuring 237

Job Carving 238

Job Sharing 238

Assistive Technology 239

Natural Supports 239

Benefits of Job Redesign 239

Summary 240 • Case Study 1 244 • Study Questions 244 • Recommended Reading 247 • Web Resources 247 • References 248

CHAPTER 11 Natural Supports in the Workplace and Beyond 250

John S. Trach *University of Illinois at Urbana–Champaign*

Natural Supports Defined 252

Why Have Processes for Natural Supports 253

How to Develop Natural Supports 254

Outcomes of Natural Supports Use 255

The Ongoing Discussion 257

Natural Supports—and the SPANS Model 257

What Types of Resources Are Natural Supports? 258

Organizational Supports 259

Physical Supports 259

Social Supports 259

Training Supports 260

Social Service Supports 260

Community Supports 261

Personal and Family Supports 261

Summary 262 • Study Questions 262 • Recommended Reading 264 • Web Resources 264 • References 264

CHAPTER 12 Supporting Students in the Transition from School to Adult Life 266

Carolyn Hughes, Barbara H. Washington, and Gaylan L. Brown
Vanderbilt University

Developing a Model of Transition Support: Bridging Research to Practice 269

The Transition Support Model: An Overview 271

Developing Support in the Environment 271

Increasing Students' Competence 275

Application of the Transition Support Model   278

Summary 280   •   Study Questions 281   •   Recommended Reading 283   •   Web Resources 284   •   References 284

CHAPTER 13   Dropout Prevention: Using Self-Determination to Achieve Desired Postschool Outcomes   288
Thomas Holub *Edgewood College* **and Frank R. Rusch** *Pennsylvania State University*

Dropping Out of High School   290

Consequences of Not Completing High School   291

Pathways to Self-Determination   292

Illustration of the Pathways Model—Mark   294

Illustration of the Pathways Model—Melissa   296

Summary 298   •   Study Questions 298   •   Recommended Reading 301   •   Web Resources 301   •   References 302

CHAPTER 14   Evaluation Practices for Transition Planning   304
Judy Elliott *Long Beach Unified School District* **and Martha Thurlow and Erin Reid** *University of Minnesota*

What Do We Know About the Transition Planning Process?   305

Definitions   307

Why Assessment and Program Evaluation Are Important During Transition   308

Poor Postschool Outcomes   308

Lack of Planning   309

Failure to Define Educational Outcomes   309

Framework for a Comprehensive Transition Assessment and Program Evaluation   311

Outcomes of Education   311

Recommended Practices   315

Using Assessment and Evaluation During the Transition Process   315

Evaluating a Program: Where to Begin   317

Impacting Program Evaluation: Proactive Planning for Success   319

Essential Components for Creating Successful Work-Based Learning Opportunities 322

Setting Up Host Employers 322

Summary 324 • Case Study 1 326 • Case Study 2 328 • Study Questions 329 • Recommended Reading 333 • Web Resources 333 • References 334

Author Index 339

Subject Index 345

Introduction to Transition Services and Legislation

PART 1

Chapter 1
Preparing Adolescents for Adult Roles

Chapter 2
Transition Legislation and Policy: Past and Present

CHAPTER 1

Preparing Adolescents for Adult Roles

Frank R. Rusch
Pennsylvania State University

Pam is 17 years old. She is a senior at Rock Island High School where she is taking general education courses in addition to a course that allows her to work part-time every day of the week. Pam is also taking a class where she works on her study skills three times a week. She is not doing very well in her general education courses, but she loves her work-study course and has learned a great deal about her interests. She really likes her work-study teacher, who spends a lot of time asking Pam what she wants and makes sure that she understands the results of her choices for herself and her family. Pam lives with her mother and grandmother. She is working in a health care and fitness center and is partly responsible for her family's household expenses. She is very confused about whom to talk to about her educational goals and finds that most of her teachers are not supportive of her interest in a career in health care. She feels that her teachers are just waiting for her to finish her last year of education and not providing her with the help she needs to find a job. Pam can't figure out whom to talk with about her needs and is frightened when she thinks about her future.

The word *adolescence* comes from the Latin verb *adolescere,* meaning "to grow into maturity" (Lerner & Steinberg, 2004). Adolescence can be viewed as a period of transition from adolescent roles and expectations to adult roles and the myriad expectations that surround adulthood. Not surprisingly, adolescents ask questions about who they are and who they will become during these periods of development, reflecting their understanding that they are changing from a child to a young adult. Pam is a typical adolescent with interests and career questions. This chapter overviews outcomes that typify Pam and her peers with disabilities. More important, this chapter and text provides some direction for educators to take when preparing students like Pam for adult roles.

There is increasing agreement that adolescence extends over many years (Levinson, Darrow, Klein, Levinson, & McKee, 1978); thus, social scientists usually differentiate among early, middle, and late adolescence. Arnett (2000), for example, suggested that early adolescence covers the period between ages 10 through 13, middle adolescence between ages 14 through 17, and late adolescence between ages 18 through the middle 20s. These periods also roughly correspond with how our society groups adolescents in educational institutions, with each of these periods (i.e., early, middle, and late adolescence) demarcating entrance, respectively, into middle schools, high schools, and postsecondary institutions, including schools that focus on specialized employment training. Schools play a major role in structuring the activities, and consequently growth, of adolescents because the objectives of middle schools, high schools, and postsecondary institutions are uniquely structured to meet the needs of adolescents as they prepare for adult roles. Middle schools prepare adolescents to think about the many options available to them, whereas high schools provide multiple opportunities for older adolescents to experience these options. Postsecondary schools prepare older adolescents to assume more narrowly identified goals.

Beyond High School focuses on the curriculum of high schools and consequently middle to late adolescence—the period that begins at approximately age 16 and continues well into the 20s. Most high schools offer three basic curricula: college preparatory courses, vocational courses, and general education courses. Approximately half of all high school students without a disability enter college after graduation from high school. Typically, these students are enrolled in the college preparatory curriculum during their high school years. The vocational curriculum is designed for students who are preparing for employment or additional training after high school that leads directly to employment. Finally, the general curriculum is geared for students who are neither bound for college nor focused on employment. These students represent a new class of students who are not engaged in high school–related activities. A large number of them drop out, as will be discussed later in this chapter as well as in Chapter 12.

Beyond High School is devoted primarily to students who are pursuing employment upon exiting high school and, therefore, are enrolled in the vocational curriculum in high school. Typically, these students spend about half their time in specialized courses (see Chapter 9), including examining alternative occupations via job tryouts and on-the-job training. The book also focuses on adolescents with disabilities. Much less is known about adolescents with disabilities than about their peers without disabilities. What we do know about older adolescents with disabilities is that they are interested in the same outcomes as their peers without disabilities, including making friends, earning money, living on their own, making their own decisions, and, possibly, continuing their education. What is less clear is why most of these outcomes are so elusive to adolescents with disabilities.

What Is the Typical State of Affairs for Youth with Disabilities?

Recent data obtained from the National Longitudinal Transition Study–2 (NLTS2; Wagner et al., 2003), as well as the data provided a decade earlier (Wagner, Blackorby, Cameto, & Newman, 1993), describe the experiences and outcomes of youth with disabilities from approximately 300 school districts across the nation. Key findings that appear unaffected by time include:

- Students with disabilities are more likely than students without disabilities to experience poverty.
- A disproportionate number of students with disabilities drop out of school, the majority leaving school as they approach their 18th birthday. (Almost 40% of students with a reported disability drop out of school.)

- Few youth with disabilities pursue additional education after high school.
- Youth with disabilities trail the general population in achieving residential independence.
- Social isolation for youth with disabilities increases over time.
- Arrest rates increase over time, with 30% of all youth with a disability reporting being arrested at some point within 3 years after leaving high school.
- The vast majority of students with a disability are unemployed or underemployed after leaving school.

Further, parents report that 60% of their children with disabilities need postsecondary services, including job skills training, help in finding a job, and assistance after finding employment up to 5 years after departing high school (Rusch & Braddock, 2004).

Secondary special education has experienced a renaissance in recent years by comparison to earlier efforts that focused on identifying youth with disabilities and ensuring that they received a free and appropriate public education (FAPE). Special education is now taking on the task of identifying adolescent-related practices and outcomes that address some of these concerns. The 1990 reauthorization of the Individuals with Disabilities Education Act (IDEA; P.L. 101–476) named the types of outcomes that public schools should be attempting to achieve, including postsecondary education, vocational training, integrated employment (including supported employment), continuing and adult education, adult services, and independent living or community participation (P.L. 101–476, 34 CFR, Section 3000.18). Unfortunately, despite legislation focused on school practice and outcomes, no significant gains are apparent in employment rates, residential participation, and social adjustment among young adults with disabilities.

We are facing a puzzling dilemma. On one hand, our schools have never been as prepared as they are today to change the long-term employment patterns of persons with disabilities, in addition to enhancing their social participation and overall health and well-being. On the other hand, we continue to miss the mark in our quest to meet the expectations of the vast majority of adolescents with disabilities who want to work or pursue additional training after high school. These expectations pose unique problems for young adults and their families because the necessary services are typically not provided by a single entity, such as a high school. After turning 21 years of age, young adults with disabilities are no longer entitled to education-related services. They are on their own as they attempt to navigate a network of loosely connected adult services agencies that provide education-related services on an eligibility, rather than a mandatory, basis.

Part of the problem may relate to treating adolescents with disabilities just like we treat adolescents without disabilities at the most critical stage of their development. Typically, youth without disabilities graduate from high school and obtain jobs or pursue postsecondary education. The network of high school services available to youth without disabilities is well known and effective. For example, high schools are prepared to provide higher education counseling as well as a vocational education. In large measure, therefore, adolescents without disabilities move on to the next chapter of their lives to engage in either employment or postsecondary education, and engagement in either direction typically leads to positive overall outcomes, including higher paying jobs, high school completion, qualifications for more advanced work opportunities, residential independence, more friendships, and fewer arrests.

Without question, current high school practices must be called into question, as they relate to preparing adolescents with disabilities to assume roles as young adults. This chapter overviews the characteristics of these adolescents, reviews prevalence figures associated with late adolescence, and concludes with an organizational model that introduces new thinking to ensure that future generations will be prepared to assume adult roles. Subsequent chapters provide expanded discussion regarding this framework.

Most students with disabilities know little about career options, their own talents, what it is really like to work, and what preparation is needed for the kinds of jobs or further education that will lead to competitive employment and a career path. High schools are often not organized or staffed to manage the transition process for students with or without disabilities; high school counselors are often overwhelmed, with an average of over 300 students per full-time staff member (Wakefield, Sage, & Coy, 2004). Therefore, high schools must explore new organizational models that move students toward their goals and aspirations. *Beyond High School* includes the best known methods for planning and preparation, placement, and supporting adolescents in transition.

WHAT DO WE KNOW ABOUT HOW TO TRAIN ADOLESCENTS WITH DISABILITIES?

Over the past 20 years, a wide range of theories have emerged to explain career development, leisure and work, and health as a result of wages earned. A number of researchers have also applied career development theory to individuals with disabilities (Hershenson & Szymanski, 1992), including the experiential differences between people with congenital and acquired physical disabilities (Hershenson, 1981). Some explanations attribute work experience history as central to eventual and long-term employment (Holland, 1985; Super, 1990). Others criticize adolescent employment among youth with disabilities prior to leaving high school, claiming that paid employment provides few benefits to their successful transition from school to work (Greenberger & Steinberg, 1986). Interestingly, employment has been seen as facilitating potentially harmful leisure activities such as engaging in delinquent activities (McMorris & Uggen, 2000).

Most recently, however, research has shown that paid work experiences of students with disabilities are highly associated with completion of high school diplomas, employment after graduation (Benz, Lindstrom, & Yovanoff, 2000), and the formation of friendships and acquaintances among coworkers that eventually promote healthy activities apart from work (Rusch, Wilson, Hughes, & Heal, 1994). In an examination of the National Education Longitudinal Study of 1988 (NELS:88) and the National Longitudinal Transition Study (NLTS) of Special Education Students, 1987–1991, Wells, Sandefur, and Hogan (2003) found that previous attempts to define what factors predicted outcomes (cf. Rusch & Phelps, 1987) had failed to consider the impact of disability and type of disability in predicting socioeconomic and personal outcomes. Wells et al. (2003) found that disability and type of disability profoundly impact adolescents' early steps toward achieving markers that define young adulthood. Students with disabilities in general are not generally engaged in work-related experiences, and students with emotional and behavioral disabilities are even less likely to be engaged in meaningful work-related experiences.

Similar findings were reported by Heal and Rusch (1995), who examined the same NLTS database. Specifically, Heal and Rusch reported that disability type accounted for the majority of post–high school job placement, with youth with mild disabilities being employed at higher rates than their peers with behavior disorders, emotional disturbance, and mental retardation. Both Wells et al. (2003) and Heal and Rusch suggested that disability and type of disability greatly overshadow race and family structure. Students with disabilities are not being prepared like their peers without a disability for adult roles.

Thus, traditional models of stratification appear not to apply to youth with disabilities. For example, Wells et al. (2003) found that 40% of young adults with disabilities were in a latent class consisting of individuals who were not working or going to school; they appeared to depend on their parents for social contact, housing, and financial support. These researchers also suggested that disabilities play an instrumental role in the transmission of intergenerational status. Thus, family status appears not to be a factor in promoting children's well-being.

In sum, divergent theories continue to surround what we know about how best to prepare adolescents with disabilities for adult roles. And it appears that disability characteristics, not current high school practices, predict future adjustment. It is important to interpret these findings as suggesting that high schools have not organized themselves in ways that would enhance or predict successful achievement of desired adult roles, but that "being disabled" is difficult to overcome when practices are not designed to maximize abilities.

OVERVIEW OF HIGH SCHOOL ATTENDANCE, PROGRAMS, AND OUTCOMES

This section provides a review of the numbers of students with and without disabilities who are attending high schools, along with their graduation and dropout rates. Additionally, recent data presented by the NLTS2 are presented. These data are based on a nationally representative sample of more than 11,000 students who were in seventh grade during the 2000–2001 school year. Finally, the outcomes associated with youth with disabilities are overviewed to provide a backdrop for why we need to consider new organizational models for providing transition services.

High School Enrollments, Graduation, and Dropouts

Table 1.1 presents a detailed overview of the total number of students with disabilities enrolled in special education (ages 14 through 21) and the numbers of students who are exiting special education (refer to columns 1, 2, and 3, respectively). These data were compiled by the Office of Special Education Programs (OSEP) of the U.S. Department of Education (2002). The columns on the far right provide a glimpse of graduation percentages, number of dropouts, and total number of students who leave special education services provided by high schools and who were enrolled in the general education curriculum. The final column represents a total count of students who have died, moved, and are unaccounted for.

As would be expected, the total number of students served drops from a high of 422,540 at age 14 to 173,169 at age 18, the age when most students leave high school. After age 18 the number of students enrolled in high school drops by over two thirds to 55,425 (age 19), followed by over 50% leaving special education between ages 19 and 20 ($N = 24,017$), and yet another 50% reduction after age 20 ($N = 10,865$).

The third column details the number of students who exit special education. As illustrated, the numbers of students who exit special education continue to increase, the majority leaving during their senior years (age 18), which represents almost 65% of the total number of students who participated the previous year. The largest percentage change appears to occur after age 18, during students' 19th year.

The primary reasons why students leave special education include earning a diploma or certificate of attendance (see columns 4 and 5), dropping out of school (column 6), and returning to the general education curriculum (column 7). As would be expected, the number the diplomas awarded is higher after students' 16th year, with a spike in the number of diplomas awarded during age 18 ($N = 62,528$), followed by 38,524 graduating with a diploma at age 19. The awarding of certificates of attendance follows a similar pattern, with the highest number of certificates awarded occurring at age 18 ($N = 10,729$), followed by age 19 ($N = 8,444$).

The numbers of students who drop out follow a similar pattern, with the majority dropping out of school during their junior ($N = 20,403$) and senior ($N = 18,783$) years. Of particular interest is the finding that the numbers of students who drop out increase from 2,631 at age 14 (typically during middle high school) to 5,646 at age 15. It appears that over 75,000 students drop out of special education across all ages in any given year. On a more positive note, more than 60,000 students who were enrolled in special education appear to return to the general education curriculum ($N = 61,380$).

TABLE 1.1 Annual Total Enrollment in Special Education, Graduations, Dropouts, and Returning to General Education From 1993 to 2001

Age (years)	Total # served[a]	Number of students exiting special education		Graduations				Dropouts		Returned to general education		Miscellaneous[b]	
				Diploma		Certificate							
14	422,540	55,078	(13.04%)[c]	52	(0.01%)	61	(0.01%)	2,631	(0.62%)	14,804	(3.50%)	37,531	(8.88%)
15	396,192	57,204	(14.44%)	65	(0.02%)	61	(0.02%)	5,646	(1.43%)	13,959	(3.52%)	37,474	(9.46%)
16	352,940	65,329	(18.51%)	643	(0.18%)	178	(0.05%)	16,227	(4.60%)	12,691	(3.60%)	35,589	(10.08%)
17	291,440	85,116	(29.21%)	23,901	(8.20%)	3,010	(1.03%)	20,403	(7.00%)	10,772	(3.70%)	27,030	(9.27%)
18	173,169	112,470	(64.95%)	62,528	(36.11%)	10,729	(6.20%)	18,783	(10.85%)	6,992	(4.04%)	13,438	(7.76%)
19	55,425	6,246	(112.70%)	38,524	(69.51%)	8,444	(15.24%)	8,771	(15.82%)	2,088	(3.77%)	4,639	(8.37%)
20	24,017	18,243	(75.96%)	8,968	(37.34%)	3,937	(16.40%)	2,889	(12.03%)	587	(2.44%)	1,863	(7.76%)
21[d]	10,865	14,484	(133.31%)	4,840	(44.55%)	3,601	(33.15%)	1,161	(10.69%)	438	(4.03%)	4,443	(40.90%)
Total 14–21[e]	1,726,588	525,612	(30.44%)	139,395	(8.07%)	30,021	(1.74%)	76,511	(4.43%)	61,380	(3.55%)	218,305	(12.64%)

Note: Data represent averages per year, calculated using congressional reports from 1993 to 2001.
[a]Total number of students served per year in special education.
[b]Total number of students exiting special education minus graduations, dropouts, and returns to general education; number represents students died, reach maximum age (accounts for most of ages 21+), or moved (accounts for most of ages 14–20).
[c]Percentages of total number served in corresponding age group.
[d]Total number served is for 21 years; all other columns are for 21 years or older.
[e]Total number served is for 14–21 years; all other columns are for 14–21 years or older.
Source: Data compiled by the Office of Special Education Programs, U.S. Department of Education, 2002.

Table 1.2 provides an overview of the total enrollment of students in general education and in special education, graduations, and dropout rates from 1993 to 2001 for students ages 14 through 18. These data show a comparison of the total number of students who are served in general education and special education. The number of students between the ages of 14 and 18 (a 5-year span) served in general education reaches about 16 million ($N = 16,077,416$) in any given year; the number of students between the same age range served in special education amounts to just over 1.6 million ($N = 1,636,291$), or about 10% of the total number of students served by the public schools.

Table 1.2 also suggests that the percentage of general versus special education students who drop out of school after age 16 is almost identical (11.25% vs. 10.17%, respectively). According to these percentages, more than 1,000,000 general education students and over 160,000 special education students drop out of high school every year. Curiously, this total is almost double the totals reported by OSEP in Table 1.1 for students with disabilities.

Overview of Employment-Related Participation After Age 14

The NLTS2 provides one of the most comprehensive overviews of adolescent participation in employment-related activities during high school. Overall, most adolescents—with and without disabilities—are participating in work-related experiences during high school. Parents of adolescents with disabilities reported that approximately 62% of their children worked for pay (Cameto, 2005) at some point during high school, increasing from 49% at age 14 to 79% at age 17. Males were slightly more likely to be employed than females (65% vs. 58%, respectively).

For youth who are employed, the average number of hours spent working totals 20 per week; 22% of youth with disabilities work 10 hours or less per week, 23% work 10–20 hours per week; 37% work 20–35 hours per week; and 18% work more than 35 hours per week. These data are of particular interest as some findings suggest that working 20 hours per week may adversely affect the school performance and engagement of an adolescent without a disability (National Research Council, 1998). That is, adolescents who work longer hours are less likely to participate in school-related activities and spend less time completing their homework, resulting in less time spent with peers and increased chances of school failure (Steinberg, 2005).

Cameto (2005) recently addressed the extent to which adolescents with disabilities worked, including (a) time spent working as a result of school-monitored work study versus self-initiated employment, (b) the characteristics of their jobs, and (c) how these work-related experiences differed for adolescents with various disabilities. Regarding employment as a result of school-arranged work study, approximately 15% of these adolescents participated in work study. The highest percentage was found for youth with mental retardation (31.7%), followed by youth with multiple disabilities (29.3%), autism (28.9%), and deaf-blindness (28%).

TABLE 1.2 Annual Total Enrollment in General and Special Education, Graduations, and Dropout Rates From 1993 to 2001

Age (years)	Total # served in gen. ed.	Total # served in spled.	Percentage spled. of gen. ed.[a]	Graduations						Dropout rates	
				Diploma			Certificate				
				Gen. ed.	Spled.	%[a]	Gen. ed.	Spled.	%[a]	Gen. ed.	Spled.
14	3,432,603	422,540	12.31%								
15	3,749,646	396,192	10.57%								
16	3,289,130	352,940	10.73%								
17	2,962,582	291,440	9.84%								
18	2,643,445	173,169	6.55%								
Total 14–21				2,572,046	139,395	5.42%	31,500	30,021	95.30%		
Total 16–24										11.25%	10.17%

Note: Data represent averages per year, calculated using congressional reports from 1993 to 2001. Gen. ed. = general education; spled. = special education.
[a] Ratio of total number of students served in special education to total number of students enrolled in general education, in corresponding age group.

Participation across all other disabilities ranged from 7.5% (speech/language impairment) to approximately 19% (visual impairment).

According to Cameto (2005), almost half of these adolescents received school credit for their work experience versus pay; 14% received payment only for their participation in employment. Employment apart from work study accounts for the majority of work-related opportunities among adolescents with disabilities. Thus, parents indicated that 54% of their teenage youth held jobs in 2001, which is comparable to the job rates of the general population of youth between the ages of 13 and 17 years of age (Marder, Wagner, & Sumi, 2003). In 1987, approximately 30% of high school sophomores and 60% of high school seniors held jobs during the school year (Mihalic & Elliot, 1997). When freelance jobs (e.g., babysitting, washing cars, mowing lawns) are factored into the types of jobs held by adolescents without disabilities, almost 90% held a job before they were 16 years old. Herman (2000) reported that 3 million 15- to 17-year-olds work during any given school year, with that number increasing to 4 million during the summer. Clearly, work is a major factor when addressing issues related to late-adolescent development.

Among youth without disabilities who work, employment has been associated with increased absenteeism from school, lower grades, diminished parental control, and increased use of tobacco and alcohol (Ianni, 1989; Manning, 1990; Steinberg & Dornbush, 1991). Steinberg and colleagues have also suggested that adolescents who work are more likely to develop negative attitudes about work (Steinberg, Greenberger, Gardugue, Ruggiero, & Vaux, 1982). The causes of these attitudes may relate to the types of jobs these youth hold. Typically, youth without disabilities hold jobs that are technically unsophisticated and menial. In part, the Fair Labor Standards Act places limits on all adolescent employment, including limiting 14- and 15-year-olds from working in manufacturing, transportation, and construction jobs as well as jobs that require operating power-driven machinery (U.S. Department of Labor, 2004). Consequently, adolescents are finding less skilled jobs that typically are considered entry-level occupations—that is, occupations that are traditionally associated with youth entering the job market to build on experiences and ultimately to move on to more sophisticated jobs. Interestingly, for adolescents with disabilities these jobs define their short- and long-term employment experiences.

The types of job that the NLTS sample of adolescents held, as reported by Cameto (2005), were typical of all youth. Regardless of whether adolescents with disabilities were employed as a result of their school arranging a work-study opportunity or whether they found their own employment, the most common types of jobs included cleaning and grounds keeping (maintenance), personal care, food service, clerical, and retail. Among adolescents without a disability, 90% work in restaurants, grocery stores, and movie theaters (retail trades and food services). In addition, girls also work as maids and child care workers, and boys work as landscape aides and in gas stations.

The benefits versus the costs of employment are still not well understood. Most believe that work is good for teenagers. Thus, it is commonly held that early work experiences provide opportunities for youth to learn responsibility, manage their time, and learn how to manage their earnings. The effect of the number of hours worked seems to be an area of growing agreement. That is, if youth, whether they have a disability or not, spend more time working than studying or engaging in typical after-school activities (joining clubs and participating in sports, for example), their grades are negatively affected as are their opportunities to interact with same-aged peers who are developing attitudes about work, leisure, and politics.

To date, there are more questions about how best to engage adolescents in our high schools in relation to adult roles than there are answers. Consequently, we are not clear on how best to organize high school curricula to provide the best chances for these youth to make a positive transition from adolescent to adult roles. For the past 20 years, the fields of special education, vocational rehabilitation, medicine, mental health/mental retardation, and career and technical/workforce education have devoted considerable attention to the needs of people with disabilities who complete high school, gain additional education, and enter the labor force. Each field has addressed this issue from its own disciplinary focus, funding stream, and sense of mission, with only limited opportunities for interdisciplinary research and testing of effective models. For example, the field of high school career and technical education, which includes growing numbers of students with special needs, continues to lack a comprehensive knowledge base of effective practices for serving transition-age youth.

The concluding section of this chapter presents an organizational model that holds promise for contributing to transition services that promote adult roles. Components of this model will be explored in depth in the remainder of this text.

EMERGING ORGANIZATIONAL MODEL-PLANNING AND PREPARATION, PLACEMENT, AND SUPPORT

Since 1983, the U.S. Department of Education has authorized the use of discretionary funding for model programs that focus on high school preparation and transition services under Part D of the Individuals with Disabilities Education Improvement Act. At least 15 different grant competitions have been funded by the Office of Special Education and Rehabilitative Services to "stimulate the improvement of and development" of secondary special education programs and "strengthen and coordinate education, training, and related services" to assist in the transition process to postsecondary education and competitive employment (Rusch & Phelps, 1987, p. 489). More than 500 model demonstration programs have been implemented in virtually every state as a result of federal funding, with New York, California,

Washington, and Pennsylvania receiving the highest number of awards (cf. Rusch & Millar, 1998).

The legacy left by over 20 years of transition-focused and federally sponsored model program research is long. Extensive reviews suggest the existence of "best practices" based on the literature (Kohler, 1993), and entire texts have been devoted to transition services (Flexer, Simmons, Luft, & Baer, 2005; Rusch & Chadsey, 1998; Test, Aspel, & Everson, 2006). However, the outcomes of youth who are the principal targets of over 20 years of federal attention have not changed, as illustrated in the previous discussion. In brief, unfortunately, adolescents with a disability are not the recipients of an education that promotes becoming self-determined; they are not being prepared to assume the roles that they have identified as being important to them; and they are not benefiting from the supports that they need as they go on to assume adult roles.

Why are high schools continuing to fail to promote the healthy adjustment of adolescents as they enter early adulthood? There is some agreement on how best to promote positive outcomes among our adolescents. Indeed, small minorities of these adolescents do find a job. What are the characteristics of model high school programs that appear to foster these better outcomes? In part, the answer lies in our earlier effort to describe how to prepare youth for "transition from school to work" (Rusch & Chadsey, 1998). We provided an overview of student-focused planning, student career plans, interagency collaboration, family involvement, and support provided after departure from high school. Our earlier text and the texts of our colleagues include helpful overviews of what we know about these topics to date. What we do know, more than at any other point in our research, is that we are not changing the post–high school outcomes of the majority of our adolescents. We are just as ineffective today as we were over two decades ago when we began to focus on secondary special education and transition services.

In contrast, the vast majority of adolescents without a disability appear to find jobs, pursue additional education, and assume adult roles after they depart high school. These youth find ways to realize their goals and ultimately become employed. They find ways to support themselves by recruiting the assistance of friends and family. Adolescents with disabilities do not assume the same level of responsibility for their futures as do their peers without disabilities. These adolescents do not assume the same level of responsibility for guiding their actual placement after departing high school. They have not identified a network of support services that they or their parents, friends, or advocates help marshal together to ensure a high level of success.

Generally, students with disabilities do not benefit from planning that focuses on their needs and desires, nor on actual preparation and placement into adult roles with the support that they need to succeed. Secondary special education continues to ignore responsibilities associated with training and education that lead

CHAPTER 1 Preparing Adolescents for Adult Roles

to young adults assuming meaningful roles in our communities. As secondary special education reconsiders its roles and responsibilities associated with high school students, we need to consider the possibility that these roles and responsibilities must extend *beyond high school.*

> *Joyce loves animals and wants a career in animal care. She is 21 years old, uses a wheelchair, and has significant cognitive disabilities. She has been around animals all her life because she lives in the country with her parents, and her family has had horses, dogs, and cats "forever." Joyce has assumed responsibility for taking care of her parents' animals for several years, including grooming and feeding them. She also volunteers about 6 hours a week at a local dog kennel where she is able to practice many of the skills she will need to become a professional dog groomer. In State College where Joyce lives, there is a dog-grooming school that provides a Dog Grooming Certificate. Joyce will not be able to take the written test because she does not read or write, but she fully expects to complete the program with the help of her transition supports aide. Joyce's parents are interested in setting up a private business for Joyce once she completes her training. Her parents have indicated that they would like to hire a couple of additional groomers to work in their grooming business with Joyce. Joyce's parents, Joyce, the high school transition program, and representatives from the local dog-grooming school have met to develop a plan for Joyce's training. Accommodations include making sure that the entire school is accessible, that Joyce has a supports aide at all times when she attends school, and that she has ample opportunity to practice all the skills she will be required to demonstrate to be a competent groomer (brushing, trimming nails, cleaning teeth, and bathing).*

The primary tenet of this text is that *every student with a disability is entitled to the belief that his or her education will result in personally meaningful outcomes.* High schools should assume the responsibility for organizing resources to help foster outcomes enjoyed by the general population of students without disabilities who leave high school, including enrolling in postsecondary education, finding employment, getting married, and adjusting to their communities as they become young adults. Figure 1.1 provides a graphic representation of this organizational model.

High schools are well equipped to offer planning and preparation-related services to students, regardless of whether they have a disability. Indeed, these two activities are defining curricular services of all high schools. Although placement

High School	Planning Preparation Placement Support	Adult Roles

FIGURE 1.1 Transition Services Designed to Promote Meaningful Community Participation

and support are not typically associated with high schools, high schools are ideally suited for assuming the lead role in organizing post–high school support associated with student-identified outcomes. High schools have established long-term relationships with organizations in their communities that provide diverse services to their student populations.

Most youth recognize that they are expected to assume a role in their community once they leave high school. These roles result in meaningful contributions, including participating in the workforce, participating in additional training that leads to employment, or attending postsecondary education institutions that ultimately lead to employment, as well as other meaningful roles. Involvement in planning and selecting meaningful activities associated with their education will result in high school students recognizing the importance of their high school–sponsored preparation because these activities are closely associated with their dreams and aspirations for the future.

Interagency planning that includes parents and adult service agencies will result in additional training or education with supports that lead to widespread understanding of the roles adult services agencies must play in the provision of services that support student-selected goals. High schools must provide new and innovative curricular structures that promote meaningful engagement of students in community activities. And, these structures must include explicit support for these students as they assume their new roles in our communities.

Summary

Most of us understand the complexities of our adult lives. For example, we know that our jobs place rigid expectations on our attendance and performance, and that there are unwritten, yet well-understood, expectations associated with workplace interactions. These jobs, roles, and expectations were learned through work experiences that began when we were young. That is, each of us managed to assume the roles we now perform as a result of our earlier work and work-related experiences. Many adolescents with varying levels of disabilities, including severe disabilities, have also found meaningful employment. However, most other adolescents with identical characteristics have failed to find employment.

Beyond High School introduces emerging, contemporary transition services that must be considered as we assume more explicitly agreed-upon high school activities. Most important, this text emphasizes the importance of investing in each of the cornerstones of an organizational model that contends that adolescents must participate in planning their high school education and training and engage in targeted training and education activities associated with their plans—two expected and typically reported activities of high schools. Additionally, the remaining cornerstones that form this foundation suggest that we must also invest in activities that result in high schools coordinating placement and follow-up support of adolescents as they assume adult roles.

CJ is ready to leave high school, and he is certain that he wants to be a truck driver. He has already enrolled in a training school that will teach him how to operate "big rigs." He was able to find this technical school because his high school offers all students placement and coordination services. CJ is thrilled because he will be moving to another community for only a short time while being trained (about 12 weeks). Then he can return to Altoona and find an apartment and stay close to his family and his girlfriend. CJ has been able to get the state department of vocational rehabilitation to pay for a large portion of his training. He said that he never heard of vocational rehabilitation and that his high school transition program helped him secure this funding. When CJ attends driving school, he will also benefit from his high school coordinating with instructors at the driving school about his educational needs, which are minimal. CJ is not a very fast reader and needs more time to read material than most. Sometimes he has to ask someone what something means. If provided a little leeway on time and a little help to understand certain questions, he typically does well enough on exams to pass them.

CJ knows he will be driving a truck one day and knows that learning to drive a truck, and meeting all of the expectations of his family, girlfriend, and friends, will be hard. But, he also knows that he is not alone; he has the support of a well-defined network of family, friends, and associates who are well aware of CJ's goals and also their roles in supporting these goals.

Study Questions

1. How do or don't adolescents with disabilities differ from their peers without disabilities in their expectations for life beyond high school?

   Much less is known about adolescents with disabilities than about their peers without disabilities. What we do know about older adolescents with disabilities is that they are interested in the same outcomes as their peers without disabilities, including making friends, earning money, living on their own, making their own decisions, and, possibly, continuing their education. What is less clear is why most of these outcomes are so elusive to adolescents with disabilities.

2. What do we know (e.g., from NLTS2 [Wagner et al., 2003]) about the experiences and outcomes of high school–age youth with disabilities?

   Students with disabilities are more likely than students without disabilities to experience poverty. A disproportionate share of students with disabilities drop out of school, the majority leaving school as they approach their 18th birthday. Almost 40% of students with a reported disability drop out of school. Few youth with disabilities pursue additional education after high school. Youth with disabilities trail the general population in achieving residential independence. Social isolation increases over time. Arrest rates increase over time, with 30% of all youth with a disability reporting being arrested three years after leaving high school. The vast majority of students with a disability are unemployed or underemployed after leaving school. Further, parents report that 60% of their children with disabilities need postsecondary services, including job skills training, help in finding a job, and assistance after finding employment up to 5 years after they have left high school.

3. What does legislation dictate for schools about outcomes?

   The 1990 reauthorization of IDEA named the types of outcomes that public schools should be attempting to achieve, including postsecondary education, vocational training, integrated employment (including supported employment), continuing and adult education, adult services, and independent living or community participation (P. L. 101–476, 34 CFR, Section 300.18).

4. How does disability type seem to affect outcomes for youth with disabilities?

   Research reports that disability type accounts for the majority of post–high school job placement, with youth with mild disabilities being employed at higher rates than their peers with behavior disorders, emotional disturbance, and mental retardation. Also, disability and type of disability greatly overshadow race and family structure. Traditional models of stratification appear not to apply to youth with disabilities. For example, family status appears not to be a factor in promoting the well-being of their children.

5. How does paid work experience influence high school–age youth with or without disabilities?

   The benefits versus the costs of employment are still not well understood. Yet, most people believe that work is good for teenagers. For example, it is commonly held that early work experiences provide opportunities for youth to learn responsibility, to manage their time, and to learn how to manage their earnings. The number of hours worked seems to be one area of growing agreement. If youth, regardless of whether they have disabilities or not, spend more time working than studying or engaging in typical after-school activities (joining clubs and participating in sports, for example), their grades are negatively affected as are their opportunities to interact with same-aged peers who are developing attitudes about work, leisure, and politics.

Among youth without disabilities who work, employment has been associated with increased absenteeism from school, lower grades, diminished parental control, and increased use of tobacco and alcohol. Research has also suggested that adolescents who work are more likely to develop negative attitudes about work. The causes of these attitudes may relate to the types of jobs these youth hold. Typically, the types of jobs that youth without disabilities hold are technically unsophisticated and menial. The types of job that the NLTS sample of adolescents held were typical of all youth, regardless of disabilities.

6. Do we know best practices that promote positive outcomes for youth with disabilities?

   Research has identified best practices based on literature reviews and analyses of final reports prepared by model program directors. In every review, textbook, or recent model program illustrations, student-focused transition planning and the completion of student-identified transition goals have been associated with improved graduation and employment/postsecondary outcomes. Unfortunately, adolescents with a disability are typically not recipients of an education that promotes self-determination.

7. How do youth without disabilities typically transition from high school to work?

   The vast majority of adolescents without a disability appear to find jobs, pursue additional education, and assume adult roles after they depart high school. We do not assume responsibility for guiding the placement of departing high school youth without disabilities. They have identified a network of support services that they or their parents, friends, or advocates help to marshal to ensure a high level of success.

8. Which components of transition services need more focused attention in the future?

   Transition services include planning and preparation, placement, and support; the first two, planning and preparation, have been the most studied best practices over the past decade. By contrast, high schools have not focused on placement of students with a disability after completing their education, nor have high schools typically collaborated with post–high school adult-oriented services in the delivery of post–high school support services.

9. What critical new role should high schools assume in a transition service model to ensure successful outcomes for youth with disabilities?

   Every student with a disability should have a place to go after departing high school, and high schools should assume the responsibility for organizing resources that ensure typical outcomes enjoyed by the general population of students without disabilities who depart high schools.

10. How should high school transition services relate to community involvement?

    Most youth recognize that they are expected to assume a role in their community after high school. These roles result in meaningful contributions, including participating in the workforce, completing additional training that leads to employment, or attending postsecondary education institutions, ultimately leading to employment, as well as other meaningful roles. High schools must provide new and innovative curricular structures that promote meaningful engagement of students in community activities.

Recommended Reading

Flexer, R. W., Simmons, T. J., Luft, P., & Baer, R. M. (Eds.). (2005). *Transition planning for secondary students with disabilities* (2nd ed.). Upper Saddle River, NJ: Merrill/Prentice Hall.

Sitlington, P. L., & Clark, G. M. (2006). *Transition education and services for students with disabilities* (4th ed.). Boston: Allyn & Bacon.

Steinberg, L. (2005). *Adolescence* (7th ed.). New York: McGraw-Hill.

Test, D. W., Aspel, N. P., & Everson, J. M. (2006). *Transition methods for youth with disabilities.* Upper Saddle River, NJ: Merrill/Prentice Hall.

Wehman, P. (Ed.). (2006). *Life beyond the classroom: Transition strategies for young people with disabilities* (4th ed.). Baltimore: Paul H. Brookes.

Web Resources

Preparing Adolescents for Adult Roles

National Center on Educational Outcomes (NCEO)

http://education.umn.edu/nceo/

NCEO provides national leadership related to the participation of students with disabilities in national and state assessments, standards-setting efforts, and graduation requirements. The website provides information about NCEO, its projects, research findings and online publications, and other related resources. The Special Topic Areas lead to additional information, including topic-specific publications that may be downloaded.

National Education Longitudinal Study of 1988

http://nces.ed.gov/surveys/nels88/

This study (NELS:88) represents the first stage of a major longitudinal effort designed to provide trend data about critical transitions experienced by students as they leave middle or junior high school and progress through high school and into postsecondary institutions or the workforce. The 2000 data were collected at a key stage of life transitions for the eighth-grade class of 1988—when most had been out of high school for nearly 8 years. Many had already completed postsecondary education, started or even changed careers, and started to form families. The public use of the 2000 (4th) follow-up data is now available.

National Longitudinal Transition Study–2 (NLTS2)

http://www.nlts2.org/index.html

Funded by the U.S. Department of Education, this study documents the experiences of a national sample of students who were 13 to 16 years of age in 2000 as they move from secondary school into adult roles.

National Youth Employment Coalition

http://www.nyec.org/

NYEC is a nonpartisan national organization dedicated to promoting policies and initiatives that help youth become lifelong learners, productive workers, and self-sufficient citizens. This site contains information on legislation, best practices, and leadership development, as well as a host of projects and initiatives.

Worksupport.com

http://www.worksupport.com/

This website provides information, resources, and research about work and disability issues. The site includes a listing of research, projects, an online store, training information, a free e-newsletter, and more.

References

Arnett, J. (2000). Emerging adulthood: A theory of development from the late teens through the twenties. *American Psychologist, 55,* 469–480.

Benz, M. R., Lindstrom, L., & Yovanoff, P. (2000). Improving graduation and employment outcomes of students with disabilities: Predictive factors and student perspectives. *Exceptional Children, 66,* 509–529.

Cameto, R. (2005). Employment of youth with disabilities after high school. In M. Wagner, L. Newman, R. Cameto, N. Garza, & P. Levine (Eds.), *Life outside the classroom for youth with disabilities. A report from the National Longitudinal Transition Study–2.* Menlo Park, CA: SRI International.

Flexer, R. W., Simmons, T. J., Luft, P., & Baer, R. M. (2005). *Transition planning for secondary students with disabilities* (2nd ed.) Upper Saddle River, NJ: Merrill/Prentice Hall.

Greenberger, E., & Steinberg, L. D. (1986). *When teenagers work: The psychological and social costs of adolescent employment.* New York: Basic Books.

Heal, L., & Rusch, F. R. (1995). Predicting employment for students who leave special education high school programs. *Exceptional Children, 61,* 472–487.

Herman, A. M. (2000). *Report on youth labor force.* Washington, DC: Department of Labor.

Hershenson, D. (1981). Work adjustment, disability, and the three r's of vocational rehabilitation: A conceptual model. *Rehabilitation Counseling Bulletin, 25,* 91–97.

Hershenson, D., & Szymanski, E. M. (1992). Career development of people with disabilities. In R. M. Parker & E. M. Szymanski (Eds.), *Rehabilitation counseling: Basics and beyond* (2nd ed., pp. 273–303). Austin, TX: PRO-ED.

Holland, J. L. (1985). *Making vocational choices: A theory of vocational personalities and work environments.* Upper Saddle River, NJ: Prentice Hall.

Ianni, F. A. J. (1989). *A search for structure: A report on American youth today.* New York: Free Press.

Individuals with Disabilities Education Act (IDEA) of 1990, Pub. L. No. 101–476, 20 U.S.C. §§ 1400 et seq.

Kohler, P. D. (1993). Best practices in transition: Substantiated or implied? *Career Development for Exceptional Individuals, 16,* 107–121.

Lerner, R., & Steinberg, L. (2004). The scientific study of adolescence: Past, present and future. In R. Lerner & L. Steinberg (Eds.), *Handbook of adolescent psychology* (pp. 124–136). New York: John Wiley.

Levinson, D., Darrow, C., Klein, E., Levinson, M., & McKee, B. (1978). *The seasons of a man's life.* New York: Knoft.

Manning, W. D. (1990). Parenting employed teenagers. *Youth and Society, 22,* 184–200.

Marder, C., Wagner, M., & Sumi, C. (2003). The social adjustment of youth with disabilities. In M. Wagner, C. Marder, J. Blackorby, R. Cameto, L. Newman, P. Levine, et al. (with M. Chorost, N. Garza, A. Guzman, & C. Sumi), *The achievement of youth with disabilities during secondary school.* A report from the National Longitudinal Transition Study–2 (NLTS2). Menlo Park, CA: SRI International. Available at http://www.nlts2.org

McMorris, B., & Uggen, C. (2000). Alcohol and employment in the transition to adulthood. *Journal of Health and Social Behavior, 41,* 276–294.

Mihalic, S. W., & Elliot, D. (1997). Short- and long-term consequences of adolescent work. *Youth and Society, 28,* 464–498.

National Research Council. (1998). *Protecting youth at work.* Washington, DC: National Academy Press.

Rusch, F. R., & Braddock, D. (2004). Adult day programs versus supported employment (1988–2002): Spending and service practices of mental retardation and developmental disabilities state agencies. *Research and Practice for Persons with Severe Disabilities, 29,* 237–242.

Rusch, F. R., & Chadsey, J. (Eds.). (1998). *Beyond high school: Transition from school-to-work.* Pacific Grove, CA: Brooks/Cole.

Rusch, F. R., & Millar, D. (1998). Emerging transition best practices. In F. R. Rusch & J. Chadsey-Rusch (Eds.), *Beyond high school: Transition from school-to-work* (pp. 36–59). Pacific Grove, CA: Brooks/Cole.

Rusch, F. R., & Phelps, L. A. (1987). Secondary special education and transition from school to work: A national priority. *Exceptional Children, 53,* 487–492.

Rusch, F. R., Wilson, P. G., Hughes, C., & Heal, L. (1994). A matched-pairs analysis of co-worker interactions in relation to opportunity, type of job, and placement approach. *Mental Retardation, 32,* 113–122.

Steinberg, L. (2005). *Adolescence* (7th ed.). Boston: McGraw-Hill.

Steinberg, L., & Dornbush, S. M. (1991). Negative correlates of part-time employment during adolescence: Replication and elaboration. *Developmental Psychology, 27,* 304–313.

Steinberg, L., Greenberger, E., Gardugue, L., Ruggiero, M., & Vaux, A. (1982). Effects of working on adolescent development. *Developmental Psychology, 18,* 385–395.

Super, D. E. (1990). A life-span, life-space approach to career development. In D. Brown & L. Brooks (Eds.), *Career choice and development: Applying contemporary theories to practice* (2nd ed., pp. 197–261). San Francisco: Jossey-Bass.

Test, D. W., Aspel, N. P., & Everson, J. E. (2006). *Transition methods for youth with disabilities.* Upper Saddle River, NJ: Merrill/Prentice Hall.

U. S. Department of Labor (2004). *Topical fact sheets # 32 and 39.* Retrieved November 22, 2004 from http://www.dol.gov/esa/fact-sheets-index.htm.

Wagner, M., Blackorby, J., Cameto, R., & Newman, L. (1993). *What makes a difference? Influence on post-school outcomes of youth with disabilities: The third comprehensive report from the National Longitudinal Transition Study of Special Education Students.* Menlo Park, CA: SRI International.

Wagner, M., Marder, C., Blackorby, J., Cameto, R., Newman, L., Levine, P., et al. (2003). *The achievements of youth with disabilities during secondary* school: *A report from the National Longitudinal Transition Study–2.* Menlo Park: CA: SRI International.

Wakefield, S. M., Sage, H., & Coy, D. R. (2004). *Unfocused kids: Helping students to focus on their education and career plans.* University of North Carolina, ERIC Counseling and Student Series Clearinghouse.

Wells, T., Sandefur, G. D., & Hogan, D. P. (2003). What happens after the high school years among young persons with disabilities? *Social Forces, 82,* 803–832.

CHAPTER 2

Transition Legislation and Policy: Past and Present

Robert A. Stodden and Kelly D. Roberts
University of Hawaii

Michael is 16 years old and was diagnosed with dyslexia at age 11. His dyslexia affects reading and writing. At age 11 Michael was placed in special education classes for English and reading.

Age 11 to the Present

Various teaching strategies and accommodations were used with Michael with minimum success. At age 14 the transition coordinator established an initial "team." Prior to calling the first IEP meeting, the transition coordinator collected information from school records, discussions with Michael's teachers, and through formal and informal communications with Michael. The transition coordinator reviewed Michael's file to determine his current level of academic performance and course load. The transition coordinator also spoke with Michael about his role in the IEP meeting. Michael had attended many meetings and understood the process and his role. Michael chose not to lead the meeting but indicated that he may want to in the future.

The initial transition team consisted of Michael, his parents, the transition coordinator, Michael's IEP teacher, and Michael's teachers. During the first meeting, the team worked to understand Michael's dreams for the future. Michael expressed his desire to become a mechanic. Michael also talked about maybe wanting to go to college but he was not sure what he would study. The team discussed the steps and additional resources or agencies that may be able to assist with both becoming a mechanic and going to college. The additional resources/agencies included the learning disability teacher consultant, vocational rehabilitation counselor, school-to-work coordinator, and the school counselor.

The team decided to try additional compensatory strategies to assist Michael with his reading difficulties. For example, it was decided that Michael would be trained on the use of text-to-speech technology to assist with his reading problems. He was also provided with a handheld spell-checker.

A draft of Michael's transition plan was developed and the team agreed to meet again within 6 months. Part of the initial transition plan consisted of the following goals established for Michael:

- *Understand the skills needed to perform jobs that Michael is interested in pursuing.*
- *Obtain career exploration and perhaps on-the-job training during high school. On-the-job training is beneficial even if Michael attends college as the job training*

provides an opportunity to develop and improve work habits while exploring possible vocations.
- *Improve social skills.*
- *Improve reading and writing skills.*

In addition to these objectives, the following supports or accommodations were to be provided:

- Extended time on tests
- Reading assignments in electronic format so Michael can use the text-to-speech software with greater ease
- Notes for lecture courses

Michael's academic schedule was developed with a focus on college preparation. In addition, during his sophomore year he will take the "school-to-work course."

Age 16

The transition coordinator prepped Michael so he could lead the transition planning meeting. Michael had recently been reevaluated and it was determined that he had made gains in both reading and writing. He continues to use the text-to-speech software and the spell-checker. He is in the school-to-work course and should be getting a part-time job by the end of the school year. Michael is still not sure if he wants to attend college immediately after high school or find employment.

Michael is still taking college preparation courses. He also continues to consider becoming a mechanic. He now views this as an achievable option and is considering going to community college to become a certified mechanic.

Applicable Legislation and Policy

- *Transition plan: IDEA and FAPE*
- *Part-time job (apprenticeship): School-to-Work Opportunities Act*
- *Testing accommodations: IDEA*
- *Assistive technology use: Technology-Related Assistance for Individuals with Disabilities Act*
- *Career and vocational training: Perkins Act*
- *Work-readiness class: Workforce Investment Act*

This chapter presents an overview of federal legislation and initiatives that have affected the evolution of secondary school-to-employment transition programs and services for individuals with disabilities. The chapter reviews the historical context of issues and legislation leading to the development of the transition initiative for youth with disabilities beginning with developments in the 1960s. The discussion includes a focus on the political climate and national policy efforts to consolidate and improve employment, rehabilitation, and education legislation to address the needs of all individuals. Further, 20 years of implementation of the "transition initiative" are discussed in relation to changes in definition, policy, and legislation.

During those 20 years, evidence has been collected regarding the use of effective practices. Such evidence-based practice has either led to the development of language found in federal and state policy guidelines or has resulted in the inclusion of such language in federal and state policy as "mandated" practice to be implemented by local education agencies and partnering entities. Examples of evidence-based practices linked to improved postschool outcomes include (a) students actively participating in transition plans developed by an interagency team with a focus on the student's future postschool goals and the necessary educational supports needed to attain those goals (Field & Hoffman, 2002; Skinner & Lindstrom, 2003); (b) students participating in career and vocational education activities, including participation in paid work experience in the community during the last 2 years of high school (Benz, Lindstrom, & Yovanoff, 2000; Wagner & Blackorby, 1996); and (c) an expansion of secondary transition services to include the participation of 18- to 22-year-old students with disabilities in 2- and 4-year postsecondary education and other lifelong learning opportunities (Hart, Zafft, & Zimbrich, 2001; Stodden & Whelley, 2004).

This chapter is divided into three key sections. The first provides an overview of early legislation in the areas of employment training, rehabilitation, and education, with a focus on policy areas that impacted the needs of persons with disabilities through the 1980s. The second section discusses the emergence of the transition initiative for youth with disabilities leading to the development of the school-to-work transition initiative within the Individuals with Disabilities Education Act (IDEA). Finally, the focus of the third section is on the expansion of disability policy in the 1990s and 2000s, presented under three categories: education, employment and training, and quality of life.

Early Legislation Related to Employment Training, Rehabilitation, and Education

This first section overviews four periods of legislative intent, beginning with support and training for veterans with disabilities (1915–1945) and ending with funds to develop transition models and practices (the 1980s).

1915–1945: Support and Training for Veterans with Disabilities

Prior to World War I, most education and rehabilitation services for persons with disabilities depended on the interest of private firms, benefactors, and individuals. In 1917, given concern that World War I veterans with disabilities would be a burden on society, the U.S. Congress passed the Smith-Hughes Act (P.L. 64-347), which provided vocational rehabilitation and employment for veterans with disabilities. This act was the first in a series of federal laws that began to influence the services and lives of persons with disabilities. In addition, the act provided the first federally supported vocational education curriculum in secondary schools in the areas of agriculture, home economics, trade, and industrial education. Soon after passing the Smith-Hughes Act, Congress passed the Smith-Sears Act in 1918 (P.L. 65-178), providing additional support for veterans with disabilities. In 1920, the Smith-Fess Act (P.L. 66-236) was passed, offering vocational training for civilians with disabilities while engaged in civil employment. Although funding and resulting benefits from the programs provided under the three acts were minimal, the legislation did provide a foundation and set precedence for future legislation.

With the advent of World War II and the need for workers in war-related industries, the LaFollette Act of 1943 (P.L. 77-113) was passed to provide vocational training for individuals who did not qualify for military service. For the first time, legislation included medically related services such as examinations, corrective surgery, and prosthetic devices. This legislation further expanded the concept of rehabilitation to include services for people with mental retardation, leading to the development of sheltered workshop services.

1946–1965: Training and Rehabilitation for Persons with Disabilities

The Vocational Rehabilitation Amendments (P.L. 83-565) were signed into law in 1954. This legislation expanded and improved vocational and rehabilitation programs, and provided funds for research and professional training. The research and professional training programs led to the development of work-study programs, sheltered workshops, job placement and work-experience activities, and employment follow-up efforts during the late 1950s.

During the 1960s, the President's Panel on Mental Retardation advocated for vocational training and supports for all persons with mental retardation. The report of the panel was supported by President Kennedy in his 1962 State of the Union address, wherein he emphasized the panel's findings and stressed a new program of public welfare, service, and training, rather than prolonged dependence. Thus, the Vocational Education Act of 1963 (P.L. 88-210) included provisions for expanded development of vocational programs and training for persons with disabilities.

The 1960s witnessed the passage of two additional pieces of legislation, the Vocational Rehabilitation Amendments of 1967 (P.L. 90-99) and 1968 (P.L. 90-391). The major provisions of these amendments included:

- Funding for rehabilitation, research, demonstration, and training projects
- Creation of programs for recruiting and training rehabilitation service providers
- Authorization of up to 10% of the funds set aside for vocational and rehabilitation programs specifically for youth with disabilities

Several reviews of programs and services resulting from legislation passed in the 1960s have indicated that this legislation had limited impact on persons with disabilities (Kohler & Rusch, 1997; Sarkees-Wincenski & Scott, 1995). Postschool outcomes for youth leaving secondary school programs failed to improve. Only a limited number of youth benefited from their education or were given access to specified training programs or services and often youth with disabilities were served in separate programs that did not result in competitive employment. Further, the Olympus Research Corporation (1974), Weisenstein (1976), and Tindall (1977) reported that states often did not use the 10% set-asides in vocational education funding for youth with disabilities, and in many cases there was a severe shortage of trained personnel in vocational programs who understood how to work with youth with disabilities. Each of these factors contributed to continuing dismal postschool outcomes for persons with disabilities.

1970s: Appropriate Access and Accommodations

During the 1970s, several pieces of landmark legislation were initiated to impact the lives of all persons with disabilities. The Rehabilitation Act of 1973, Sections 503 and 504 (P.L. 93-112), provided significant changes in the training and hiring of persons with disabilities. Specifically, Section 503 stipulated that businesses with federal contracts were to initiate an affirmative action plan for the purpose of hiring, recruiting, training, and promoting persons with disabilities. Section 504 of the act provided for significant changes in the training and hiring of persons with disabilities by ensuring that training institutions and employers not discriminate against persons with disabilities solely by reason of their disability. Also, for the first time, emphasis was placed on meeting the needs of those with the most severe disabling conditions.

In 1971, the concept of career education was introduced to the disability field "as the totality of experiences through which one learns about and prepares to engage in work as part of his or her way of living" (Hoyt, 1975, p. 17). For example, federal Office of Career Education was established to guide states in implementing programs, including (a) encompassing the total curriculum of the school and providing a unified approach to education for life; (b) encouraging all members of the community to share responsibility for learning within classrooms, homes, private and public agencies, and the employment community; (c) providing for career awareness, career exploration, and skills development at all levels and ages; and (d) encouraging all teachers to review their subject matter for its career implications. Special educators embraced the concept of career education (Clark, 1979) as a method for linking academic and vocational preparation for youth with disabilities. Unfortunately, due to a lack of a specific federal mandate and accompanying federal funding, career education programs had minimal impact on the education of adolescents with disabilities (Brolin, 1982).

In 1973, the Comprehensive Employment and Training Act (CETA; P.L. 93-203) took the place of many programs and functions established under employment and job training legislation during the 1960s. The primary purpose of CETA was to provide comprehensive worker services to alleviate the high unemployment rates of the early 1970s.

Specifically, the act was intended to address the needs of unemployed youths and adults who had no occupational skills and, thus, were not in a position to contribute to the development of the nation's economy. Although not specifically targeted for youth with disabilities, this legislation provided services, programs, and training opportunities that benefited this population. Later, the Job Training Partnership Act of 1982 (P.L. 97-300) reshaped the original CETA programs and provided significant funding for job training and placement programs directly benefiting youth with disabilities.

In 1975, the Education for All Handicapped Children Act[1] (P.L. 94-142) was passed to reduce the disparities in educational opportunity between children with disabilities and other children. This legislation provided partial federal funding to states, which in turn were to ensure students received a free appropriate public education (FAPE). One of the criteria of FAPE was the development of an individualized education program (IEP) for each child with a disability; for adolescents and young adults with disabilities, the IEP could include career and vocational objectives if such an education was deemed appropriate by the IEP planning team. Further requirements of P.L. 94-142 centered on ensuring the rights of children with disabilities and their parents and guardians. Thus, the law outlined due-process procedures for parents to express concerns or complaints with respect to student identification, evaluation, placement, and educational programming.

In 1976, the Vocational Education Act (P.L. 94-482) was amended, resulting in increased funding for vocational education programs and the continued 10% designated set-aside for youth with disabilities. Further, this amendment established the recognition of a need for cooperative working relationships between vocational education and other job training and employment programs conducted in the Department of Labor. Much of the legislation that guided programs in the 1970s served as a guidepost for more focused and refined legislation proposed and passed in the 1980s.

---

[1] The Education for All Handicapped Children Act (P.L. 94-142) passed in 1975, was retroactively renamed the Individuals with Disabilities Education Act (IDEA) to eliminate the use of the word *handicapped* and to use people-first language in the title. *IDEA* or *P.L. 94-142* will be used throughout this chapter.

1980s: Funds to Develop Transition Models and Practices

During the 1980s, previous legislation was further refined and refocused on what students with disabilities need to successfully prepare for and transition from the education years to adult life. In 1984, the Carl D. Perkins Vocational Education Act (P.L. 98-524) was passed with the intent to

> assure that individuals who are inadequately served under vocational education programs are assured access to quality vocational education programs, especially individuals who are disadvantaged, who are handicapped, men and women who are entering non-traditional occupations, adults who are in need of training and retraining, individuals who are single parents or homemakers, individuals with limited English proficiency, and individuals who are incarcerated in correctional institutions. (P.L. 98-524, Section 98, Stat. 2435)

The act extended the provisions of the Vocational Education Act of 1963 (P.L. 88-210) by mandating vocational assessment, counseling, support, and transition services for youth identified as disabled and disadvantaged. Further, the act mandated planning and coordination with other federally funded programs. Vocational goals and objectives were to be included in each student's IEP, and training was to be provided in the least restrictive environment. Record keeping and service delivery under the Perkins Act were to be coordinated in states and local education agencies with special education requirements mandated under P.L. 94-142. Table 2.1 provides a summary of the historical context of issues and legislation leading to the development of the transition initiative.

EMERGENCE OF THE TRANSITION INITIATIVE FOR YOUTH WITH DISABILITIES

During the early 1980s the transition initiative for youth with disabilities began to emerge. For example, in 1983, P.L. 94-142 (Education for All Handicapped Children Act) was amended with a new Section 626, titled "Secondary Education and Transition Services for Handicapped Youth" (Education of the Handicapped Act Amendments, 1983). Section 626 authorized federal funds for grants to demonstrate support and coordination among education and adult service programs designed to assist youth with disabilities to transition from secondary school to postsecondary education, employment, and community services. The purpose of Section 626 was to stimulate improvement and development of programs for youth with disabilities in secondary schools and to strengthen and link between secondary education, training, and related services. Briefly, the intent was to assist students with disabilities in the transition to postsecondary education, vocational training, competitive employment, continuing education, or adult services.

Madeliene Will, assistant secretary for the Office of Special Education and Rehabilitation Services (OSERS) during the early 1980s, was a key figure in creating a national priority in the area of transition for youth with disabilities. Thus, she was instrumental in establishing the intent of new policy and providing guidance

TABLE 2.1 *Legislative Path to the Transition Initiative in IDEA*

1915–1945		
Focus on support and training for veterans with disabilities	1917	Smith-Hughes Act (P.L. 64-347)
	1918	Smith-Sears Act (P.L. 65-178)
	1920	Smith-Fess Act (P.L. 66-236)
	1943	LaFollette Act (P.L. 77-113)
1945–1965		
Focus on training and rehabilitation for persons with disabilities	1954	Vocational Rehabilitation Amendments (P.L. 83-565)
	1963	Vocational Education Act (P.L. 88-210)
	1967	Vocational Rehabilitation Amendments (P.L. 90-99)
	1968	Vocational Rehabilitation Amendments (P.L. 90-391)
1970s		
Focus on appropriate access and accommodations for persons with disabilities	1973	Rehabilitation Act (Sections 503 & 504; P.L. 93-112)
	1973	Comprehensive Employment and Training Act (P.L. 93-203)
	1975	Individuals with Disabilities Education Act (P.L. 94-142)
	1976	Vocational Education Amendments (P.L. 94-482)
1980s		
Authorized funds to develop transition models and practices	1982	Job Training Partnership Act (P.L. 97-300)
	1983	Individuals with Disabilities Education Act (P.L. 98-199)
	1984	Carl D. Perkins Vocational and Technical Act (P.L. 88-210)
1990s		
Transition defined and mandated consistency established across other legislation	1990	Individual with Disabilities Education Act (P.L. 101-476)
	1990	Americans with Disabilities Act (P.L. 101-336)
	1992	Rehabilitation Act Amendments (P.L. 102-569)
	1993	Job Training Reform Act (P.L. 102-367)
	1994	National Service Trust Act (P.L. 103-82)
	1994	School-to-Work Opportunities Act (P.L. 103-239)

to demonstration projects developing the initiative. The new priority (Will, 1984) was established "to strengthen education, training, and support services for youth with disabilities and to support their successful transition from school to the adult world of independent work and living" (p. 12). The priority included specific recommendations to create secondary school curricula with relevancy to the workplace, to improve postsecondary services, and to develop incentives for employers to hire youth with disabilities. The recommendations were based on three areas of perceived need that guided the formulation of OSERS transition policy during the 1980s: (a) a need to focus on all students with disabilities, (b) a need to address the complexity of postschool services, and (c) the goal of employment and independent living.

To address the needs and recommendations of the OSERS transition priority, a model was offered to guide states and local education agencies in planning and

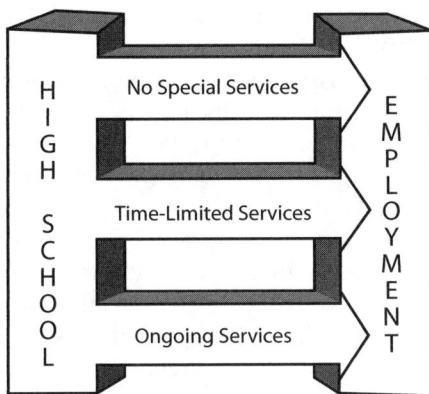

FIGURE 2.1 OSERS Transition Model
Source: Will, 1983.

designing programs and services. As illustrated in Figure 2.1, the model presented secondary school preparation as the foundation for successful transition with a focus on curriculum content in special education and vocational education. Will (1983) argued that students must leave school with entry-level skills that are salable in the local community. Employment was depicted as the resulting goal of transition services and supports. The following three levels of intervention were described for youth with disability as they sought to transition from secondary school to adult work environments: (a) transition without special services, (b) transition with time-limited services, and (c) transition with ongoing services.

During initial implementation of the OSERS transition model, activities concentrated on research, demonstration, and development projects in support of new programs and services in states. Numerous research and demonstration projects resulted in refinements of the OSERS transition model, as well as new models that often took a broader perspective of transition, focusing on several quality-of-life issues surrounding youth with disabilities. These projects added clarity and definition to the transition initiative, which would guide further policy development in the late 1980s and early 1990s (Table 2.1).

EXPANSION OF DISABILITY POLICY IN THE 1990S AND 2000S

In the early 1990s IDEA provided important new policy direction to guide the delivery of special education services, including a range of outcomes expected as a result of obtaining an effective education. Other pieces of generic legislation began to reflect the values of the transition initiative as policy and legislation evolved throughout the early 1990s. Further, education, employment, and human service legislation began to complement and embrace common issues and values necessary for cooperation between related government departments and programs to more effectively serve persons with disabilities.

Disability policy and legislation in the mid-1990s expanded or broadened much of the intent established in legislation during the preceding 20 years. Two forces contributed to shifts in thinking about disability policy as major pieces of legislation approached reauthorization in the mid-1990s. These shifts were attributed to (a) the perceptions of diverse groups of individuals (parents of children with disabilities, general education advocates, and special education and related services advocates) representing more than 20 years of research and experience with disability programs and services; and (b) a changing political climate that influenced prevailing perceptions of the federal role in defining education, health, and human services for persons with disabilities.

Other chapters in this text will focus on the results of research and experience with disability programs and services. The following section presents perceptions drawn from years of research and experience and factors of political climate that influenced reauthorization of various pieces of legislation. For example, the federal political climate of the mid-1990s significantly impacted state and local school districts as characterized by the following descriptors:

- A desire to downsize the federal role (mandates for services and findings) in education, health, and human services, allowing states greater power to determine eligibility for, and the scope of such services
- A desire to reduce costs at the federal level for education, health, and human services, while also reducing the costs to states for implementing unfunded federal mandates
- A desire to consolidate programs and budgets under single generic authorizations, thereby eliminating conflicting eligibility and funding tracks for numerous employment, training, and education programs
- A desire to focus on broad generic services addressing the needs of all persons eligible for programs and services, thus removing program earmarks and separate funding floors for programs for persons with disabilities and other special-needs groups
- A desire to focus on results and the benefits of federally funded programs on intended individuals

The views of policy groups focusing on services and programs for individuals with disabilities in the mid-1990s were characterized by the following descriptors:

- A desire of generic service providers (general education, health, and human services) to impact disability legislation, which had traditionally been freestanding, with separate funding streams and administrative structures
- A desire of policy makers to impact the numerous and conflicting requirements found across pieces of legislation addressing the education and

employment needs of persons with disabilities and other special needs groups
- A desire of parents of children with disabilities to reinforce the principle of inclusion and the participation of their children within general education curriculum frameworks and community employment settings, including the provision of necessary supports and services for children and youth with disabilities to self-determine and attain desired goals and outcomes
- A desire of professional advocacy groups to focus on the interests and abilities of persons with disabilities to assume satisfying and productive roles in their schools and communities instead of focusing on deficits and disability categories
- A desire of legislators to focus on the results and outcomes of programs and services for children and youth with disabilities rather than on the process that was used to conduct the program

The political climate and views of policy groups highly influenced the reauthorization of the IDEA. Other federal legislation of the 1990s followed the direction and intent of IDEA, thereby representing a major shift in public policy with regard to persons with disabilities. The majority of legislation that has had an impact on transition is entitlement acts. The exception to this is the Americans with Disabilities Act (ADA) of 1990 (P.L. 101-336). The ADA is a civil rights bill that guarantees individuals with disabilities certain rights under the law. ADA and other pieces of legislation implemented in the 1990s and 2000s that impacted the transition initiative and services are presented under three headings: education, employment and training, and quality of life.

Education

Two key pieces of education legislation were reauthorized in the 1990s and early 2000s: IDEA and the Elementary and Secondary Education Act (ESEA), renamed No Child Left Behind (NCLB).

IDEA 1990. In 1990 P.L. 94-142 was reauthorized as IDEA. Since its implementation in 1975, IEPs have been a requirement for all children and youth with disabilities eligible for special education services. Each student's IEP must include (a) a statement of the student's present level of educational performance; (b) annual goals and short-term objectives for reaching the goals; (c) specific special education and related services to be provided, and the extent of participation in general education; (d) projected dates for initiation and duration of services; and (e) criteria and procedures for determining whether short-term objectives have been met.

The IDEA 1990 reauthorization mandated that the IEP include a required statement of transition services for each student by age 16 and younger, if appropriate. This statement was to include the needed transition services and, if appropriate, a statement of each public agency's and each participating agency's responsibilities or linkages, or both, before the student leaves the school setting. Additionally, if the IEP team determined that services were not needed in one or more of the areas specified (instruction, community experiences, employment, and other postschool adult living objectives), the IEP must include a statement to that effect and the basis on which the determination was made (Individuals with Disabilities Education Act of 1990, P.L. 101-476, 34 CFR, Section 300.18).

Further, transition services in IDEA 1990 were defined as:

> a coordinated set of activities for a student, designed within an outcome oriented process, which promotes movement from school to post-school activities, including postsecondary education, vocational training, integrated employment (including supported employment), continuing and adult education, adult services, independent living, or community participation. The coordinated set of activities must: (a) be based on the individual student's needs; (b) take into account student preferences and interests; and (c) must include instruction, community experiences, the development of employment and other post-school adult living skills, and functional vocational evaluation. (IDEA 1990, P. L. 101-476, 34 CFR, Section 300.18)

Traditionally, the IEP was designated as a planning document for a maximum period of one year focusing on annual goals broken into short-term objectives. With the addition of the transition services requirements, planning for youth with disabilities took on a longer time period, with goals spanning several years. That is, for the first time, educators at the high school level were asked to orient their planning toward students' life after secondary school, including statements of needed transition services, agency responsibilities, and linkages to services within other agencies. By defining transition services, and by requiring a statement of such services in the student's IEP, the 1990 reauthorization of the IDEA did more than any of the previous amendments to promote the development of educational programs focused on postschool goals (see Table 2.2). These changes underscored the importance of the transition initiative as part of the delivery of special education services to youth with disabilities.

Changes in the transition initiative language of IDEA 1997 included:

- Planning for postschool transition earlier based on significant evidence that many youth with disabilities drop out of school prior to the initiation of transition planning activities (beginning at age 14 subsequently changed back to age 16 in the 2004 reauthorization).
- Ensuring that youth with mild disabilities are included in transition planning activities and/or services; many generic career and vocational education programs had not been linked or coordinated with transition activities for youth with mild disabilities.
- Ensuring that transition planning and service provision activities are presented in conjunction or collaboration with secondary school academic and vocational curriculum requirements as many of the benefits of the transition initiative had little or no impact on, or perceived relevance to, educational planning activities.

TABLE 2.2 *Progress of the Transition Initiative Within IDEA*

1975 IDEA (P.L. 94-142)	1983 IDEA (P.L. 98-199) Reauthorization	1990 IDEA (P.L. 101-476) Reauthorization	1997 IDEA (P.L. 105-17) Reauthorization	2004 IDEA Reauthorization
• Ensured FAPE for children with disabilities • Outlined due process procedures • Established an individualized education program (IEP) for each child with a disability	• Federal funds were provided to demonstrate transition models • OSERS transition model was developed • Transition outcomes were specified in legislative language	• Transition services were defined in legislation • Legislation included a statement of needed transition services in the IEP for each student, age 16 or younger • Promoted educational planning focused on postschool goals	• Focused on self-determination for students and families in transition planning • Focused on short- and long-range goals rather than objectives within the IEP • Focused on student planning and participation in the general education curriculum • Focused on integrating transition planning within the process of educational planning starting at age 14 years • Based educational planning and programming on postschool results	• Focused on protecting civil rights • Clarified roles and responsibilities • Ensured quality services and instruction at all stages of education • Improved discipline and school safety • Integrated IDEA provisions within NCLB • Defined transition planning to begin at age 16

- Linking transition planning activities and resulting services to the educational expectations of youth with disabilities during the secondary school years. This change in legislative language was based on several advocacy and parent/family groups who questioned the role of transition services within IDEA, as they were viewed by many as educational legislation.

Changes in IDEA 1997 that impacted the IEP process included:

- Focus on integrating planning for the transition needs of students with disabilities within the structure of the IEP process. This is to include "a statement of the transition service needs of the child under the applicable components of the child's IEP, that focuses on the child's courses of study, such as participation in advanced-placements courses or a vocational education program" (IDEA 1997, P.L. 105-17).

- Focus on planning within the IEP process for student participation within the general education curriculum, including advanced placement courses, vocational education, and school-to-work programs. The IEP team was instructed to provide a description of modifications to the course of study in which the student would participate and that would lead to a successful transition from secondary school to postschool adult environments.
- Focus on the involvement of postschool agencies in the transition planning and service provision process for the student with a disability no later than age 16 ("a statement of interagency responsibilities or any needed linkages").
- A requirement that states develop a statement regarding the transfer of rights under IDEA to the student on reaching the age of majority.

The section of IDEA 1997 that described the discretionary programs was significantly restructured (including Section 626, which provided authorization of demonstration, outreach, and systems-change grants in the area of transition) with the intent of organizing such programs as supportive activities leading to improved services and results for children and youth with disabilities. Further, the intent was to organize the various discretionary programs in a manner that could be defended as a necessary support package to implementation of Part B within yearly fiscal Appropriation Committee allocations. The restructured discretionary programs within IDEA 1997 were organized to provide new opportunities for the transition initiative to emerge as a more expansive and powerful force in support of improved educational results for youth with disabilities. Throughout the act, the focus on improving educational and transitional results for children and youth with disabilities was established to guide accountability and quality assurance activities within states as they sought to determine and measure student expectations, including postschool expectations and results. This could serve as an opportunity for those working with the transition initiative to contribute to the development of educational quality assurance and accountability models in states. Further, the new components in the section on IEPs for youth in secondary school provided an opportunity to apply transition postschool expectations to influence and determine educational curriculum decisions when planning for youth with disabilities.

IDEA 2004. IDEA 2004 focused on reinforcing several areas of the national disability policy, as follows: (a) protecting the civil rights of students with disabilities; (b) further clarifying the roles and responsibilities of students, parents, teachers, administrators, and school districts; (c) ensuring quality services and instruction at all stages of education for children with disabilities; (d) making improvements in the areas of discipline and school safety; and (e) integrating IDEA provisions within the Elementary and Secondary Education Act[2] (ESEA; P.L. 101-110).

---

[2]The Elementary and Secondary Education Act (ESEA) was named the No Child Left Behind Act (NCLB) in 2001.

A comparison of the transition provisions of IDEA 1998 and the reauthorized IDEA 2004 shows that the following areas of the policy were impacted:

- Definition of transition was adjusted toward a results-oriented process "that is focused on improving the academic and functional achievement of the child with a disability" (Section 602(34) Definition of Transition Services).
- When a student's eligibility for special education services is ending, a summary of the student's academic achievement and functional performance, including recommendations for how to assist the student in meeting postsecondary goals, is to be prepared (Section 614(B)(ii)).
- Planning for transition services will begin not later than the first IEP, to be in effect when a child is 16 years of age (Section 614(d)(1)(A)). Further, the IEP should include "appropriate measurable postsecondary goals" (aa), "and transition services (including course of studies) needed to assist the child in reaching those goals" (bb).

Even though the changes associated with transition made to IDEA in 2004 were minor, they reflected the concerns of educators, parents of youth with disabilities, and postsecondary program providers to simplify the transition planning process and improve the linkages of secondary school personnel with postsecondary program providers.

Elementary and Secondary Education Act: Reauthorized as the No Child Left Behind Act of 2001. The No Child Left Behind (NCLB) Act of 2001 focused on addressing the achievement gap between disadvantaged, minority, and special education students and their peers. Four major areas included (a) improving student and school accountability for academic results, (b) providing increased flexibility and control to local school districts, (c) increasing school choices and options for parents, and (d) placing an emphasis on proven, research-based teaching methodology.

Efforts were also undertaken to align segments of IDEA with the requirements of NCLB. NCLB placed a mandate on states to develop academic standards for all public elementary school and secondary school children in subjects determined by the state, but including at least mathematics, reading or language arts, and (beginning in the 2005–2006 school year) science. All children, including those with disabilities, are expected to achieve the standards (i.e., the same knowledge, skills, and levels of achievement). Success in meeting the standards/expectations is measured through large-scale state assessment systems, which provide data for each school, district, and state, in determining their adequate yearly progress (AYP). In turn, NCLB required schools to use AYP data as the measure of accountability for rewarding or penalizing administrators and teachers.

NCLB made it clear that students with disabilities were to participate within statewide assessment systems, as well as state accountability systems and AYP data reporting. These mandates, along with the need for schools and states to achieve AYP, have increased the importance of students with disabilities having meaningful access to the general curriculum. Unfortunately, many students with disabilities do not receive adequate accommodations or alternate forms of assessment necessary for them to demonstrate their knowledge, move to the next grade, and eventually graduate from high school (Stodden, Jones & Chang, 2002). Many educators and parents of youth with disabilities have voiced concerns over the need for schools to maintain a focused balance between standards-based academic instruction and functional life skills training necessary to succeed in postschool environments.

Employment and Training

The 1990s represent an important and one of the most active legislative periods in the 20th century. This period started with civil rights legislation (the Americans with Disabilities Act of 1990), with five additional employment and training laws being introduced.

Americans with Disabilities Act (ADA) of 1990 and Rehabilitation Act Amendments of 1992. The Americans with Disabilities Act (ADA) of 1990 (P.L. 101-336) and the Rehabilitation Act Amendments of 1992 (P.L. 102-569) further reinforced the shift away from focusing on what people could *not* do, to what persons with disabilities *could* do to contribute to their own quality of life and to society in general. These legislative acts recognized that a disability in no way diminishes the rights and desires of persons with disabilities to live independently, make choices, and pursue a meaningful life in their community. The intent across these pieces of major disability legislation was to reflect the broad values of community inclusion, full participation, self-determination with meaningful and informed choices, and the involvement of families and community members as natural supporters in all phases of life.

The ADA, an umbrella civil rights law signed in 1990, prohibited discrimination against people with disabilities in the areas of private employment, public accommodation and services, transportation, and telecommunications. The Rehabilitation Act Amendments of 1992 (P.L. 102-569) extended the policy directions of promoting improved quality-of-life outcomes for individuals with disabilities. Developed to be consistent with IDEA of 1990, they included several provisions to reinforce the success of youth with disability in the workforce. Specifically, the Rehabilitation Act provisions sought to define transition services in the same language as IDEA, and to link agencies and services provided by rehabilitation and education programs. Further, the amendments required states to plan and define how the two service systems would collaborate and coordinate in the provision of transition services.

These policy changes promoted a shift in philosophy and values impacting the way persons providing programs and services perceived individuals with disabilities. Each of the legislative acts supported self-determination and the importance of including individual preferences and desires in service delivery plans. Specifically, the IDEA sought student and family participation in the development of IEPs and stipulated that educational programs must be developed on the basis of postschool transition goals that reflect students' needs, preferences, and interests. Similarly, the Rehabilitation Act Amendments of 1992 focused on consumer-oriented services that supported the needs of persons with disabilities to participate in a satisfying, quality life.

Workforce Investment Act (WIA) of 1998. The goal of the Workforce Investment Act (WIA; P.L. 105-220) was to create a seamless workforce system by consolidating numerous federally funded programs and services into a one-stop service delivery model. Thus, under WIA, individuals (including persons with disabilities) should be able to access employment, training, educational support, and other human resource–related services at one location. All services must include and accommodate the needs of individuals with disabilities. The transition service requirements of Title I of WIA are available to youth ages 14 to 21.

WIA was designed to provide educational services that include tutoring, study skills training, instruction leading to completion of secondary school including dropout prevention strategies, alternative secondary school services, and leadership development opportunities. In addition to the educational services provided under WIA, workforce preparation was also provided to include summer employment opportunities that are directly linked to academic and occupational learning, paid and unpaid work experiences, and occupational skills training. Additional transition-related services provided under WIA include intake and orientation, initial assessment, job search and placement assistance, comprehensive guidance and counseling that may include drug and alcohol abuse counseling and referral and career counseling, adult mentoring for the period of participation and subsequent periods for a total of not less than 12 months, and follow-up services for not less than 12 months after completion of participation as appropriate.

WIA programs create lifelong access to career development assistance in that services are not only available at the time of transition from secondary school to postsecondary education and adult employment, but eligible persons may access these services throughout their adult lives. In addition to having a strong intersection with IDEA's transition goals, WIA-sponsored youth program models offer youth with disabilities additional resources (National Center on Secondary Education and Transition, 2002). Since vocational rehabilitation is one of the key components within WIA's workforce investment system, those services are to be available via the one-stop centers.

Ticket to Work and Work Incentives Improvement Act of 1999. Historically, young persons with disabilities have been plagued with the fear that their health insurance and other disability supports would be lost when they transitioned from high school to work or postsecondary education. The Ticket to Work and Work Incentives Improvement Act of 1999 (P.L. 106-170) was passed to assist individuals who enter the workforce and/or postsecondary education so they would not immediately lose their Medicare or Medicaid coverage. Under this legislation, Medicare coverage may be extended for 4.5 years for people in the disability insurance system who return to work and/or postsecondary education. In addition, the legislation created a new Medicaid buy-in demonstration to assist people whose disability is not so severe that they cannot work. This Medicaid buy-in allows individuals to work while continuing to maintain their health care coverage.

Job Training Reform Act of 1993. The Job Training Reform Act of 1993 (P.L. 102-367) provided funds for Job Corps Centers designed to serve disadvantaged young people who need additional education, vocational and social skills training, and other assistance in order to take part in meaningful employment, return to school, or enter the armed forces.

National Service Trust Act of 1994. The National Service Trust Act of 1994 (P.L. 103-82) created a voluntary national service program offering opportunities for individuals to provide community service in exchange for scholarships to attend college (each individual could receive up to $5,000 a year for a maximum of 2 years).

The Workforce Development Act of 1995. The Workforce Development Act of 1995 (S. 143) sought to amend Title I of the Rehabilitation Act, which authorized rehabilitation programs to assist individuals with disabilities in preparing for and securing employment. Under this legislation, a separate authorization at the federal level would be maintained to continue vocational rehabilitation services under state grant programs. As a job training program, vocational rehabilitation services were to be coordinated as much as possible with the comprehensive workforce development system to be established in each state. The amendments sought to ensure the planning processes, timelines, and accountability measures of the vocational rehabilitation system were consistent with the purposes of the Workforce Development Act.

Other amendments to the Rehabilitation Act ensured that vocational rehabilitation representatives participated in the state's overall employment and training efforts and provided technical assistance regarding provision of services to individuals with disabilities in the overall state system. These changes mandated that vocational rehabilitation programs work with the larger employment and training systems in each state, while retaining their own statutory authority and funding stream.

Quality of Life

Legislation that emphasized making choices and utilizing technology complete this section of the chapter.

Technology-Related Assistance for Individuals with Disabilities Act (Tech Act) of 1988 and 2004. The Technology-Related Assistance for Individuals with Disabilities Act of 1998 (P.L. 100-407) was signed into law by President Reagan on August 19, 1988.

The original intent of the law was to assist states in developing comprehensive programs for technology-related assistance and promote the availability of technology to individuals with disabilities and their families. Federal funding provided under the Tech Act has provided support for systemic change within the states while establishing systems to help individuals with disabilities obtain access to assistive technology (AT).

The 2004 reauthorization of the Tech Act refocused the act on direct aid to individuals to ensure that even more individuals with disabilities have access to the technology they need. This reauthorization has the potential to greatly influence the transition of youth with disabilities to productive post–high school outcomes through the provision of AT that can level the playing field and provide access to increased opportunities.

Real Choices Systems Change Initiative Within the Centers for Medicare and Medicaid Services (CMS). During the late 1990s Medicare and Medicaid programs were reorganized within a new agency referred to as the Centers for Medicare and Medicaid Services (CMS) under the U.S. Department of Health and Human Services (Centers for Medicare and Medicaid Services, n.d.). As part of the New Freedom Initiative (2003), the CMS awarded numerous Real Choice Systems Change Grants for Community Living. The intent of these grants was to help enable persons with disabilities reside in their own homes and participate fully within their community of choice. Further, demonstration grants were issued to states to improve the direct-service community workforce, enabling community-based providers to test new strategies for recruiting, training, and retaining direct-service workers. Each of the CMS grant initiatives reinforced the values of consumer choice, self-determination, and consumer authority over the funds and personnel involved in their living and employment support. Youth preparing to transition from secondary school into postschool communities and employment found the need to learn the new information and skills required within the new CMS-sponsored support models.

Summary

If the education, employment, health, and human service policy shifts of the early 2000s continue to expand, major changes in services and supports will be evident for persons with disabilities. Legislators and the general public want a major change in the perceptions held of persons with disabilities and the way programs have been structured and funded to support their equal participation, ownership, and performance in education and training programs. New policy initiatives must build on past decades of progress toward equal access and full participation for persons with disabilities, while continuing to promote performance and excellence for all youth. Efforts to maintain this policy balance in the future raise a number of issues or concerns to be addressed by advocates, policy makers, and others outlined as follows:

1. There is a continued need for a coordinated system of education and work preparation programs and services implemented under a unified vision and purpose, with a focus on the importance of learning and successful transition into the workforce. Such an effort must present a strong and consistent vision of quality education for all children and youth, resulting in an improved range of options and quality of life for all students leaving the secondary school years.

Currently, policy, legislation, and funding streams for special programs within education (including transition, work preparation, rehabilitation, and special education) remain separate and autonomous, and often have conflicting purposes and overlapping initiatives. As each legislative initiative and its constituents seek to carve out their own place and identity within the bureaucracy of federal programs, separate boundaries become a sign of success and status. Efforts in the late 1990s to consolidate and coordinate work preparation programs encountered major legislative difficulty because of the inability of policy makers to give up the current separate program structures in favor of visualizing and conceptualizing a service system consisting of a coordinated and integrated sequence of education, employment training, and community living supports.

2. There is a need to conduct inclusive discussions and build consensus concerning use of the term *all* when referring to the participation of children and youth with special needs in education, employment training, and community programs. Because many children and youth with special needs (including youth with disabilities) have traditionally been served under separate funding streams and program models, many policy and program personnel have yet to shift their perception of youth with disabilities as being included in legislative and program language. With the shift away from federally mandated special fiscal set-asides and specific earmarks for different groups of individuals, it will be important that this discussion be inclusive and focus on the broad range of services and supports necessary to achieve equity and excellence for *all* children and youth.

3. There is a need to refocus resources and program agendas from the arena of dependency (i.e., welfare, social work, social services) to the arena of supports and accommodations, leading to independence and self-determination and sufficiency (i.e., improved education and training programs) in programs for persons with disabilities and other special needs. It is difficult for policy makers to understand that persons with special needs should self-determine and be independent when programs continue to distribute funds and follow guidelines that support dependency.

4. There is a need to focus on person outcomes and results from, and satisfaction with, participation in education and training programs. If policy makers and

the public become increasingly more frustrated with the poor outcomes of our educational system, this may lead to less advocacy and support for addressing the needs of special populations. As schools and vocational training programs seek to respond to this frustration, it is important that the balance of equity (program access and participation) and excellence (improved outcomes) is maintained for *all* students.

5. There is a need to capture the evidenced-based practices and supports that have been generated through the separate special needs programs and OSEP-supported transition initiative to ensure that such practices are used to improve general education curriculum sequences and generic work preparation programs. Much has been learned about meeting the educational and training needs of children and youth with disabilities; it would be extremely inefficient not to access and apply this knowledge as we move toward serving *all* children and youth within a coordinated and integrated system of education and training.

Over the past several decades, disability policy related to education, rehabilitation, training, and preparation for adulthood has been addressed within multiple pieces of legislation, and administered by numerous government departments and programs. Education, health, employment, and human service legislation has shifted from little or no focus on children and youth with disabilities to a commitment to several special authorizations, and fiscal and programmatic set-asides within more generic legislation.

As many separate government program structures and funding streams evolved to ensure that children and youth with disabilities received special education and training supports, it has became increasingly clear that policy and regulations often did not support positive and efficient outcomes for persons with disabilities. Efforts to consolidate legislation and programs meeting the needs of *all* children and youth within a coordinated system of integrated services and supports remain a challenge for policy makers in the 21st century.

Joanne is a 21-year-old college sophomore who has cerebral palsy. She lives at home with her parents and two younger siblings. Joanne's parents are her biggest allies. Her verbal communication is limited. She cannot walk and uses a powered wheelchair. Joanne has good dexterity in her right hand. She has used a variety of electronic augmentative communication devices beginning in fourth grade. She now uses a powerful augmentative communication device with MinSpeak. Joanne also uses word predication software on her computer to minimize the number of key strokes required to type longer words. Joanne wants to become an accountant.

High School to College Transition

At age 16, Joanne's team began planning with her for her transition from high school to college. Her IEP included a specific transition plan. This plan detailed who and what agencies were to be involved and their responsibilities. Joanne's team consisted primarily of the following individuals:

Name	Position
Joanne	Student
Cheryl and Ted	Parents
Vicki	IEP teacher
Leo	Transition coordinator
Kerry	Occupational therapist
Lisa	Physical therapist
Mike	Speech therapist
Brian	Vocational rehabilitation counselor
Elizabeth	Teacher
Tom	Teacher
Sue	School counselor

Note: Additional teachers attended meetings throughout Joanne's high school career, but Elizabeth and Tom were two consistent team members.

With the goal of attending college and becoming an accountant, Joanne was in a college preparation program of study throughout high school. She generally performed in the average or slightly above-average range academically. Each year the school counselor provided a teacher in-service training to assist teachers recognize and accommodate Joanne's needs to ensure she would receive a free appropriate public education (FAPE). Joanne required numerous accommodations that she and the school counselor worked together to get implemented. For example, in courses where note-taking was necessary, Joanne was provided notes taken by another student in the class. Joanne also needed assistance with getting prepared for class, for example, getting her books and homework out of her backpack. In general, students assisted with these tasks. All of Joanne's teachers were aware that Joanne used an augmentative communication device. Protocol was established in each class that allowed Joanne to use her augmentative communication device and say "speak," similar to other students raising their hand. Once Joanne said "speak," the teacher would call on her the same as any student with his or her hand raised. The same protocol was used in group discussions and projects. Joanne used a computer to do in-class assignments. She also used a computer at home to complete her homework. She could use the computer independently.

During the summer between 11th and 12th grade Joanne attended a summer college experience program. For 2 weeks, she attended college from 9:00 a.m. to noon. During this time she received information on disability support services; received training in self-advocacy, self-determination, and management skills; and became acclimated with the college campus.

While Joanne was a senior in high school, the disability support coordinator from the college where Joanne was enrolling attended a transition planning meeting. Joanne was prepared to self-advocate, as she had practiced these skills throughout high school. Using her augmentative communication device, she told the counselor exactly what her needs were and what supports she needed to be successful in college. The disability support coordinator and Joanne communicated regularly via e-mail after this initial meeting. This e-mail contact helped relieve some of Joanne's and her parents' apprehension. Through these communications, the supports and accommodations Joanne needed to succeed in postsecondary education were in place when she began her first year.

Supports at the postsecondary education level include:

- *Notetakers.*
- *In-class assistance in getting prepared for each class session.*
- *Assurance that the classrooms where the classes were to be held are accessible.*
- *Assurance that the restrooms are accessible.*
- *Textbooks and materials available electronically. Although not mandatory, the availability of information in electronic format enables Joanne to be more independent.*
- *Faculty awareness that it takes Joanne longer to respond to in-class discussions because she uses an augmentative communication device. Faculty is asked to use the protocol used in high school: When Joanne says "speak," they call on her.*

In addition to these supports, the vocational rehabilitation (VR) agency agreed to provide support for Joanne's augmentative communication device. This includes repairs and updated equipment if necessary. Joanne was allowed to take her augmentative communication device with her when she graduated from high school.

Joanne wanted to live on campus but due to a lack of accessible housing, this was not an option. She is living at home. The local independent living center is working on getting Joanne into her own apartment. Joanne receives transportation assistance, in the form of vouchers, from VR. Thus, she is able to take the accessible cab service to and from campus.

Study Questions

1. Who was impacted by the Smith-Hughes Act? Why was the act important?

   The Smith-Hughes Act, passed in 1917, impacted the lives of veterans with disabilities. This act was important for three major reasons. First, the act provided vocational rehabilitation and employment specifically for veterans with disabilities. Second, this law was the first in a series of three to influence the services and affect the lives of all individuals with disabilities. Furthermore, these three acts established the groundwork and set precedence for future legislation. Last, the Smith-Hughes Act federally supported vocational education curricula in secondary schools covering content in the following areas: agriculture, home economics, trade, and industrial education.

2. What were the major provisions of the Vocational Rehabilitation Amendments of 1967 and 1968?

   There were three major provisions of the Vocational Rehabilitation Amendments of 1967 and 1968. The amendments included (a) funding for rehabilitation, research, demonstration, and training projects; (b) creating programs to recruit and train rehabilitation service providers; and (c) allowing for up to 10% of funds allocated for vocational and rehabilitation programs to be used specifically for youth with disabilities.

3. What was the focus of the Rehabilitation Act of 1973, Sections 503 and 504?

   Both Sections 503 and 504 of the Rehabilitation Act of 1973 mandated that changes be made in the training and hiring of individuals with disabilities. Both sections of the act highlight the importance of meeting the needs of *all* individuals with disabilities. Specifically, Section 503 required that businesses having federal contracts initiate affirmative action plans with the intent of hiring, recruiting, training, and promoting individuals with disabilities. Section 504 made modifications to guarantee that both training institutions and employers did not discriminate against an individual based on the fact that he or she had a disability.

4. Describe the OSERS transition model that was developed in 1980.

   The goal of OSERS was to create secondary school curricula with relevancy to the workplace, improve postsecondary services, and develop incentives for companies to hire students with disabilities. The expectations that guided OSERS transition policy included focusing on students with disabilities, addressing the complex issues of postschool services, and improving employment and independent living. The model viewed secondary school preparation as the key to a successful transition. Employment after school was the main goal. Last, this model provided three levels of intervention

CHAPTER 2 Transition Legislation and Policy: Past and Present 49

with hopes of reaching this goal: transition without services, transition with limited services, and transition with ongoing services.

5. How was transition defined by the IDEA reauthorized as P.L. 101-476 in 1990?

   In 1990, IDEA defined transition as a coordinated set of activities that aimed to improve the educational planning for individuals with disabilities when moving from school to postschool activities. Postschool possibilities included postsecondary education, vocational training, integrated employment, continuing and adult education, adult services, or independent living or community participation. Furthermore, IDEA stated that these activities must be based on the student's individual needs, consider student preferences and interests, and include instruction, community experiences, the development of employment and other postschool adult living skills, and functional vocational evaluation.

6. What were the views of policy groups in the mid-1990s concerning services and programs for individuals with disabilities?

   In the mid-1990s policy groups advocated for appropriate services and programs for individuals with disabilities. Efforts included (a) service providers impacting disability legislation, (b) policy makers addressing education and employment needs of individuals with disabilities, (c) parents of children with disabilities promoting the idea of inclusion and participation of their children in the general education or community employment settings while receiving support needed to achieve desired goals, (d) advocacy groups focusing on interests and abilities of individuals with disabilities to ensure they are active in school and community settings, and (e) legislators focusing on outcomes of services for children and youth with disabilities.

7. What were the broad policy shifts in the IDEA reauthorization of 1997?

   There were several policy shifts in the IDEA 1997 reauthorization. These shifts required that (a) transition planning begin at age 14 rather than 16, (b) students with mild disabilities be active participants during the transition planning process, (c) students participate in the general education curriculum (i.e., academic and vocational curriculum), and (d) educational planning and programming focus on postschool outcomes.

8. How did IDEA 1997 make improvements in addressing issues with the IEP for youth in secondary school settings?

   IDEA 1997 made several improvements to address issues during the IEP process that impacted students in secondary schools. These improvements included (a) integrating planning for transition needs of students with disabilities during the IEP process, (b) having students actively participate in the general education curriculum with the necessary modifications to succeed, (c) involving agencies in the IEP process prior to the child turning 16, and (d) mandating that states develop a statement related to the transfer of rights to the student upon reaching the age of majority.

9. What was the intent behind restructuring the discretionary programs in the IDEA reauthorization of 1997? Within what context were the discretionary programs described?

   The discretionary programs were restructured in 1997 with the intent of reframing programs such as supportive activities for students with disabilities. They also wanted to reorganize transition programs so they could be seen as a necessary support package. Finally, they were improved to provide new opportunities for transition so it would seen as a powerful source of support, establish accountability models, and include postsecondary expectations in IEPs.

10. What are issues or concerns to be addressed by disability policy in the 21st century?

    A. In 2001, the New Freedom Initiative supported the integration of persons with disabilities into all aspects of American life, increasing access to assistive technologies; expanding educational opportunities; increasing the ability of Americans with disabilities to integrate into the workforce; and promoting increased access into daily community life.

    B. In 2001, the No Child Left Behind Act focused on addressing the achievement gap between disadvantaged, minority, and special education students and their peers.

    C. In 2004, the Individuals with Disabilities Education Improvement Act of 2004 focused on reinforcing several areas of the national disability policy; protecting the civil rights of students with disabilities; further clarifying the roles and responsibilities of students, parents, teachers, administrators, and school districts; ensuring quality services and instruction; making improvements in discipline and school safety; and integrating IDEA provisions within the Elementary and Secondary Education Act.

Recommended Reading

Brucker, D. L. (2004). Informing the development of employment programs for persons with disabilities: A case study analysis of the definitions, uses and implications of idea of suitable employment. *Journal of Vocational Rehabilitation, 21,* 137–147.

Etscheidt, S. (2006). Issues in transition planning: Legal decisions. *Career Development for Exceptional Individuals, 29,* 28–47.

Imber, S. C. (2003). Independent educational evaluations under IDEA '97: It's a testy matter. *Exceptional Children, 70,* 27–44.

Mull, C. A. (2003). The role of technology in the transition to postsecondary education of students with learning disabilities: A review of the literature. *Journal of Special Education, 37,* 26–32.

Sitlington, P. L. (2003). Postsecondary education: The other transition. *Exceptionality, 11,* 103–113.

Web Resources

Transition Legislation and Policy

Council for Exceptional Children (CEC)

http://www.cec.sped.org

CEC examines policy issues, develops appropriate responses to those issues, and influences local, state, provincial, and federal legislation. CEC's Legislative Action Center is an important resource for up-to-date information related to impending legislation.

National Center on Secondary Education and Transition (NCSET)

http://www.ncset.org

NCSET coordinates national resources, offers technical assistance, and disseminates information related to secondary education and transition for youth with disabilities in order to create opportunities for youth to achieve successful futures.

National Council on Disability (NCD)

http://www.ncd.gov

NCD makes recommendations to the president and Congress to enhance the quality of life for all Americans with disabilities and their families. NCD's overall purpose is to promote policies, programs, practices, and procedures that guarantee equal opportunity for all individuals with disabilities, regardless of the nature or severity of the disability.

Rehabilitation Research and Training Center, University of Hawaii at Manoa

http://www.rrtc.hawaii.edu

The vision of the National Center is to move beyond what has and has not worked in the past, toward a new system of educational supports for people with disabilities in the 21st century. Postsecondary programs' teachers, support persons, and agency providers must focus on the use of individualized supports and technology to meet each student's needs and promote a successful transition to a chosen career.

Thomas: Legislative Information (the Library of Congress)

http://thomas.loc.gov

Thomas was founded in 1996 and has continued to expand the scope of its reach to include information on all facets of the legislative process, including bills and their interpretation, congressional alignment to pending and passed legislation, and more.

References

Americans with Disabilities Act of 1990, Pub. L. No. 101-336, 42 U.S.C.A. §§ 12101 *et seq.*, 104 Stat. 327 (1991).

Benz, M., Lindstrom, L., & Yovanoff, P. (2000). Improving graduation and employment outcomes of students with disabilities: Predictive factors and student perspectives. *Exceptional Children, 66*(4), 509–529.

Brolin, D. (1982). *Vocational preparation of persons with handicaps.* Columbus, OH: Bell & Howell.

Carl D. Perkins Vocational Education Act of 1984, Pub. L. No. 98-524, § 98, Stat. 2435.

Centers for Medicare and Medicaid Services (CMS). (n.d.). Retrieved December 11, 2004, from http://www.cms.hhs.gov/

Clark, G. M. (1979). *Career education for the handicapped child in the elementary school.* Denver, CO: Love.

Comprehensive Employment and Training Act (CETA) of 1973, Pub. L. No. 93-203.

Education for All Handicapped Children Act of 1975, Pub. L. No. 94-142, 20 U.S.C. §§ 1401 *et seq.*

Education of the Handicapped Act Amendments of 1983, Pub. L. No. 98-199.

Elementary and Secondary Education Act (No Child Left Behind) 2001, Pub. L. No. 107-110 § 626.

Field, S., & Hoffman, A. (2002). Preparing youth to exercise self-determination: Quality indicators of school environments that promote the acquisition of knowledge, skills and beliefs related to self-determination. *Journal of Disability Policy Studies, 13*(2), 113–118.

Hart, D., Zafft, C., & Zimbrich, K. (2001). Creating access to college for all students. *The Journal for Vocational Special Needs Education, 23*(2), 19–31.

Hoyt, K. B. (1975). *An introduction to career education.* Washington, DC: U.S. Government Printing Office.

Individuals with Disabilities Education Act (IDEA) Amendments of 1997, Pub. L. No. 105-17, 20 U.S.C. §§ 1400 *et seq.*

Individuals with Disabilities Education Act (IDEA) of 1990, Pub. L. No. 101-476, 20 U.S.C. §§ 1400 *et seq.*

Individuals with Disabilities Education Improvement Act of 2004, H.R. 1350, 108th Cong. (2004).

Job Training Partnership Act of 1982, Pub. L. No. 97-300, 29 U.S.C. §§ 1501 *et seq.*

Job Training Reform Act of 1993, Pub. L. No. 102-367.

Kennedy, J. F. (1962). *State of the union address.* Retrieved December 10, 2004, from http://odur.let.rug.nl/~usa/P/jk35/speeches/jfk62.htm

Kohler, P. D., & Rusch, F. R. (1997). Secondary education programs: Preparing youth for tomorrow's challenges. In M. C. Wang, M. C. Reynolds, & H. J. Walber (Eds.), *Handbook of special and remedial education: Research and practice* (2nd ed., pp. 108–130). New York: Elsevier Science.

LaFollette Act of 1943, Pub. L. No. 77-113.

National Center on Secondary Education and Transition: Staff, 2002. Available at http://www.ncset.org

National Service Trust Act of 1994, Pub. L. No. 103-82.

New Freedom Initiative Report Delivering on the Promise. (2003). Retrieved December 11, 2004, from http://www.whitehouse.gov/news/freedominitiative/freedominitiative.html

No Child Left Behind Act of 2001, Pub. L. No. 107-110.

Olympus Research Corporation. (1974). *An assessment of vocational programs for the handicapped under Part B of the 1968 Amendments of the Vocational Education Act.* Salt Lake City, UT: Author.

Rehabilitation Act Amendments of 1992, Pub. L. 102-569, 29 U.S.C §§ 701 *et seq.*

Rehabilitation Act of 1973, Pub. L. No. 93-112, 29 U.S.C. §§ 503 and 504 *et seq.*

Sarkees-Wincenski, M., & Scott, J. L (1995). *Vocational special needs* (3rd ed.). Homewood, IL: American Technical Publishers Incorporated.

Skinner, M. E., & Lindstrom, B. D. (2003). Bridging the gap between high school and college: Strategies for the successful transition of students with learning disabilities. *Preventing School Failure, 47*(3), 132–137.

Smith-Fess Act of 1920, Pub. L. No. 66-236.

Smith-Hughes Act of 1917, Pub. L. No. 64-347.

Smith-Sears Act or Soldiers Rehabilitation Act of 1918, Pub. L. No. 65-178

Stodden, R. A., Jones, M. A., & Chang, K. B. T. (2002). *Services, supports, and accommodations for individuals with disabilities: An analysis across secondary education, postsecondary education, and employment.* Honolulu: University of Hawaii, Center on Disability Studies. Retrieved December 20, 2004, from http://www.rrtc.hawaii.edu/products/phases/phase3.asp

Stodden, R. A., & Whelley, T. A. (2004). Postsecondary education and persons with intellectual disabilities: An introduction. *Education and Training in Developmental Disabilities, 39* (1) 6–15.

Technology-Related Assistance for Individuals with Disabilities Act of 1988, Pub. L. No. 100-407, 29 U.S.C. §§ 2201 *et seq.*

Technology-Related Assistance for Individuals with Disabilities Act (Tech Act) of 2004, H. R. 4278, 108th Cong., 2d Sess. H.R. 4278.

Ticket to Work and Work Incentives Improvement Act of 1999, Pub. L. No. 106-170.

Tindall, L. W. (1977). *Vocational/career education programs for persons with special needs in Wisconsin's vocational technical and adult districts.* Madison: Wisconsin State Board of Vocational, Technical, and Adult Education.

Vocational Education Act Amendments of 1976, Pub. L. No. 94-482.

Vocational Education Act of 1963, Pub. L. No. 88-210.

Vocational Rehabilitation Amendments of 1954, Pub. L. No. 83-565.

Vocational Rehabilitation Amendments of 1967, Pub. L. No. 90-99.

Vocational Rehabilitation Amendments of 1968, Pub. L. No. 90-391.

Wagner, M., & Blackorby, J. (1996). Transition from high school to work or college: How special education students fare. *The Future of Children: Special Education for Students with Disabilities, 6*(1), 103–120.

Weisenstein, G. R. (1976). Vocational education for exceptional person: Have educators let it drop through a crack in their services continuum? *Thresholds in Secondary Education, 2,* 16–17.

Will, M. (1983). *OSERS programming for the transition of youth with disabilities: Bridges from school to working life.* Washington, DC: Office of Special Education and Rehabilitative Services.

Will, M. (1984). *Supported employment for adults with severe disabilities: An OSERS program initiative.* Washington, DC: Office of Special Education and Rehabilitation Services.

Workforce Development Act of 1995, § 143.

Workforce Investment Act (WIA) of 1998, Pub. L. No. 105-220, 29 U.S.C. §§ 2810 *et seq.*

Student Involvement, Planning, and Assessment

PART 2

Chapter 3
Person-Centered Career Planning

Chapter 4
Building an Employment Vision: Culturally Attuning Vocational Interests, Skills, and Limits

Chapter 5
Working with Parents: Using Strategies to Promote Planning and Preparation, Placement, and Support.

CHAPTER 3

Person-Centered Career Planning

Martin Agran
University of Wyoming
and
Michael Wehmeyer
University of Kansas

Roberto is 14 years old. He receives special education services under the category of mental retardation and has extensive and pervasive support needs. He attends his neighborhood junior high school. His expressive language is satisfactory (although his expressions consist mostly of three- to five-word statements), he has a generally positive affect, and he enjoys interacting with his junior high peers. On several occasions he has said that when he grows up he would like to have a job. At his IEP meeting, it was decided to divide his school day as follows: four periods in general education, two in resource, and one in-school job. At the meeting several different types of work activities were discussed (e.g., library, counselor's office, greenhouse). When asked which of these he liked the most, Roberto indicated that he liked to be in the greenhouse. Based on his preference and input provided by his parents and team, it was determined that the greenhouse would provide an optimal learning experience.

One of the difficulties Roberto experiences in school is frustration and confusion resulting from problems in following task sequences. Greenhouse duties include watering, planting, selling plants, cleaning, and transplanting, among others. The team was concerned that Roberto may have difficulty completing each of these tasks. Although the team was confident that the teacher assigned to the greenhouse would provide appropriate support, and typical students will be available to assist as needed, all team members felt strongly that every effort should be made to teach Roberto to direct and manage his own behavior. It was determined that after task analyses were developed for all assigned work tasks, a self-instruction sequence for each task would also be developed. Roberto would be taught to verbalize these self-instructions prior to and during the execution of a job task. The self-instructions would provide him with self-generated verbal prompts to remind him of the required response sequence needed for each task. Rather than rely on and, most important, become too dependent on prompts delivered by others, the self-instructions will allow Roberto to prompt and support himself.

The employment outcome data for people with disabilities suggest that they continue to be at a great disadvantage compared to their nondisabled peers (Harris, 2004; Wehman, 1996; Wehmeyer, Agran, & Hughes, 1998). Only 35% of individuals with disabilities are employed full- or part-time; they are twice as likely to drop out of school; more than three times as many people with disabilities live in poverty; and the majority of individuals with disabilities appear to be dissatisfied with their life situation (Harris, 2004). In general, the transition outcome data for persons with disabilities suggest disappointing findings as discussed in Chapter 1.

A major reason for this dismal situation is that the educational process does not adequately prepare students with disabilities to become self-determined so that, in turn, they can better identify what they want to achieve at work and in the community and how to achieve such goals (Wehmeyer et al., 1998). Students remain unsure of their capabilities and interests and have difficulty advocating for their needs and making adjustments during the early stages of their life (Agran, 1997).

In recent years, educators, service providers, parents, and administrators have become committed to investigating ways to promote person-centered planning, self-advocacy, and self-determination for students with disabilities. We discuss each of these points in the following sections.

WHAT IS SELF-DETERMINATION?

Webster's Dictionary (Gove, 1967) defines self-determination as the "determination of one's acts or states by oneself without external compulsion" (p. 2059). The noun *determination* has a number of meanings that influence a person's understanding of this definition. To make a determination means to come to a decision or to render a judgment. To act with determination means to be firm in one's resolve and resolute. One might reasonably conclude that self-determination means to make one's own decisions or to act resolutely. However, the source of the word *determination* is the philosophical doctrine of *determinism*.

According to determinism, actions are *caused* by events or natural laws that precede or are antecedent to the occurrence of the action. Behavior, then, is governed by these other events or natural laws. Consider the role of genetics in human behavior as an example of determinism. We know that people act in certain ways because of their genetic makeup. Genes, thus, are determinants of human behavior; they cause human behavior. In our modern era, we understand that human behavior has lots of potential causes or determinants: genes, neurochemicals, past experience, parenting behaviors or cultural norms, religious beliefs, psychological states, emotions, and so forth.

Thus, self-determination means more than simply that action is volitional; it implies that action is in some way caused (e.g., determined) by the self. This self-caused action is, by definition, set in opposition to other-caused action. The self versus other dichotomy is not just equivalent to saying that self-determination refers to actions that are caused by forces inside the person versus forces outside the person, because genes, neurotransmitters, and other determinants are clearly internal to the person. Instead, the notion of self-determinism is linked to the capacity of humans to, in a sense, override other forces or determinants to act based on their own will. That is why the term *volition* is important in understanding self-determination. Volition refers to making conscious choices or the actual power to make conscious choices, or will. (For an extensive treatment of definitional and theoretical models of self-determination, see Wehmeyer, Abery, Mithaug, & Stancliffe, 2003.)

Why is all this important? Because too often self-determination is misunderstood to mean simply making complex decisions, setting goals, solving problems, acting independently, and so forth. The literature talks about self-determined people engaging in these often complex, metacognitively based activities as a means to control their lives. However, many individuals with developmental disabilities cannot solve complex problems or make complex decisions independently. If self-determination is understood solely to mean doing these types of actions and thus controlling one's life, it is unlikely that many people with disabilities will be able to become self-determined.

When we say that self-determination refers to people acting volitionally, based on their own will, is this applicable for people with disabilities? The clear answer is yes. People with significant disabilities can be supported to act more volitionally. Decisions about their lives can be made taking into account their preferences and interests, thereby enabling them to act based more on their own will and their own volition.

Wehmeyer (2002) defined self-determined behavior as referring to "volitional actions that enable one to act as the primary causal agent in one's life and to maintain or improve one's quality of life." Simply put, the crux of the meaning of self-determination is that self-determined people act volitionally as causal agents in their lives. The adjective *causal* is defined as expressing or indicating cause; showing the interaction of cause and effect. The term *agent* is a noun that means one who acts or has the authority to act or, alternatively, a force or substance that causes change. Self-determined people are *causal agents* in their lives. They act "with authority" to make or cause something to happen in their lives. But causal agency implies more than just causing action; it implies that the individual who makes or causes things to happen in his or her life does so with an eye toward *causing* an effect to accomplish a specific end or to cause or create change; in other words, he or she acts volitionally and intentionally. Causal agency, as opposed to implying strictly that an individual simply caused some event to happen, implies that action was purposeful or performed to achieve an end.

Self-determination emerges across the life span as children and adolescents learn skills and develop attitudes that enable them to be causal agents in their lives. These attitudes and abilities are the component elements of self-determined behavior. They include choice making, self-advocacy, problem solving, decision making, goal setting, and so forth—skills that are particularly important to the emergence of self-determined behavior.

This chapter discusses the importance of incorporating efforts to promote self-determination into the transition process. After discussing the importance of active student involvement, evidence is presented on the effects of instruction to promote self-determination on learning and skill development in transition, school, and community contexts. Second, the value of person-centered planning in the transition process is discussed, and the contributing roles of component elements of self-determined behavior are examined. Third, varying procedures to promote self-determination are presented.

Active Student Involvement

The Individuals with Disabilities Education Act (IDEA) Amendments of 1997 (P.L. 105-17) required that all students with disabilities ages 14 and above be invited to participate in meetings where their individualized education programs (IEPs) are discussed and that decisions at these meetings be based on the students' interests and preferences (34 CFR Section 300.344(b)(1) and Section 300.29). Because student involvement in goal setting and self-evaluation is at the very heart of transition planning (Wehmeyer & Schwartz, 1998), this mandate sought to maximize the meaningful involvement of transition-age youth with disabilities in the transition planning process.

Concurrent with this initiative has been an emerging focus on promoting the self-determination of students with disabilities. That is, there has been the realization that to ensure that students with disabilities achieve relevant and meaningful transition outcomes in school, work, and in the community, we must maximize their participation in decisions that affect their lives, impact their learning, and enhance their independence. Committed efforts must be made to enable these students to become more self-determined (Hughes & Carter, 2000; Wehmeyer et al., 1998; Wehmeyer & Sands, 1998). These efforts include teaching students to advocate for their own needs and wishes, make decisions about current and future concerns, set appropriate goals for themselves, monitor their performance, identify solutions to present or future problems, verbally direct their own behavior, reinforce themselves, and evaluate their own performance goals (Agran, 1997). These strategies have been referred to as student-directed learning strategies.

Although longitudinal data on the relationship between self-determination and transition outcomes are limited, findings reported by Wehmeyer and colleagues (1998) have suggested that students who are more self-determined attain more positive transition outcomes. For example, Wehmeyer and Schwartz (1997) measured the self-determination (SD) of 80 students with learning disabilities or mental retardation and then examined adult outcomes 1 year after they left high school. Students in the high SD group were more than twice as likely (80% of sample) as youth in the low SD group to be employed (40% of sample) and earned, on average, $2 per hour more than students in the low SD group who were employed. Wehmeyer and Palmer (2003) conducted a follow-up study examining the adult status of 94 students with cognitive disabilities 1 and 3 years after graduation. One year after high school, students in the high SD group were disproportionately likely to have moved from where they were living during high school, and by the third year they were still disproportionately likely to live somewhere other than their high school home, and were significantly more likely to live independently. For employed students, those scoring higher in self-determination made statistically significant advances in obtaining job benefits, including vacation, sick leave, and health insurance, an outcome not shared by their peers in the low SD group.

Further, greater involvement in transition planning by youth with disabilities holds a promise for better postschool outcomes, which traditionally have been disappointingly poor for individuals with disabilities (Mason, McGahee-Kovac, Johnson, & Stillerman, 2002). As Mason, Field, and Sawilowsky (2004) noted, the planning and interactive skills used at transition planning meetings are particularly important for students to acquire given that they will be called on to use these skills in future meetings with vocational rehabilitation counselors, postsecondary instructors, and employers.

To promote the meaningful involvement of students in the transition planning process and to maximize opportunities to enhance their self-determination, committed efforts have been made in preparing students to be more fully involved in transition planning meetings and, increasingly, to learn to lead their own meetings (Agran & Smith, 2004; Allen, Smith, Test, Flowers, & Wood, 2001; Martin & Marshall, 1996; Mason et al., 2002; Powers, Turner, Matuszewski, Wilson, & Phillips, 2001; Snyder & Shapiro, 1997; Zhang, Katsiyannis, & Zhang, 2002).

Mason et al. (2002) taught 43 students, most with learning disabilities, skills to become more involved in transition planning. As a result, the students reported they understood the IEP process better, were more aware of their disabilities and the accommodations they needed, and learned how they could better prepare for planning meetings. Konrad and Test (2004) taught seven students with learning disabilities to draft their own IEPs following a template. Benz, Lindstrom, and Yovanoff (2000) reported higher graduation scores for students involved in IEP development. Additional benefits reported by researchers include higher levels of goal attainment (Powers et al., 2001); improved self-advocacy and communication skills, as well as increased status and recognition (Mason et al., 2002); and increased attendance at IEP meetings (Johnson & Sharpe, 2000). As Mason et al. (2004) suggest, positive transition and educational outcomes for youth with disabilities appear to be positively associated with active IEP involvement and self-determination activities.

EVIDENCE OF THE IMPORTANCE OF SELF-DETERMINATION: STUDENT-DIRECTED LEARNING

Concurrent with efforts to maximize student involvement in transition planning has been a strong commitment to defining and tailoring instruction to enable students to become more self-determined. Most important, this has involved the identification and subsequent teaching of strategies that enable students to regulate and manipulate instructional cues, prompts, consequences, and to monitor and evaluate their own task performances. Students have been instructed to use a variety of student-directed learning strategies that enable them to regulate their own behavior and, by doing so, support them to become active participants in their own learning. Specifically, these student-directed learning strategies aim to teach students to set appropriate goals, monitor their progress toward those goals, identify solutions to present or future problems, direct their own behavior, reinforce themselves, and evaluate their own performance, respectively.

There is a growing body of research suggesting that student-directed learning strategies may greatly enhance a student's participation in transition and general education learning experiences. For example, McGlashing-Johnson, Agran, Sitlington, Cavin, and Wehmeyer (2003) taught four secondary-level students with extensive to pervasive support needs to monitor their work performance. The students were involved in a variety of community-based job placements. Three of the students achieved mastery levels of performance, and the fourth student performed at a considerably higher level after the intervention than in baseline. Similarly, Hughes et al. (2002) investigated the effects of goal setting and self-monitoring instruction on the conversational skills (i.e., initiating conversations) of five high school students with extensive support needs (e.g., severe mental retardation, autisticlike behavior). Prior to instruction, the students performed the target behavior at low frequency levels (i.e., 0%). After receiving instruction, their performance increased dramatically, ranging from approximately 60% to 100%. Gilbert, Agran, Hughes, and Wehmeyer (2001) taught five middle school students with severe disabilities to self-monitor a set of classroom survival skills in their general education classrooms (i.e., Spanish, reading, history). Target behaviors included greeting teachers and students, using a day planner, and responding to questions. All students increased their performance levels of all target behaviors, and all reported that the instruction they received made them feel a part of their classes and increased their level of classroom participation. Copeland, Hughes, Wehmeyer, Agran, and Fowler (2002) taught four high school students with mental retardation a set of self-regulation strategies (i.e., goal setting, self-monitoring, goal evaluation) to increase their level of performance of specified study skills (e.g., responding to worksheets, reading comprehension). The instruction produced immediate effects, increasing all students' report card grades to satisfactory levels. Last, Agran, Blanchard, Wehmeyer, and Hughes (2001) taught six secondary-level students with varying disabilities to use several student-directed learning strategies (i.e., goal setting, self-monitoring, problem solving) to achieve selected transition, academic, study, and social skills. All students increased their performance levels from 0 to 20% to 100%.

Person-Centered Planning

Wehmeyer (2002) noted that efforts to promote self-determination seek to shift the responsibility for educational and lifestyle planning from the service provider to the service recipient; in the case of schools, this means from educators and parents to students. Person-centered planning, similarly, seeks to identify a desirable vision for an individual based on his or her history, preferences, dreams, fears, and needs (Holburn, 2002; 2000b) and by doing so, to empower and motivate the individual to construct a life that is aligned with his or her values, self-knowledge, and sense of efficacy. Student-led transition planning is a manifestation of person-centered planning. By giving the student a primary role in the planning process, person-centered planning serves to yield a "self" rather than "other" lifestyle.

According to Schwartz, Jacobson, and Holburn (2000) and Menchetti (2001), person-centered planning involves the following basic principles:

1. The person's activities, services, and supports are based on his or her dreams, preferences, interests, and capacities.
2. The person and other people important to him or her are included in planning, have the opportunity to exercise control, and make informed decisions.
3. The person is provided opportunities to make meaningful choices based on his or her experiences.
4. The person uses when appropriate natural and community supports.
5. Activities, supports, and services are determined to foster skills to promote personal relationships, community inclusion, dignity, and respect.
6. The person's opportunities and experiences are maximized, and flexibility is enhanced within existing regulatory and funding constraints.
7. Planning is collaborative and involves an ongoing commitment to the person.
8. The person is satisfied with his or her personal relationships, home, and daily routine.

By ensuring that transition and educational planning is driven by these values and assurances, it is believed that the individual's vision can be realized and self-determination enhanced. But what is the nature of the relationship between person-centered planning and self-determination?

Wehmeyer (2002) noted that person-centered planning and student-directed transition planning have developed with similar missions and, therefore, suggested that a merger of the two might be more powerful. Though both value and aim to maximize the extent to which planning involves the person with a disability, the two approaches differ. Wehmeyer explained this difference in terms of whether the approach is ostensibly focused on opportunity enhancement or capacity enhancement. An *opportunity-enhancement approach*, or person-centered planning, places emphasis on organizational or environmental changes to help ensure that a person's vision can be realized. A *capacity-enhancement approach*, or student-directed transition planning, on the other hand, sees the value of teaching learning and support strategies that allow a person to manage his or her own behavior (e.g., self-instruction) and manipulate or modify relevant environments (e.g., self-reinforcement).

The opportunity-enhancement aspects of person-centered planning processes maintain that providing people with disabilities with ample opportunities and appropriate supports may be sufficient to allow them to become self-determined.

In contrast, a capacity-enrichment orientation does not totally negate the importance of opportunity but suggests that a person's execution of component elements of self-determined behavior—for example, goal setting, decision making, or self-monitoring—will enable the individual to better access resources, information, and relationships, and eventually enhance individual self-determination.

A related difference between the two approaches is based on the independence–interdependence continuum. Although it is inaccurate to expect that a student with a disability has to be totally autonomous to be self-determined (Wehmeyer, 1998), a capacity-enrichment approach seeks to maximize autonomy and independence by instructing individuals to acquire a repertoire of student-directed learning strategies and self-regulatory skills that they can consistently use across community settings. An opportunity-enrichment approach, instead, puts greater emphasis on the interdependent end of the continuum and believes that support from stakeholders remains the key to self-determination.

Ultimately, the relationship of opportunity to capacity is a symbiotic one, in which both must interact if transition-age youth are to become successful. To achieve the outcome that the educational programs of students with mental retardation reflect an individualized, appropriate education program that is driven by the general curriculum and by unique student learning needs, Wehmeyer, Sands, Knowlton, and Kozleski (2002) recommended that the IEP process embody principles of both person-centered and student-directed planning, to be a person-centered, student-directed process. Mithaug (1996) referred to an appropriate fit between capacity and opportunity as a "just-right" match, and it is critical that students understand this relationship. The following section describes instructional procedures designed to optimize this connectivity.

Recommended Practices

Teaching Needs

Although efforts to promote student self-determination have been going on for more than a decade, few teachers feel competent to teach their students to either be more involved in their IEP meetings or to learn self-advocacy and other skills leading to enhanced self-determination. For example, Wehmeyer and Schwartz (1998) reported that, in a review of 136 transition plans, they found no goals related to promoting self-determination or self-advocacy. Although the reasons were not provided, it appears that teachers do not know how to teach skills that enhance self-determination to their students. Also, Agran, Snow, and Swaner (1999) reported that 55% of teachers surveyed indicated that self-determination-related skills were not included in their students' IEPs, and 59% indicated they spent little or no time discussing issues pertaining to self-determination with their students. Additionally, in a national survey involving over 1,200 respondents, Wehmeyer, Agran, and Hughes (2000) found that although 60% of respondents were familiar with the term *self-determination*, a third indicated that no goals pertaining to promoting self-determination were included in their students' IEPs, one third did not involve their students in any kind of educational planning, and a large number of respondents noted that they did not believe their students would benefit from such instruction. An additional but related finding was that 41% of these teachers reported they did not have sufficient training or experience in teaching skills, such as student-directed learning strategies, that would lead to enhanced self-determination, nor were they aware of available instructional materials in this area.

In another survey, Thoma, Nathanson, Baker, and Tamura (2002) found that the majority of teachers in their sample did not believe they knew enough to successfully provide instruction to promote self-determination. Also, over 90% of their respondents were not familiar with any of the curricula or tools used to teach person-centered planning, self-advocacy, or student preparation for IEP meetings. Last, Mason et al. (2004) reported that only 22% of the teachers in their sample said they were prepared to teach their students skills to promote student self-determination.

In all, despite the current interest in student-directed learning and self-determination, the data reported to date suggest that efforts to promote these outcomes for students with disabilities—particularly students with moderate to severe disabilities—are at best underutilized and are often given low instructional priority. This is ironic, considering that a growing body of literature has demonstrated the positive effects of self-determination instruction for students with significant disabilities (see Agran, King-Sears, Wehmeyer, & Copeland, 2003; Wehmeyer & Sands, 1998). The following section describes ways to enhance self-determination and student-directed learning.

Teaching Skills to Promote Self-Determination

Student-directed learning strategies have demonstrated efficacy across a wide age range of transition skills and students with varying support needs, and have been well validated and supported in the literature (see Agran et al., 2003; Agran & Wehmeyer, 1999; Hughes & Carter, 2000; Wehmeyer et al., 1998). Among the strategies that promote component elements of self-determined behavior that have been extensively investigated are goal setting, self-monitoring, self-evaluation, self-reinforcement, self-instruction, antecedent cue regulation, and problem solving. These strategies aim to teach students to set appropriate goals for themselves, monitor their performance, identify solutions to present or future problems, verbally direct their own behavior, reinforce themselves, or evaluate their own performance, respectively. A description of each follows.

Goal Setting. Goal setting is an essential skill for person-centered career planning. Inherent in goal setting is the realization that there is a discrepancy between "where I am" and "where I want to be." The anxiety created by this discrepancy has been shown to motivate people toward change. Students need to be provided with learning opportunities so they can realize the discrepancies they experience between what they have and what they want. They must learn and be given opportunities to practice goal-setting strategies to achieve self-selected goals and enhance their self-efficacy, independence, and self-direction. Many students with disabilities, especially students with severe disabilities, have not had an opportunity to learn how to set their own goals, or lack the skills associated with goal setting. However, evidence strongly suggests that implementing the procedures in this strategy will enhance transition outcomes.

Although only a few studies have examined the effects of goal setting on task performance for students with moderate to severe disabilities, the findings to date are promising. Copeland and colleagues (2002) taught four high school students with mental retardation, who were enrolled in general education classes (cosmetology and hairdressing), to assist in setting performance goals for themselves. First, the trainer presented a rationale for the intervention and provided a definition and an example of a goal (e.g., "something you try to achieve, such as working to save money to buy a CD player"). The participants were then shown a list of their scores on modified worksheets during baseline and were asked to provide input in setting a performance goal (i.e., the letter grade they would like to make on each daily worksheet). Using a goal-evaluation sheet, the trainer marked the percentage in the number column corresponding to the letter grade selected by participants (e.g., "90%") to provide the participants a visual representation of their goals. Improved performance for all participants was reported. In a similar study, Wehmeyer, Hughes, Agran, Garner, and Yeager (2003) taught four high school students with mental retardation participating in general education to select performance goals for themselves. Among the target behaviors were holding head upright, increasing eye contact, and increasing attendance. Improvements were reported for all students.

Last, Agran and colleagues (2001) taught four students, labeled as having autism, intellectual disabilities, or multiple disabilities, to set their own goals. The students participated in general education life skills, science, and English classes. The students were taught to identify a target behavior they wanted to improve. Three of the students were aware of their instructional needs and required little support in considering target behavior options; the fourth student required a higher level of teacher assistance. Each student set a personal goal of correctly performing the target behavior at least 80% of opportunities. Immediate and dramatic changes were reported for all students. The students indicated that they appreciated playing a goal-setting role.

Goal setting ultimately allows students to both establish performance standards for themselves, a task traditionally done by teachers, and to evaluate how well they are progressing relative to the standards. Thus, goal setting has great utility in placing responsibility for learning and career planning with the student.

Self-Monitoring. Self-monitoring consists of a student's self-observation of a target behavior followed by recording the behavior's occurrence. The strategy requires that a student understand and successfully implement two functions: (a) recognizing that the desired or goal behavior was or was not performed, and (b) accurately recording the occurrence on a card or chart. Essentially, any discrete behavior (i.e., a response that has a distinguishable beginning and end) that can be operationally defined can be self-monitored. Recommended target behaviors may include practically any behavior that the student would like to increase or decrease. For example, Gilbert et al. (2001) taught five middle school students with severe intellectual disabilities, served in general education classrooms, to monitor a set of classroom "survival skills." The survival skills included a variety of academic, social, and behavioral skills. Positive changes were reported for all students, with behavior maintaining at 100%.

Self-monitoring produces behavior change because it may serve as a discriminative stimulus and, thus, cue the desired response. The self-monitoring process allows the student to recognize the specific target behavior, as well as to remind him of the present and future contingencies that exist in the environment (i.e., "If I perform this response, this will happen.") The target behavior is more likely to occur when this information is available to the student. Malott (1984) suggested that students with disabilities often have difficulty responding as desired because the available reinforcing contingencies are too delayed or ineffective. Self-monitoring may serve as a mediator because it reminds the student that when the behavior is performed, a desired consequence is made available. In a work setting in which the student receives little or no supervision (and consequently, feedback), self-monitoring allows the student to provide to himself feedback on his work performance.

Self-Evaluation. Self-evaluation involves comparing the behavior being monitored with the student's desired goal. It is an important component of the self-determination because it keeps the student constantly aware of whether she is meeting a desired goal. This is critical to the planning process because it informs the student whether or not the self-selected goal is being achieved. Thus, self-evaluation provides the student with a standard to assess his or her behavior (Agran, 1997). If the standard is not being met, the comparison may serve a corrective function. If it is being met, it serves as a reinforcing event and promotes the likelihood of the behavior being performed in the future. Consequently, it functions as a feedback loop, which provides the student with the appropriate consequence. Of practical significance is the fact that the student provides herself with the feedback and is not dependent on a teacher or other individual to do so.

Self-evaluation lends itself well to target behaviors that can be observed and recorded—behaviors that can be self-monitored. For example, in one application of self-evaluation conducted by the authors, a student was taught to give herself the correct amount of insulin at lunch time (Agran, Blanchard, & Wehmeyer, 2000). Information was collected from the student, her mother, and a doctor to develop a list of steps that guided her through the process. The list consisted of the following steps: (a) use the access kit (which included the supplies to test her blood, a chart to determine how much insulin to take and when to take it, a chart giving her information about her carbohydrate intake for the lunch meal, and her insulin and syringe); (b) test blood, (c) write down blood level; (d) find blood level on the chart; (e) follow what the chart says; (f) find lunch items on the chart and add the correct number of carbohydrates for the meal; (g) divide the total by five; (h) turn the syringe to the correct number of units; and (i) give herself the insulin.

The decision to teach the student to self-evaluate was based on the medical implications of making an error. The goal was to become 100% proficient in following the procedures outlined—anything less than that could have life-threatening consequences. The strategy proved to be successful.

In another investigation of the effects of a self-regulation strategy on the behavior of three adolescents with development disabilities served in general education, the students were taught to compare their self-monitored records to goals they had previously established for themselves (Wehmeyer, Hughes, et al., 2003). Target behaviors included not touching others, decreasing inappropriate verbalizations, increasing on-task behavior, decreasing disruptive behavior, and improving listening skills. The students compared their monitoring forms with those of a second observer, and determined if their performance met the selected goal. The self-evaluative intervention produced strong changes for all target behaviors.

Essentially, the same procedure to teach self-monitoring is used to teach self-evaluation. However, the student is taught to discriminate and record the occurrence of the target behavior and to discriminate whether the frequency of its occurrence as reflected in the recordings meet the specified criterion.

Self-Reinforcement. Self-reinforcement represents a major component of most conceptualizations of self-determination. Evidence suggests that it is as effective as, if not more effective than, teacher-delivered reinforcement. Self-reinforcement involves a system whereby students can reinforce their own behavior immediately (Wehmeyer et al., 1998). For example, students are always present to administer their own consequences or feedback, so the possibility of lost reinforcement is greatly minimized. Students often have difficulty acquiring desired outcomes because the natural consequences are too delayed, too small, or not achievable. Self-reinforcement essentially changes that by providing immediate feedback (Malott, 1984). As mentioned previously, students may work in settings where reinforcement is rarely delivered. Self-reinforcement allows the student to essentially create a reinforcement-rich work setting.

As with self-monitoring and self-evaluation, self-reinforcement is not acquired automatically. Most individuals, with or without disabilities, are not experienced in overtly reinforcing themselves. However, even individuals with the most extensive support needs can systematically be taught to reinforce themselves. For example, Lagomarcino and Rusch (1989) taught a student with profound mental retardation to reinforce himself by placing a coin into an empty slot in a board after completing a work task. The intervention increased the student's productivity.

Self-Instruction. Self-instruction involves teaching students to make task-specific statements out loud prior to their performance of a task. That is, they are taught to tell themselves what they have to do. These verbal statements allow students to direct and manage their own behavior as if they were being verbally directed by a teacher. By having the response consistently paired with the stimulus condition (the self-instruction), it is hoped that the likelihood of the response being performed is increased. (The case study of Roberto at the beginning of the chapter describes an application.)

Many students with disabilities have difficulty with problem solving and short-term memory retention; self-instruction provides additional information (verbal cues) to promote desired responding. It allows the student to verbally rehearse what he needs to do and to engage in meaningful problem solving. Because human behavior is largely controlled by language, self-instruction allows students to control their own behavior—a valued skill if someone is to become more self-determined. Self-instruction involves a two-step process: teaching the student to produce the self-instructions and then to complete the task.

Because language and thought are integrally linked, self-instruction has also been thought of as a verbal mediator that can regulate or control behavior (Whitman, 1990). Rather than serving as a cue to trigger the desired behavior, the self-instruction changes the way the student thinks about a phenomenon or behavioral event. In effect, self-instruction allows the student to think aloud.

Self-instruction can be used to teach a wide variety of skills (Agran & Moore, 1994). As indicated previously, if you can define the target behavior, the relevant self-instruction can be easily identified. Typically, self-instruction applications have followed a problem-solving approach in which the student is first taught to identify a problem. Such a problem may be a condition that prevents the student from completing a task (e.g., "I don't work fast enough. What am I doing wrong?"), or the realization that the student lacks some knowledge relevant to completion of the task (e.g., "I want to learn how to prepare food but I don't know how"). The student is then taught to identify a solution to the problem (e.g., "I'll find out how to make sandwiches"). Finally, the student is taught to tell himself what to do (e.g., "Now, I'll start making the sandwich").

Typically, self-instructions are comprised of complete phrases or sentences. They need to contain sufficient information so that the student can attend to the salient dimensions of the task. For students with limited language capacity, it may be necessary to shorten the self-instructions and use only a word or two. For example, if the student has difficulty saying, "I need to make sure I have all bread types to make sandwiches," it may be necessary to teach the student only to say "different bread on counter."

Antecedent Cue Regulation. The use of antecedent cues—that is, picture cues—is highly recommended. There are many applications in the transition research literature to support the use of picture cues as a means to promote student competence and independence. They provide students—particularly students with severe learning needs—an easy-to-use learning strategy and memory aid.

From symbols designating accessible parking areas to restroom signs to computer icons, picture cues and symbols serve as easily identified stimuli that provide information about a task, operation, place, or function. They portray or illustrate exactly what one has to do, and may be of great value to a student required to complete a complex task sequence. Independent of teacher assistance, the student can literally cue or prompt her behavior and determine her own success in completing a work task.

Picture cues include a variety of presentation formats: graphic symbols, simple line drawings, published instructional materials, magazine pictures, single photographs, and detailed photographic sequences, among others. Some students respond better to one method than another. Consequently, it is recommended that the visual method the student responds to best be determined. Unless the picture cues are already available, preparation of these cues may involve some cost: purchase of film, time to take photographs, processing, and so on.

Instruction involves two phases. First, the student has to be taught to identify the picture, and to follow the picture sequence correctly if more than one picture is shown. It is assumed that the student will be able to match the picture to the stimulus condition or task, but in some instances this level of instruction may also need to be provided. Second, the student is taught to refer to the picture and perform the response pictured. In the second phase the student is reinforced for following the picture cues and performing the illustrated pictures.

Many students have difficulty making discriminations. An advantage of using picture cues is that they alter the stimulus conditions that precede the target behavior by limiting the range of discriminative stimuli present in the environment (Agran & Martin, 1987). That is, they limit the number of discriminative stimuli the student may attend to. In short, the pictures enhance the likelihood that the student attends to the relevant stimuli associated with the task, which are illustrated in the cues, and remind the student of the relevant dimensions.

To promote generalization, students should be encouraged to refer to the pictures across different settings and situations. An advantage of picture cues is that they may serve as common stimuli across settings and, thus, promote generalized responding.

Problem Solving. Functioning successfully at school and in the community requires the ability to come up with multiple solutions to multiple problems (Agran & Hughes, 1997); unfortunately, youth with disabilities have considerable difficulty in this area. When confronted with problems at school, work, or in the communities, these individuals often respond impulsively without weighing the consequences of their actions, or do not respond at all. In short, many students with disabilities do not know how to identify problems or find ways to resolve those problems. Problem solving is the means by which students can meet their goals and, ultimately, become self-determined. It represents the student's key to success in the community and at work.

Similar to the other strategies discussed, problem solving can be systematically taught. The model described next presents a model to teach these skills.

Self-Determined Learning Model of Instruction. Wehmeyer and colleagues (Mithaug, Wehmeyer, Agran, Martin, & Palmer, 1998; Wehmeyer, Palmer, Agran,

Mithaug, & Martin, 2000) developed a model of teaching students to problem solve. The model, called the self-determined learning model of instruction, was derived from an earlier instructional model, the adaptability instruction model (Mithaug, Martin, & Agran, 1987; Mithaug, Martin, Agran, & Rusch, 1988).

The model consists of a three-phase instructional process. Each instructional phase presents a problem to be solved by the student. The student solves each problem by posing and answering a series of four student questions per phase. Each question is linked to a set of teacher objectives. Additionally, each instructional phase includes a list of educational supports that teachers can use to instruct students on how to self-direct their learning. In each phase, the student is the primary agent in decision making and developing an appropriate action plan. (The case study of Veronica at the end of the chapter illustrates an application of this model.)

The student questions are constructed to direct the student through a problem-solving sequence in each phase. The solutions to the problems in each phase lead to the problem-solving sequence in the next phase. Their construction was based on a theory in the problem-solving and self-regulation literature suggesting that there is a sequence of thoughts and actions, a means–ends problem-solving sequence that must be followed for any person's actions to produce results that satisfy his or her needs and interests. Thus, teachers implementing the model teach students to solve a sequence of problems to construct a means–ends chain—a causal sequence—that moves them from where they are (an actual state of not having their needs and interests satisfied) to where they want to be (a goal state of having those needs and interests satisfied) by having students answer the questions that connect their needs and interests to their actions and results via goals and plans.

To answer the questions in this sequence, students must regulate their problem solving by setting goals to meet needs, constructing plans to meet goals, and adjusting actions to complete plans. Thus, each instructional phase poses a primary problem the student must solve (What is my goal? What is my plan? What have I learned?), which, in turn, leads to additional problems or concerns that have to be addressed. The questions differ from phase to phase, but represent identical steps in the problem-solving sequence. That is, students answering the questions must (a) identify the problem, (b) identify potential solutions to the problem, (c) identify barriers to solving the problem, and (d) identify consequences of each solution. These steps are fundamental in any problem-solving process and form the means–end problem-solving sequence represented by the student questions in each phase.

Ultimately, the soundness of a person-centered career plan depends on the student's level of awareness of his or her career preferences and interests, as well as knowledge of his or her skills, competencies, and experiences. Problem solving provides a means for students to learn from their experiences and increase their knowledge about themselves. With this information students can construct plans that are truly based on their wishes and interests, and that, ideally, can be supported by the stakeholders in their communities.

Summary

Thoma and Getzel (2005) interviewed a sample of individuals with disabilities involved in varying types of postsecondary education. The majority identified the instruction they received to promote self-determination as being most critical for their success. In particular, they stressed the importance of learning to problem solve, learning more about themselves, setting goals, and learning a variety of self-management (self-directed) strategies, the strategies discussed in this chapter. The participants in this investigation represented a restricted sample, and further replications are warranted. Yet, the findings underscore the importance of self-directed learning. Self-determination has received a great deal of attention and has achieved a best practice status in the area of transition services (Wehmeyer & Schwartz, 1997). Nevertheless, as discussed in this chapter, few teachers are systematically teaching their students self-directed learning strategies to promote transition outcomes. This is troubling in light of the fact that the skills associated with enhanced self-determination and student-directed learning are positively associated with desirable transition outcomes.

The strategies described in this chapter provide students with skills that will allow them to identify and develop transition goals, self-direct their learning, and monitor and evaluate their own performance. Student self-determination is promoted only if transition team members and other stakeholders are supportive of students' wishes, interests, and actions. Without such support transition programs will continue to be directed by others. The student-directed learning strategies described here provide the means for students to drive their own programs and achieve self-selected goals—the purpose of transition services.

Veronica, a 17-year-old, is diagnosed as having a mild disability. She is highly verbal, has excellent social skills, and is an active contributor at IEP meetings; especially, she likes to tell the team how she sees her future. Although her grades are low, she is planning to receive her diploma the following year. She receives educational services in a neighborhood high school. She spends three out of seven periods in general education content classes, one period in resource room, one period in a special class, and two periods in a cooperative work experience. In her cooperative work experience she is being exposed to three different work situations: a fast-food restaurant, a grocery store, and a discount store. Although Veronica enjoys all these work experiences, working at the discount store is her favorite. She likes the fact that the store has so many things to sell and gives her the opportunity to smile and talk to customers.

Veronica expresses the concern that she is usually asked to straighten shelves or do cleanup work at the discount store. She would really like to be a cashier, but she is uncertain what that involves. After discussing her wish with team members, it was decided that the necessary training be provided. Additionally, the team wanted Veronica to have as much responsibility as other team members for monitoring and evaluating her own performance. The team decided that Veronica should be taught to apply the self-determined learning model of instruction to guide her instruction. That is, she would set relevant goals for herself, develop an action plan to learn how to be a cashier, and, last, evaluate how well she did after a given training period.

Study Questions

1. Why do you believe the lack of skills in component elements of self-determined behavior, like self-advocacy or goal setting, is associated with poor transition outcomes?

    Without these skills students have difficulty knowing what they want to get out of life and how to set their transition goals. This will result in disengagement and lack of motivation to succeed as they transition from school to work and community living.

2. What is the value of person-centered planning?

    It allows a student to identify a vision for his future. By developing his own plan, the student will feel empowered and motivated.

3. What is the difference between opportunity enhancement and capacity enhancement in person-centered planning?

    Opportunity enhancement seeks to provide students with sufficient supports and opportunities to pursue desired goals and interests. In contrast, capacity enrichment focuses on systematically teaching students a set of self-directed learning strategies to employ to achieve self-selected goals.

4. Why is it important to teach students to set goals for themselves?

    It allows them to set performance standards for themselves and to evaluate their progress relative to these standards.

5. What is the value of self-monitoring?

    Self-monitoring allows students to determine that a desired or goal behavior has been performed. Also, it may serve as a discriminative stimulus and cue the desired response.

6. What is the difference between self-monitoring and self-evaluation?

    Self-monitoring teaches students to record or tally the frequency of occurrence of a target behavior, whereas self-evaluation involves monitoring relative to a standard.

7. What is the advantage of self-reinforcement?

   It allows the student to immediately reinforce a desired behavior and, in doing so, increase the likelihood that the behavior will occur in the future.

8. How does self-instruction facilitate learning and task performance?

   It provides students with verbal cues to prompt desired responding. Additionally, by providing additional information, it facilitates problem solving and short-term memory retention.

9. What is the value of antecedent cue regulation in transition programs?

   It represents a means by which students can refer to easily identified stimuli that provide essential information about a work task.

10. Why is the self-determined learning model of instruction of value to students in transition programs?

    The model allows students to identify goals, develop action plans, and evaluate their progress in achieving their goals. It serves as a self-regulated problem-solving procedure, and is aligned with person-centered planning.

Recommended Reading

Agran, M., King-Sears, M. E., Wehmeyer, M., & Copeland, S. (2003). *Teachers' guides to inclusive practices: Student-directed learning*. Baltimore: Brookes.

Field, S., & Hoffman, A. (1996). *Steps to self-determination*. Austin, TX: PRO-ED.

Halpern, A., Herr, C. M., Wolf, N. K., Lawson, J. D., Doren, B., & Johnson, M. D. (1997). *Next S.T.E.P.: Student transition and educational planning*. Austin, TX: PRO-ED.

Martin, J. E., Huber-Marshall, L., Maxson, L., & Jerman, P. (2000). *ChoiceMaker self-determination curriculum*. Longmont, CO: Sopris West.

Wehmeyer, M., Agran, M., & Hughes, C. (1998). *Teaching self-determination to students with disabilities: Basic skills for successful transition*. Baltimore: Brookes.

Web Resources

Person-Centered Career Planning

Beachcenter.org, University of Kansas

http://www.beachcenter.org

The Beach Center on Disability consists of a rehabilitation research and training center on policies and families, funded by the National Institute on Disability and Rehabilitation Research, U.S. Department of Education; doctoral training programs and research initiatives funded by the Office of Special Education, U.S. Department of Education; and a research center on the ethical, legal, and social implications of the Human Genome Project, funded by the National Human Genome Project Institute, National Institutes of Health.

Child Development and Rehabilitation Center, Oregon Health and Science University

http://cdrc.ohsu.edu/

The CDRC improves the lives of individuals with disabilities or special health needs through leadership and effective partnerships with individuals, families, communities, and public and private agencies. It serves as an exemplary local, state, and national resource through a commitment to excellence in interdisciplinary clinical practice, research, education, policy development, and community service.

Self-Determination and Transition Projects, Wayne State University

http://www.coe.wayne.edu/

Out of the conviction that education is the means by which human circumstances can be improved, the college prepares professionals who have the commitment and competence to help people acquire the knowledge, skills, and understandings necessary to participate in and contribute to a complex changing society. To achieve this mission the college is committed to excellence in teaching, research, and service.

Self-Determination Synthesis Project, University of North Carolina at Charlotte

http://www.uncc.edu/sdsp/home.asp

The UNC at Charlotte, with a grant from the Office of Special Education Projects, U.S. Department of Education, is conducting a review and synthesis of the knowledge base and best practices related to self-determination (SD) and self-advocacy (SA) interventions in order to improve, expand, and accelerate the use of this knowledge by the professionals who serve children and youth with disabilities and the parents who rear, educate, and support their children with disabilities.

References

Agran, M. (1997). *Student-directed learning: Teaching self-determination skills*. Pacific Grove, CA: Brooks/Cole.

Agran, M., Blanchard, C., & Wehmeyer, M. (2000). Promoting transition goals and self-directed learning model of instruction. *Education and Training in Mental Retardation and Developmental Disabilities, 35*, 351–364.

Agran, M., Blanchard, C., Wehmeyer, M., & Hughes, C. (2001). Teaching students to self-regulate their behavior: The differential effects of students vs. teacher-delivered reinforcement. *Research in Developmental Disabilities, 22*, 319–332.

Agran, M., & Hughes, C. (1997). Problem-solving. In M. Agran (Ed.), *Student-directed learning: Teaching self-determination skills* (pp. 171–198). Pacific Grove, CA: Brooks/Cole.

Agran, M., King-Sears, M. E., Wehmeyer, M., & Copeland, S. (2003). *Teachers' guides to inclusive practices: Student-directed learning*. Baltimore: Brookes.

Agran, M., & Martin, J. E. (1987). Applying a technology of self-control in community environments for mentally retarded individuals. In M. Hersen, R. M. Eisler, & P. M. Miller (Eds.), *Progress in behavior modification* (pp. 108–151). Beverly Hills, CA: Sage.

Agran, M., & Moore, S. (1994). *How to teach self-instruction of job skills*. Washington, DC: American Association on Mental Retardation.

Agran, M., & Smith, M. (2004). Student-directed IEPs: "It's my life." *Innovations*. (Jefferson City: Missouri Department of Education.)

Agran, M., Snow, K., & Swaner, J. (1999). Teacher perceptions of self-determination: Benefits, characteristics, strategies. *Education and Training in Mental Retardation and Developmental Disabilities, 34*(3), 291–301.

Agran, M., & Wehmeyer, M. (1999). *Teaching problem solving to students with mental retardation*. Washington, DC: American Association on Mental Retardation.

Allen, S. K., Smith, A. C., Test, D. W., Flowers, C., & Wood, W. M. (2001). The effects of "self-directed IEP" on student participation in IEP meetings. *Career Development for Exceptional Individuals, 71*, 219–277.

Benz, M., Lindstrom, L., & Yovanoff, P. (2000). Improving graduation and employment outcomes of students with disabilities: Predictive factors and students' perspectives. *Exceptional Children, 66*, 509–529.

Copeland, S. R., Hughes, C., Wehmeyer, M. L., Agran, M., & Fowler, S. E. (2002). An intervention package to support high school students with mental retardation in general education classrooms. *American Journal on Mental Retardation, 107*, 32–45.

Gilbert, G. H., Agran, M., Hughes, C., & Wehmeyer, M. (2001). The effects of peer delivered self-monitoring strategies on the participation of students with severe disabilities in general education classrooms. *Journal of the Association for Persons with Severe Handicaps, 26,* 25–36.

Gove, P. B. (1967). *Webster's third new international dictionary of the English language unabridged.* Springfield, MA: Merriam-Webster.

Harris, L. (2004). *2004 National Organization on Disability/Harris survey of Americans with disabilities.* Washington, DC: National Organization on Disability.

Holburn, S. (2002). How science can evaluate and enhance person-centered planning. *Research and Practice for Persons with Severe Disabilities, 27,* 250–260.

Holburn, S. (2002b). Person-centered planning must evolve: Rejoinder to O'Brien, Evans, Halle and Lowrey. *Research and Practice for Persons with Severe Disabilities, 27,* 272–275.

Hughes, C., & Carter, E. W. (2000). *The transition handbook: Strategies high school teachers use that work!* Baltimore: Brookes.

Hughes, C., Copeland, S. R., Wehmeyer, M. L., Agran, M., Cai, X., & Hwang, B. (2002). Increasing social interaction between general education high school students and their peers with mental retardation. *Journal of Developmental and Physical Disabilities, 14,* 387–402.

Individuals with Disabilities Education Act (IDEA) Amendments of 1997, Pub. L. No. 105-17, 20 U.S.C. 1400 et seq.

Johnson, R. D., & Sharpe, N. M. (2000). Analysis of local education agency efforts to implement the transition services requirements of IDEA of 1990. In D. R. Johnson & E. M. Emmanuel (Eds.), *Issues influencing the future of transition programs and services in the United States* (pp. 31–48). Minneapolis: University of Minnesota.

Konrad, M., & Test, D. W. (2004). Teaching middle school students to use an IEP template. *Career Development for Exceptional Individuals, 27,* 101–124.

Lagomarcino, T. R., & Rusch, F. R. (1989). Utilizing self-management procedures to teach independent performance. *Education and Training in Mental Retardation, 24,* 297–305.

Malott, R. W. (1984). Rule-governed behavior, self-management, and the developmentally disabled: A theoretical analysis. *Analysis and Intervention in Developmental Disabilities, 4,* 199–209.

Martin, J. E., & Marshall, L. H. (1996). ChoiceMaker: Infusing self-determination instruction into the IEP and transition process. In D. J. Sands & M. L. Wehmeyer (Eds.), *Self-determination across the life span: Independence and choice for people with disabilities* (pp. 211–232). Baltimore: Brookes.

Mason, C., Field, S., & Sawilowsky, S. (2004). Implementation of self-determination activities and student participation in IEPs. *Council for Exceptional Children, 70,* 441–451.

Mason, C. Y., McGahee-Kovac, M., Johnson, L., & Stillerman, S. (2002). Implementing student-led IEPs: Student participation and student and teacher reactions. *Career Development for Exceptional Individuals, 25*(2), 171–192.

McGlashing-Johnson, J., Agran, M., Sitlington, P., Cavin, M., & Wehmeyer, M. (2003). Enhancing the job performance of youth with moderate to severe cognitive disabilities using the self-determined learning model of instruction. *Research and Practice for Persons with Severe Disabilities, 28,* 194–204.

Menchetti, B. M., & Piland, V. C. (2001). Transition assessment and evaluation: Current methods and emerging alternatives. In S. Alper, D. L. Ryndak, & C. N. Schloss (Eds.), *Alternative assessment of students with disabilities in inclusive settings* (pp. 220–255). Boston: Allyn & Bacon.

Mithaug, D. E. (1996). The optimal prospects principle: A theoretical basis for rethinking instructional practices for self-determination. In D. J. Sands & M. L. Wehmeyer (Eds.), *Self-determination across the life span: Independence and choice for people with disabilities* (pp. 147–165). Baltimore: Brookes.

Mithaug, D. E., Martin, J. E., & Agran, M. (1987). Adaptability instruction: The goal of transition programming. *Exceptional Children, 53,* 500–505.

Mithaug, D. E., Martin, J. E., Agran, M., & Rusch, F. R. (1988). *Why special education graduates fail.* Colorado Springs, CO: Ascent Publications.

Mithaug, D. E., Wehmeyer, M., Agran, M., Martin, J. E., & Palmer, S. (1998). The self-determined learning model of teaching: Engaging students to solve their learning problems. In M. Wehmeyer & D. J. Sands (Eds.), *Making it happen: Student involvement in educational planning* (pp. 299–328). Baltimore: Brookes.

Powers, L. E., Turner, A., Matuszewski, J., Wilson, R., & Phillips, A. (2001). TAKE CHARGE for the future: A controlled field-test of a model to promote students' involvement in transition planning. *Career Development for Exceptional Individuals, 24*, 89–103.

Schwartz, A., Jacobson, J. W., & Holburn, C. S. (2000). Defining person-centeredness. *Education and Training in Mental Retardation and Developmental Disabilities, 35*, 235–249.

Snyder, E. P., & Shapiro, E. S. (1997). Teaching students with emotional/behavioral disorders the skills to participate in the development of their own IEPs. *Behavioral Disorders, 22*, 246–256.

Thoma, C. A., & Getzel, E. E. (2005). "Self-Determination is what it is all about": What post-secondary students with disabilities tell us are important consideration for success. *Education and Training in Developmental Disabilities, 40*, 234–242.

Thoma, C. A., Nathanson, R., Baker, S. R., & Tamura, R. (2002). "Self-determination: What do special educators know and where do they learn it?" *Remedial and Special Education, 23*, 242–247.

Wehman, P. (1996). *Life beyond the classroom: Transition strategies for young people with disabilities.* Baltimore: Brookes.

Wehmeyer, M., Agran, M., & Hughes, C. (1998). *Teaching self-determination to students with disabilities: Basic skills for successful transition.* Baltimore: Brookes.

Wehmeyer, M. L. (1998). Self-determination and individuals with significant disabilities: Examining meanings and misinterpretations. *Journal of the Association for Persons with Severe Handicaps, 23*, 5–16.

Wehmeyer, M. L. (2002). The confluence of person-centered planning and self-determination. In C. S. Holburn & C. Vietz (Eds.), *Person-centered planning: Research, practice, and future direction* (pp. 51–69). Baltimore: Brookes.

Wehmeyer, M. L., Abery, B., Mithaug, D. E., & Stancliffe, R. J. (2003). *Theory in self-determination: Foundations for educational practice.* Springfield, IL: Charles C Thomas.

Wehmeyer, M. L., Agran, M., & Hughes, C. (2000). A national survey of teachers' promotion of self-determination and student-directed learning. *Journal of Special Education, 34*, 58–68.

Wehmeyer, M. L., Hughes, C., Agran, M., Garner, N., & Yeager, D. (2003). Student-directed learning strategies to promote the progress of students with intellectual disability in inclusive classrooms. *International Journal of Inclusive Education, 7*, 415–428.

Wehmeyer, M. L., & Palmer, S. B. (2003). Adult outcomes for students with cognitive disabilities three years after high school: The impact of self-determination. *Education and Training in Developmental Disabilities, 38*, 131–144.

Wehmeyer, M. L., Palmer, S. B., Agran, M., Mithaug, D. E., & Martin, J. (2000). Teaching students to become causal agents in their lives: The self-determined learning model of instruction. *Exceptional Children, 66*, 439–453.

Wehmeyer, M. L., & Sands, D. J. (1998). *Making it happen: Student involvement in education planning, decision making, and instruction.* Baltimore: Brookes.

Wehmeyer, M. L., Sands, D. J., Knowlton, H. E., & Kozleski, E. B. (2002). *Teaching students with mental retardation: Providing access to the general education curriculum.* Baltimore: Brookes.

Wehmeyer, M. L., & Schwartz, M. (1997). Self-determination and positive adult outcomes: A follow-up study of youth with mental retardation or learning disabilities. *Exceptional Children, 63*, 245–255.

Wehmeyer, M. L., & Schwartz, M. (1998). The self-determination focus of transition goals for students with mental retardation. *Career Development for Exceptional Individuals, 21* (1), 75–86.

Whitman, T. L. (1990). Self-regulation and mental retardation. *American Journal on Mental Retardation, 94*, 347–362.

Zhang, D., Katsiyannis, A., & Zhang, J. (2002). Teacher and parent practice on fostering self-determination of high school students with mild disabilities. *Career Development for Exceptional Individuals, 25*(2), 157–169.

CHAPTER 4

Building an Employment Vision: Culturally Attuning Vocational Interests, Skills, and Limits

James E. Martin, Lee L. Woods, and Lorraine Sylvester
University of Oklahoma

What is the purpose of special education? IDEA 2004 defines the purpose of special education as providing individually designed special education and related services to prepare children with disabilities for further education, employment, and independent living. Each child with a disability, who is at least 16 years old (14 years old in many states; Grack, 2005), will receive transition services to improve academic and functional behaviors to facilitate transition from school to postsecondary education, employment, and independent living. IEP teams develop transition goals and activities based on students' needs while considering their interests, skills, and limits as identified by student-expressed interests, transition assessment, and parental input (Johnson, 2005). Identification of employment interests, skills, and limits, mediated by needs, produces a vision of post–high school employment life to answer the question "What job do I want to do when I'm out of school?"

Thus, to answer this question, students must learn their employment interests, skills, and limits via an employment preference and transition assessment process that considers family cultural values (Leake & Black, 2005; Valenzuela & Martin, 2005). Teachers and employment specialists must know the meaning of the following concepts and how they apply to the transition process:

- *Interests:* job characteristics, setting, and tasks students are enthusiastic about
- *Skills:* behaviors and attitudes associated with positive supervisor on-the-job evaluations
- *Limits:* necessary behaviors that students do not have or do not use when required for positive job performance

Students learn their interests, skills, and limits as they participate along with their family in a vocational preference instructional and assessment process. This process provides students the opportunity to consider a range of job options that match their interests, skills, and limits (Martin, Mithaug, Husch, Frazier, & Marshall, 2003). Educators in turn include information gained from the preference process into the present levels of academic achievement and functional performance, need, and strength sections of IEP documents. Eventually, this information merges with suggestions from family and educators to become the student's employment vision.

Who provides the information that produces an employment vision? Does it come from just the student? Do educators provide input? What about family needs, interests, and dreams? IDEA 2004 suggests that students primarily develop their employment vision with assistance from transition assessments and parental input. Yet, increasing numbers of students in U.S. schools come from family backgrounds where their post–high school decisions derive from cultural expectations, needs, and interests of the family. The complexity of the employment vision development process emerges when school-based individualistic decision making, which teaches students to develop their own employment vision, meets a family-centered or collectivist decision-making process. That is, employment visions from a collectivist *perspective do not derive from individual decisions, but from decisions that meet the needs and interests of the family (Leake & Black, 2005).*

This chapter begins with two case studies—one exemplifies the student-directed transition decision-making process; the other represents a family-centered collectivist decision-making process. We examine how these two students, their families, and educators developed postschool transition employment goals. Last, we discuss the importance of culturally attuning the transition planning process to develop an employment vision for all students.

Julie—A 17-Year-Old Who Wants to Become a Chef

Hi! My name is Julie. I am a 17-year-old girl in the 11th grade. I have had help at school with my learning disabilities since the third grade, and my teacher is helping me write this story. I have attended my IEP meetings since the fifth grade and have been leading my IEP meetings for the past 2 years. When I first learned how to do this it was scary, but now I wouldn't have it any other way. About 3 years ago, when I was a freshman, I learned what my disability really means. Until then I simply thought I was stupid and couldn't do well in school. After I learned about my learning disability and how to become a self-advocate, I realized that I could be successful at school and in my adult life after I leave high school.

My family is very supportive and encourages me to be independent and make my own decisions. My parents have always had hopes and dreams for my future, and have given suggestions and guidance regarding my life after high school, but they expect that I will make my own decisions regarding college, a job, and where and how I will live.

I have been thinking for several years about what I want to do after high school. At first I wanted to be a nurse like my mom. She arranged for me to do some volunteer work at the hospital so I could see what it was like. It was okay, but there was a lot of gross stuff, and way too much paperwork! I decided to look into what I really liked to do . . . cook! Last year I started studying the "culinary arts" at the career technology center. My dream now is to attend a cooking school when I graduate next year. I want to get a job working in one of the nice restaurants in the canal area of the city. Who knows? Maybe someday I'll even own my own restaurant. I've participated in a transition class that helped me figure out what I wanted to do for a job. You'll see some of what I did.

I've always been encouraged to speak up for myself. My teacher says I'm a self-advocate. At school I learned how to lead my own IEP meetings. My teacher helped me learn how to describe my learning disability at the IEP meeting. I learned that my visual processing is in the superior range, while auditory processing, short-term memory, and written language are "areas of concern." I just know that it's hard for me to remember stuff and someone else must double-check my writing before I turn papers in to catch my mistakes. I am very organized (I get that from my mom), and I am a hard worker. My grades aren't too bad. I take tests in the resource room so I can have extra time. I can have a notetaker in class so I can concentrate on what the teacher is saying without thinking about writing. But you know what? I don't like to use a notetaker because it becomes too easy for me to daydream. At my next IEP meeting I'm going to tell my team that I no longer want a notetaker. Instead, I think I'll record the lessons so I can listen to important sections at home when I get ready for tests or have to write papers.

Each semester I talk to my teachers and explain to them my disability and the accommodations I need to be successful in their classes. At first this was hard to do. But my special education teacher coached me in what to say and now I would not have this any other way. She told me that I should learn to do this while in school so that I would know how to ask for accommodations when I'm at a job site. At the IEP meetings I also report on my goals, and talk about the new goals I have for the future. I need to continue to work on my writing, learn how to cook, and get a summer restaurant job. I like being able to lead my own IEP meeting rather than have others talk about me and make decisions for me. I now sit at the head of the IEP meeting table and lead my own meeting!

Christopher—A 17-Year-Old Who Likes to Fish

I am Brenda Alvarez. I work at the high school as a parent liaison. I am helping Christopher's mother write this story because she speaks little English and doesn't write it at all. Although I'm writing this, the thoughts are all from Christopher's mom.

Christopher was born in the Philippines. On the day he was born, the possibilities for his future seemed limitless. Everything seemed perfect. His entrance into the world was smooth. We were thrilled with this beautiful boy and imagined him doing great and wonderful things for his family and our village, for which we would be so proud. We imagined him swimming in the ocean, building his first vinta (a small sailboat), and sailing in front of our house with his friends. We dreamed that he would learn to fish and be very proud to have his first fish for supper. His grandparents and the other elders in our village would teach him their compassionate and caring ways. Someday, he might become a leader in our village. He has done great and wonderful things with his life; we continue to be proud of his accomplishments, but our dreams are different now than when he was first born.

The path we took in life was nothing like we had expected. That path took us to the United States when Christopher was just 3 years. We came to America to live with family members and to seek medical treatment so that Christopher could walk. In the Philippines, we take care of our sick until they die, and our family and community help anyone in need. But we had heard that miracles happen and that life is better in the United States. My older son went to the United States after graduating from the University of Manila. He said that Christopher could get lots of medical and educational help in the United States. We left everything and everybody we knew behind, including Christopher's grandparents and cousins, and went to the United States to live with our oldest son and his family. Christopher had several surgeries on his legs. He can now walk with support and a short distance by himself. We doubt we'll ever return to the Philippines. Our new life is here in America.

Christopher is now 17 years old and is in his second year in high school. His teachers tell us that he has moderate mental retardation. He still sees a physical therapist weekly to build his leg muscles. He can walk, but tires after walking a few blocks without support. He loves camping, fishing, and watching wrestling matches on TV. Many people in the city and in his school think he is dumb and stupid when they see him walk with his shaky movements or listen to his thick speech. Some kids tease him. He does understand what we say to him, and we understand him. Others could too if they would just take the time to listen. Christopher understands and speaks Tagalog, the language we spoke at our home in the Philippines. We still speak Tagalog around the house and with our family. Christopher learned to speak English at his school but he doesn't read much. When we go to stores, Christopher often talks for us because he speaks English better than my husband and me.

When Christopher began school, we went to meetings to determine what was best for him. There were lots of people, so many experts, at the meetings. Christopher has always had extra help at school, and he spends time in classes with other kids who aren't smart. But Christopher is smart. He helps me remember things at home. He lets me know when his baby sister cries or wakes up. He helps me clean and works in our store. In school, his needs are met, and he is treated well. After he turns 21, he will leave high school. He won't have a diploma but will have a paper saying he attended high school. His teachers want him to do more on his own. They want him to get a job and earn money. What can he do by himself? They talk about him living on his own. If we were back home in the Philippines, he would live with us, fish, and help his family. I am afraid for him to work among strangers. We want him to work for us in our small grocery store. Christopher is confused because the school wants him to decide where he wants to work and live after leaving high school. At home we tell him that he will live and work with his family and his church.

Summary

These case studies represent just two of the varied transition situations that face secondary educators. Julie will primarily determine her postsecondary transition goals with support from her family and educators. Christopher's story shows the need for educators to culturally attune the transition planning process. Let's now examine the transition process these two students experienced in school.

Julie's Example: Building an Employment Vision for a Student with Mild Disabilities Who Will Make Her Own Decisions with Family Support

Middle School Career Exploration

The evolution of Julie's employment vision formally began in middle school. Her school district uses ACT's Educational Planning and Assessment System (EPAS) to provide a longitudinal, systematic approach to prepare students for high school and transitions into adult life. In eighth grade Julie took the ACT EXPLORE assessment, which estimated her English, math, reading, and science performance. It examined her proposed high school course of study with recommended courses, and it provided a profile of her initial career interests. Like many students her age, Julie had limited exposure to the world of work, but she still expressed an interest in various occupations.

The EXPLORE test allowed Julie a formal opportunity to begin thinking about career possibilities. Her career profile showed interest in health care (nursing), medical diagnosis and treatment (veterinarian), crafts and related trades (chef or cook), and management (hotel or motel management). Julie's English class required that she research her top three EXPLORE career choices, write a paper on what she learned, and present the results to the class. This integrated interdisciplinary assignment met several English and counseling state content standards.

Julie first went to America's Career Infonet on the Internet (http://acinet.org/acinet/videos.asp) and watched career and job skills videos describing her top job choices. She also watched a few others that interested her. This free website provides videos for hundreds of job clusters and specific jobs and skills. Second, Julie visited the U.S. Department of Labor, Bureau of Labor Statistics' Occupational Outlook Handbook website (http://www.bls.gov/oco/home.htm). She looked up each of her top jobs to learn the training or education needed, earnings, expected job prospects, job details, and work conditions. Third, Julie and her mom both completed the Casey Life Skills functional transition assessment (http://www.caseylifeskills.org). This free Internet assessment determined the daily living, self-care, social relationships, communication, and work and study skills that Julie can do and those she still needs to learn. Julie and her mom used their home computer to complete the online assessment; the computer automatically scored and e-mailed the results to their e-mail accounts and Julie's teacher. Julie and her mom had fun comparing their results. Julie thought she did better on many of the items than her mom did. Last, Julie spent a few hours shadowing her mom while she worked at the hospital during a school-sponsored "take your child to work day."

After completing her research, Julie typed her paper and presented the results of her career exploration process to her English class. Julie realized the science classes that she would have to take for a career in health care would be tough, but she thought she could handle them. After watching her mom and other nurses at the hospital, however, Julie realized she would not like all the paperwork, the smell, and other tasks that bothered her. After initially considering being a nurse, she changed her mind.

At her middle school to high school transition IEP meeting, Julie presented to the IEP team what she learned through her career exploration English project. The Casey Life Skills assessment provided a list of transition strengths and needs that Julie asked to be included in her IEP. Several of the needs grew into goals that she would try to attain her first year. Julie expressed to the team that she would like to go to culinary school after graduating high school, and that she would like to become a chef. The postschool transition goals provided the IEP team direction in developing a course of study that included culinary art classes at the career technology center and a culinary-oriented work experience program.

High School Exploration and Preparation

The following three sections provide an overview of how Julie was invested in the transition class, when she took her interest inventory, and when updates were scheduled during high school.

Transition Class. First-year students with learning disabilities at Julie's high school take a required transition class. This class teaches students to understand their disability, how to actively participate in their IEP meetings and work to attain their own goals, and to develop their postschool transition goals and course of study. The teacher uses an employment program called Choosing Employment Goals (Marshall, Martin, Maxson, & Jerman, 1997) to teach students to identify and express their employment interests, skills, and limits.

To begin the employment section of the class, students learn to identify their initial employment goals. To do this, Julie first watched a video that depicts high school students using their interests, skills, and limits to determine their postsecondary transition goals. Julie then learned how to complete the Choosing General Goals process which asks her to identify her employment interests, skills, requirements, and limits. If Julie does not know the answer to a Choosing Goals question, that unanswered question becomes a goal. Julie knew that she was interested in becoming a chef (see Figure 4.1). She answered yes to question 1—"Do I know my interests?" She answered no to question 2—"Do I know what is required to do this?" She then set a goal to find out the requirements involved in becoming a chef. She identified her skills and verified that she had the skills to meet the job requirements. She recognized that her writing and short-term memory are limits, but she did not think they would cause any problems. By using the Choosing Goals process she established the goal to visit a restaurant, interview a chef, and continue learning how to become a chef.

By visiting the job site students discover the job's requirements, gather information about job characteristics, and learn about the actual work environment

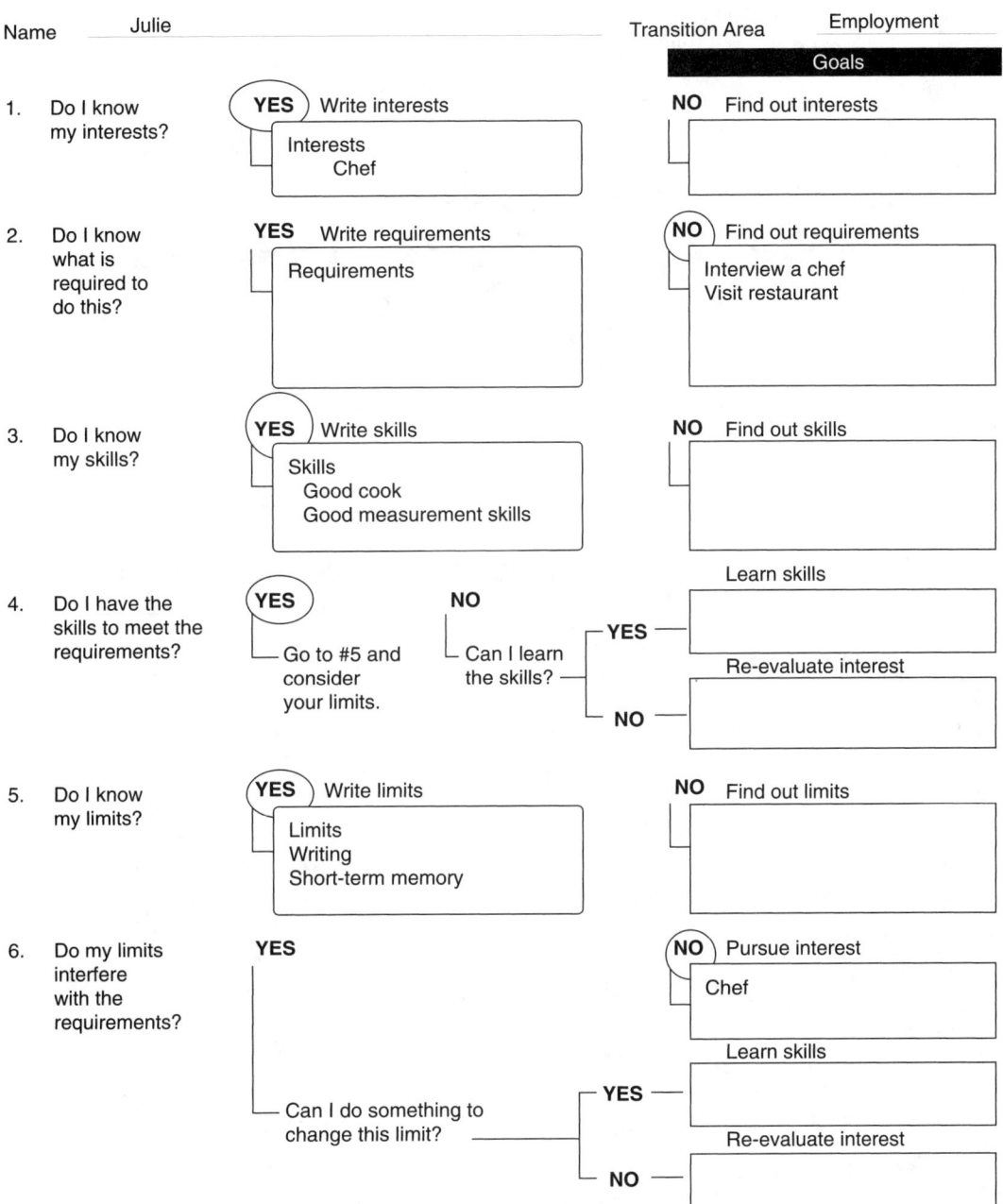

FIGURE 4.1 Choosing General Goals Worksheet
Source: Sample created from Marshall et al. (1997).

FIGURE 4.2 Job Characteristics I Like Worksheet
Source: Sample created from Marshall et al. (1997).

Name: Julie   Date: 2-27-06   Site: LeFood

	Circle the job characteristic or characteristics you like best. **What I Like**	Circle the job characteristic or characteristics that best describe what is at this job. **What Is There**	Circle YES if what you circled in the first two columns is the same. Circle NO if it is not. **Matches**
1.	work alone / (lots of people around)	work alone / (lots of people around)	(YES) NO
2.	quiet workplace / (noisy workplace)	quiet workplace / (noisy workplace)	(YES) NO
3.	(weekdays only) / weekends too	weekdays only / (weekends too)	YES (NO)
4.	easy job / (challenging job)	easy job / (challenging job)	(YES) NO
5.	dress up for work / (do not dress up) / wear uniform	dress up for work / do not dress up / (wear uniform)	YES (NO)
6.	(standing up) / sitting down / moving around	(standing up) / sitting down / moving around	(YES) NO
7.	work mornings / (work afternoons) / (work nights)	work mornings / (work afternoons) / (work nights)	(YES) NO
8.	(co-workers my age) / co-workers not my age	(co-workers my age) / co-workers not my age	(YES) NO
9.	(thinking work) / physical work	(thinking work) / physical work	(YES) NO
10.	(detail important) / detail not important	(detail important) / detail not important	(YES) NO
11.	(job same every day) / job different every day	(job same every day) / job different every day	(YES) NO
12.	(work with people) / (work with things)	(work with people) / (work with things)	(YES) NO
13.	important to work fast / (not important to work fast)	(important to work fast) / not important to work fast	YES (NO)
14.	(little supervision) / a lot of supervision	(little supervision) / a lot of supervision	(YES) NO
15.	work outside / (work inside)	work outside / (work inside)	(YES) NO

Percentage of Matches

Directions:

- Write the total number of matches from your Matches column on line **(a)**.
- Enter **(a)** into your calculator and push the "+" button.
- Enter 15 into your calculator and push the "=" button.
- Push the "×" button, enter "100."
- Push the "=" button. This is your percentage.
- Place your percentage in the shaded oval area marked **(b)**.
- Draw a line where your % Matches falls on the scale. Shade from 0% to your percentage to see how well the job matches what you like.

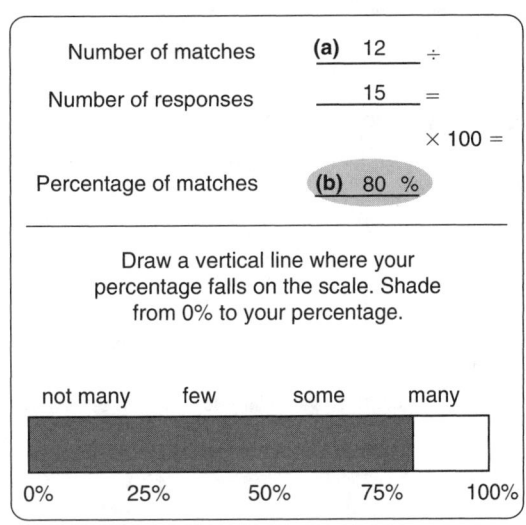

traits. Before going to visit the restaurant to shadow the chef and interview her, Julie identified the job's characteristics she thought she would like (see Figure 4.2). She indicated that she would like to work inside, with lots of people, in a noisy place. After spending time observing the chef in the kitchen and talking with her afterward, she completed the characteristic assessment form. Comparing the characteristics she initially preferred to those that existed at the restaurant, Julie determined the degree a job at this restaurant matched her characteristic interests. This restaurant matched 80% of her initial characteristic preferences. In future job site visits, Julie completed a characteristic assessment match at each job site she visited, with each match adding to her vocational assessment portfolio. By the time she left high school, she had established the job sites that provided her the best characteristic match.

While watching the chef work at the restaurant, Julie completed the Dream Job Shadowing Worksheet (see Figure 4.3). This form provided Julie a means to identify specific aspects of the job. She identified the job duties, and the necessary social, personal, and work skills, and from conversations with those around her,

FIGURE 4.3 Dream Job Shadow Worksheet
Source: Sample created from Marshall et al. (1997).

Name ___Julie_____ Date ___2/28/2006_____

Job Site ___LeFood_____ Job Title ___Chef_____

WORK	**What is the daily routine of this job?**
	Check inventory, order supplies, take deliveries, oversee kitchen staff, prepare meals according to recipes.

SOCIAL	**Is this person required to talk to supervisors, coworkers, customers?**
	Limited talk with customers, but talks a lot with supervisor and coworkers.

PERSONAL	**How does this person present himself/herself (example: dress, attitude)?**
	Uniform clean (at least at the start of the shift) and professional. Gets along well with coworkers.

JOB DUTIES	**What are the job duties (things you must be able to do)?**
	Prepare meals, follow recipes, direct kitchen staff, manage leftover food to limit waste, check inventories, order supplies.

ATMOSPHERE	**What is the work atmosphere? Is it very structured with many safety and work rules, or is it more relaxed and less structured?**
	Lots of safety rules, but the kitchen staff jokes around and has fun except when they are really busy.

JOB CHARACTERISTICS	What are the job characteristics (example: working alone or with lots of people)?

The job is inside, working with several people, it can get hot and crowded, it's important to work fast, it's a challenging job, lots of standing, you wear a uniform, there are lots of safety rules, you work nights, weekends, and holidays, and it can be noisy.

REQUIREMENTS	What experience, education, or training is required for this job?

Degree from vo-tech, college, or culinary arts school and apprenticeship.

REQUIREMENTS	How often do people get hired for this job?

Varies, but skilled chefs are usually in good demand.

REQUIREMENTS	What is the pay range for this job?

Average $14.75 per hour. Range $8.28–$26.75 per hour. Depends on the restaurant and area.

Can I do this job? (YES) NO   *Why or why not?*   I have (or can learn) the skills and I have a strong desire to become a chef.

Do I like this job? (YES) NO   *Why or why not?*   It's what I want to do, I love to cook and I like the restaurant environment.

FIGURE 4.4 Dream Job Informational Interview Worksheet
Source: Sample created from Marshall et al. (1997).

Name Julie	Date 2/28/2007

Site & Job Title LeFood - Chef			
Requirement Questions	**Would I like this?**	**Could I do this?**	**Teacher Comments**
1. What are the job duties? Prepare meals, create recipes, coordinate work of kitchen staff, estimate food requirements, order supplies.	(Yes) No	(Yes) No	
2. What are the training or educational requirements of the job? Culinary Arts degree from vocational school college, or professional culinary institute, followed by apprenticeship.	(Yes) No	(Yes) No	May need accommodations for written work requirement
3. What experience must people have to start here? Food prep, line cook, or other kitchen work experience.	(Yes) No	(Yes) No	
4. What are the physical demands of the job (lifting, standing, etc.)? Standing for hours at a time, lifting heavy pots and pans, may have to work in close quarters near hot stove.	(Yes) No	(Yes) No	
5. What are the hours of the job? May include early mornings, late nights, weekends and holidays. Might work 12-hour shifts.	Yes (No)	(Yes) No	
6. What kinds of equipment (vehicles, machinery, computers, etc.) must a worker be able to operate to do the job? Variety of pots, pans, cutlery, and other equipment including ovens, broilers, grills slicers, grinders, and blenders.	(Yes) No	(Yes) No	
7. Are there other jobs in this field that might have fewer requirements? Food prep, cooks, and line cook.	Yes (No)	(Yes) No	

Work Skills Questions	Would I like this?	Could I do this?	Teacher Comments
1. How important are speed and accuracy on this job? Very important.	(Yes) No	(Yes) No	
2. What are the company safety practices? Employees must complete annual safety program.	(Yes) No	(Yes) No	
3. What is the daily routine of the job? Inspect/order food for prep, run the kitchen and direct kitchen help, prepare meals.	(Yes) No	(Yes) No	
4. What are the reading, writing, and math requirements of the job? Reading/writing recipes, orders, measurement and money skills.	(Yes) No	(Yes) No	Julie has good math skills. The reading and writing demands should be manageable.
Social Skills Questions			
1. Do workers have contact with customers? If yes, what is the policy for customer interaction? Minimal contact with customers.	(Yes) No	(Yes) No	
2. Is there time for coworkers to talk to one another? Some during slow business hours.	(Yes) No	(Yes) No	
3. Does the company have social activities? No official ones.	(Yes) No	(Yes) No	
Personal Skills Questions			
1. What is the dress code? Chef uniform.	(Yes) No	(Yes) No	
2. What kind of personal traits must workers have to do this job? Must love cooking, good organizational skills.	(Yes) No	(Yes) No	
3. What things must workers have (uniforms, lunch, special shoes, tools, etc.)? Chef uniform, rubber-soled shoes.	(Yes) No	(Yes) No	

FIGURE 4.4 (continued)

Company Policy and Atmosphere Questions	Would I like this?	Could I do this?	Teacher Comments
1. How often do people get hired? Varies, employment outlook good for skilled chef.	Yes	Yes	
2. What is the entry level wage for this job? $10.50 per hour.	Yes	Yes	Wage varies greatly by type of restaurant and geographical region.
3. What benefits can workers at this site receive? Full-time chefs get medical and dental benefits. Free meals.	Yes	Yes	Varies by employer.
4. What kind of training do workers receive? Good knife techniques, safe food handling, proper use and care of equipment.	Yes	Yes	
5. Are workers closely supervised? Entry level and sous chefs supervised closely by master chef.	Yes	Yes	
6. How are workers evaluated? New chefs are evaluated monthly by master chef.	Yes	Yes	
7. **Is there a possibility of promotion?** Yes, to master or executive chefs.	Yes	Yes	
Summary			
1. Would I like this job? (Yes) No Why or why not? I love to cook and like the restaurant atmosphere.	(Note: Consider the number of times you chose "Yes" and "No" in the "Would I like this?" column and the teacher comments.) Why or why not?		
2. Could I do this job? (Yes) No Why or why not? I answered yes to all (all training).	(Note: Consider the number of times you chose "Yes" and "No" in the "Could I do this?" column and the teacher comments.) Why or why not?		

she found out about pay and how often someone is hired to work in the kitchen. After her observation she spent a few minutes with the chef and conducted a dream job interview (see Figure 4.4). Here Julie found out the specific training requirements, physical demands of the job, work hours and conditions, need for specific skills, starting pay, and benefits. For each interview question she had to indicate on the form if she liked what she found out, and if she could do what she had just discovered. At the end of the interview she decided that she liked this job and could do it.

Interest Inventory. All students in the 10th grade at Julie's high school take the ACT plan assessment. The plan updates the information from the middle school EXPLORE assessment. Julie's results showed that her career interests had become more focused. Nursing dropped out of her list. Her top interest areas now included crafts and related trades (chef or cook) and management (hotel or motel management) jobs. The plan advised Julie on her current academic performance in relation to career possibilities and postsecondary education plans. Specifically, her plan indicated that her math and science scores were below the benchmark scores that show readiness for college-level work, supporting Julie's change of job interest from nursing to cooking.

Update. During Julie's last 2 years of high school she successfully completed four semesters of culinary arts classes at the career technology school. With recommendations from her career tech culinary arts teachers, her supervisor at the restaurant where she worked part-time, and her teachers, Julie got accepted into a regional culinary school. Julie graduated from the culinary school and is now working as an assistant chef at a popular restaurant in the canal area of the city.

CHRISTOPHER'S EXAMPLE: BUILDING AN EMPLOYMENT VISION FOR A STUDENT WITH MENTAL RETARDATION FROM A COLLECTIVIST DECISION-MAKING FAMILY

Middle School Career Awareness

Christopher's middle and high school life school program established a sequenced career exploration and placement program so that students could leave high school with a successful community job matching their interests, skills, and limits. While in middle school, students first experience typical entry-level jobs that exist in their community and determine their preference for these jobs. Second, during their first 2 or 3 years of high school, students explore jobs they like in more depth. Third, students become employed at their preferred sites and receive support from school staff. Last, on-the-job support transfers to adult agency staff when students exit high school.

The four-stage career awareness, exploration, and placement model enabled many students to exit high school with a paid job that matched their interests, skills, and limits. The life skills educators and administrators realized that for some students from a collectivist family background, individual student interests must be considered relative to family interests and needs. With the help of parent liaisons and frequent teacher and parent interactions, school staff learned to understand family dynamics, and the family's needs, dreams, and interests. They also asked the family to understand the need for their son or daughter to experience a wide variety of jobs while going to school.

Students at Christopher's urban middle school speak 97 different languages in their homes. The school established a parental outreach program to help facilitate student success. Parental liaison teachers play an important role in this process. Prior to the start of Christopher's first year in middle school, a parent liaison visited him and his parents to learn parental expectations and needs, and to inform the parents of the school's expectations and procedures. During this visit the parent liaison asked the parents to describe their vision for Christopher's life after leaving high school. The liaison learned that his parents want Christopher to work in their family store and to live with them. The liaison told Christopher and his parents that the life skills program would provide him many opportunities to learn how to interact with the community, and to be as independent as possible. The parents learned that the school could arrange transportation for them to attend school parent nights and Christopher's educational meetings.

During middle school Christopher participated in the life skills program's community-based career awareness and exploration process, which enabled him to begin becoming aware of available community jobs and his initial job interests. Once or twice a month Christopher used the Choose and Take Action vocational assessment software (Martin et al., 2004) to choose an entry-level job he would like to visit (see Figure 4.5 for a listing of job sites, characteristics, and activities). The Choose and Take Action process combines interactive software with community experiences to enable individuals with mental retardation and other moderate to severe disabilities to make practical career choices. Students watch video segments, select a job that matches their interests, watch or do the selected job at a community site, evaluate the experience, and then make new choices based on what they learned. The Choose and Take Action instructional activities taught Christopher numerous self-determination skills, including:

- Choosing from a variety of work options
- Planning whether he wanted to watch or do the activity
- Completing the plan in the community setting
- Evaluating what he liked and did not like about the setting, activity, and worksite characteristics, and how he did while he was at the setting
- Using the information gained in the experience to make the next choice

CHAPTER 4 Building an Employment Vision

Settings	Activities	Characteristics
Car repair shop	Bag items/bring carts	Big open space
Child care center	Care for animals	Small space
Construction site	Care for people	Clean
Factory	Care for plants	Messy
Greenhouse	Cleanup	Few people
Grocery store	Clear tables	Many people
Hospital	Filing	Inside
Hotel	Handle materials	Outside
Janitorial service	Heavy cleaning	Noisy
Landscape company	Laundry	Quiet
Office	Move things	Wear own clothes
Restaurant	Do paperwork	Wear a uniform
Store	Stock shelves	
Vet office	Wash dishes	
	Yard work	

FIGURE 4.5 Community-Based Job Settings, Characteristics, and Activity Matrix
Source: Adopted from Martin et al. (2004).

The Choose and Take Action process includes four steps. Christopher completed the first two steps, choice making and plan development, in one session, then repeated this over the years he attended school.

Step 1: *Choice Making.* During choice making, Christopher viewed pairs of randomly presented videos showing different employment settings, activities, and job characteristics (see Figure 4.6). From each pair, he selected the one he liked the best. After viewing all the videos once, the chosen videos were paired and Christopher chose again. This continued until he picked one final video. He then developed a plan.

Step 2: *Plan.* During the planning part of the program, Christopher determined if he wanted to *watch* someone do the activity at the selected setting or if he wanted *to do* the activity. A printed plan shows what Christopher chose: the setting, activity, two

FIGURE 4.6 Screen Shot of Choose and Take Action Vocational Assessment Software Program
Source: From Martin et al. (2004).

characteristics, and whether he wanted to watch or do the activities. Evaluation questions regarding these choices are also printed on the plan.

Step 3: *Try It.* Based on the plan, Christopher went into the community to "try it" at the chosen setting.

Step 4: *Evaluate.* Christopher, with his teacher's guidance, evaluated the experience, and then entered that information into the computer.

The videos gave Christopher more information than illustrations or pictures of employment sites, but they still did not exactly replicate community settings. Christopher had to go to the settings and *try it* to make his choice meaningful.

The Choose and Take Action software recorded Christopher's choices and created reports that detailed his interests. The software graphed the results on simple bar graphs (see Figure 4.7) and provided the teachers detailed reports. Reports and graphs helped Christopher, his parents, and his IEP team witness his emerging interests and skill trends. The teacher included these reports, including the instructor's evaluations and observations, in his assessment portfolio. This

CHAPTER 4 Building an Employment Vision

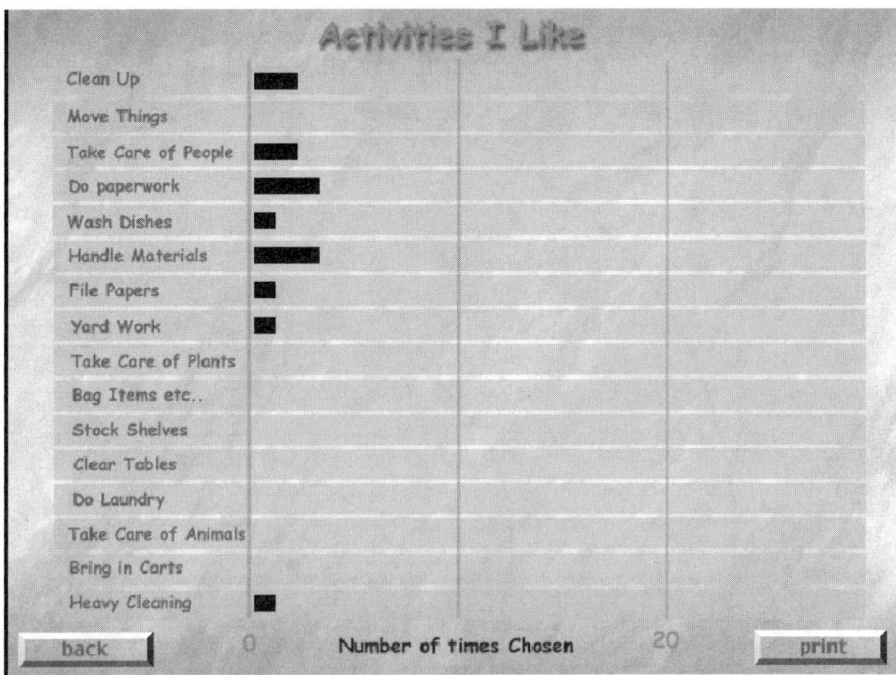

FIGURE 4.7 Screen Shot of Choose and Take Action Activity Preferences Bar Chart After One Completed Trial
Source: From Martin et al. (2004).

provided information about Christopher's preferences to discuss with his parents and to add to the planning process at IEP meetings. When Christopher's teacher or parent liaison discussed the Choose and Take Action results with his parents, they showed them how Christopher learned that he liked specific job characteristics, job tasks, and job sites. The teachers talked about the family's dream for Christopher to work in their store, and pointed out that he had the opportunity to learn about working in their store as well as other jobs.

At Christopher's middle to high school transition IEP meeting the team reviewed his vocational interest portfolio, and discussed with Christopher and his family his postschool employment vision. Christopher's special education teacher used the Employment Vision Circle (Sylvester, Martin, & Woods, 2006) to identify the family, educator, and student employment visions (see Figure 4.8). Christopher's mother said that the family wanted him to work in the fish section of their store when he leaves high school. Christopher said that he did not know what he would like to do. His teacher identified the preferred choices that Christopher made while using the Choose and Take Action process. After discussing the different viewpoints, the team decided that the employment postschool goal would be to

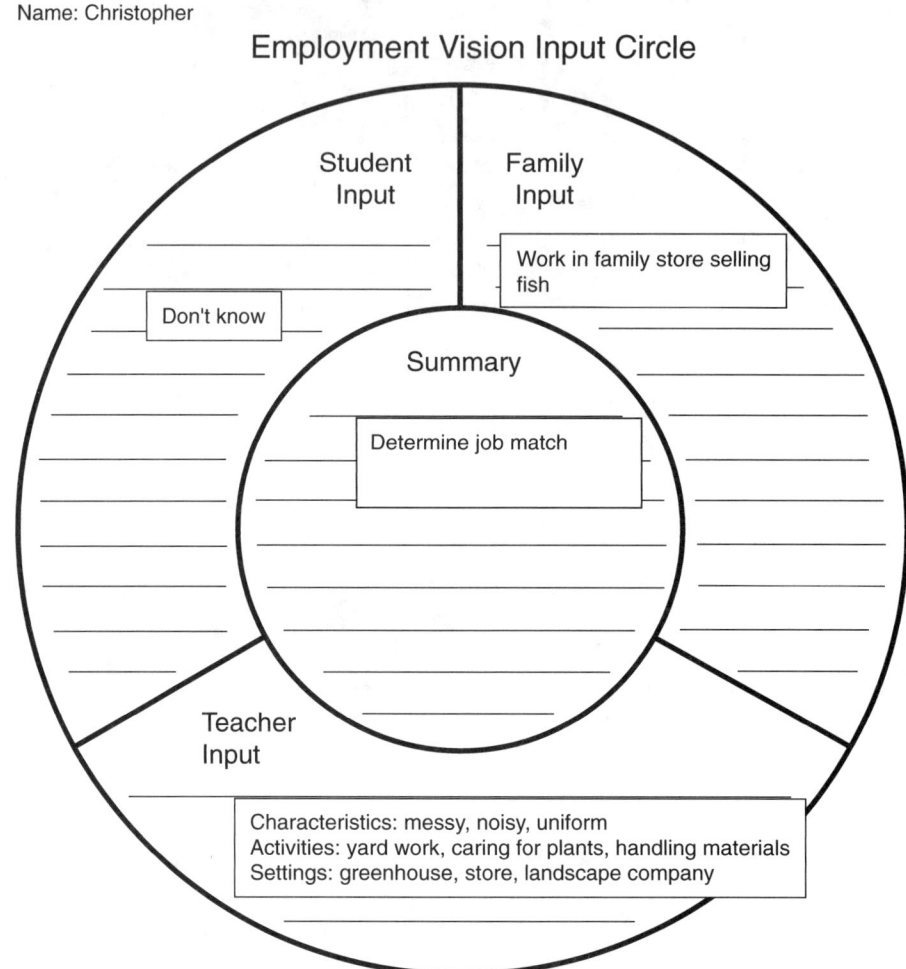

FIGURE 4.8 Employment Vision Input Circle to Help Determine Postschool Employment Goal
Source: From Sylvester et al. (2006).

determine a good job match because it was too early to pick a specific job and that he needed to explore jobs in more depth before making a decision.

High School Career Exploration Year 1

The high school career exploration program for the first year of high school expanded on what Christopher had started in middle school. Each month he continued using the Choose and Take Action software to choose a job site to visit.

CHAPTER 4 Building an Employment Vision

Rather than just visiting the job site for a few minutes as he had done in middle school, Christopher spent a few hours a week for 5 weeks at the chosen job site doing various tasks. A school job coach supervised his work and made certain the jobs he completed did not take away work from any job site employees. Each Monday his teacher gave him illustrated tasks, jobs, and characteristics assessments taken from the *Self-Directed Employment* handbook (Martin, Mithaug, Oliphint, Husch, & Frazier, 2002), which Christopher used to identify what he liked before going to job sites. At the end of the week, Christopher compared what he liked to what existed at the job site. This produced a percentage match indicating his interest in the site. Rather than using the illustrated assessment tools that came with the *Self-Directed Employment* handbook, Christopher's teacher downloaded vocational illustrations from the Self-Directed Employment website and created an individualized characteristic, task, and job site assessment match process (http://brookespublishing.com/picturebank/) to match his locations (see Figure 4.9 for an example task match assessment). Each week she graphed Christopher's assessment results and placed the results in his growing vocational assessment portfolio.

Tasks I Like

What I Like (Circle what you like)

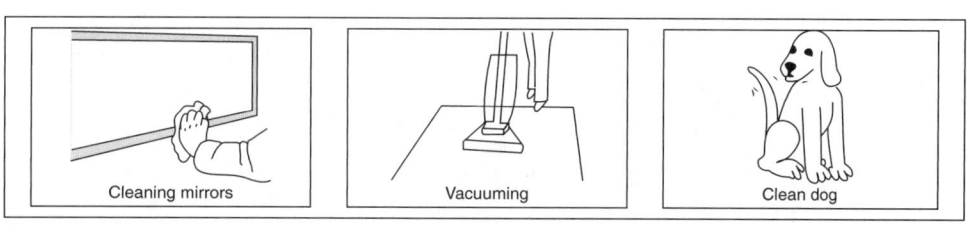

What's Here (Circle what is at this job site)

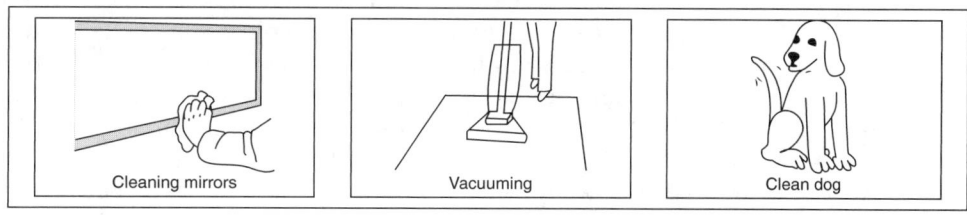

How Many matches?

0   1   2   3

FIGURE 4.9 Teacher-Made Task Match Assessment
Source: Created from illustrations in Martin et al. (2002).

Years 2 and 3. Christopher's second-year career exploration program continued the year 1 career exploration activities and added one component—self-evaluation of his work and social and personal skills. At the end of his work shift Christopher evaluated what he thought of his work performance and then compared them to those completed by his job coach to determine if they matched. Christopher's teacher developed the job evaluation form to match his work needs using the process described in the *Self-Directed Employment* handbook (Martin et al., 2002), and downloaded illustrations (http://brookespublishing.com/picturebank/) to develop the individualized evaluation form (see Figure 4.10). She also graphed the percentage of matches between Christopher and his job coach, and the job coach's evaluations. These data went into the assessment portfolio to document Christopher's performance at each exploration job site.

Year 3 Until Exit. Midway through Christopher's third high school year, his IEP team met to review his progress and to develop a new IEP. Christopher's teacher began the meeting by discussing his postschool employment goal. She first summarized the vocational assessment data collected since Christopher had come to high school:

- Favorite Characteristics: speed not important, working with family, wear a uniform
- Favorite Job Settings: store, vet office, auto repair shop
- Favorite Job Tasks: stocking shelves, talking to customers, wrapping packages
- Work Performance: accuracy okay; speed concern if job demands quick response
- Social Performance: talk too much at times
- Personal Performance: wear same clothes too often without washing

She then asked Christopher what job he wanted. Using the illustrated assessment forms, Christopher said that his first choice would be to work in a store stocking shelves or working with fish. His second choice would be working at a vet office helping take care of animals. His third choice would be working in a sports equipment store stocking shelves or helping in the fishing department. His mother indicated that they would like Christopher to work in the family store helping in the fish department. Christopher went to work part-time in the afternoons and weekends at his family's store. A school job coach provided follow-up services once or twice a week. Because he worked with family members, they provided any necessary on-the-job supports. Christopher attended high school through his 21st year. Follow-up evaluations indicated that his work, social, and personal behaviors matched job expectations and that he enjoyed the job. He went to work full-time at the store immediately after leaving school.

Job Site Self-Evaluation Form

Location: Date: Student:

My Evaluation	Job Coach Evaluation	Match
Person running — **FAST**	Person running — **FAST**	YES
Slow — **SLOW**	Slow — **SLOW**	NO
Dirty — **DIRTY**	Dirty — **DIRTY**	YES
Clean person — **CLEAN**	Clean person — **CLEAN**	NO
Man singing — **HAPPY**	Man singing — **HAPPY**	YES
Upset person — **UPSET**	Upset person — **UPSET**	NO
NUMBER YES MATCH =		
PERCENTAGE YES MATCH =		

FIGURE 4.10 Teacher-Made Job Site Self-Evaluation Assessment
Source: Created from illustrations in Martin et al. (2002).

CULTURALLY AND LINGUISTICALLY DIVERSE STUDENTS, THEIR FAMILIES, AND TRANSITION

Estimates suggest that if current trends continue, by the year 2040 over half of the K–12 school population will be comprised of culturally and linguistically diverse (CLD) students (Archer, 2000; Leake & Black, 2005; Sue, Bingham, Porché-Burke, & Vasquez, 1999). CLD students may broadly be defined as students who are not regarded as Caucasian or White; however, students who are considered White may also fall into the CLD category if they are outside the mainstream of American culture (Leake & Black, 2005). Interrelationships between culture, transition programs, self-determination, and the IEP process influence the postschool outcomes for CLD students with IEPs (Leake, Black, & Roberts, 2004; Trainor, 2002). Postschool outcomes for CLD students with disabilities include lower rates of postsecondary education participation, lower rates of employment, and a lower percentage of workers earning more than minimum wage compared to students with disabilities identified as White (Wagner, Newman, Cameto, & Levine, 2005).

Practitioners must know how best to involve CLD families and students with IEPs in IEP meetings and transition planning, but little empirical guidance exists on how to do this. White school culture and the collectivist values characteristic of many other cultures create a barrier preventing CLD students from successfully engaging in the transition planning process. Martin (personal communication, March 18, 2006) tells about a conversation he had with special education teachers at a small-town school where almost 60% of the students in elementary school are Native American; yet the percentage drops to about 15% during the high school years. When asked about this drop, the teachers told him that many of the Native American families want their children to only learn basic academics, then return home to learn the traditional ways. They are afraid that if they stay in school they will not learn the traditional ways and will move away from home.

How can we be sure students with disabilities from CLD backgrounds move from high school into a happy, secure, and culturally meaningful adult life? Moving through and planning for life after high school is a challenge for almost all teenagers and their families. Students with disabilities and their families have an even more difficult time understanding and positively impacting the transition from high school given their disability-related constraints. Yet another layer of frustration and difficulty occurs for students with disabilities and their families from CLD backgrounds. For these teenagers, the challenges may seem insurmountable as the student moves from high school into adulthood.

Helping students with disabilities from CLD backgrounds understand and manage the transition process while maintaining familial and cultural connections is difficult. Success requires that the student, family, teachers, and other significant people in the student's life develop common visions for the student's future.

While addressing the student's interests, skills, and limits, these visions can be attuned to the student's cultural traditions.

Individualism and Collectivism

Best practice transition methods and materials teach students to set goals and plan for their future using self-determination practices that promote individualism (Trainor, 2002; Valenzuela & Martin, 2005; Zhang, 2005). This means that students with disabilities are encouraged and expected to make their own decisions and attain their own goals. Self-determination practices that utilize personal decision making, self-evaluation, self-awareness, self-knowledge and self-advocacy support an individualistic perspective (Frankland, Turnbull, Wehmeyer, & Blackmountain, 2004). Students from CLD families, however, are more likely to demonstrate "collectivist" values, or interdependence with family, neighbors, or tribe (Black, Mrasek, & Ballinger, 2003). Thus, when determining their post–high school goals and directions, students from collectivist backgrounds consider their own role in terms of their family or community group, with the group's well-being as the priority (Ewalt & Mokuau, 1995; Leake et al., 2004). They often do not see themselves separate from their tribe or family—their tribe or family tends to define who they are and what they will do.

At issue in this distinction between individualistic or collectivist cultural values is the reality that cultural values fall on a continuum between the two. That is, students are not one or the other, not just individualist or collectivist. At different times they typically move from one to the other, or meld individualistic and collectivist characteristics for more effective interactions or to meet particular needs (Leake & Black, 2005). Individuals from both an individualistic and collectivist perspective undergo "cultural frame-switching" from collectivist to individualist and back when expectations and situations demand (LaFromboise, Coleman, & Gerton, 1993; Ramirez-Esparza, Gosling, Benet-Martinez, Potter, & Pennebaker, in press). This ability to frame-switch enables individuals, especially those from a collectivist background, to interact successfully within and with an individualist school society.

Cultural Reciprocity

Concerted effort to work with families, or to link students with peers, mentors, or other culturally relevant role models, can help ensure success in achieving postsecondary outcomes. Nevertheless, even without culturally specific mentors or professionals, sensitive use of cultural reciprocity will enable teachers and professionals to successfully engage students and their families from many diverse cultures. Cultural reciprocity coupled with student-directed and other self-determination strategies will ensure better outcomes for these students.

Cultural reciprocity involves getting to know and understand each family's uniqueness and recognizing that teacher, student, and family variables of cultural identity interact to form a relationship in which all voices are heard and respected (Harry, Rueda, & Kalyanpur, 1999). In cultural reciprocity, our self-awareness and subtle awareness of differences in others has universal applicability in that it ensures that all families and personnel feel empowered (Leake & Black, 2005). This empowerment is part of effective self-determination strategies, regardless of the cultural diversity exhibited by the student and family, and the professionals supporting each student.

Cultural reciprocity provides the basis for mutual understanding between students with disabilities from culturally diverse backgrounds and teachers and other professionals from mainstream American culture (Kalyanpur & Harry, 2004). This process goes beyond just being aware of cultural differences. It must start with an awareness of our own cultural background and orientation. This may be like asking a fish to describe water, as the old saying goes, and some may be so immersed in their worldview that they are unaware that values that are an integral part of their lives do conflict with values of others from different backgrounds. Many members of the American mainstream culture may not consider themselves as belonging to a particular culture, and individualistic values may exist outside the level of conscious awareness (Sue et al., 1999).

We cannot, and should not, be expected to change our own cultural orientation to match those of our students and families. However, once we understand our own cultural background, we can prevent it from dictating our perceptions of people from other cultural backgrounds. Acknowledging cultural differences first, and then determining why it is important to the student and family will lead to collaborative understanding all around (Harry et al., 1999).

Effective transition strategies typically involve identifying the student's and family's dreams and apprehensions about the future. It also involves identifying the student's interests, preferences, and strengths, as well as particular challenges and necessary supports in terms of technology, services, and people to overcome or manage these challenges. IDEA recognizes the importance of all these issues, a shared vision, in its primary planning tool, the IEP. Yet, students from CLD backgrounds continue to leave high school without achieving personal and culturally relevant outcomes. What can we do to ensure that the vision remains alive and constant for these students with a disability, their families, and teachers?

Several lesson packages are available that help students develop the self-determination and self-advocacy skills needed to achieve postsecondary employment outcomes. However, these materials typically emphasize individualistic decision making and fail to take into account family needs and interests. Thus, they usually stress the students' role in identifying and achieving goals based on how they value themselves, usually apart from their family. Valued qualities associated with self-determination include individualism, self-help, personal control over the environment, goal setting and attainment, competition, and future orientation (Zhang, 2005). However, CLD families may find the individualistic nature of self-determination models and the focus on independence and choice to be at odds with their values (Trainor, 2002). Valued qualities in this view include understanding one's role within the group, responding to the needs of others, and abilities to work as a team member (Leake & Black, 2005). Ewalt and Mokuau (1995) discussed this latter view as the antithesis to individual choice and self-determination. However, they go on to state that improving a student's self-direction may require a strengthening of the student's connection with and commitment to the group, as opposed to causing a disintegration of these connections.

Although instructional strategies typically address students' unique learning issues relative to their disability, they are not as responsive to cultural differences. The ability of the student and teacher to understand the impact of disability on learning and achieving future adult outcomes within the context of the student's unique familial and cultural background is critical to the success of the transition planning process. Self-determination, usually defined from a mainstream individualistic perspective that emphasizes the student's personal control and free choice in decision-making processes, is also an integral part of a collectivist perspective. That is, students from collectivist backgrounds can benefit from instructional strategies that teach self-determination with critical modifications to include giving priority to the group's well-being (Leake & Black, 2005). Regardless of the cultural values system practiced by students with disabilities, their families, teachers, or other helping professionals, these relationships must be based on trust and mutual respect.

Currently, a limited knowledge base and few practical strategies exist to help families and professionals involved with this unique group of youths from CLD backgrounds. Culturally attuning identification of barriers beyond the disability, and some initial suggestions for ameliorating these barriers in education for students with disabilities from CLD backgrounds are emerging. Recognizing that this barrier exists is a start. Removing the barrier requires attention to and strategies for teaching students how to achieve their postsecondary employment visions through a process that culturally attunes their interests, preferences, and strengths. This process must occur within the context of the student's and family's cultural perspective, which is likely to be collectivist, rather than individualistic in nature.

Summary

This chapter presented two case studies—Julie and Christopher's—with detailed examples of how each student's goals were addressed. Attending a transition class that provided opportunities for students to visit worksites and complete interest inventories led to Julie successfully completing four semesters of culinary arts classes that led to her becoming an assistant chef. Christopher's path began in middle school and included life skills training, community-based career exploration and planning, and eventually participating in work options that led to Christopher making informed choices. Important to making career decisions is our ability to understand and appreciate culturally and linguistically diverse students, their families, and the transition process. The second half of this chapter provided discussion on emerging questions and potential considerations related to cultural diversity.

Study Questions

1. What is the general objective of transition services?

   Each child with a disability, who is at least 16 years old (14 years old in many states [Grack, 2005]), receives transition services to improve academic and functional behaviors to facilitate transition from school to post-secondary education, employment, and independent living.

2. How are transition goals developed?

   IEP teams develop transition goals and activities based on students' needs while considering their interests, skills, and limits as identified by student-expressed interests, transition assessment, and parental input (Johnson, 2005). An employment preference and transition assessment process also considers family cultural values.

3. How can students get a first orientation about job skills of particular jobs of interest?

   America's Career InfoNet on the Internet (http://acinet.org/acinet/videos.asp) offers career and job skills videos that illustrate job choices. This free website provides videos for hundreds of job clusters and specific jobs and skills.

4. How can students obtain information about requirements of particular jobs of interest?

   The U.S. Department of Labor, Bureau of Labor Statistics' Occupational Outlook Handbook website (http://www.bls.gov/oco/home.htm) provides information on training or education needed for specific jobs, along with earnings, expected job prospects, job details, and work conditions.

5. How can students decide if a specific job of interest would be a good personal match?

   By visiting the actual job site students discover the job's requirements, gather information about job characteristics, and learn about the actual work environment traits. They can determine the degree a job at this site matches their characteristic interests. By the time students leave high school, they may clearly establish the job sites that provide them the best characteristic match.

6. How can a dream job interview be helpful?

   During a dream job interview, students can find out the specific training requirements, physical demands of the job, work hours and conditions, need for specific skills, starting pay, and benefits. For each interview question, students can indicate if they liked what they found out, and if they feel they could do what they had just discovered. At the end of the interview they may decide if they really liked this job and could do it.

7. What are characteristic postschool outcomes for culturally and linguistically diverse (CLD) students with disabilities?

   Postschool outcomes for CLD students with disabilities include lower rates of postsecondary education participation, lower rates of employment, and a lower percentage of workers earning more than minimum wage compared to students with disabilities identified as White (Wagner et al., 2005).

8. What can be reasons for those characteristic outcomes?

   Students from CLD families are more likely to demonstrate collectivist values, or interdependence with family, neighbors, or tribe (Black et al., 2003). When determining their post–high school goals and directions, students from collectivist backgrounds consider their own role in terms of their family or community group, with the group's well-being as the priority (Ewalt & Mokuau, 1995; Leake et al., 2004). They often do not see themselves separate from their tribe or family—their tribe or family often defines who they are and what they will do.

9. How can CLD students with disabilities be helped to overcome barriers to their self-determination?

   Concerted effort to work with families or to link students with peers, mentors, or other culturally relevant role-models can help ensure success in achieving post-secondary outcomes. Sensitive use of cultural reciprocity will enable teachers and professionals to successfully engage students and their families from many diverse cultures. Cultural reciprocity coupled with student-directed and other self-determination strategies will ensure better outcomes for these students.

10. What is a key factor to success of the transition planning process for CLD students with disabilities?

    Although instructional strategies typically address the student's unique learning issues relative to their disability, they may not be as responsive to cultural differences. The ability of the student and teacher to understand the impact of disability on learning and achieving future adult outcomes, within the context of the student's unique familial and cultural background, is critical to the success of the transition planning process.

Recommended Reading

Agran, M., & Moore, S. (1994). *How to teach self-instruction of job skills.* Washington, DC: American Association on Mental Retardation.

Hughes, C., & Carter, E. W. (2000). *The transition handbook: Strategies high school teachers use that work!* Baltimore: Brookes.

Web Resources

Culturally Attuning Vocational Interests, Skills, and Limits

America's Career InfoNet

http://acinet.org/acinet/videos.asp

This free website provides over 400 career cluster, job, and skill videos in both English and Spanish. Each 2- or 3-minute video provides an overview about the topic, needed requirements for the job, and job duties.

Casey Life Skills Assessment

http://www.caseylifeskills.org

The site provides a free and easy-to-use assessment for students, their parents, and teachers to discover what students need to learn to prepare for their adult life after high school. It provides detailed assessment results and teacher lesson plans. The assessments can be customized by using several assessment supplements, including specialized assessment questions for Native Americans, pregnant girls, and adolescent parents. The assessments can be viewed in Spanish or English.

Self-Directed Employment: A Handbook for Transition Teachers and Employment Specialists

http://brookespublishing.com/picturebank/

The site provides free downloadable vocational illustrations to depict job tasks, objects, people, places, and characteristics. The illustrations are then infused into the Self-Directed Employment vocational assessment and on-the-job assessment process.

U.S. Department of Labor, Bureau of Labor Statistics, Occupational Outlook Handbook (OOH), 2006–2007 Edition

http://www.bls.gov/oco/home.htm

This free website provides information on the training or education needed for most jobs, earnings, expected job prospects, job details, and working conditions.

References

Archer, J. (2000). Competition is fierce for minority teachers. *Education Week, 19,* 32–33.

Black, R. S., Mrasek, K. D., & Ballinger, R. (2003). Individualist and collectivist values in transition planning for culturally diverse students with special needs. *The Journal for Vocational Special Needs Education, 25,* 20–29.

Ewalt, P. L., & Mokuau, N. (1995). Self-determination from a Pacific perspective. *Social Work, 40,* 168–175.

Frankland, H. C., Turnbull, A. P., Wehmeyer, M. L., & Blackmountain, L. (2004). An exploration of the self-determinaton construct and disability as it relates to the Dine (Navajo) culture. *Education and Training in Developmental Disabilities, 39,* 191–205.

Grack, A. (2005). *What states either have, or plan to adopt, legislative or regulatory language requiring secondary transition.* Minneapolis, MN: North Central Regional Resource Center.

Harry, B., Rueda, R., & Kalyanpur, M. (1999). Cultural reciprocity in sociocultural perspective: Adapting the normalization principle for family collaboration. *Exceptional Children, 66,* 123–136.

Individuals with Disabilities Education Improvement Act of 2004, H. R. 1350, 108th Congr. (2004).

Johnson, D. R. (2005). Key provisions on transition: A comparison of IDEA 1997 and IDEA 2004. *Career Development for Exceptional Individuals, 28,* 60–63.

Kalyanpur, M., & Harry, B. (2004). Impact of the social construction of LD on culturally diverse families: A response to Reid and Valle. *Journal of Learning Disabilities, 37,* 530–533.

LaFromboise, T., Coleman, H. L., & Gerton, J. (1993). Psychological impact of biculturalism: Evidence and theory. *Psychological Bulletin, 114,* 395–412.

Leake, D., & Black, R. (2005). *Cultural and linguistic diversity: Implications for transition personnel.* National Center on Secondary Education and Transition, Essential Tools: October 2005. Retrieved January 12, 2006, from http://www.ncset.org/publications/essentialtools/diversity/default.asp

Leake, D., Black, R., & Roberts, K. (2004). Assumptions in transition planning: Are they culturally sensitive? *Impact, 16*(3), 1, 28–30.

Marshall, L. H., Martin, J. E., Maxson, L. L., & Jerman, P. A. (1997). *Choosing employment goals.* Longmont, CO: Sopris West.

Martin, J. E., Marshall, L. H., Wray, D., Wells, L., O'Brien, J., Olvey, G., et al. (2004). *Choose and take action: Finding the right job for you.* Longmont, CO: Sopris West.

Martin, J. E., Mithaug, D. E., Husch, J. V., Frazier, E. S., & Marshall, L. H. (2003). The effects of optimal opportunities and adjustments on job choices of adults with severe disabilities. In D. E. Mithaug, D. Mithaug, M. Agran, J. E. Martin, & M. Wehmeyer (Eds.), *Self-determined learning theory: Predictions, prescriptions, and practice* (pp. 188–205). Mahwah, NJ: Erlbaum.

Martin, J. E., Mithaug, D. E., Oliphint, J. H., Husch, J. V., & Frazier, E. S. (2002). *Self-directed employment: A handbook for transition teachers and employment specialists.* Baltimore: Brookes.

Ramirez-Esparza, N., Gosling, S. D., Benet-Martinez, V., Potter, J. P., & Pennebaker, J. W. (in press). Do bilinguals have two personalities? A special case of cultural frame-switching. *Journal of Research in Personality.* Retrieved January 24, 2006, from http://www.sciencedirect.com

Sue, D. W., Bingham, R. P. Porché-Burke, L., & Vasquez, M. (1999). The diversification of psychology: A multicultural revolution. *American Psychologist, 54,* 1061–1069.

Sylvester, L., Martin, J. E., & Woods, L. L. (2006). *Student-directed transition planning: A means for students, families, and teachers to plan for life after high school.* Norman: University of Oklahoma, Zarrow Center for Learning Enrichment. Retrieved from http://www.ou.edu/zarrow/SDT_IEP!!_.html

Trainor, A. T. (2002). Self-determination for students with learning disabilities: Is it a universal value? *Qualitative Studies in Education, 15*(6), 711–725.

Valenzuela, R. L., & Martin, J. E. (2005). The Self-Directed IEP: Bridging values of diverse cultures and secondary education. *Career Development for Exceptional Individuals, 28,* 4–14.

Wagner, W., Newman, L., Cameto, R., & Levine, P. (2005). *Changes over time in the early postschool outcomes of youth with disabilities. A report of findings from the National Longitudinal Transition Study (NLTS) and National Longitudinal Transition Study–2 (NLTS2).* Menlo Park, CA: SRI International. Retrieved January 25, 2006, from http://www.nlts2.org/

Zhang, D. (2005). Parent practices in facilitating self-determination skills: The influence of culture, socioeconomic status, and children's special education status. *Research and Practice for Persons with Severe Disabilities, 30,* 154–162.

CHAPTER 5

Working with Parents: Using Strategies to Promote Planning and Preparation, Placement, and Support

Wendy Parent, Denise Gossage, and Molly Jones with Patty Turner, Chris Walker, and Renee Feldman
University of Kansas

Sara is a cheerful, friendly, and inspiring young woman who has a smile for everyone and a positive outlook on life. She is 27 years old and has a disability label of Down syndrome. Sara works as a file clerk in the Medical Records Department of a hospital part-time earning $9.55 an hour with vacation, sick, insurance, and retirement benefits. She has been employed in this position for one year. Her parent always had hopes and dreams for her. In looking back over the years, it is interesting to see how they arrived at this juncture.

From the time Sara was an infant her mother (Linda) volunteered time, always kept in contact with her therapists and teachers, and provided her with outside school experiences with "regular kids." During her school years, she was mainstreamed into PE and music. Linda always attended IEP meetings and didn't just accept what the teachers presented but brought up suggestions and concerns. As junior high approached, Linda did a great deal of lobbying to get Sara into better programs. When in high school, Sara was fortunate to have a teacher who believed that all of her high school students should be treated as "normal" students. This was the first teacher who practiced full inclusion. Through a local college Sara joined Best Buddies and had three or four different girl buddies that she socialized with.

When Sara was 16, she moved to another state with her family. Sara's previous teacher wrote to the new teacher telling her not to underestimate Sara's capabilities as she was quiet. Later, Linda asked the new teacher if she had read the note. She admitted that she didn't but she came to the realization that the former teacher was right. Her new teacher worked hard at treating special education students normally. This teacher worked closely with the general education teachers and placed students in appropriate integrated classes. In her junior year Sara started job training. She went to various jobs for several months and did a variety of jobs, none of which really excited her or had any growth potential. She never complained but the jobs weren't exactly stimulating. Sara had a job coach with her, and Linda kept in contact with the job coach regularly.

As Sara became close to aging out of the school's 18–22 program, the job coach approached a local hospital about a job in the cafeteria for Sara. Sara worked there for 6 months with a job coach and no pay; however, as school ended the cafeteria was willing to keep Sara on as a paid employee. She had a job coach from the local county for 1 month and then worked on her own. It took a long time, but someone finally realized that Sara could read. When they started a new delivery system Sara was elevated to deliver meals to the patient rooms. She had to read the room number and bed number. This was quite a promotion for her and went well for 6 years until a new cafeteria manager decided that she didn't want Sara in the cafeteria.

This was another situation where going to the mat was worth it. Sara's family met with hospital administration, the board, the local TV news station, and also *pursued legal action. They arranged for an employment specialist to analyze different jobs at the hospital and negotiate a position. The position required learning the procedures and equipment handling, including adapting the workplace procedures and equipment. Sara's case was reopened with vocational rehabilitation services and Sara was able to obtain job coach support from the local supported employment provider. This job has turned out to be good for Sara, the hospital, and service providers. It impacted local job coach activities as Sara's new position was more sophisticated and detailed than what the coaching support services were used to. The coaching services were required to upgrade their approach to meeting Sara's new job training requirements.*

It is clear to Sara's family that positions for individuals with disabilities require individualized approaches and supports. Sara's parents were a great resource for job leads. They learned that it is very important to establish jobs before leaving the school-supported job placement activities as it becomes more difficult to get services after leaving. Among the biggest supporters for Sara were the teachers who believed in her and worked with the school system to encourage appropriate mainstreaming and typical experiences. Sara's parents found talking with other parents of children with special needs was very helpful.

Sara's parents have been involved in Sara's education from day one, keeping in contact with the school from the principal on down. They tried to provide Sara with a variety of opportunities, both after school and out of school. This required Sara's parents to provide transportation and be available to help out if circumstances changed. Being cooperative and realistic and maintaining expectations were real assets. Making contacts through the system was advantageous to Sara's family and knowing the rules and regulations governing special education was extremely important in helping effectively work the system. Sara's parents' role did not end when Sara transitioned from school to adulthood. They have been and continue to be involved, making contacts with adult service personnel, providing support at home and at her job, monitoring her employment situation, helping her stay connected with friends and the community, and working hard to keep her employed.

Families' involvement in their son's or daughter's education is a critical factor related to school success (Henderson & Mapp, 2002; National Parent Teacher Association [PTA], n.d.). Students benefit from family involvement as indicated by better academic performance, better attendance, lower dropout rates, increased likelihood for higher education, and improved attitudes (National Alliance for Secondary Education and Transition [NASET], 2005). For students with disabilities, in particular, family support and involvement contributes to successful transition and positively impacts postschool outcomes (deFur, 2005; Johnson, 2003;

Kim & Morningstar, 2005; Kim & Turnbull, 2004; National Center on Secondary Education and Transition [NCSET], 2004; Nisbet, Covert, & Schuh, 1992).

Parents play a significant role in transition as indicated by the overwhelming support for their involvement evident through legislation, research, outcomes, and student testimony (Carol, 2005; Carter, n.d.; Kohler & Chapman, 1999; NASET, 2005; NCSET, 2004). They bring a wealth of knowledge, experience, and documented evidence of what works and what does not work. In addition, parents are a source of continuity and consistency in the young adult's life that can be a key link among changing education and adult service personnel as well as an ongoing and constant source of support (deFur, 2005). All too often, without the involvement of parents a very different outcome or scenario than the one described for Sara is likely to occur in the young person's life ("Family perspectives on inclusion," 2005).

Family well-being has been shown to be impacted by transition success (Blacher, 2001; Chambers, Hughes, & Carter, 2004). Individuals with disabilities are part of a larger family system; therefore, what affects one member greatly influences the other members of that system. The quality of life of all persons is a critical consideration and targeted outcome of transition (Kim & Turnbull, 2004; Turnbull et al., 2005). Family-centered approaches that encourage family and individual involvement and address the needs of all persons foster parent–professional partnerships that promote positive postschool experiences (Kohler & Chapman, 1999; Turnbull, Turnbull, Erwin, & Soodak, 2006). Feelings of equality, mutual trust, respect, valuing of each other's contributions, a sharing of power, and a sense of give-and-take are essential for building productive and mutually satisfying relationships (Caplan, Hall, Lubin, & Fleming, 1997; deFur, Todd-Allen, & Getzel, 2001; Henderson & Mapp, 2002; PACER Center, 2004b; SRI International, 2005).

Families and students see employment as a primary goal and expectation of transition activities (Brooke, Barcus, & Inge, 1992; Chambers et al., 2004; Cooney, 2002; Kraemer & Blacher, 2001; "Family perspectives on inclusion," 2005). Supported and customized employment are two proven approaches for assisting individuals with disabilities in becoming competitively employed (Office of Disability Employment Policy, 2004; Wehman, Sale, & Parent, 1992). The basic idea behind both employment approaches is knowing what the potential employee wants and needs, what the employer wants and needs, and supporting or negotiating any differences between the two. As a result of these service modalities, many youth and adults who might otherwise be sitting home or spending their days in sheltered workshops are now working successfully at real businesses in the community (Wehman, 2001; WESTAT, 2005).

Supported employment has been a service option available to persons with disabilities for a long time and is responsible for many individuals working today who were previously considered unemployable (Bellamy, Rhodes, Mank, & Albin, 1988; Rusch, 1992; Rusch & Braddock, 2004; Wehman & Kregel, 1985). It is characterized by competitive employment in community businesses with training and support provided by a skilled job coach for as long as the individual is employed. Supported employment is for individuals who need help finding a job, intensive support to learn the job, and ongoing follow-along support in order to keep their job. It is based on the premise that individuals do not have to "get ready" for work but receive the necessary supports that bridge the gap between their skills and the job requirements once they are employed. Job coach assistance is provided more intensely at first, followed by intermittent ongoing support once the individual is able to complete the job. Examples of some of the supports that may help someone perform a job include advocacy, natural supports, assistive technology, job modifications, job sharing, rehabilitation engineering, compensatory strategies, and behavioral training techniques. Each of these supports are discussed in detail in this text. Important to parents, these supports must become part of a family's knowledge base.

In recent years, the idea of customized employment has gained increasing attention (Callahan, 2002; Luecking & Tilson, 2002; Office of Disability Employment Policy, 2004). An initiative by the U.S. Department of Labor, customized employment is considered to be an effective approach for all individuals who have support needs as a result of their life circumstances. It is characterized by competitive employment in integrated businesses with individualized support built on the relationship between an applicant and specific employer, meeting the needs of both. Thus, it is a value exchange between the employer and employee based on the unique needs and contributions of the individual and the discrete and emerging needs of the employer. Customized employment represents the best of what we know about employing individuals with disabilities, building on the proven practices of supported employment to include carved and created jobs, resource ownership, and self-employment strategies (Callahan & Rogan, 2004).

RECOMMENDED PRACTICES

Information is readily available describing what transition is, why it is important, how to implement effective transition planning, and how positive postschool outcomes can be achieved (Cameto, 2005; Hughes & Carter, 2000; Luecking & Certo, 2004; Rusch, Destefano, Chadsey-Rusch, Phelps, & Szymanski, 1992; Wehman, 2001b).

These resources are often targeted for students, family members, and teachers to equip them with the knowledge and strategies they need to make transition happen for themselves, their loved ones, and all students with a disability. However, even with this knowledge of what leads to positive postschool outcomes, transition planning is often less than effective, resulting in students exiting school only to sit home, attend sheltered work and day programs, live with families or in more restricted settings, be unemployed, and have their name added to long waiting lists.

Too many youth and adults who have a disability express a need for employment supports and without them cannot find or keep jobs. Employment rates are low (see Chapter 1) as compared to people who do not have a disability—a figure that has changed little over time (Louis Harris Poll, 2004; National Council on Disability [NCD], 2002).

Parents have and continue to find it increasingly difficult to promote positive outcomes for their children for a number of reasons, including (a) lack of a single agency responsible for transition, (b) fragmented service delivery systems, (c) shortages of qualified staff, (d) different and conflicting agency criteria for service delivery, (e) low expectations of what students can do, (f) interagency turf issues, (g) inadequate financial resources, (h) lack of knowledge of what other organizations have to offer, (i) poor student and family preparation and involvement, and (j) perpetuation of the status quo. The disturbing fact is these are the same issues that have plagued transition efforts for many years. Although transition activities vary in school systems nationwide, it is likely that most would identify one or more of these factors as significantly hindering what they were trying to accomplish.

Despite documentation of the problems and information, demonstrations, and resources that prove what works, transition best practices do not filter down to the implementation level on a consistent basis. As Rusch suggests in Chapter 1, the educational system does not provide appropriate planning services, or appropriately prepare youth for adult roles. It also fails to provide placement services and the supports needed to retain employment gains. Teachers report lack of time, inadequate support from administrators, and insufficient preparation as factors hindering their ability to implement quality transition services (General Accounting Office [GAO], 2003; Morningstar & Kleinhammer-Tramill, 2005; NCD, 2004). Families express concern that they are not involved in their son or daughter's transition planning activities as much as they would like (Everson & McNulty, 1992; Lankard, 1994). This chapter takes a decidedly focused approach to offering suggestions that students, schools, and school administrations should consider to buttress the need for better planning, preparation, placement, and support. The following sections detail each of these three levels.

Student-Level Strategies

We propose a process that does not depend on knowing everything or solving all of the problems plaguing transition. The process does require that programs support a way of thinking about transition that drives the entire system. This process can be used as a means to leverage systems to be more responsive to the needs and desires of students and their families. It is multifaceted and offers the benefit of addressing one student at a time while impacting change and lives beyond the targeted individual. The effectiveness of the process is that it does not rely on:

- knowing about all the potential resources, but on learning through the power of community;
- having all the services and supports available, but on creating options through the strength of the group;
- making sure all the pieces are in place, but on filling in the gaps with the expertise and connections of the team; and

- everyone believing in the possibilities, but on the persuasiveness and enthusiasm of the one who does.

This process suggests that the most powerful technique for implementing effective services is through teaming and collaboration. Both of these important concepts are discussed in the next section. Our approach is one where we make sure that the role of families is considered in both processes discussed in Chapters 6 and 7. Teaming and collaboration promote innovative employment and identifying needed creative supports. We recommend that parents organize, energize, individualize, and materialize. Each is discussed below.

Organize. Teaming can be initiated by a family member or a student directly or indirectly by making a suggestion to the teacher, transition coordinator, case manager, or other community or agency representative. Individuals to invite include school personnel, vocational rehabilitation counselor, benefits planner/navigator, supported employment provider, mental health/mental retardation/developmental disability agency representative, friends and family, an employer or member of the business sector, and others whose input and contributions are relevant.

Personal telephone calls made by parents are most helpful for encouraging individuals to attend. Explaining the purpose as needing their expertise to assist a student with becoming employed is often an attractive selling point. Additionally, having parents or their children conducting the meeting often enhances participation of everyone in attendance. It is likely that meetings will take approximately 2 hours. Asking participants to provide several convenient times over a 2-week period is often the best way to coordinate everyone's busy schedules.

Energize. Parents can set the tone of the meeting with an attitude of optimism and an agenda that identifies employment as the intended outcome. The focus of the meeting is not to determine the possibility or consideration of employment or to discuss barriers. The meeting is an effort to establish employment as the desired outcome of the individual's education and the meeting is a forum for figuring out how to accomplish this goal. A helpful starting point is for the student and family member(s) to share what the student likes, what his strengths and interests are, what his dreams and expectations are, and what he thinks might be important in talking about employment. The gathering of individuals around a single employment interest, such as law or art or cars, provides a forum for brainstorming, pooling resources and ideas, and sharing creative energy built on the experiences and knowledge of such a diverse group. The enthusiasm tends to be contagious and fosters productivity through the direct contributions of some and the response to peer pressure by others. Figure 5.1 outlines transition tips that parents can implement to increase their child's chances for success.

> Mary's mom indicated a critical need for a summer program for her 19-year-old daughter with a physical disability, preferably a job. But no job coach or supported employment resources were available and vocational rehabilitation services had

> - Prepare your child for major changes, such as going to a different school, changing jobs, or moving. Visit the school with the child so he can see where things are, like restrooms, counselors' offices, or libraries. Ask the job coach or teacher to take the student to a new job site before he is expected to perform the job tasks.
> - Observe transition programs carefully and try to avoid having your child "warehoused" if at all possible. Transition is a crucial time in your child's life and off-campus activities are vital to preparing her for adult life.
> - Ask the school to begin transition services as early as possible.
> - Begin working toward a goal of employment early. Identify areas that need work and find the techniques and personnel to work on them. Insist on activities during the day that will expose your child to work settings. Early in the transition process, if your child is able, have him take classes that could point to possible careers such as a greenhouse science class. See if your child can find work opportunities within the school such as working in the AV room or helping the office staff.
> - Don't be afraid to go to the top if necessary. If there is a problem, the first person to talk to should be your child's teacher, then the director of special education in the school. If you still are not satisfied, go to the head of special education in the district. They need to hear about individual situations and they are in a position to make changes.
> - Request that your child be given a vocational assessment upon entering high school to learn what areas she needs support in (to be included in the transition plan) so that she can develop the necessary skills to become employed. These skills could be work related, independent living, and community access. Often, schools do vocational assessments only when students are ready to graduate, which is much too late for the assessment to have any value.

FIGURE 5.1 Transition Tips for Parents

refused services earlier than midway through her last year of school at age 22. During the team meeting, the teacher mentioned a paid job at her community-based instruction site; the speech therapist stated she knew a college student interested in special education who might like to be a job coach; a friend and recreational therapist volunteered to support Mary in an inclusive recreational program; and vocational rehabilitation agreed to open her case and begin the process for permanent employment prior to leaving school.

Individualize. Out of the meeting ideas emerge, and through brainstorming the group realizes that everyone is connected to someone who is potentially instrumental in providing services. Narrowing down options into a workable plan, including how the plan will be implemented, is an essential next step. It is critical to draft an individual plan (see Chapter 4) that includes action steps, persons responsible, a timeline, and expected outcomes to ensure all pieces come together, particularly because traditional service delivery systems may not be responsible for coordinating the employment activities. A detailed plan will be needed to guide the team's efforts and ensure employment outcomes in areas that participants may not be familiar with. In addition, people with varying levels of expertise may be needed to make the employment situation happen. Furthermore, the plan serves as a blueprint for students and family members, putting them in the driver's seat as they direct the steps and activities that will enable them to achieve their employment goal.

> Keith, a young man with autism, loved music and through his team's brainstorming started his own self-employment venture in the recording industry where he is known as the Music Man. The teacher took the lead to pull together an employment team meeting. A friend on the team knew of someone who owned a coffee shop that brought in bands for entertainment. Another member knew of a professional consultant in the music industry. Keith's father offered to provide job coach support and manage the business. An acquaintance of one member was connected to the local college student union who could link with student musicians, and the family knew a member of their church who could share music resources and recording opportunities. Several members knew of possible marketing channels; the rehabilitation counselor suggested "starting your own business classes" through the small business development centers; the benefits navigator explained the impact of business ownership on SSI and Medicaid benefits; and resources for purchasing recording equipment and ideas for an accountant/bookkeeper were explored.

It is important to note that all of the specifics regarding the individual's employment do not need to be solved during the team meeting; however, it is critical to make sure that each one is raised, documented as an action step, and assigned as homework for one interested member to investigate.

Materialize. Too often, the best laid plans are just that: plans with no results. To ensure that employment outcomes are realized, a follow-up meeting must be scheduled. Many of the action steps are only the beginning, and once the information is brought back to the group, additional brainstorming and discussion are necessary. Often, new persons with specific knowledge or expertise may be invited to participate in subsequent meetings to fill an identified need of the group. For example, somebody may share types of jobs in a particular line of work, another may have found out what local business demands, still another may have identified a business open to creative job carving and, finally, someone who is employed in that field may give personal insight.

It is likely that the information generated at this meeting will dictate the development of a new plan or additional steps within the existing plan, taking it to another level closer to the targeted goal. Typically, the nature of the employment situation becomes clearer and greater emphasis is placed on who will actually develop the job, what supports are needed to maintain employment, and what are funding options to cover certain costs (e.g., travel, uniforms, and additional training). Remember, the energy and resourcefulness of the team continues to be the driving force behind the development of new and creative ideas that go beyond traditional disability service delivery systems, instead relying on generic, disability, and natural services, supports, and dollars. An added benefit is the shared contributions of the group with participating agencies offering to fund and/or provide all or part of specific components of the plan. Combined with resources available to the general community and a network of family and friends, the result is a collaborative effort and creative competitive employment outcome. Several meetings may be required before this point is reached, however.

> Cindy, a young woman with a cognitive disability, was interested in books and magazines even though she wasn't able to read. Her family wanted her to work and pushed for employment. The school helped identify job leads and shared assessment information. A job was negotiated at a local coffee shop, and Cindy's Book Nook was born. Vocational rehabilitation purchased magazine racks and start-up books and magazines; the developmental disability agency provided job coach support; Cindy's friend who was a bookkeeper volunteered to help her manage her books; the coffee shop owner offered to ring up her sales on the cash register for a small administration fee; and coworkers provided assistance on the job. Cindy is on the employer's payroll during the 20 hours she is at work and is self-employed the remaining hours when she is not there, allowing her to invest her profits and expand to other coffee shops in the area.

School-Level Strategies

As the transition years are approached, family members have many questions regarding the school's and community's plans for preparing their child for adult life. (See Figure 5.2 which lists transition tips for teachers.) Family members want information and need to take advantage of everything they can get. These avenues for information exchange offer family members a two-way street, providing them with a mechanism for sharing their own information and agenda with school personnel. Several classroom and school-based initiatives can provide this opportunity. These include parent forums, resource fairs, college nights, transition councils, parent resource networks, community contacts, and parent connections and support groups.

Parent Forums. These regularly scheduled meetings allow family members to communicate with special educators in a format similar to, but larger than, an IEP meeting without the goal-setting pressures and time constraints. Outreach efforts that rely on multiple formats to get the word out, such as notes with the student, mailed letters, school newspaper announcements, and posting flyers around town, are most inviting and effective at increasing family participation. Forums offer parents an opportunity to meet and connect with other parents who have a child with a similar disability or who might be experiencing similar issues.

Resource Fairs. These are annual events where for-profit and nonprofit organizations set up display tables and panels or presenters speak to parents about current or future topics of interest. Agencies representing local community options are

FIGURE 5.2 Transition Tips for Teachers

- Social skills training is crucial to students' success. This should be a major part of the transition process and should begin early. The schools' job is to prepare students for adult life and social skills frequently affect success at a job.
- Avoid "warehousing" students in a classroom if possible. Transition is for learning how to function as an adult in the outside world, not the artificial world of a high school campus.
- Begin working on transition services as early as possible. This gives students several years to work on practical skills needed to be employable and independent.
- During high school, in a student's schedule, find the right balance of academic and practical living or working skills to match what might be the student's needs as an adult. Don't underestimate the student and deprive him of an education, but at the same time don't ignore the skills that will allow him to function in the community either.
- Fill the time during the day with valuable activities, taking into account the student's stamina and capacity. In high school, suggest the child take classes that can point to possible job or career directions, such as a greenhouse science course, which could lead to jobs at florists or small farming operations, rather than more rigorous and abstract classes, unless there is a strong possibility that the student will be able to complete a postsecondary program leading to a technical certificate or an associates or bachelor's degree.
- Seek opportunities for the student to function in postsecondary settings. Look for opportunities for her to volunteer, work, take classes, do independent study, or participate in social activities on campus. Provide the necessary support for the student, and work with people on campus who are willing to include transition students.
- Consider the timing of activities. The time of day when the student does his best work should be when his most important activity happens. For example, if the student has a promising job opportunity and works best midmorning, schedule the job for that time of day. It is probably not a good idea to have a high-demand activity right after lunch.
- If changes are necessary in the student's schedule, be sure the student, the parents, and all staff members involved are informed of what the changes will be, why they are necessary, how they will improve the situation, and when they will start.
- If it is possible to find someone from outside the school doing a job or other activity that is interesting and appropriate for the student, let the student work with that person, having the aide fade away as quickly as possible.
- At the beginning of the school year, and whenever a new person joins the staff or personnel at a job, introduce administrators, supervisors, and new people to the student, providing them with information about the student that will help them understand her.
- Keep in mind that for those students who live entirely in the present, a paycheck in 2 weeks doesn't mean much when right now they are doing something they hate. They need to learn to accept delayed rewards because that is the way of the world, but consider their ability to understand that concept at this point in their lives.
- Prepare the student for unpredictable changes, such as the absence of a teacher or job coach due to illness. Have a clear plan and make sure the student understands it, maybe even allowing him to participate in creating the plan if possible. Practice the plan.
- When the student visits unfamiliar locations with school personnel, on the first day they find a place where the student can go if she becomes uncomfortable or needs a break. This location could be a

corner of the room, next to a cabinet, just outside the front door of a business—anyplace that is safe, comfortable for the student, and acceptable to the person accompanying the student.

- If you need a behavior plan, be sure it is simple enough so that all the participants can and will make use of it. Review its effectiveness often and make changes as necessary. Keeping elements of the plan that are no longer effective may not only waste time but also can create problems. Make sure the student understands the plan to the best of his ability. Report changes to everyone who will be affected, including aides, job coaches, employers, general education teachers who have the student in their classes, and administrators.
- Identify areas the student needs to work on to make her more employable. Find the techniques and personnel to work on them. Remember that for some students learning takes longer, so getting an early start will give them more time to develop good behaviors.
- Help the parent find summer activities. Offer an extended school year, explaining the benefits clearly.
- Teach students work-acceptable use of downtime including how to use vending machines. Most employee break rooms have these machines.

also available to share information on the services they provide, such as employment; housing; leisure, recreation, and social opportunities; postsecondary education; early childhood education; guardianship; special needs; advocacy; financial planning; and day services.

College Nights. College night is a yearly workshop and informal discussion with representatives from colleges, universities, community colleges, and technical schools about opportunities at the postsecondary level and the support services offered for students with disabilities. Information can include how to access postsecondary services, rights and responsibilities, required documentation, and types of support resources available.

Resource fairs and college nights are wonderful ways for parents to be exposed to potential options after school and to see some of the people or agencies that would become more involved with their child in the future. By asking questions and following through with their suggestions, family members can learn more and more about community offerings. Contacting and talking with individuals introduced at these two events allows both parties to exchange ideas.

Transition Councils. A transition council made up of representatives from the community is a good forum for communication among the agencies that participate. The activities the council as a whole conduct are valuable to the community in terms of disseminating information and connecting various professional entities, making them more effective in their own functions. It is also an effective means for parents to share their feelings and experiences as well as to bring up issues regarding a specific student or situation.

It is important to note that family members often do not become involved in transition councils if they are not actively seeking parent members and don't effectively reach out to them. A useful way to accomplish transition council work is to establish subcommittees around specific tasks or topics, such as employment, university connections, external funding, the business community, and so on. The council functions as an advisory board for these subcommittees. In some circumstances, family members may be the catalyst by suggesting that the school start a transition council, indicating who might serve and what the agenda items may include.

Parent Resource Networks. Started by parents, these groups offer a way to establish communication among parents. Interested family members can sign up to be part of the network. One group was started by parent members of the transition council and offered the use of its website as the primary mode of communication. The network provides a means of sharing information with a larger group of parents who want to be involved but may not like to attend meetings. This group can serve as a pool from which to draw participants for specific projects as well as a possible stepping-off point from which to form a separate parent-run transition coalition. The website can serve as a forum for parents to connect with each other regarding specific issues that occur in their children's lives without having to attend meetings where the bulk of the time is spent discussing issues other than the individual parent's needs. It also serves as an excellent mechanism for information dissemination and resource sharing. In addition, the parent resource network can act as a body or as a large group of individuals expressing concerns to the legislature and the school board about policy.

Community Contacts. Family members need to advocate to get community agencies to step in and help out. As individuals and groups, parents can communicate with legislators, city governments, community leaders, and policy makers, making them aware of the issues facing transition-age youth and the needs of family members, schools, and service providers.

One way some parents are coming together and connecting with their communities is through "small towns," building on the concept of natural supports and wrapping the small-town philosophy of neighbors taking care of one another around each individual with a disability (Solomon, 2005).

Parent Connections and Support Groups. These provide opportunities for sharing and gathering information. Many support groups have guest speakers who discuss a variety of topics, including IDEA, behavior intervention, job coaching, school vocational programs, and so on. If parents from several school districts come together, they may learn about a vocational program being offered in another school district but not in theirs. Parents can then ask their school system to provide that program. Parents might also know of businesses that they frequent or own that might offer a job lead for their son or daughter.

District-Level Strategies

Family members can also assume leadership roles within their school communities. The shortage of leadership and lack of trained staff in the area of transition offer family members excellent opportunities to fill in the gaps by assuming such roles (Everson & McNulty, 1992; NCSET, 2004; PACER Center, 2004a). Additionally, family members in leadership positions can affect the direction of transition activities by interjecting their own interests as well as promoting new agendas related to employment and postsecondary education. One unique and effective way of accomplishing this is to start a parent-led transition coalition.

Parent-run coalitions offer several advantages. First, family members give a face and a name to the issue of transition. The ambiguity of the transition process becomes real and tangible when aligned with individuals who are experiencing it. Second, family members' ideas are not colored by the perceived constraints of a big system such as budgeting, paperwork, liability, scheduling, and so on. Typically, they come with fresh thoughts and a "can do" attitude regarding expectations for their son or daughter. Third, family members bring a wealth of knowledge of community contacts and supports that they have developed over the years of being the parents of a child with a disability. Fourth, there is often a lot of finger pointing between agencies. Family members are not necessarily school district employees and, therefore, may be viewed as potential consumers modifying the focus of the interagency dynamics. Fifth, family members may bring a more focused leadership to a transition coalition as they have a very good reason to do it well. Finally, having a group of parents voice concern over an issue or make a suggestion is often much more powerful than one parent making the same statement at an IEP meeting.

Getting Started. Developing a transition coalition can feel like an overwhelming endeavor. Parents have a full life and other responsibilities; despite the desire it is one more task and a lot of work. One important consideration is to think of the transition coalition as one big transition meeting—for the parents' own child and many others. Once the coalition is up and running, many parents feel that the benefits gained for their own son or daughter, special education students, and the school as a whole far outweigh the initial start-up efforts and growing pains.

Suggestions for interested parents to consider include the following:

- Start making a list of hopes and dreams for your child. This is the transition plan. Think about whose help you would need to make those dreams come true for you and your child. Those are the members of the transition coalition.

- Talk with other parents and community members about starting a small group. Talk to your child's teacher.
- The parents and their child with a disability can be the focus of the first coalition meeting. Everybody will be at the table working toward a common purpose rather than spending a lot of time trying to figure out what the coalition should look like.

Moving Forward. Scheduling the meeting is frequently reported to be the most challenging part of the process. School personnel can often provide insight on arrangement details to make it a little easier. Things to consider include (a) location (community building, agency, or school); (b) date (Mondays and Fridays tend to be the least desirable); (c) time (afternoons may allow more people to participate); (d) frequency and length (perhaps once a month for 2 hours to start); (e) refreshments (always a nice bonus, especially if contributions can be identified); and (f) membership (ask around, make it known, contact specific individuals by phone). During the first meeting, it is helpful to establish a regular meeting schedule for at least a 6-month period.

Suggestions for moving forward are as follows:

- To get started, bring together people with similar interests. The group will expand as word gets out and others come. Group evolution will result in a core group of committed members who regularly participate.
- Allow a meeting or two for people to get to know each other, build rapport, share their accomplishments, and discuss their challenges. Surprisingly, there will be a great deal of similarity across the experiences of participants and agencies.
- Facilitate the group to set a clear vision, mission, and goals.
- Start on the front line, one student at a time, identifying and addressing real issues, such as transportation, job searches, and college or university involvement during high school.

Due to confidentiality, students' names may not be mentioned; however, the issues can be discussed as they are sure to extend beyond the particular student.

Continuing. Over time, the group will bond together in its common purpose. Membership will stabilize, and a more formal process will emerge. Often, the issues raised at one meeting will drive the agenda for the next. In addition, some long-term, ongoing projects are likely to be the focus of the group. Guest speakers are an excellent way to bring information and training to participants. The following is an example of the mission, goals, and meeting agendas for a parent-led council, the Athens Council for Transition (ACT).

> *The mission of ACT is to ensure meaningful transition for every student in the Clarke County School District.* Meaningful *is defined as the opportunity to obtain the highest level of independent functioning and productive activity possible for each student.*

Goals for Current Academic Year

- Provide training to teachers regarding transition process and resources available.
- Explore ongoing funding sources needed to carry out our mission.
- Host parent meetings to explain transition and related issues.

January Agenda

- Introductions
- Review and assess goals
- Transition training for teachers
- Student cases
    - Student (Q) and the student's mother will present the student's case regarding the transition process
- Update on upcoming parent workshops
- Student Recognition Celebration
- Announcements

February Agenda

- Introductions
- Review and assess goals
- Update on Q's transition
- Guest speakers
    - Housing and Economic Development
    - Transit Authority
- Parent workshops
- Announcements

Parent-run coalitions can impact the bigger issue of transition in the community as follows:

- Establish a collaboration with city or county leisure services and the school district:
    - Combine leisure services summer camp and school district extended-school-year services. The school district provides meals and the space. The cost of staff and transportation is split equally. The camp curriculum is tailored to meet IEP goals.
    - The Graduation Recognition Program is a collaborative effort to recognize the achievements of graduating students with disabilities. Students are given the opportunity to thank others and talk about postgrad plans. Recent graduates are also given the chance to talk to about what their life is like after high school.
- Establish a collaboration with the Transit Authority; it provides free training passes for students in the vocational training program, Youth Apprenticeship Program, transitioning students who are employed, etc.
- Cosponsor an annual transition expo to provide information to parents, teachers, and community members about the resources and supports available for individuals with disabilities in the local and surrounding areas.

- Advocate with the school district to commit to training and hiring of transition-age youth with disabilities.
- Problem solve solutions for individual student issues related to employment, thereby impacting policies and practices that influence all students who could potentially be affected.

Melvin is a bright young man with distinct interests and preferences. He often finds pleasure in the simple things in life: Mountain Dew, swinging, and credit card applications. Michael has autism, which significantly limits his ability to lead an independent life. In addition, his family life is tumultuous; he often told his teacher that he wanted to move out and have his own room. After a visit with the adult service provider, Melvin, who rarely expresses his wants and needs, looked at his teacher and said, ". . . makes me glad."

Because there were so many challenges for Melvin, his teacher began working with the agency social worker to research options, contact community agencies, and pool resources to help him. The teacher and social worker worked together with Melvin's caretaker to complete the necessary paperwork for services. Unfortunately, they kept hitting dead ends. Despite Melvin's significant needs and limitations due to his autism, he was not eligible to receive services through the agency because he did not have a diagnosis of mental retardation. If Mental Retardation and Developmental Disabilities (MRDD) deemed him ineligible for services, where could he receive services? The team did not give up. The director at the agency offered to serve Melvin using private funds as he was not eligible for a state waiver or a grant in aid slot. Problem solved, or so we thought. We were told that there were hundreds of individuals with an MR diagnosis throughout the state who were waiting for services and that Melvin could not take their slot because he had a disability label of autism. Now the advocacy campaign began in earnest. Members of the council presented Melvin's case to regional and state-level policy makers and wrote letters on his behalf. The parent-led transition council did not take no for an answer, and Melvin is now receiving services from the adult service provider while still enrolled in school.

Summary

This chapter has provided numerous strategies that can be used by parents, teachers, and administrators at several levels of potential influence. To provide students with the best opportunities to promote employment we suggested that parents organize, energize, individualize, and materialize. Parents must organize themselves to obtain desired outcomes and coalesce themselves to make sure that there is enough continuous energy to meet established goals. Making sure that the student is kept in mind, all parties should remain focused on achieving the agree-upon goals. Parent forums, resource fairs, college nights, and transition councils were some of the topics outlined to promote school-level change. District-level strategies were also presented with ideas that included how to help organize an academic year to promote meaningful outcomes for students.

Study Questions

1. What does supported employment mean?

   Supported employment has been a service option for a long time and is responsible for many individuals working who were previously considered unemployable. It is characterized by competitive employment in community businesses with training and support provided by a skilled job coach for as long as the individual is employed. Supported employment is for individuals who need help finding a job, intensive support to learn the job, and ongoing follow-along support in order to keep the job. It is based on the premise that individuals do not have to "get ready" for work but receive the supports that bridge the gap between their skills and the job requirements once they are employed.

2. What is customized employment?

   Customized employment is considered an effective approach for all individuals who have support needs as a result of their life circumstances. It is characterized by competitive employment in integrated businesses with individualized support built on the relationship between an applicant and specific employer, meeting the needs of both. It is a value exchange between the employer and employee based on the unique needs and contributions of the individual and the discrete and emerging needs of the employer.

3. What percentage of youth with severe disabilities is currently competitively employed, and what factor could play an important role in raising the statistics?

   According to national postschool data for youth with severe disabilities, only 13% are competitively employed 2 years after school exit (Certo et al., 2003). For youth leaving school, competitive work prior to graduation or exit is the most critical factor for avoiding these staggering statistics (Johnson, 2003; Wehman, 2001a; Wehman & Revell, 1997).

4. What are parent forums and what support do they offer?

   These regularly scheduled meetings allow family members to communicate with special educators in a format similar to, but larger than, an IEP meeting without the goal-setting pressures and time constraints. Outreach efforts that rely on multiple formats to get the word out, such as notes with the student, mailed letters, school newspaper announcements, and posting flyers around town, are most inviting and effective at increasing family participation. Forums offer parents an opportunity to meet and connect with other parents who have a child with a similar disability or who are experiencing similar issues.

5. What are parent resource networks and how do they differ from meeting-type forums?

   Started by parents, these groups offer a way for communication among parents. Interested family members can sign up to be part of the network. The network provides a means of sharing information with a larger group of parents who want to be involved but may not like to attend meetings. This group can serve as a pool from which to draw participants for specific projects as well as a possible stepping-off point from which to form a separate parent-run transition coalition. It is important that the network offer parents something more than just being able to participate in other people's projects. If a website is used it can serve as a forum for parents to connect with each other regarding specific issues that occur in their children's lives without having to attend meetings where the bulk of the time is spent discussing issues other than the individual parent's needs. It also serves as an excellent mechanism for information dissemination and resource sharing. In addition, the parent resource network can act as a body or as a large group of individuals expressing concerns to the legislature and the school board about policy.

6. What are possible advantages of family involvement in the transition process?

   First, family members give a face and a name to the issue of transition. The ambiguity of the transition process becomes real and tangible when aligned with individuals who are experiencing it. Second, family members' ideas are not colored by the perceived constraints of a big system such as budgeting, paperwork, liability, scheduling, and so on. Typically, they come with fresh thoughts and a can-do attitude regarding expectations for their son or daughter. Third, family members bring a wealth of knowledge of community contacts and supports that they have developed over the years of being parents of a child with a disability. Fourth, there is often a lot of finger pointing between agencies. Family members are not necessarily school district employees and, therefore, may be viewed as a potential consumer modifying the focus of the interagency dynamics. Fifth, family members may be more focused individuals to lead a transition coalition. They have a very good reason to do it well. Finally, having a group of parents voice concern over an issue or make a suggestion is often much more powerful than one parent making the same statement at an IEP meeting.

7. How can parents increase opportunities for their child to develop social skills?

   Parents should insist the school place the child in settings where she can interact not only with peers but also with people who are older and younger. In the child's life outside school, parents can find ways for her to interact with people in the community, such as ordering food at restaurants, paying for items at the store, or checking out library books. The child also should have opportunities to help others, to make her feel important and useful and take the focus off herself.

8. How can parents support the transition process in collaboration with the school?

   Parents can ask the schools to begin transition services as early as possible and request that their child be given a vocational assessment upon entering high school to learn in what areas he needs support (to be included in the transition plan) so that he can develop the skills needed to become employed. These skills could be work related, independent living, or community access. Parents should identify areas that need work and find techniques and personnel to work on them. Parents should also insist on activities during the day that will expose their child to work settings. Early in the transition process, if a child is able, he should take classes that could point to possible careers such as a greenhouse science class. Also, there may be work opportunities within the school such as working in the AV room, or helping out the office staff.

9. How can parents help their child handle challenging situations in the transition to work?

   Most of the time, parents should place only the amount of responsibility on the child that she can handle successfully, ramping it up as her abilities improve, but sometimes it is good to challenge her beyond what has been expected. It is never a good idea to add new challenges before special events that affect the child emotionally, either positively or negatively, such as a major vacation or moving to a new residence. Instead, expectations should be lowered. Parents can learn from difficult situations and review them with the child or with a spouse or friend. Mechanical problems that could have caused misbehavior should be considered first. There is no need to delve into deep psychological causes for an outburst if the problem is as simple as lost lunch money. Parents can then find out what they could have done differently, if anything, to have made the situation better or teach the child how she could have affected the outcome in a better way.

10. What opportunities might exist for a high school student in postsecondary settings?

    Opportunities might include volunteering, auditing classes, and participating in social activities.

Recommended Reading

Turnbull, A., Turnbull, R., Erwin, E., & Soodak, L. (2006). *Families, professionals, and exceptionality: Positive outcomes through partnerships and trust* (5th ed.). Upper Saddle River, NJ: Merrill/Prentice Hall.

Turnbull, A. P., Brown, I., & Turnbull, H. R. (Eds.). (2004). *Family quality of life: An international perspective.* Washington, DC: American Association on Mental Retardation.

Turnbull, H. R., Turnbull, A. P., Shank, M., & Smith, S. (2007). *Exceptional lives: Special education in today's schools* (5th ed.). Upper Saddle River, NJ: Merrill/Prentice Hall.

Wandry, D., & Pleet, A. (Eds.). (2003). *A practitioner's guide to involving families in secondary education.* Arlington, VA: Council for Exceptional Children.

Web Resources

Working with Parents

Beach Center on Disability

http://www.beachcenter.org

The Beach Center on Disability consists of a rehabilitation research and training center on policies and families, funded by the National Institute on Disability and Rehabilitation Research, U.S. Department of Education; doctoral training programs and research initiatives funded by the Office of Special Education, U.S. Department of Education; and a research center on the ethical, legal, and social implications of the Human Genome Project, funded by the National Human Genome Project Institute, National Institutes of Health.

National Dissemination Center for Children with Disabilities (NICHCY)

http://www.nichcy.org

NICHCY serves the nation as a central source of information on disabilities in infants, toddlers, children, and youth; IDEA, which is the law authorizing special education; No Child Left Behind (as it relates to children with disabilities); and research-based information on effective educational practices.

Parent Advocacy Coalition for Educational Rights (PACER)

http://www.pacer.org

The mission of PACER Center is to expand opportunities and enhance the quality of life of children and young adults with disabilities and their families, based on the concept of parents helping parents.

Parent Educational Advocacy Training Center (PEATC)

http://www.peatc.org

PEATC assists the families of children with disabilities through education, information, and training. PEATC builds parent–professional partnerships to promote success in school and community life through information and assistance to families in understanding and negotiating the education and service systems for their children with disabilities; training for families and professionals that model partnerships and encourage active learning; and collaboration with and technical assistance to schools, state and local agencies, parent resource centers, and community organizations.

References

Bellamy, G., Rhodes, L., Mank, D., & Albin, J. (1988). *Supported employment: A community implementation guide.* Baltimore: Brookes.

Blacher, J. (2001). Transition to adulthood: Mental retardation, families, and culture. *American Journal on Mental Retardation, 106*(2), 173–188.

Brooke, V., Barcus, M., & Inge, K. (1992). *Consumer advocacy and supported employment: A vision for the future.* Richmond: Virginia Commonwealth University, Rehabilitation Research and Training Center on Supported Employment.

Callahan, M. (2002). *Employment: From competitive to customized.* Retrieved September 30, 2004, from http://ruralinstitute.umt.edu/transition/art_employcustomized.asp

Callahan, M., & Rogan, P. (2004). Customized employment—a discussion. *Choose Work, 15*(2–3), 8.

Cameto, R. (2005, April). The transition planning process. *National Center on Secondary Education and Transition NCTS2 Data Brief, 4*(1). Retrieved September 14, 2005, from http://www.ncset.org/publications/printresource.asp?id=2130

Caplan, J., Hall, G., Lubin, S., & Fleming, R. (1997). *Literature review of school–family partnerships.* North Central Regional Educational Laboratory. Retrieved November 17, 2005, from http://www.ncrel.org/sdrs/pidata/pi01trev.htm

Carol, K. (2005). Strategies for helping young adults in transition: A mother's wisdom. *Tash Connections, 31*(7/8), 12–13.

Carter, S. (n.d.). *The impact of parent/family involvement on student outcomes: An annotated bibiliography of research from the past decade.* Eugene, OR: Consortium for Appropriate Dispute Resolution in Special Education (CADRE).

Certo, N. J., Mautz, D., Pumpian, I., Sax, C., Smalley, K., Wade, H., et al. (2003). A review and discussion of a model for seamless transition to adulthood. *Education and Training in Developmental Disabilities, 38*(1), 3–17.

Chambers, C. R., Hughes, C., & Carter, E. W. (2004). Parent and sibling perspective on the transition to adulthood. *Education and Training in Developmental Disabilities, 39*(2), 79–94.

Cooney, B. F. (2002). Exploring perspectives on transition of youth with disabilities: Voices of young adults, parents, and professionals. *American Association on Mental Retardation, 40*(6), 425–435.

DeFur, S. H., Todd-Allen, M., & Getzel, E. E. (2001). Parent participation in the transition process. *Career Development for Exceptional Individuals, 24*(1), 19–36.

Everson, J. M., & McNulty, K. (1992). Interagency teams: Building local transition programs through parental and professional partnerships. In F. R. Rusch, L. DeStefano, J. Chadsey-Rusch, L. A. Phelps, & E. Szymanski (Eds.), *Transition from school to adult life: Models, linkages, and policy.* Sycamore, IL: Sycamore Publishing.

Family perspectives on inclusion and transition. (2005, July/August). *TASH Connections, 31*(7/8).

General Accounting Office. (2003, July). *Special education: Federal actions can assist states in improving postsecondary outcomes for youth.* Washington, DC: Author.

Henderson, A., & Mapp, K. L. (2002). *A new wave of evidence: The impact of school, family, and community connections on student achievement.* Austin, TX: Southwest Educational Development Laboratory.

Hughes, C., & Carter, E. (2000). *The transition handbook: Strategies high school teachers use that work!* Baltimore: Brookes.

Johnson, J. (2003). *Parent and family guide to transition education and planning: What parents and families need to know about transition education and planning for youth with disabilities.* Retrieved November 22, 2005, from http://www.rohan.sdsu.edu/-jrjohnso/SFTEPl/SFTEP1.htm

Kim, K., & Morningstar, M. E. (2005). Transition planning involving culturally and linguistically diverse families. *Career Development for Exceptional Individuals, 28*, 92–103.

Kim, K. H., & Turnbull, A. (2004). Transition to adulthood for students with severe intellectual disabilities: Shifting toward person–family interdependent planning. *Research & Practice for Persons with Severe Disabilities, 29*(1), 53–57.

Kohler, P., & Chapman, S. (1999). *Literature review on school-to-work transition.* Champaign: University of Illinois at Urbana–Champaign, National Transition Alliance, Transition Research Institute.

Kraemer, B. R., & Blacher, J. (2001). Transition for young adults with severe mental retardation: School preparation, parent expectations, and family involvement. *American Association on Mental Retardation, 39*(6), 423–435.

Lankard, B. A. (1994). *Parents and the school-to-work transition of special needs youth.* Retrieved November 14, 2005, from http://npin.org/library/pre1998/n00159/n00159.html

Louis Harris Poll. (2004). Retrieved from http://www.nod.org/content.cfm?id=1537

Luecking, R., & Certo, N. (2004). Integrating service systems at the point of transition for youth with significant support needs: A model that works. *American Rehabilitation, 27*(1), 2–9.

Luecking, R., & Tilson, G. (2002). *A practical introduction to customized employment.* Baltimore: TransCen, Inc.

Morningstar, M. E., & Kleinhammer-Tramill, J. (August, 2005). Professional development for transition personnel: Current issues and strategies for success. *National Center on Secondary Education and Transition Data Brief, 4*(4). Retrieved November 14, 2005, from http://www.ncset.org/publications/printresource.asp?id=2440

National Alliance for Secondary Education and Transition. (2005). *National standards & quality indicators: Transition toolkit for systems improvement.* Minneapolis, MN: National Center on Secondary Education and Transition.

National Center on Secondary Education and Transition. (January, 2004). *Current challenges facing the future of secondary education and transition services for youth with disabilities in the United States,* (Discussion paper). Minneapolis, MN: Author.

National Council on Disability. (2002, June). *Letter to the Honorable Elaine L. Chao.* Retrieved November 30, 2005, from http://www.ncd.gov/newsroom/correspondence/2002/chao_06-28-02.htm

National Council on Disability. (2004). *Improving educational outcomes for students with disabilities.* Retrieved April 27, 2005, from http://www.ncd.gov/newsroom/publications/2004/educatio noutcomes.htm

National Parent Teacher Association. (n.d.). *National standards for parent/family involvement programs.* Retrieved November 22, 2005, from http://www.pta/org/archive_article_details_11 18251710359.htm

Nisbet, J., Covert, S., & Schuh, M. (1992). Family involvement in the transiton from school to adulthood. In F. R. Rusch, L. DeStefano, J. Chadsey-Rusch, L. A. Phelps, & E. Szymanski (Eds.), *Transition from school to adult life: Models, linkages and policy.* Sycamore, IL: Sycamore Publishing.

Office of Disability Employment Policy. (2004). *Customized employment Q and A.* Washington, DC: Author.

PACER Center. (2004a). *Increasing parent involvement on special education and disability-related interagency committees, councils and boards.* Bloomington, MN: Author.

PACER Center. (2004b). *Parent keys to success in the parent–school partnership.* Minneapolis, MN: Author.

Rusch, F. R., & Braddock, D. (2004). Adult day programs versus supported employment (1988-2002): Spending and service practices of mental retardation and developmental disabilities state agencies. *Research and Practice for Persons with Severe Disabilities, 29*(4), 237–242.

Rusch, F. R. (1992). *Supported employment: Models, methods, and issues.* Sycamore, IL: Sycamore Publishing.

Rusch, F. R., DeStefano, L., Chadsey-Rusch, J., Phelps, L. A., & Szymanski, E. (1992). *Transition from school to adult life: Models, methods, and policy.* Sycamore, IL: Sycamore Publishing.

SRI International. (2005, June). *Changes over time in the early post school outcomes of youth with disabilities.* Menlo Park, CA: Author.

Turnbull, A., Turnbull, R., Erwin, E., & Soodak, L. (2006). *Families, professionals, and exceptionality: Positive outcomes through partnerships and trust* (5th ed.). Upper Saddle River, NJ: Merrill/Prentice Hall.

Turnbull, A. P., Turnbull, H. R., Agosta, J., Erwin, E., Fujiura, G., Singer, G., et al. (2005). Support of families and family life across the lifespan. In C. Lakin & A. P. Turnbull (Eds.), *National goals and research for persons with intellectual and developmental disabilities* (pp. 217–256). Washington, DC: American Association on Mental Retardation.

Wehman, P. (2001a). *Life beyond the classroom: Transition strategies for young people with disabilities* (3rd ed). Baltimore: Brookes.

Wehman, P. (Ed.). (2001b). *Supported employment in business: Expanding the capacity of workers with disabilities.* St. Augustine, FL: Training Resource Network, Inc.

Wehman, P., & Kregel, J. (1985). A supported work approach to competitive employment of individuals with moderate and severe handicaps. *The Association for Persons with Severe Handicaps, 10*(1) 3–11.

Wehman, P., & Revell, W. G. (1997). Transition into supported employment for young adults with severe disabilities: Current practices and future directions. *Journal of Vocational Rehabilitation, 8*(1), 65–74.

Wehman, P., Sale, P., & Parent, W. (1992). *Supported employment: Strategies for integration of workers with disabilities.* Boston: Andover Medical Publishers.

WESTAT. (2005). *Evaluation of disability employment policy demonstration programs, final report.* Rockville, MD: Author.

Building Teams and Interagency Coordination

PART 3

Chapter 6
Using Interagency and Interdisciplinary Teams to Enhance Transition Services

Chapter 7
Interagency Collaboration: It Takes Communication to Support Transitions

CHAPTER 6

Using Interagency and Interdisciplinary Teams to Enhance Transition Services

Jane M. Everson and Joy Ivester
University of South Carolina School of Medicine
and
Joan D. Guillory
Louisiana State University Health Sciences Center

Across the United States, cities, counties, and other municipalities struggle continuously to assess needs, budget resources, create policies, and oversee a broad array of quality services for their communities and citizens. In the areas of human and social services, community-level professionals have acknowledged that interagency and interdisciplinary teaming can enhance the planning, delivery, and evaluation of these services. As a result, teamwork is considered an effective practice with regard to affordable housing, assistive technology, early intervention, family support, high school to adult life transition, postsecondary education, public health, public transportation, workforce development, as well as in many other service areas.

In recognition of its critical role, the broad concepts of interagency and interdisciplinary teamwork have been promoted in an abundance of professional literature. However, much of this literature promotes the concept of teamwork, while paying minimal attention to the process and outcomes of teamwork. This has frustrated the ability of professionals and other advocates to apply teamwork experiences and skills to interagency and interdisciplinary services and outcomes.

This chapter provides education and adult services personnel, families, self-advocates, and other community advocates with a foundation on which to build community-level teamwork activities that will enhance interagency and interdisciplinary services and outcomes for all of a community's citizens, including those with disabilities. Specifically, the chapter (a) provides an overview of selected community development terminology and concepts; (b) describes how community development and teaming practice can be applied successfully; (c) presents case studies of communities and transition-age students to illustrate concepts and recommended practices; and (d) summarizes findings across the case studies that may be applicable to other communities.

OVERVIEW OF COMMUNITY DEVELOPMENT AND TEAMWORK CONCEPTS

Communities provide a variety of services in order to meet the wants and needs of their citizens. Ideally, such services promote characteristics that define the community as an attractive place to live, to relocate to, or in which to invest business and other economic development resources. These characteristics include, among other things, effective roads and transportation systems, cultural and recreation amenities, quality schools and high levels of educational attainment, quality health and medical facilities and services, a stable workforce and low unemployment rates, low levels of poverty, high median household incomes, high rates of homeownership, and low crime rates.

Professionals who are concerned with disability services, individuals with disabilities, and their families desire the same quality of life indicators for their communities. However, like many distinct populations they often desire additional and specific services, such as more affordable accessible transportation services, case management services, supported employment services, and supported living services.

Researchers in community development (e.g., Coleman, 1988; Florida, 2002; Morse, 2004; Putnam, 1995; Putnam & Feldstein, 2003; Sirolli, 1998; Wachter & Tinsley, 1996) have identified several concepts that help determine quality of life in communities. Across these diverse researchers and their disciplines, some of the most commonly promoted concepts are civic engagement, community connections, and social capital. Each of these concepts, summarized in the following pages, is a building block for community-level teamwork practices. In order for education professionals and other community advocates who are concerned with transition services to move from endorsing teamwork to practicing teamwork, they must be skilled in operationalizing these concepts within their repertoire of transition planning skills.

Civic Engagement

Desirable community outcomes are more likely to occur in "civically engaged" communities (e.g., Morse, 2004; Putnam, 1995; Putnam & Feldstein, 2003; Schorr, 1997; Wachter & Tinsley, 1996). Civically engaged communities are communities where people feel that they are a part of their communities, where citizens not only have expectations of entitlements to community services, but also where they feel reciprocal responsibilities to give back to their communities.

Civic engagement may take many forms and may be measured by rates of volunteerism with organizations (e.g., Habitat for Humanity and Special Olympics) as well as participation in business, civic, faith-based, and service groups (e.g., churches, rotary, scouts, chambers of commerce, and neighborhood watch). Civic engagement may also include participation in less formal groups and activities such as athletic leagues, community gardens, and book clubs. Finally, civic engagement may be measured by broader indicators, such as rates of participation during local blood drives, rates of attendance at school- or church-sponsored community events, and rates of voting in local elections.

Community Connections

Researchers also agree on the importance of connections among diverse community citizens. The term "community connections" defines the extent to which community members and members of diverse groups interact and appreciate each other's histories, values, talents, expectations, and needs. Community connections may be measured by a number of quantifiable variables; for example, the number and variety of faith-based organizations and members, social change organizations and members, and cultural and civic organizations and members. It may also be measured by more qualitative descriptors, such as "friendly and welcoming people," "close-knit families," and "people who are appreciative of diversity."

Social Capital

Together, civic engagement and community connections yield a third concept known as *social capital* (Coleman, 1988). Social capital refers to a community's formal and/or informal network of organizations that coordinate and cooperate to collectively achieve mutually desired community benefits. One way to better understand the concept is to contrast it with *physical capital*. Whereas physical capital refers to investment in infrastructure such as buildings and roadways, social capital refers to investment in networks and relationships among organizations and individuals. Social capital, then, is the glue that holds society together, the sum of active connections among organizations and people (Putnam, 2000). It is characterized by shared values and behaviors, trust, and communication. The desired product of social capital investment is the binding together of networks of people, organizations, and communities in such a way that they work together toward mutually desired outcomes.

Putting It All Together: Community Development

In response to these observations, advocates across multiple disciplines have suggested community development as a specific and proven approach to building civic engagement, community connections, and social capital (e.g., Kretzman & McNight 1997; Morse, 2004; Putnam & Feldstein, 2003). Briefly, community development is a set of strategies used by local communities to (a) focus attention on the community's assets and strengths, (b) combine resources, and (c) encourage self-determination and grow leadership among the citizenry. The goal of community development is to empower communities both to identify and to address their own unique service needs. A related goal is to develop and establish an interagency and interdisciplinary teamwork infrastructure that enables a community to address future needs (Everson, Guillory, & Ivester, 2005).

Teamwork: A Critical Component

Teamwork is a critical component of community development, and interagency and interdisciplinary teamwork, in turn, are critical components of transition services. *Interdisciplinary* is used to refer to a group of two or more people who come together representing two or more disciplines or fields of study. Similarly, *interagency* refers to two or more people who come together representing two or more agencies or organizations. During its initial meetings, a team that is both interdisciplinary and interagency in makeup may have more in common with a group of business leaders and elected officials visiting a foreign country to negotiate a trade deal than with a human services team. Some members may be meeting each other for the first time—learning each other's names and position titles, and attempting to understand how these new members and new agencies relate to them. They may be hearing discipline-specific and agency-specific acronyms, policies, and procedures for the first time and be attempting to understand how these ideas fit within their own professional paradigms. Trust may be low, expectations may be high, and communications are likely to be misunderstood.

Specific to high school to adult life transition services, Everson and Guillory (1998) define a collaborative interagency and interdisciplinary team as

> —a group of individuals and organizations who come together to address a common need and agree to pursue a common goal. Over time and with much effort, the group becomes a team if its members agree to common values and a mission, set clear goals and objectives, design an organizational structure and operating procedures, develop common communication patterns, and pursue agreed-upon roles and activities. If the team maintains these characteristics and self-monitors and assesses its activities and outcomes, it will become an effective team that may accomplish improved transition services, improved transition outcomes, and other systems-change results. (p. 301)

This definition will be used in this chapter to identify the group of people who come together regularly and frequently to address one or more identified service needs that respond to the wants and needs of a community's citizens, including transition-age youth with disabilities.

As the definition implies, teamwork is hard work, but it is neither magical nor mysterious. When teams apply the concepts discussed in this chapter, members will learn to trust and to communicate with each other, to take action toward common goals, and to evaluate and celebrate successes in their communities.

Tuckman (1965) proposed a teamwork model that is as applicable today as it was when he first proposed it more than 40 years ago. He suggested that all teams progress through five predictable stages: forming, storming, norming, performing, and disbanding. Everson and Guillory (2002) applied this model with new and veteran teams who chose to participate in Louisiana's 5-year statewide systems change project on transition services. In the process, they identified specific developmental milestones for teams to pursue within each stage, as illustrated in Table 6.1. Because the transition process covers several years, the topic of disbanding is not relevant. Tuckman (1965) proposed a model that allowed teams to form and ultimately disband once they achieved their goals.

COMMUNITY-LEVEL TEAMWORK: RECOMMENDED PRACTICES

In 2003, the University Centers for Excellence in Developmental Disabilities Education, Research, and Service (UCEDDERS) in South Carolina and Louisiana collaboratively implemented a 33-month project funded by the U.S. Department of Health and Human Services. The project used the teamwork model proposed by Tuckman (1965) and expanded on by Everson and Guillory (2002), combined with the community development concepts defined earlier in this chapter, to develop teams in four communities across the two states. The project's goal was to

TABLE 6.1 *Teamwork Stages and Milestones*

The Forming Stage

Milestone #1: Initiating a Team
- What is our community need?
- How will this team address this need better than individual agencies or organizations?

Milestone #2: Planning and Holding an Initial Organizational Meeting
- Who is the target population to be impacted by the identified needs?
- What is the geographic area or community to be served by the proposed team?
- Which core agencies or stakeholders will serve as members of the proposed team?

Milestone #3: Planning and Holding Additional Follow-Up Meetings
- What are the critical team development and organizational activities that an interagency team must address during the forming stage?

Milestone #4: Confirming the Team's Membership
- How can a team secure commitment from individuals and member agencies regarding their continued membership?

The Storming Stage

Milestone #1: Developing Values/Mission Statements
- What do we value as a team?
- Why do we exist?

Milestone #2: Conducting Needs Assessments
- What are the specific needs faced by the target population in our community?

Milestone #3: Setting Team Goals/Developing Team Action Plans
- What future desired outcomes will our team pursue in order to address the identified needs of the target population?
- How will our team monitor and document our progress toward these outcomes?

Milestone #4: Developing Team Structural/Operating Procedures
- Who will be in charge of running our team meetings?
- How often will we meet?
- How will we develop our agendas?
- How will we accomplish our work efficiently?
- How will we make decisions?

Milestone #5: Practicing Effective Meeting Processes, Communication Skills, and Conflict Management Skills
- How will our team conduct itself before, during, and after meetings?
- How can we ensure that our communications as a team enhance our efforts rather than detract from them?
- How will team members ensure that we continue to pull in the same direction rather than in different directions?

The Norming Stage

Milestone #1: Using Action Plans
- How will our team know and track the status of our efforts?
- How will we determine "next steps" and any needed changes?

Milestone #2: Using a Case Study Approach
- How can we maintain a focus on achieving outcome goals?
- How can we ensure that we are addressing the assessed needs of the target population?

TABLE 6.1 (*continued*)

Milestone #3: Field-Testing, Evaluating, and Revising Policies and Procedures
- Based on our case studies, what policies and/or procedures may need to be changed or developed?
- How can we study and document the potential effects of these changes or additions?
- Based on our field-test, what policy and/or procedural revisions or additions are supported or warranted?

Milestone #4: Developing Interagency Agreements
- Do we want and need to formalize our values, mission, goals, and agreed-on responsibilities in an interagency agreement?
- What would be the benefits of doing this?
- Are there any disadvantages to consider?

The Performing Stage

Milestone #1: Using Planning Strategies to Maintain a Team's Direction and Focus
- How can our team avoid becoming too specialized or too isolated within the larger community?
- How can we systematically and effectively address external resistance so that we can continue to maintain our team's direction and focus?

Milestone #2: Using Self-Monitoring and Evaluation Strategies to Maintain a Team's Direction and Focus
- How does our team periodically assess whether we are doing what we set out to do?
- How does our team assess whether our actions are making positive differences in the lives of our target population?

Milestone #3: Guiding a Team Through Disbandment
- Once our team has accomplished what it set out to do, what happens next?
- If our team decides to disband, how should we go about it?

---

guide all four teams through a community development process that would enhance civic engagement and community connections for the community's citizens.

The project was designed purposefully to function beyond traditional approaches designed to promote community inclusiveness of citizens with disabilities. Instead, the project was designed to help communities build their social capital so that *all* citizens, including those with disabilities, would become more civically engaged and, thus, more contributing and connected citizens within their communities. The project's underlying premise was that all communities and all citizens have unique capacities and needs. That is, every citizen has something to give to a community as well as a need to receive something from a community. Further, communities will be able to mobilize their social capital toward desired outcomes only when all citizens are afforded opportunities to exercise self-determination, display leadership, and participate as members of community-level teams. Therefore, a basic premise of activities at all four sites was that citizens with and without disabilities must contribute equally to and benefit from teamwork activities.

For illustrative purposes, we describe the activities of one community in South Carolina and one community in Louisiana. Andersonville County[1] in South

---
[1] Although these case studies are based on real communities, students, and teaming activities, the communities' and students' names and some of the descriptive information have been changed.

Carolina identified a need for expanded recreation opportunities for young adolescents, whereas Jenkins Parish (County) in Louisiana identified a need for expanded housing options for adults with low incomes.

GETTING STARTED: ARE WE FORMING, STORMING, NORMING, OR PERFORMING?

How might a brand-new team get started? How might a struggling team become more productive? First, team leaders should use the milestones in Table 6–1 to identify at which stage the team is currently operating. If the team is newly forming or within a year of forming, the answer is probably self-evident—the team is in the forming stage. But for veteran teams the answer may not be so obvious. Teams that have been in existence for a year or longer, even as long as 10 years, are equally as likely to be operating in the storming stage as they are in the norming or performing stage. Robbins and Finley (2001) remind us that most teams spend three fifths of their time in the storming stage, either because they never progress beyond this stage or because at some point members become complacent and the team regresses.

Whenever possible, both newly forming and veteran teams should consider using external facilitators to guide them through forming and storming teamwork activities. Alternatively, teams who must rely on their leaders to serve as facilitators, instead of external consultants, are advised to choose leaders with the training and personal characteristics necessary to serve as a skilled facilitator. Along with this chapter, *The Facilitator's Handbook* (Justice & Jamieson, 1999) and the websites at the conclusion of this chapter provide excellent resources for team leaders to consider.

A team may identify its level of functioning by conducting a self-assessment. Facilitated by team leaders, teams might begin by asking individual members to self-assess whether they think the team has accomplished the necessary milestones within each stage, followed by a full team discussion of areas of agreement and disagreement. This task will result in lively discussion and, perhaps, equally as lively disagreement! The end result will be an appreciation among team members of the team's history, accomplishments, strengths, and opportunities for growth and improvement.

Developing a Shared Foundation: Core Elements

Building on the stages described in Table 6.1, project staff next identify five core elements to be implemented by team leaders and members. Team activities to accomplish these elements are presented in Table 6.2 as examples only and are not intended to be comprehensive. Instead, specific strategies used by teams should be developed, implemented, and evaluated based on each team's unique history, membership, goals, actions, and outcomes.

TABLE 6.2 *Core Elements of Community Development and Suggested Technical Assistance Strategies*

Core Element #1: Communities must support the development of multiconstituency teams.
- Identify community leaders from various constituencies and meet with them to assess the community's history and experiences with interagency teams.
- Partner with community leaders to hold community forums to identify preliminary community needs, available resources, and potential stakeholders.
- Identify one or more key stakeholders to help initiate and organize a new team *or* partner with already existing teams and ask key leaders to endorse a subcommittee or task force structure to address identified needs and goals.
- Have initial stakeholders and/or existing teams identify the roles/affiliations of stakeholders that need to be included to ensure that the team/subcommittee/task force is multiconstituency.
- Use team assessment tools to assess an existing team's level of functioning.
- Confirm the team's membership and roles by developing a written membership list and description of membership roles.
- Obtain letters of support or memorandas of agreement from agencies to secure commitment for team representatives.
- Identify resources to support the participation of parents, families, and self-advocates (e.g., travel stipends, flexible meeting schedules, meeting room accessibility, and communication accommodations).
- Use teambuilding and icebreaker activities to build relationships and commitment, define roles, and develop team ground rules and norms.

Core Element #2: Teams must define and support roles for all citizen stakeholders to assume.
- Identify all stakeholders and identify potential roles for everyone by inviting representatives from all potential stakeholder groups to participate in community forums or focus groups.
- Invite members of all stakeholder groups to serve on advisory councils, task forces, and subcommittees.
- Provide all stakeholders with necessary information and opportunities to make comments during public hearings and to provide input to written plans.
- Investigate needs and provide all necessary supports in order to promote participation by all stakeholders (e.g., transportation, child care, stipends, ASL interpreters, accessible locations, large-print or Braille materials, etc.).
- Encourage and support stakeholders to respond to community needs surveys/assessments.
- Invite stakeholders to review draft surveys, plans, and/or reports before they are publicly disseminated.

Core Element #3: Teams must agree on one or more identified needs that, if addressed, will positively enhance the quality of life of all citizen stakeholders.
- Hold a series of community forums or focus groups to identify and prioritize general community needs.
- Use need-specific assessment tools across services to identify and prioritize specific community needs.
- Use brainstorming, consensus building, voting, or other team procedures to reach agreement on and to prioritize goals.
- Have stakeholders ask their corresponding constituencies to provide input and feedback via mail, telephone, or electronic surveys or questionnaires, mail-in postcards, group voting and consensus techniques, and so on in order to identify and prioritize general and/or specific community needs.

Core Element #4: Goal setting and action planning are essential tools in addressing needs and attaining desired goals.
- Encourage the team to self-assess its level of attention to community experiences, community behaviors, and community values as they apply to all of its community citizens regarding the identified needs.
- Support the team in developing, implementing, and evaluating community development plans to address desired goals and outcomes.
- Use brainstorming, consensus building, voting, and other team procedures to develop goals.
- Use organizational tools such as Gantt charts and planning timelines to define action steps and timelines for goals.
- Use conflict management tools such as GAP analysis and force field analysis to problem-solve goals.

- Use implementation tools such as action plans and team goals monitoring worksheets for the team to self-assess its progress toward its targeted goals.
- Be prepared to assist the team to adjust timelines and to revise and/or to set different goals, as needed.

Core Element #5: Desired solutions to identified needs must include measurable outcomes for people, systems, and processes.
- Use the community development evaluation matrices to assist the team in monitoring, evaluating, and reporting three outcome areas: consumer, systems, and process.
- Use a case study approach to track and evaluate the impact of team activities on stakeholders.
- Use a case study obstacle and opportunities map to help identify common themes related to resources, barriers, strategies, and services/supports across the targeted case study individuals.
- Based on field-test with case study individuals, assist the team in identifying any policies and/or procedures that may need to be revised or developed.
- Develop a plan for the team to expand from the case study individuals to the community at large.

Once teams have identified the stage at which they are operating, team leaders use the activities listed in Table 6.2 to develop a common foundation for teamwork. Team leaders, again serving as facilitators, describe these core elements and engage the team in discussion. For newly forming teams, these discussions should take place early in the teams' development to ensure mutual understanding of goals, roles, and processes. For veteran teams, these discussions should take place immediately following the self-assessment activity. Next, team leaders seek endorsement of core elements from all team members by facilitating discussions about developing value and mission statements, or, if the team has developed them already, reviewing, revising, and recommitting to them.

Moving Through the Stages: Developing Work Plans

Once core elements have been endorsed, team leaders use the next few meetings to develop *work plans* (also known as *action plans*). We define a work plan as a time-bound strategic plan, developed and endorsed by the full team, that includes goals, objectives, team members responsible for completion of objectives, timelines for completion of objectives, and mechanisms for monitoring and recognizing completion. A work plan should incorporate strategies such as those included in Table 6.2, individualized to the needs and preferences of the entire team. Once developed, a work plan provides team leaders and other members with a one-year or multiple-year map of expected activities and outcomes. The work plan also serves as a guide for establishing subcommittees, developing agendas for specific meetings, assessing barriers and progress, and documenting and celebrating accomplishments.

Case Study Overviews

Community Needs and Demographics

Jenkins Parish. Jenkins Parish (County) is a sprawling urban community adjacent to the city of New Orleans. In 2003, its population was estimated at 455,500 and its unemployment rate was 4%. The median household income was $40,536, with approximately 15% of the population living in poverty.

In 2003, the Jenkins Parish Affordable Housing Task Force, a newly created and loosely organized group, had been attempting for several months to form a team to address the housing needs of citizens with low incomes. Although Jenkins offered citizens a mixture of housing options, the need for affordable housing for those who were elderly and/or had disabilities continued to rise due to the limited availability of funds and programs.

Andersonville County. Andersonville is a rural county with a population of 24,000 located in the southwest quadrant of South Carolina. In 2003, the unemployment rate was 7%, the median household income was $23,000, and 17% of children under the age of 18 lived in poverty. Andersonville, the county seat, exudes a small-town feeling, and faith-based social capital is particularly strong. In 1995, Andersonville leaders established an interagency and interdisciplinary team whose mission was to build a healthy community by coordinating and communicating resources among the various organizations. In 2003, the veteran team identified a community need for recreation activities that would promote healthy adolescent behaviors and outcomes, but team members were unsure how to move the team from being a resource-sharing team to an action-oriented team.

The Forming Stage: Establishing Community-Level Teams

According to Everson and Guillory (2002), the forming stage is characterized by a team's completion of four major activities: (a) initiating the team; (b) planning and holding an initial organizational meeting; (c) planning and holding at least three additional meetings focusing on the team's goals, roles, and processes; and (d) confirming the team's structure and membership.

In 2003, when the project began, Andersonville had a community team that had been in operation for 10 years and Jenkins Parish had a team that had been in existence for 3 months. Thus, this chapter illustrates activities of both a newly forming team and a veteran team.

During the forming stage, teams must dedicate their resources to becoming a team. Work plans should focus on the major forming stage activities: (a) initiating a team in the community where a team did not exist; (b) planning and holding meetings to discuss the community need and the community development approach; (c) planning and holding additional, follow-up meetings to coalesce the team; and (d) confirming the team's membership (Everson & Guillory, 2002).

An important aspect of confirming membership was inclusion of representatives from all stakeholder groups knowledgeable about the identified service needs. In Andersonville, this meant that culturally diverse adolescents and their families, community recreation providers, high school teachers, and transition personnel were all invited to join the team. In Jenkins Parish, this meant that age-diverse renters and homeowners with low incomes, community housing professionals, building and construction officials, school system representatives, families of transition-age students, and elected officials were invited to join the team.

The outcomes desired from these forming meetings are to (a) confirm the team's commitment to a community development approach, (b) confirm the team's commitment to its previously identified community need, and (c) finalize the team's membership and structural and operating procedures.

Jenkins Parish. A Parish Resolution formally established the Jenkins Parish Affordable Housing Task Force. However, little work was accomplished and an external facilitator was provided to guide teamwork activities. With guidance, the original, struggling task force convened a second, much smaller executive committee, with membership drawn from the larger team. Next, the executive committee formed four planning subcommittees, two focusing on homeownership and two focusing on rental housing, with membership drawn from the original task force. To ensure coordination across the four subcommittees, members of the executive committee and the original task force also agreed on communication and data-sharing procedures during and between meetings.

Once established, the executive committee moved quickly through typical forming stage activities (i.e., setting meetings, identifying members). Within two meetings and 2 months, the executive committee agreed to a meeting format and schedule and committed resources to conducting an extensive local housing needs assessment.

Andersonville County. Andersonville, the veteran team, readily agreed on the community's need for expanded recreation opportunities, but it took four team meetings and approximately 4 months to reach consensus on how to best structure the team's efforts. Ultimately, a recreation subcommittee of the larger team was established. As in the Louisiana community, membership was drawn from the larger and, in this case, well-established community team. However, the subcommittee's membership was expanded to include members with special interest in recreation and in disabilities, stakeholders who were not well represented on the larger team.

The Storming Stage: Getting Down to Work

The storming stage of team development is a period of intense planning and negotiation, and typically a challenging time for everyone. Everson and Guillory (2002) suggested that teams that have addressed all forming activities and that continue to meet monthly or every other month will need approximately 10 meetings and between 10 to 20 months to complete all storming activities. The authors listed five major activities that must occur during the storming stage: (a) developing values and mission statements; (b) conducting needs assessment activities; (c) setting goals and developing action plans; (d) developing structural and operating procedures; and (e) practicing effective meeting, communication, and conflict management skills.

As predicted, all four teams spent a significant amount of time in the storming stage. In fact, at the conclusion of the 33-month project, two of the four teams were either still in the storming stage or had regressed back to the storming stage. Only Andersonville and Jenkins had transitioned to the third stage, the norming stage.

Jenkins Parish. By the nature of each community's unique needs and demographics, their approaches to assessing their needs were similarly unique. Jenkins embarked on the most extensive needs assessment, researching and compiling extant data to write and make public a 45-page blueprint addressing the community's need for affordable, safe, and quality housing.

Within 2 months of the executive committee's establishment, membership for the four subcommittees was confirmed. Each subcommittee agreed to adopt the mission set by the full task force:

> To conduct activities that would result in a written document that summarizes the corresponding resources, barriers, and prioritized strategies, as well as identifies measurable recommendations, to increase affordable, safe, and quality housing options in Jenkins for persons with very low, low, and moderate incomes, including persons with disabilities and persons who are elderly.

Over the next 4 months, the subcommittees met regularly, using written work plans to structure their meetings. Eventually, the four complementary subcommittees joined forces, resulting in one homeownership subcommittee report and one rental housing subcommittee needs report. Next, the executive committee compiled the two reports into a single document, and the Jenkins team made public a blueprint that included (a) two overarching recommendations requiring future action of the local governing body that had established the team, the Jenkins Parish Council; and (b) five long-term goals with 23 associated short-term objectives to address the community's housing needs. Within 2 more months, the parish council adopted the recommendations and five implementation subcommittees were established to address the corresponding goals and objectives.

During the storming period, several noteworthy events occurred. First, local elections resulted in major changes in the local governmental administration. The executive committee capitalized on this opportunity by requesting that the newly elected parish president convene a meeting of the full task force so that a formal status report about activities could be shared.

A second noteworthy occurrence emerged when members of the executive committee were asked to share their teaming experiences with other community groups. Members reported on several observations that they attributed to their successes: (a) a third-party facilitator (i.e., project staff) was vital during the team's first 12 to 18 months; (b) a subcommittee structure was beneficial in managing conflicts and in reaching consensus; (c) although members were reluctant to take on leadership roles, they recognized that it was essential to maintain efforts over time; (d) collaboration was effective in maximizing expertise and resources; and (e) effective meeting and communication skills were a key component of growth.

A third noteworthy occurrence was that the Jenkins team began to address consumer outcome goals, in addition to team development goals, within its work plan. For example, it began measuring changes in the numbers of people receiving Section 8 housing vouchers, the numbers of people with low incomes receiving mortgages, and the numbers of consumer complaints about housing services. In addition, it invited team members to share stories of individuals whose housing opportunities were positively impacted by the team's efforts.

> Delia is a shy 21-year-old woman who has been diagnosed with moderate mental retardation and legal blindness. Delia attended special education classes at her local high school and graduated in 2004 with an occupational diploma. While in high school, Delia completed a home economics class. In this course, she learned how to prepare a monthly budget, complete credit card applications and use credit wisely, and read and evaluate apartment rental and mortgage loan applications. She volunteered with church members for Habitat for Humanity. She attended a 5-day youth leadership forum where she learned about community living and employment opportunities enjoyed by other adults with disabilities. With support from her IEP team, Delia began using several low-vision devices to help her work and live more independently. As a result of her high school program and her IEP/transition planning activities, Delia began to think about living in an apartment as a desirable high school outcome.
>
> During her final year of high school, Delia secured a part-time job with a fast-food restaurant. Delia's employer and coworkers were enthusiastic about her work, and she received many positive evaluations. With help from her teacher, Delia established a checking account and secured a credit card with a $250 credit limit. With help from her IEP team, Delia was placed on the waiting list for a Section 8 rental voucher program.
>
> Upon graduation from high school, Delia secured a 30-hour-a-week job at a restaurant located on a public bus route, and within 18 months, she became eligible for a rental voucher. Within an additional 2 months, Delia moved into a one-bedroom apartment within walking distance from her job. Like many young renters, Delia lives on a tight budget and realizes that she must work diligently and make budget choices in order to remain independent. She receives weekly case management services to help her with budgeting, shopping, housekeeping, and traveling to and from medical appointments.
>
> Shortly after moving into her apartment, Delia was invited to share her story with members of the Jenkins Task Force. She urged them to "tell everyone [in high school] about this [Section 8 voucher] program!" She continued, "I like decorating the way I want and eating with my friends at my house." Her mother adds, "Now, Delia is saving $25 a month and bugging us about buying a house. I told her, 'Keep working and we'll see'!"

As a result of these activities and milestones, the Jenkins team began to emerge from the storming stage and enter the norming stage. As it made the transition, members celebrated that they were making progress on 17 of their 23 objectives, and with support from community members like Delia, they were monitoring and evaluating their outcomes in a more person-centered manner.

Andersonville County. Andersonville conducted a significantly less extensive, but equally community-driven, assessment of recreation needs. Team members surveyed adolescent participants during local recreation events and conducted small focus groups of adolescents and their families. These focus groups were held at middle schools, high schools, and in local recreation centers and were structured to include diverse members of the community, including individuals with disabilities.

Team structure and goal setting were critical storming activities for Andersonville. By the time it moved from the forming stage to the storming stage, the Andersonville Recreation Coalition had begun to meet regularly apart from the larger community team. These meetings were cofacilitated by project staff and team members (for example, teacher, special education administrator and school psychologist) and the school system's transition coordinator. The transition coordinator served as the liaison between the two groups.

The Andersonville team set three goals: (a) to increase the participation of all adolescents in existing recreation activities; (b) to increase the use of Andersonville's park and recreation centers; and (c) to make available new, alternative recreation activities in addition to those currently offered. During its fifth meeting, members easily reached consensus that these goals would address the identified community need. Andersonville pursued many other typical storming activities during this time period. For example, it began using an action planning form to record its activities and progress and established ground rules for its meetings. In summary, during the storming period, Andersonville became a team.

The Norming Stage: Beginning to Address Systems Changes in Communities

According to Everson and Guillory (2002), hard work and observable results characterize the norming stage. Thus, goals, roles, and processes become clear and operational, and conflicts and tensions diminish as members begin to feel loyalty and even affection for each other and for the team. Further, teams are able to confidently use their work plans to track their accomplishments, to identify and tackle needed next steps, and to determine whether changes or adjustments are warranted. Effective meeting skills, communication skills, and conflict management skills become second nature to both leaders and members at large. In addition, teams that successfully begin to transition from the norming stage to the performing stage are well positioned to self-monitor and evaluate their activities and progress. Most central to the norming stage, however, members begin to enjoy their work and each other.

Jenkins County. As the Jenkins team began to emerge from the storming stage and enter the norming stage, members were working hard on 17 of their 23 objectives. During the norming stage, the five implementation subcommittees began realizing consumer outcome goals. In addition, with encouragement from project staff, team members began to recognize potential use for evaluation data. Most of the five subcommittees began to agree that systems outcomes must be viewed as a means of attaining consumer outcomes. That is, it was recognized that systems outcomes were important to document, but that they were not ends in and of themselves.

Although work plans remained an integral part of the process, the Jenkins team created a visual tool to assist members in focusing on outcomes. The tool "A Snapshot in Time" allowed members to document the status of goals, to identify systems and consumer milestones, and to determine tasks and timelines necessary to reach the targeted outcomes.

This tool assisted team members in adopting a case study approach to further assist members in making the transition from focusing only on systems goals to focusing on both consumer and systems outcome goals. Adoption of a case study approach meant that the team considered case studies of individuals such as Delia during meetings to illustrate how housing policies and programs were and were not meeting citizens' needs. Over time, additional members began to embrace case study data as a major means of evaluating activities and driving systemic change.

In addition, A Snapshot in Time assisted the team in beginning to self-monitor its goals and objectives. While none of the goals was eliminated, timelines for many objectives were extended. Also, A Snapshot in Time assisted the team in self-monitoring its structure. Although over 25% of the 23 targeted objectives had already been achieved and another 44% were well under way, the team decided that the remaining objectives would benefit from being assigned to the executive committee. That is, as the team continued to flourish in the norming stage, the role of the executive committee took on additional importance, and several members emerged as team leaders, allowing project staff to reduce their efforts with the team.

As the project concluded, several areas needing policy and procedural attention had been identified and transferred to the executive committee. In addition, the formation of two regional teams to expand activities beyond Jenkins Parish was under way: (a) a regional Community Development Financial Institution (CDFI) Collaborative; and (b) a regional Individual Development Account (IDA) Collaborative. The executive committee began discussing the need for a systematic "close-out plan," as there was general agreement that the team had accomplished what it set out to do. As part of the plan, a formal report to include both systems and consumer outcomes was developed and disseminated to the full

Jenkins Parish Affordable Housing Task Force, to the parish administration and council, and to other interested parties. Rather than completely disband, the executive committee agreed to continue to operate in order to field-test some of the identified policies, procedures, and programs with case study individuals.

Andersonville County. During the norming stage, the Andersonville Recreation Coalition continued to meet regularly, to experience positive and productive meetings, and to realize both consumer and systems outcomes. Coalition leaders began using their action plans to focus meeting agendas and to self-monitor progress toward their goals. In addition, the team formalized its structure and commitment by developing an interagency agreement that detailed each member's roles and responsibilities and was signed by each participating agency.

As they began self-monitoring their activities, members began adjusting their activities to achieve more person-centered consumer outcomes. For example, the team's initial activities included organizing and sponsoring new recreation events, such as special movie nights at the local recreation center. As they evaluated these activities, they recognized that attendance from the target population was poor. After assessing reasons for the poor attendance with the target population, the team redirected its activities. Instead of offering entirely new, additional activities, it began partnering with other community recreation providers and collaborating to enhance and market existing recreation activities to the target population. For example, Andersonville's new activities included working with a local teen pregnancy project to host a mother–daughter fashion show and working with the local art guild's art classes and events. As a result of the team's collaborative activities with other providers, participation from the target population increased and the team began to build community interest in and support for local recreation activities that included young adults with disabilities, but that were not designed specifically for them.

> Logan is a 15-year-old in his second year at his local high school. Logan is deaf and has been diagnosed with attention deficit hyperactivity disorder (ADHD). With assistance from an American Sign Language (ASL) interpreter, he attends English, biology, and American history classes with his high school peers, and he participates in a study skills/self-determination class with other students who have learning needs. Logan is an outgoing and inquisitive teenager who enjoys "hanging out with other guys." He has both friends who are deaf and friends who are hearing, and several have learned some elementary sign language skills. Logan takes medication to help him control his impulsive behaviors and his temper. Nevertheless, he has been arrested twice for destruction of school property and for setting off the school's fire alarm.
>
> Logan participated in some of Andersonville's needs assessment activities, and his assessment that "there is nothing fun to do on weekends" was echoed by many other teenagers. When asked what he would most enjoy doing, Logan suggested a list of activities, for example, attending NASCAR events in neighboring communities, playing nighttime basketball, attending dance contests, and participating in computer game competitions. Some of these events were

available locally, but Logan and other teenagers did not have transportation or money for registration fees. Other activities were not available or were available on very limited schedules.

As a result of needs assessment and collaborative planning activities, Logan's IEP team was able to provide him with training on using the telephone relay service to plan weekend activities with his friends and to negotiate transportation with friends and public transit services. Within a year, Logan had joined a new intramural basketball league at the local recreation center that met weekly throughout the winter. The center also offered, and Logan participated in, a summer motorsports recreation program that enabled teens to learn about potential NASCAR careers, refine their mathematics skills, and attend local NASCAR events. In addition, Logan attended several monthly teen dance events, and helped recreation center leaders organize a computer game competition and an ASL conversational course.

As team members began to self-monitor and evaluate their activities using case studies such as Logan's, overall progress was noted on all three goals.

Specifically, the community calendars developed by the team had been disseminated to a broader audience, including classroom teachers and churches throughout the county. In addition, the weekly local newspaper began to publish the calendar as a public service announcement and teachers encouraged teens to use it as a planning tool. As a result of the team's activities, the calendar was now more expansive, advertising a broad assortment of classes and events requested by teens like Logan, which contributed to an increase in communitywide attendance of target youth, including those with disabilities. Further, the team collaborated in writing and submitting a grant proposal designed to increase accessibility of one of the county park's walking trails. Even though the grant was not funded, the team joined with the local garden club to plan and implement this activity.

As the Andersonville team navigated the norming stage, it became apparent that members and the community at large were thriving on the social capital available in this small, cohesive community. The community's size provided enhanced opportunities for "between meetings" and informal communication among team members. In addition, the closeness of the community encouraged accountability within the group and beyond to the town residents.

Summary

The goal of the South Carolina and Louisiana community development project was to implement a community development approach in four communities across two states that would create civic engagement and community connections for all citizens. During the project's tenure, project staff and the participating teams succeeded in incorporating a community development approach into teaming activities and, in the process, learned several valuable lessons about community building and community connections for citizens with disabilities, including the following:

- Community development is a proven framework for strengthening a community's roles in assuming responsibility for addressing issues impacting local citizens. The approach implemented by project staff in South Carolina

and Louisiana lent itself equally well to a variety of community issues, to team members representing a broad range of teaming experiences, to both large and small teams, and to existing, veteran teams, as well as to newly forming and less experienced teams.
- Contributions of transition-age youth and adults with disabilities may take many forms, including participation in community forums or focus groups; serving on community teams, executive committees, advisory committees, task forces, and/or subcommittees; providing input at public hearings and to written plans; responding to community needs surveys and assessments; and/or reviewing reports prior to public dissemination.
- Community connections are critical in order for all citizens, including those with disabilities, to fully participate in community development activities. Teams that truly embrace the value and power of community connections are more willing to provide the support necessary for all citizens to serve in some appropriate capacity.
- Successful completion of the critical forming stage activities will lay the foundation for more effectively accomplishing team activities during the later stages of teaming. However, for most team members, it is not until they reach the storming stage that they truly understand and appreciate the activities that they dedicated so much time and energy to during the forming stage. External facilitation and technical assistance can help ensure strong team development during the forming stage.
- Each stage offers teams unique challenges and distinct opportunities. Some teams may regress back into earlier stages, particularly the storming stage, especially if changes in membership, administration, goals, and so on occur. In fact, many teams find themselves dealing with some storming stage activities throughout their existence. For far too many teams, the struggles experienced as they attempt to address storming stage activities result in their undoing. Indeed, it is not uncommon for teams to collapse and to terminate their efforts during the storming stage, more so than during any of the other stages. As a result, external facilitation and technical assistance are crucial during this stage.
- Members of teams that reach the norming stage often find that they enjoy not only their work but also working with each other. Because they now operate successfully as teams, this is the stage where members get to invest time and resources to address the needs and goals that brought the teams together in the first place. This is where real systems change work begins to be accomplished. For many teams, the norming stage ends only if it reverts back to an earlier stage, if it reaches the performing stage, or if it decides to disband.
- Members of teams that do reach the norming and performing stages may eventually agree to disband once their teams' work has been accomplished. However, this often proves to be a difficult, but necessary and sensible

decision. If the decision to disband is reached, steps should be taken by teams to recognize the hard work and contributions of the members, to celebrate their accomplishments and successes, and to acknowledge and share what members learned as part of this positive teaming experience.
- Although it is not uncommon for individual team members or agencies to want to be in positions of power, or to be in control, this does not necessarily translate into a willingness or ability to take on leadership roles, which require skills, capacities, commitments, obligations, and responsibilities.
- Team members, regardless of their previous histories, varied teaming experiences, and current skill levels, readily attribute much of their effective team process successes to a common strategy—the use of a work plan or action plan. This simple, yet valuable, tool provides a straightforward, diplomatic way to guide team members to take needed actions and to follow through on agreed-upon tasks before the next scheduled meeting or some other determined timeframe.
- Teamwork is critical to the ongoing success of transitioning high school students with disabilities. Teams that address consumer outcomes, especially via a case study approach, describe themselves as more committed to their causes, reinvigorated and further motivated, and better able to sustain their momentum and direction over time. These teams are also more likely to describe their teams as successful in improving postschool outcomes among young adults with disabilities.
- Self-monitoring and self-evaluation activities are equally important, yet distinctly different in their purposes and uses by teams. Even though they are interrelated in their design and utility to teams, both can prove to be daunting, overwhelming, and intimidating undertakings. However, teams that do successfully conduct self-monitoring and self-evaluation activities confirm and validate how equally rewarding and powerful such activities can be.

Study Questions

1. What are the defining characteristics of a community development approach? How might they be applied to and incorporated within high school to adult life best practices and expected outcomes within your own community?

   Briefly, community development is a set of strategies used by local communities to focus attention on the community's assets and strengths, to combine resources, and to encourage self-determination and grow leadership abilities among the citizenry. Teamwork is a critical component of community development, and interagency and interdisciplinary teamwork, in turn, is a critical component of transition services. Community development also embraces civic engagement, community connections, and social capital. These are all familiar concepts in transition best practices associated with self-determination, self-advocacy, and community participation and presence.

2. What are the essential features of a well-functioning team? Cite examples of teams within your community that are functioning at various stages of development. Brainstorm potential strategies for addressing problems and for supporting growth.

Everson and Guillory (1998) define a collaborative interagency and interdisciplinary team as

> a group of individuals and organizations who come together to address a common need and agree to pursue a common goal. Over time and with much effort, the group becomes a team if its members agree to common values and a mission, set clear goals and objectives, design an organizational structure and operating procedures, develop common communication patterns, and pursue agreed-upon roles and activities. If the team maintains these characteristics and self-monitors and assesses its activities and outcomes, it will become an effective team that may accomplish improved transition services, improved transition outcomes, and other systems-change results. (p. 301)

Tuckman (1965) proposed a teamwork model that is as applicable today as it was when he first proposed it more than 40 years ago. He suggested that all teams progress through five common, predictable stages. He labeled these stages forming, storming, norming, performing, and disbanding.

3. Brainstorm various roles that transition-age youth could play with local teams that would benefit their community connections as well as the team's development.

Contributions of transition-age youth and adults with disabilities may take many forms, including participation in community forums or focus groups; serving on community teams, executive committees, advisory committees, task forces, and/or subcommittees; providing input at public hearings and to written plans; responding to community needs surveys and assessments; and/or reviewing reports prior to public dissemination.

4. What is the relationship between a student's self-determination abilities and his or her involvement in local community development and team activities? Brainstorm high school curriculum ideas and teaching methods that may be used by educators and other transition personnel to enhance self-determination abilities among high school youth.

Every citizen has something to give to a community as well as a need to receive something from a community. Further, communities are able to mobilize their social capital toward desired outcomes only when all citizens are afforded opportunities to exercise self-determination, display leadership, and participate as members of community-level teams. Therefore, a basic premise of these case studies was that citizens with and without disabilities must contribute equally to and benefit from teamwork activities. Self-determination instruction and opportunities provided as part of a comprehensive high school/transition program help youth gain the knowledge, skills, and behaviors necessary to be full community members.

5. Professionals who are concerned with disability services, individuals with disabilities, and their families desire services that are quality-of-life indicators for their communities. However, they may desire additional services and outcomes that specifically address the wants and needs of citizens with disabilities. What are some examples?

   These may include, for example, accessible transportation services; case management services that embrace housing, transportation, and medical resources for citizens with low incomes; supported employment services; and supported living services that embrace workforce development and affordable housing resources.

6. What is meant by the term *civic engagement?* How can civic engagement be measured?

   Civically engaged communities are communities where people feel that they are part of their communities, where citizens not only have expectations of entitlements to community services, but also feel reciprocal responsibilities to give back to their communities. Civic engagement may be measured by rates of volunteerism with organizations as well as participation in business, civic, faith-based, and service groups. Civic engagement may also include participation in less formal groups and activities such as athletic leagues, community gardens, and book clubs. Finally, civic engagement may be measured by broader community indicators; for example, rates of participation during local blood drives; rates of attendance at school- or church-sponsored community events; and rates of voting in local elections.

7. What is meant by a community's social capital?

   Social capital refers to a community's formal and/or informal network of organizations that coordinate and cooperate to collectively achieve mutually desired community benefits.

8. What typically happens during the storming stage of team development?

   Everson and Guillory (2002) suggested five major activities that must occur during the storming stage: (a) developing values and mission statements; (b) conducting needs assessment activities; (c) setting goals and developing action plans; (d) developing structural and operating procedures; and (e) practicing effective meeting, communication, and conflict management skills.

9. What stage of team development is most vulnerable to the collapse or termination of teamwork?

    For far too many teams, the struggles experienced as they attempt to address storming stage activities result in their undoing. Indeed, it is not uncommon for teams to collapse and to terminate their efforts during the storming stage, more so than during any of the other stages. As a result, external facilitation and technical assistance are crucial during this stage.

10. What steps should be taken if a team decides to disband?

    Members of teams that reach the norming and performing stages may eventually agree to disband once their work has been accomplished. This often proves to be a difficult, but necessary and sensible decision. If the decision to disband is reached, steps should be taken by teams to recognize the hard work and contributions of the members, to celebrate accomplishments and successes, and to acknowledge and share what members learned as part of this positive teaming experience.

Recommended Reading

Everson, J. M., & Guillory, J. D. (1998). Building statewide transition services through collaborative interagency teamwork. In F. R. Rusch & J. Chadsey-Rusch (Eds.), *Beyond high school: Transition from school to work* (pp. 299–317). Pacific Grove, CA: Brooks/Cole.

Everson, J. M., & Guillory, J. D. (2002). *Interagency teaming: Strategies for facilitating teams from forming through performing.* New Orleans: Louisiana State University Health Sciences Center, School of Allied Health Professions, Human Development Center.

Everson, J. M., Guillory, J. D., & Ivester, J. (2005). *Community development in action: Illustrations from communities in South Carolina and Louisiana.* Columbia: University of South Carolina School of Medicine, Center for Disability.

Justice, T., & Jamieson, D. W. (1999). *The facilitator's handbook.* New York: American Management Association.

Schorr, L. B. (1977). *Common purpose: Strengthening families and neighborhoods to rebuild America.* New York: Anchor Books/Doubleday.

Wachter, M. I., & Tinsley, C. (1996). *Taking back our neighborhood: Building communities that work.* Minneapolis, MN: Fairview Press.

Web Resources

Using Interagency and Interdisciplinary Teams to Enhance Transition Services

Community at Work

http://www.communityatwork.org

Community At Work specializes in group decision making. Clients usually need help solving complex problems that cannot be solved by traditional hierarchical structures.

Corporation for National and Community Service (CNCS)

http://www.nationalservice.org

CNCS provides opportunities for Americans of all ages and backgrounds to serve their communities and country through three programs: Senior Corps, AmeriCorps, and Learn and Serve America. Members and volunteers serve with national and community nonprofit organizations, faith-based groups, schools, and local agencies to help meet community needs in education, the environment, public safety, homeland security, and other critical areas.

Interaction Institute for Social Change (IISC)

http://www.interactioninstitute.org

IISC has seen the power of bringing together key stakeholders to create a shared vision and the strategies and plans to achieve that vision. Its work resonates with the literature on social capital development, community building, deliberative democracy, civic engagement, governance, regional stewardship, and good, old-fashioned social change.

References

Coleman, J. C. (1988, January). Social capital in the creation of human capital. *American Journal of Sociology, 94*, S95–S120.

Everson, J. M., & Guillory, J. D. (1998). Building statewide transition services through collaborative interagency teamwork. In F. R. Rusch & J. Chadsey-Rusch (Eds.), *Beyond high school: Transition from school to work* (pp. 299–317). Pacific Grove, CA: Brooks/Cole.

Everson, J. M., & Guillory, J. D. (2002). *Interagency teaming: Strategies for facilitating teams from forming through performing.* New Orleans: Louisiana State University Health Sciences Center, School of Allied Health Professions, Human Development Center.

Everson, J. M., Guillory, J. D., & Ivester, J. (2005). *Community development in action: Illustrations from communities in South Carolina and Louisiana.* Columbia: University of South Carolina School of Medicine, Center for Disability Resources.

Florida, R. (2002). *The rise of the creative class: How it's transforming work, leisure, community, and everyday life.* Boulder, CO: Perseus Books.

Justice, T., & Jamieson, D. W. (1999). *The facilitator's handbook.* New York: American Management Association.

Kretzman, J. P., & McNight, J. (1997). *Building communities from the inside out: A path toward finding and mobilizing a community's assets.* Chicago: Acta Publications.

Morse, S. W. (2004). *Smart communities.* San Francisco: Jossey-Bass.

Putnam, R. D. (1995, January). Bowling alone: America's declining social capital. *Journal of Democracy, 6*(1), 65–78.

Putnam, R. D. (2000). *Bowling alone in America: The collapse and revival of American communities.* New York: Simon & Schuster.

Putnam, R. D., & Feldstein, L. M. (2003). *Better together: Restructuring the American community.* New York: Simon & Schuster.

Robbins, H., & Finley, M. (2001). *The new why teams don't work.* San Francisco: Berrett-Koehler.

Schorr, L. B. (1977). *Common purpose: Strengthening families and neighborhoods to rebuild America.* New York: Anchor Books/Doubleday.

Sirolli, E. (1998). *Ripples from the Zambezi: Passion, entrepreneurship, and the rebirth of local economies.* British Columbia: New Society Publications.

Tuckman, D. W. (1965). Developmental sequence in small groups. *Psychological Bulletin, 63*, 384–399.

Wachter, M. I., & Tinsley, C. (1996). *Taking back our neighborhood: Building communities that work.* Minneapolis, MN: Fairview Press.

CHAPTER 7

Interagency Collaboration: It Takes Communication to Support Transitions

Caren L. Sax and David A. Noyes
San Diego State University

There is no shortage of legislation, policies, research, and recommended strategies on the importance of supporting students with disabilities as they move beyond high school and enter adult life. The statistics clearly indicate that the post–high school outcomes for these students should be improved in the following areas: high school graduation rates; enrollment in postsecondary education; options for employment and career development; and community integration related to housing, recreation, and an improved quality of life. Given the amount of attention paid to this subject, why do the options remain limited for so many youth with disabilities? Researchers offer many reasons and recommend a wide range of solutions; however, when it comes to reevaluating practice, altering routines, and restructuring systems, practitioners often feel powerless to effect change.

This chapter offers one perspective on producing change through the use of the basic art of communication and creating relationships that foster collaboration among the many stakeholders involved in the transition process.

THE NEED FOR COLLABORATION

The law is very specific about the requirement for interagency cooperation and collaboration in the area of transition. For example, IDEA 1997 (P.L. 105-17) required that the individualized transition plan (ITP) include statements outlining (a) the projected services that the student needs to make a successful transition to adult life, and (b) interagency responsibilities or linkages that support the provision of services. Reauthorized in 2004, IDEA retained the language from 1997 specifying that "if an adult partner agency [e.g., department of rehabilitation (DR)] does not fulfill the agreed-upon services, the educational agency must reconvene the IEP team and develop alternative methods to meet the transition objectives" (Wright, 2004, p. 15). This requirement is aimed at preventing cross-agency finger pointing and blaming that typically occurs when transition services are not provided. When plans are not implemented or fail to produce the desired outcomes, families and students are unsure whom to hold accountable. Ultimately, the educational agency is responsible for arranging transition services (Noyes & Sax, 2004).

In addition to IDEA 2004, the 1998 Rehabilitation Act Amendments (P.L. 105-166) required stakeholders to work together in building a coordinated service delivery system to assist all students with disabilities as they prepare for employment and independence while in school and after they leave the school setting. The Rehab Act defined "transition services" as

> a coordinated set of activities for a student, designed within an outcome-oriented process, that promotes movement from school to postschool activities, including

postsecondary education, vocational training, integrated employment (including supported employment), continuing and adult education, adult services, independent living, or community participation. (Sec. 7(37))

Collaborating across agencies and systems makes sense for everyone, particularly for the student and family facing the move beyond high school. Yet, collaboration often remains unobtainable as students, families, teachers, administrators, and adult service providers struggle with translating legislation and theory into practice.

The National Council on Disability and the Social Security Administration (NCD/SSA, 2000) assembled a Transition–Post School Outcomes Team to review and analyze research from 1975 to 2000 regarding the outcomes of transition, postsecondary education, and employment for individuals with disabilities aged 14 to 22. Team members identified what was working and what should work, and presented recommendations for local, state, and national action. Among these findings, the report highlighted interagency collaboration as a key component.

Under the "what works" category, the report referred to the expansion of school-to-work transition services for youth with disabilities during the 1980s. During that time, state and local efforts focused on improving high school curriculum to include real-life work and community experiences, and increasing student and family participation in the process. Concerted efforts were made "to increase the level and intensity of interagency cooperation among educators, employers, and community service agencies in addressing the transition needs of secondary students with disabilities" (NCD/SSA, 2000, p. 7).

Included in the "what should work" category, a summary of educational research from the 1990s produced a list of strategies designed to lead to successful outcomes for students beyond high school, including gainful employment. Again, the involvement of students, families, businesses, and community representatives was a key factor in successful interagency transition teams.

The outcomes team concluded that barriers continued to limit successful postschool outcomes despite federal legislation, research efforts, and evidence of promising practices. Among the 12 conclusions suggested for why these barriers persisted were references to the lack of interagency collaboration, specifically that "vocational rehabilitation and other community service providers have limited involvement in the transition process on a national scale" (NCD/SSA, 2000, p. 32). The report recommended the promotion of transition partnerships among stakeholders and the increase of opportunities for "local intermediaries" as brokers who promote individualized transition planning and implementation.

Similarly, in the National Disability policy progress report (NCD, 2004), the findings were all too familiar: "Despite government efforts to address transition through more effective cooperation between educational, rehabilitation, and other adult service systems, smooth transition from secondary school to post-school pursuits for people with disabilities has remained elusive in all too many cases" (p. 8). Issues that require particular attention and that depend on interagency cooperation include transferring assistive technology from schools to adult service systems, clarifying the financial responsibilities for each system, and creating a better understanding of shared responsibility and shared accountability across systems (NCD, 2002).

The recommendations related to students with disabilities as they move from school to adult life consistently reflect the need for effective communication, collaboration, and accountability across all the systems responsible for preparing these youth for full participation in society. The next section addresses strategies for improving this communication.

USE OF DIALOGUE

The need for achieving mutual understanding remains substantial, especially as budgets grow tighter and resources are spread thinner. One successful strategy for elevating the level of understanding is through the use of dialogue. Dialogue, as explained by one of the world's most famous public opinion experts, Daniel Yankelovich, is a practical tool for anyone to use. Yankelovich (1999) explains his understanding of dialogue as follows: "Most people have two purposes for doing dialogue: to strengthen personal relationships and to solve problems" (p. 12). He also described what dialogue is not:

> Dialogue is not, however, an arcane and esoteric form of intellectual exercise that only the few can play. It is not, in fact, an instrument of decision making, which always involves considerations of power and interest—issues that interfere with dialogue. And it is not a negotiating device that seeks agreement leading to action. (p. 15)

Other scholars representing a variety of backgrounds and professions have explored the use of dialogue in this same context. From the philosopher Martin Buber to the management expert Peter Senge, many thinkers have referred to the contribution of dialogue to their respective fields. David Bohm, a theoretical physicist, discovered that "world-class physicists develop their most creative ideas not in solitary thought but through dialogue with one another" (Yankelovich, 1999, p. 23). Bohm (1996) suggested that dialogue has a deeper connotation than is commonly used. For example, "the object of a dialogue is not to analyze things, or to win an argument, or to exchange opinions. Rather, it is to suspend your opinions and to look at the opinions [of others] and to see what all that means" (p. 26). Moreover, Bohm contended that if we take the time to understand what all our opinions mean, we can share a common content whether we agree on everything or not. The dialogue moves more creatively in a different direction out of which may emerge some new understanding. If interagency collaboration is going to be effective, then dialogue is necessary to gain mutual understanding of goals, outcomes, and assumptions that each of the stakeholders brings to the table.

Interagency Dialogue and Collaboration

An example of the use of interagency dialogue is presented here to demonstrate an effective strategy for building trust among stakeholders, challenging the status quo, and achieving better outcomes for students with disabilities as they enter adulthood. The context for using dialogue is the transition service integration model, conceptualized in 1996 to foster both the joint investment and the responsibility required to facilitate a seamless transition from school to adult life for students with significant support needs (Certo, Pumpian, Fisher, Storey, & Smalley, 1997). The project, as funded by the U.S. Department of Education (Pumpian, Certo, & Sax, 1996–2004), addressed the fragmentation of services among the primary systems responsible for transition: public schools, department of rehabilitation (DR), and developmental disability systems (DDS). The model has been integrated into existing practice, continuing beyond the funded projects.

The goal of the project was to effect a systems change by increasing the level of collaboration and cooperation among the three agencies prior to the student's aging out or exiting the public school system. Partnerships were formed between schools and community rehabilitation programs (e.g., nonprofit agencies) in order to develop job sites for students prior to their exit from school. Using the job as an anchor, students, families, and staff identified other activities (e.g., postsecondary education, recreation, and options for community integration) to complete individualized weekly schedules. Funding arrangements for continued support through rehabilitation and/or developmental disability systems were determined and in place by the time of graduation. Strategies such as early intervention, creative funding, and regular interagency committee meetings were used and resulted in seamless transitions, employment, and other quality postschool outcomes for the majority of students (Certo et al., 2003; Noyes & Sax, 2004).

Given that the model was introduced in more than a dozen sites in California and other states and evolved differently in each location, the strategies recommended here are based on the experience of the authors and the teams with which they interacted. The recommendations include guidelines for initiating and maintaining dialogue with the systems stakeholders (e.g., personnel from schools, adult support agencies, rehabilitation, developmental disabilities) who are critical to effectively supporting students beyond high school. The process and progress of the interagency team interactions reflect the stages described in Chapter 6, including the use of external facilitators, identification of common goals, and commitment to a long-term effort.

Cofacilitation. Using cofacilitators to initiate the dialogue and maintain the momentum is an effective strategy on several levels. First, identifying two individuals as facilitators who bring specific expertise and experience that complement one another (e.g., special education and rehabilitation) builds both rapport and credibility. Ideally, the facilitators provide an objective perspective from outside the respective systems, or can at least temporarily "switch hats" to function outside their typical roles. Second, by working as a team, facilitators can model collaboration. That is, they demonstrate the ability to learn from one another as they check for understanding. Moreover, the power of observation is strengthened when one of the facilitators monitors the reactions of the group while the other is speaking. It is important for the group to get to know the facilitators as individuals who are equally invested in the process. An environment of speaking directly and openly to one another is encouraged, bridging any distance that might be felt due to perceived status, official position, or other such misperceptions.

Preparation. The process of dialogue begins with preparation that includes gaining understanding from many perspectives. Most school district representatives are likely to argue that a collaborative agreement is in place; however, when asked whether such an agreement has resulted in seamless transitions for students with significant support needs, it is doubtful that all partners would agree that outcomes are adequate.

In preparing for assembling an interagency group, the facilitators begin with a review of documents that provide a historical context (e.g., prior or existing agreements, program reviews, training materials that have been adopted, and needs assessments if available). Talking individually with representatives of the primary stakeholder groups to determine the status of the existing collaboration provides insight into the consistencies and inconsistencies among their points of view. Facilitators should use these conversations to identify the most appropriate individuals to become involved in the ongoing dialogues (i.e., those who are willing and able to make the commitment to the process).

Facilitators may also want to gather information from others who have been involved peripherally in the process. For example, when we worked as cofacilitators to revive an interagency team that was unable to reach agreement on its collaborative transition agreement, we talked with colleagues who had provided training and technical assistance to the stakeholders in another context. These "outsiders" provided critical insight about the political context, personal relationships, and resource issues that had influenced both the development and the demise of past collaborative efforts. This proved to be vital information before starting a new form of dialogue with individuals who tended to be skeptical and suspicious of one another. Contact with representatives of each of the stakeholder groups in advance of the first interagency meeting should be scheduled to clarify the goals and expected outcomes. Participants typically need reassurance that the interagency team's goals are consistent with their own.

Meetings. After identifying the participants for the interagency dialogue, the facilitators begin designing the agenda for the first meeting, offering the information to the various representatives beforehand in order to build trust that the facilitators are operating in an open manner. If there is a history of noncooperation or failure to follow through on commitments, participants need time to rebuild confidence in one another as well as in the process. The facilitators play a key role in creating the unique atmosphere in which dialogue is conducted. The features of dialogue that distinguish it from discussion, debate, or other deliberations include "equality and the absence of coercive influences; listening with empathy; and bringing assumptions into the open" (Yankelovich, 1999, pp. 41–45). As the meetings unfold, the facilitators must verify the presence of all three of these requirements and, if they are missing, must figure out how to include them.

Given that the participants represent and are influenced by different organizational cultures, structures, language, and acronyms, the group must be prepared to reconcile some amount of historical dissonance. Aligning the stakeholders in identifying and implementing shared vision and complementary outcomes is the major task at hand. Even when participants have opposing points of views about how goals should be accomplished, they can often see the legitimacy of each other's perspectives. Sharing common concerns and offering mutual acknowledgment go a long way toward demonstrating respect and empathy, and help move the group into meaningful dialogue. (See Table 7.1 for a quick guide to the use of dialogue.)

Dialogue in Action

The following three case study composites show the level of interagency agreements and collaboration that developed as a result of the transition service integration dialogue.

TABLE 7.1 *Quick Guide to Dialogue*

Tasks	Strategies
Identify facilitators	Use individuals who bring expertise, experience, and credibility; who are skilled at facilitating dialogue
Identify participants (from various stakeholder groups)	Use individuals who have knowledge of the process, who are familiar with current and past status, and are invested in the success of the approach; include individuals who have authority to make changes
Prepare for meetings	Gather history from participants individually to gain various perspectives; review documents when available (memorandums of understanding or other agreements; exit data); clarify purposes for dialogue; identify potential "historical dissonance"
Conduct meetings	Create atmosphere of trust, openness, transparency of process; share goals/outcomes and find commonalities; assess current strategies related to outcomes to find out what has to be changed, enhanced
Build in continuity	Design continuous feedback loops to build on knowledge, success, and challenges; communicate on a regular basis to maintain trust, report on efforts and outcomes

Traditional Process Before Interagency Dialogue

A story about Diego, a composite character representing typical student experiences, will help illustrate the traditional transition process prior to engagement in the transition service integration dialogue.

> Diego, age 22, has moderate mental retardation and has been participating in his school's transition class since he was 18. He is scheduled to exit from the public school system in June and has worked in several school-based employment sites over the past 3 years. Diego does well at his current job at a music store in a local mall and likes it very much, but the job does not belong to him. The job is designated as a training site used by many of the students in this class.
>
> The transition teacher has arranged for a planning meeting in April and has invited Diego, his family, the service coordinator from DDS, and a representative from DR. Assuming that all of the parties involved agree that supported employment is an appropriate goal for Diego after he leaves school, an application will be made for vocational rehabilitation services. The application process and eligibility determination for rehabilitation services can take up to 60 days. Diego and his family are encouraged to visit adult agencies in their area to discuss supported employment options and to decide who would provide the best services for Diego to find and maintain employment.
>
> By June, rehabilitation services are authorized for Diego, and an adult agency begins to provide job development and identify an appropriate employment match. Diego exits school and stays at home while a job is identified. After 2 months of waiting, he is offered a job at a sheltered workshop until a community placement is found. Diego and his family refuse this option, feeling that this is a step backward, as Diego was already working successfully in the community while he was in school. Two more months pass, leaving Diego bored and his family frustrated. Momentum and motivation are lost.

Diego's story helps illustrate a critical issue in transition planning. Due to delayed interagency collaboration and planning, too many students experience this "black hole" at the end of their school career. Much of the progress many students make during their school-based work experiences in the community is interrupted at the time of transition. Traditionally, students age out of school transition programs when they turn 22 and are referred to an appropriate adult "receiving agency" (a program providing services in the community). In general, students like Diego must usually leave current employment because it is part of the school-training program used by other students. The exiting student typically has to start over with new program staff (usually strangers), start a new job with a new job coach (once a job is identified), and begin to establish relationships with new coworkers. Thus, any natural supports that had been developed at the job site are lost.

Meaningful Dialogue

The transition service integration model—generated as a result of interagency dialogue and established procedures and practices during the year prior to graduation, typically at age 21—helps develop vocational, social, and recreational activities that students can maintain when they leave public schools. The services are tailored to the individual. In addition, school and adult agency staff begin working proactively with families to address student and family concerns and fears about losing Social Security Insurance (SSI) benefits. Work incentives are explained fully, and families are supported to obtain appropriate income exemptions. Vague reassurances that a student will always be better off working are not enough to overcome this significant barrier to employment. Families must be shown the actual numbers, as illustrated in Latisha's and Josh's stories that follow.

One important change made to implement this model is for DR to fund the receiving supported employment agency working with the student during the last year of transition. This ensures continuity; that is, any job or social/recreation activity the agency was able to establish goes with the student. The year is also used to build natural supports for these activities in the environment that the student will be accessing as an adult. The school staff members who know the student best would still be on hand that year to assist in these activities.

> Latisha, diagnosed with moderate mental retardation, was in her third year of the transition program when she was referred for services from the DR. The transition program was completely community based (off campus), and during the last 2.5 years Latisha had tried out many jobs at school-subsidized training sites. At the time of application for DR services, Latisha was working at a local grocery store with two other students. She was well liked by the other store employees, loved her work, and the store manager decided that she wanted to offer Latisha a permanent job if supported employment assistance was available.
>
> Because of the influence of the transition service integration model, the local DR had already established a policy of overlapping services during the student's final year in public education. Supported employment services could begin and the job could be acquired as long as Latisha was in her final year of school. Unfortunately, Latisha was still 16 months from exiting public education according to her individualized education program (IEP). The transition team did some brainstorming, and the DR counselor asked if it was possible to change the exit date. Instead of leaving the school system the following June, would Latisha and her family agree to exit in December, thus qualifying her for immediate assistance with supported employment services and allowing Latisha to have the job she so much desired?
>
> Latisha, her family, and the rest of the IEP team quickly agreed to this simple solution. Latisha was hired and remained a valuable employee well past graduation. In addition, because an adult agency was able to begin support in March with her vocational needs, the school staff was freed up to spend time working on Latisha's other goals in her IEP. The transition team was able to provide some "social coaching," assisting Latisha in getting involved in a swimming program at the local YWCA and taking a computer class at a community college. The school staff was able to develop natural supports at these sites so the activities could be sustained once staff faded away at school exit (similar to job coaching). These efforts provided a seamless transition for Latisha—her first day with the adult service system looked no different than her last day in the public education system.

Impact on SSI. Latisha's family was initially concerned about her Supplemental Security Income (SSI) benefits and whether working would jeopardize them in any way. The transition team was well informed about the benefits of working and alleviated the family's fears. Before working, Latisha received approximately $600.00 in SSI benefits because she was living at home. Working 20 hours a week at $6.75 an hour, Latisha would earn about $567.00 a month in wages (based on 4.2 weeks per month). SSI excludes the first $65.00 of earnings (earned income exclusion), then deducts $1.00 for every $2.00 earned from the monthly benefit until this zeros out. In this case, $567.00 minus $65.00 equals $502.00 divided by 2 equals $251.00.

Latisha's monthly SSI check would be reduced by $251.00—from $600.00 to $349.00. But with her earnings of $567.00, combined with the $349.00 SSI adjusted benefit, Latisha and the family could see that the actual monthly income would be $926.00—an increase of $326.00.

> Josh is a 21-year-old male who was born with cerebral palsy. Josh is a personable young man with mental retardation who uses a powered wheelchair for mobility and needs assistance from personal attendants and family members with eating and toileting. In addition, Josh's speech is difficult to understand. The school had provided an augmentative communication device that Josh had spent considerable time customizing for his personal use.
>
> At the time of application for DR services, Josh was 8 months away from exiting the public school system. Josh was working 6 hours a day, 5 days a week at a large retail store as a greeter. School staff helped support Josh with his eating and toileting needs at work, and the employer was willing to hire him permanently if support could continue once he graduated. Supported employment was not a real option as local employment agencies typically will not assist with toileting, and job coaching was not needed as Josh knew his job. Josh and his transition team met and decided that perhaps the best solution was to hire one of his personal attendants to come to the job site to assist him with his personal needs. Josh was willing to apply for the Impairment Related Work Expense (IRWE) exemption from SSI. In essence, if Josh paid his attendant $10.00 an hour to come in each day for 2 hours (including travel time), it would cost him only $5.00. SSI shares the cost (see "SSI Implications" for the breakdown).
>
> With the attendant care in place, the next barrier was related to Josh's assistive technology. The communication device was purchased by the school and, according to existing practice, Josh would leave it behind when he graduated. DR could begin an evaluation and the purchase of new equipment, but then it would have to be customized again to fit Josh's needs and personality. He did not want to start over. Through interagency collaboration and dialogue, the local DR office and school district negotiated a process whereby DR could purchase the equipment based on a standard schedule of depreciation. The school district registered as a vendor for DR, supplied its tax ID number, and the purchase occurred. This creative thinking led to a new process for students to keep their assistive technology equipment when they exited the public school system. As a result, Josh was able to accept the permanent job and remained employed after graduation.

SSI Implications. Josh, working 30 hours per week at $6.75 an hour, earned approximately $850.00 a month (based on 4.2 weeks a month). Less the $65.00 initial exclusion, his countable income was down to $785.00. The IRWE allowed 10 hours a week (times 4.2 weeks) for personal attendant care on the job site, a total of 42 hours a month at $10.00 an hour minus another $420.00 deduction, which dropped his countable income down to $365.00, divided by 2 equals $182.50. Previously, his monthly SSI check was $600.00 because he still lived at home. Less $182.50, the new SSI amount was $417.50. Taking Josh's earnings of $850.00 less actual attendant pay of $420.00 equals $430.00, plus the new SSI amount of $417.50 brings a new monthly total income of $847.50 ($247.50 more than the previous SSI payment alone).

Summary

The case studies illustrate several examples of creative interagency collaboration and the use of Social Security work incentives that led to improved outcomes for students in transition. New regulations or policies were not needed to implement these changes, only a planned and meaningful process of dialogue between relevant stakeholders that could question business as usual.

Traditionally, DR did not begin funding supported employment services for students until they left the public school system. There was a myth that it was illegal to do so. The dialogue process raised the question, and a local DR administrator had the courage to say why not? She believed that this approach would improve employment outcomes by allowing adult agencies to work side by side with teachers and families the last year of school. Her leadership led to a statewide memorandum that clarified this approach as an acceptable and appropriate practice throughout the state.

Dialogue also created the opportunity to think differently about school-purchased assistive technology and about school exit dates. Why not ask DR to purchase the personalized equipment from the school on a depreciation schedule? Why start over if the student is happy with his or her piece of equipment? Further, every student may not need to attend a full 4 years of transition programming. If a good job opportunity can be obtained for a student through early intervention of a supported employment agency as in Latisha's case, why not go after it if the other goals of the IEP have been addressed? The last year of school typically starts at age 21 for students in transition class, but it could also start at age 20, 19, or 18. The IEPs can become more individualized to access appropriate services at appropriate times.

Interagency partners often attend IEP meetings, but typically the discussion focuses on what each brings to the table based on current practice with little opportunity or motivation to question why we do what we do. Assigned, accountable facilitators are needed to cross these agency boundaries and conduct a proactive dialogue process. Bureaucracies are slow to change, but change is possible by collectively questioning our interagency transition process and identifying leaders willing to take some risk in each of the systems. The first step is to make the time to have dialogue with each other in order to produce new outcomes.

Study Questions

1. What is meant by overlapping services the final year of school? Why is this beneficial for students? For families?

   Teachers know the students and families best. They can leverage their relationships and bring on adult agency staff in a nonthreatening manner. Students can participate in their regular school job sites while a permanent job is identified. School staff can help adult agency staff problem solve areas of concern (e.g., transportation, hygiene, behavior). Teachers can help build a schedule of nonwork activities around the permanent job schedule once it is identified. Families continue to receive support from the school, and students can return to the school program that last year if the permanent job is lost, and the agency can then begin to find another job. The school serves as a safety net that last year, allowing students and families to take a chance on adult agency services they might not otherwise take. Early supported employment funding from DR makes this possible.

2. Does a student who receives services from DDS have to stay in school until he or she is 22?

   According to our sources, this is a family's choice. There may be subtle (or overt) pressure to do so, but this is another myth that can be challenged.

3. Why is purchasing existing adaptive equipment important for students in transition?

   Comfort level and familiarity are key factors, alleviating stress for students. Using existing equipment also avoids unnecessary evaluations.

4. What is meant by social coaching?

   It is similar to job coaching, but for nonwork activities. Social coaching helps a student attend a regular activity in the community, develops natural supports, then fades away. School staff can focus on this while an adult agency takes care of the employment support.

5. Why are families so fearful of losing Social Security benefits? Why do you have to be so specific about the impact on the dollar amount of the SSI check?

   Many families depend on the income for monthly expenses—part of the family budget. The student receives the check and, therefore, will have more control of his or her money. The family needs specific help on understanding and negotiating these implications.

6. Why doesn't this dialogue process just happen naturally?

   The process takes significant time, effort, planning, and commitment to making change. It is difficult to offer an objective perspective on why things are working or not working without taking responsibility for some of the difficulties.

7. How can cross-agency training help the transition process?

   Assumptions are typically held that individuals from one agency are familiar with and understand how other agencies operate. For example, transition teachers are expected to be familiar with the way in which the DR and the DDS each conduct intakes and assessments and provide services; however, this is not always the case. Just as teachers may not understand the intricacies, policies, and procedures of these systems, similarly, professionals representing these agencies may be unfamiliar with the demands, requirements, and restrictions that govern teachers on a daily basis. Teaching one another how their respective systems work goes a long way toward establishing procedures that work for everyone. Common planning documents have been developed as a result of cross-agency training.

8. What are the main distinctions between dialogue and debate?

   According to Daniel Yankelovich (1999), the following distinctions are made (pp. 39–40):

Debate	**Dialogue**
Assuming that there is a right answer and you have it	Assuming that many people have pieces of the answer and that together they can craft a solution
Combative: attempting to prove the other side wrong	Collaborative: working together toward common understanding
Assuming it's about winning	Assuming it's about exploring common ground
Listening to find flaws and make counterarguments	Listening to understand and to find meaning and agreement
Defending assumptions as truth	Revealing assumptions for reevaluation
Critiquing the other side's position	Reexamining all positions
Defending one's own views against those of others	Admitting that others' thinking can improve on one's own
Searching for flaws and weaknesses in other positions	Searching for strengths and value in others' positions
Seeking a conclusion or vote that ratifies your position	Discovering new options, not seeking closure

9. Why is the technique of cofacilitation advantageous in dialogue?

   Using cofacilitators to initiate the dialogue and maintain the momentum is an effective strategy on several levels. First, identifying two individuals as facilitators who bring specific expertise and experience that complement that of the other, builds both rapport and credibility. Second, by working as a team, facilitators can model collaboration. That is, they demonstrate the ability to learn from one another as they check for understanding. Moreover, the power of observation is strengthened when one of the facilitators monitors the reactions of the group while the other is speaking.

10. Why is it important to facilitate even small steps of dialogue in challenging existing systems?

    Bureaucracies are slow to change, but change is possible by collectively questioning our interagency transition process and identifying leaders willing to take some risk in each of the systems. The first step is to make the time to have dialogue with each other in order to produce new outcomes.

Recommended Reading

Brown, C., & Miller, J. (Eds.). (2002). *Investing in the transition of youth with disabilities to productive careers*. Hot Springs, AR: Twenty-Eighth Institute on Rehabilitation Issues.

Clark, H. B., & Davis, M. (Eds.). *Transition to adulthood: A resource for assisting young people with emotional or behavioral difficulties*. Baltimore: Brookes.

Sax, C., & Thoma, C. *Transition assessment: Wise practices for quality lives*. Baltimore: Brookes.

Wheatley, M. J. (2002). *Turning to one another: Simple conversations to restore hope to the future*. San Francisco: Berrett-Koehler.

Yankelovich, D. (1999). *The magic of dialogue: Transforming conflict into cooperation*. New York: Simon & Schuster.

Web Resources

Interagency Collaboration

National Center on Secondary Education and Transition: Creating Opportunities for Youth with Disabilities to Achieve Successful Futures

http://www.ncset.org/

NCSET coordinates national resources, offers technical assistance, and disseminates information related to secondary education and transition for youth with disabilities in order to create opportunities for youth to achieve successful futures.

On-Campus Outreach (OCO): Supporting Transition Best Practices in Post-Secondary Settings for Students with Significant Disabilities

http://www.education.umd.edu/oco/training/pubs/relpubs.html

Supported at the University of Maryland through a federal grant from the U.S. Department of Education's Office of Special Education Programs, the purpose of OCO is to provide information and support to programs and personnel that provide services to public school students ages 18–21 with significant disabilities in postsecondary settings such as colleges, universities, or other community locations.

President's Committee for People with Intellectual Disabilities

http://www.acf.hhs.gov/programs/pcpid

PCPID, formerly the President's Committee on Mental Retardation (PCMR), is a federal advisory committee established by presidential executive order to advise the president of the United States and the secretary of the Department of Health and Human Services on issues concerning citizens with intellectual disabilities, coordinate activities between different federal agencies, and assess the impact of their policies on the lives of citizens with intellectual disabilities and their families.

ThinkCollege.net: Access to College by Students with Intellectual Disabilities

http://www.thinkcollege.net/

The site is divided into sections for students, family members, and professionals and features a searchable database, discussion board, listserv, and resource section with links to other sites and a bibliography listing related publications.

Viewpoint Learning: Insight Through Dialogue

http://www.viewpointlearning.com/

The website features resources on understanding and implementing dialogue in organizations.

Wrightslaw on Transition

http://www.wrightslaw.com/info/trans.index.htm

Wrightslaw provides legislative information on transition laws and policies, legal interpretations, and additional resources including free publications on transition planning and implementation.

Youthhood.org: Where Teens Prepare for Life After High School

http://www.youthhood.org/

Registration is available for youth and teachers at this site. It can be accessed by youth independently or with a mentor, family member, or friend to find out more about what other youth are doing, career opportunities, personal growth, and so on. The site is funded by the U.S. Department of Education's Office of Special Education Programs.

References

Bohm, D. (1996). *On dialogue.* London: Routledge.

Certo, N. J., Mautz, D., Pumpian, I., Sax, C., Smalley, K., Wade, H., et al. (2003). A review and discussion of a model for seamless transition to adulthood. *Education and Training in Mental Retardation and Developmental Disabilities, 38*(1), 3–17.

Certo, N. J., Pumpian, I., Fisher, D., Storey, K., & Smalley, K. (1997). Focusing on the point of transition: A service integration model. *Education and Treatment of Children, 20*(1), 68–85.

Individuals with Disabilities Act (IDEA) Amendments of 1997, Pub. L. No. 105-17, 20 U.S.C. §§ 1400 *et seq.*

National Council on Disability. (2002). *National Council on Disability feature: Youth with disabilities have special concerns.* Retrieved January 23, 2005, from http://www.ncd.gov/newsroom/news/2002/f02-383.htm

National Council on Disability. (2004). *National disability policy: A progress report December 2002–December 2003.* Retrieved January 29, 2005, from http://www.ncd.gov/newsroom/publications/2004/ProgressReport2004.htm

National Council on Disability and Social Security Administration. (2000). *Transition and post-school outcomes for youth with disabilities: Closing the gaps to post-secondary education and employment.* Retrieved January 23, 2005, from http://www.ncd.gov/newsroom/publications/2000/transition_11-01-00.htm

Noyes, D., & Sax, C. (2004). Changing systems for transition: Students, families, and professionals working together. *Education and Training in Mental Retardation and Developmental Disabilities, 39*(1), 35–44.

Pumpian, I., Certo, N. J. & Sax, C. (1996–2004). *Focusing on the point of transition: A service integration model.* Washington, DC: U.S. Department of Education, Office of Special Education and Rehabilitation Services.

Rehabilitation Act Amendments of 1998, Pub. L. No. 105-166.

Yankelovich, D. (1999). *The magic of dialogue: Transforming conflict into cooperation.* New York: Simon & Schuster.

Assessment, Work Experience Opportunities, Job Placement, and Student Support

PART 4

Chapter 8
Transition Assessment: Emerging Guidelines and Promising Practices

Chapter 9
Work-Based Learning: Developing Work Experience Opportunities for Transitioning Students

Chapter 10
Job Placement and Job Redesign

Chapter 11
Natural Supports in the Workplace and Beyond

Chapter 12
Supporting Students in the Transition from School to Adult Life

Chapter 13
Dropout Prevention: Using Self-Determination to Achieve Desired Postschool Outcomes

Chapter 14
Evaluation Practices for Transition Planning

CHAPTER 8

Transition Assessment: Emerging Guidelines and Promising Practices

Bruce M. Menchetti
Florida State University

Systematic and comprehensive transition assessment has potential to expand life opportunities for students with disabilities. When conducted effectively, transition assessment can provide important information needed for making critical life decisions, such as how to prepare for postsecondary education and employment. In addition, the information gathered through the transition assessment process can be useful to many different people—teachers, students, family members, employers, adult service providers, and other members of the community who have a stake in students with disabilities making a successful transition from school to postschool activities. For these reasons, it is important to understand the legal requirements, assessment theories and approaches, professional guidelines, and data collection methods that shape comprehensive transition assessment. This chapter provides a broad overview of the procedures that should be considered when developing portfolios or profiles. After a discussion of legal requirements that are influencing transition assessment, career development models of assessment are reviewed, followed by an overview of person-centered approaches. This chapter concludes with a discussion of consensus building and emerging best practice related to developing an individualized transition profile.

LEGAL REQUIREMENTS IMPACTING TRANSITION ASSESSMENT

The Individuals with Disabilities Education Improvement Act of 2004 (IDEA 2004; P.L. 108-446) included several provisions related to transition services that have implications for transition assessment. As in earlier versions of IDEA (1990 and 1997), transition services defined in IDEA 2004 largely remained a process of identifying and coordinating all the activities necessary for a student to obtain socially important and personally satisfying postschool outcomes. IDEA 2004 suggested some appropriate outcomes of the transition process, including postsecondary education, vocational education, competitive employment, adult education, adult services, independent living, and community participation. Recognizing that individual students would require a variety of services and activities to obtain appropriate postschool outcomes, IDEA suggested that transition services include school-based instruction, related services and therapies, community experiences, and the development of daily living skills, employment, and other adult living objectives. Finally, to facilitate identification of appropriate services among all these options, IDEA 2004 recognized that students would require a specialized assessment focused on transition.

Accordingly, IDEA 2004 specified that transition planning in a student's IEP must be based on age-appropriate transition assessments. One purpose of the transition assessments would be to gather the information necessary to identify measurable postsecondary goals on a student's IEP. In addition, according to IDEA 2004, transition assessment must be broadly focused in order to determine the most appropriate array of possible transition services. Although it appears, based on these legal requirements, that IDEA 2004 intended transition assessment to be comprehensive and broadly focused, the question is, what areas should be addressed by a comprehensive transition assessment? The legal requirements of IDEA 2004 also offer some answers to this question.

Neubert (2006) pointed out that IDEA 2004 slightly changed the definition of transition services from the definitions offered in IDEA 1990 and 1997. Some of these changes have implications for identifying the areas to be addressed by transition assessment. Among the changes pointed out by Neubert in the IDEA 2004 definition of transition service was a focus on improving both the academic and functional achievement of the child with a disability. The dual focus on scholastic and functional skills implies that these broad areas and the many respective component skills comprising these areas should be included in a comprehensive transition assessment.

IDEA 2004 also changed the requirement for student involvement in transition service planning (Neubert, 2006). Prior to 2004, transition services were required to be based on a student's preferences and interests. This requirement moved schools to involve students with disabilities in transition planning as a means of ascertaining their postschool preferences and interests. Taking the next step, IDEA 2004 also decreed that transition services be based on a child's strengths along with preferences and interests. Specifically, IDEA 2004 stated that transition services must be "based on the individual child's needs, taking into account the child's strengths, preferences, and interests" (Neubert, 2006, p. 44). This new requirement has implications for the type of assessment approaches and tools comprising transition assessment by suggesting that assessment should highlight a student's talents, abilities, and accomplishments.

The time when transition is addressed in a student's IEP has also been changed by IDEA 2004 (Neubert, 2006; Test, Aspel, & Everson, 2006). Test et al. pointed out that IDEA 2004 eliminated transition planning as part of the IEP at age 14, instead mandating that transition services should be planned in "the first IEP in effect when a student turns 16 years old" (p. 22). It is important to note, however, that Test et al. still recommend the practice of beginning transition planning as early as possible, and early planning is allowable under IDEA 2004. Because transition planning must be guided by assessment, it is important to begin the process of transition assessment as early as possible for individual students.

In summary, Salvia and Ysseldyke (2004) suggested that much assessment practice in special education is the direct result of legislation. Federal special education legislation has many implications for transition assessment. Given the link between practice and legislation, the transition-related requirements of IDEA 2004 should be used by professionals to shape the form and function of a comprehensive transition assessment for students with disabilities. Seven major implications of IDEA 2004 for transition assessment are:

- Transition planning should begin as early as possible, but no later than the first IEP to take effect when a student turns age 16.

- Transition planning must be based on age-appropriate transition assessments.
- Transition assessment should be broadly focused and comprehensive in coverage.
- Transition assessment should guide the identification of measurable postsecondary goals on the student's IEP.
- Transition assessment should focus on areas needed to improve both academic and functional skill outcomes for students with disabilities.
- Transition assessment should allow for identification of a student's postschool interests and preferences.
- Transition assessment should use methods that highlight a student's strengths, abilities, talents, and accomplishments.

LONGITUDINAL APPROACHES TO TRANSITION ASSESSMENT

Whereas federal legislation requires that transition planning begin no later than the first IEP to take effect when a student turns age 16, many transition experts believe that students with disabilities can benefit from a much earlier and longitudinal approach to transition planning and service provision (Amos, 2006; Clark, Carlson, Fisher, Cook, & D'Alonzo, 1991; Repetto & Correa, 1996). However, transition services that produce a broad range of desirable postschool outcomes have not always been the constant focus of educational programs for children with disabilities.

Pointing to a gap in transition services occurring in the elementary and middle school grades, Amos (2006) suggested "not responding to the need for transitions education and services between early childhood and secondary leaves a gap in student learning" (p. 113). Amos proposed three strategies to reduce fragmentation of services and build a more cohesive education system that values successful postschool outcomes for students with disabilities: (a) nurturing the active and continuous involvement of families in the IEP process; (b) promoting early and ongoing collaboration with local and state agencies; and (c) early and continued participation of students in their IEPs (e.g., by introducing teachers, stating their likes and dislikes, setting their own goals). It is important to note that family involvement, interagency collaboration, and student participation in planning have been identified by several researchers as transition practices that produce successful adult outcomes for students with disabilities (Hasazi, Furney, & DeStefano, 1999; Kohler, 1998).

Continuous emphasis on transition planning and services from elementary through middle and high school grades has promise for improving a student's eventual adult outcomes (Kohler, 1998). Consequently, transition assessment practices should begin early and continue over time. This will focus a student's educational program on outcomes that are desirable to the student, the family, and society.

Career Development Models of Assessment

For over 20 years, proponents of career development theory have called for assessment beginning in the elementary school and continuing through adulthood (Sitlington, Brolin, Clark, & Vacanti, 1985) for students with disabilities. Specifically, assessment of a student's career development focuses on the ongoing process of developing all life roles including worker, family member, lifelong learner, participant in social and interpersonal networks, and community citizen (Sitlington & Clark, 2006).

The Council for Exceptional Children's (CEC) original Division on Career Development defined assessment as "a developmental process beginning in the elementary school and continuing through adulthood" (Sitlington et al., 1985, p. 3). Later, the Division on Career Development and Transition, still using the career development model, defined transition assessment as "the ongoing process of collecting data on the individual's strengths, needs, preferences, and interests as they relate to the demands of current and future working, educational, living, and personal and social environments" (Sitlington, Neubert, & Leconte, 1997, p. 71). Similarly, Clark (1998) suggested that transition assessment address all the life span transitions from childhood through adulthood and that assessment information be used to make the transitions successful and satisfying to individual students.

The career development model provides many challenging guidelines for transition assessment. Models of transition assessment based on career development theory have called for (a) early and ongoing assessment; (b) a broad focus on all the life roles that students encounter as they move across the life span; (c) measurement of a student's strengths, needs, preferences, and interests; and (d) the use of data to develop IEP goals that are results oriented and personally satisfying to individual students.

Transition assessment based on career development theories and practices can provide useful information to a variety of transition stakeholders and may be used to expand life opportunities for students with disabilities. It is not surprising, then, that other transition assessment approaches share many characteristics of the career development assessment model.

Person-Centered Approaches

Person-centered planning shares many important features with the career development model. Person-centered planning has been proposed as a suitable conceptual framework for transition assessment (Garcia & Menchetti, 2003; Menchetti & Piland, 2001). Although used most frequently to guide assessment of students with severe disabilities and significant transition service needs, recently the person-centered approach has been recognized as playing an important role in incorporating student choice in the transition assessment process (Sitlington & Clark, 2006). Indeed, some have suggested that person-centered planning has applications to a broader population of students with disabilities (Menchetti & Piland, 2001; Sax, 2002).

Person-centered planning is a continuous process of information gathering and decision making. It uses a support network comprised of highly committed people who are knowledgeable and supportive of ways to improve the quality of life of the individual with the disability (Garcia & Menchetti, 2003). The support network is comprised of family, friends, teachers, rehabilitation counselors, employers, and any other members of the community who are committed to helping the individual with the disability. Garcia and Menchetti listed the following features of person-centered planning: (a) an effort to increase participation of individuals with disabilities in life planning and decision making; (b) a focus on the preferences, interests, strengths, and abilities of the individual with a disability; (c) the development of a vision of a positive future lifestyle for the individual; and (d) a continuous process of meeting, planning, evaluating, and revising actions to move the individual toward his or her vision for the future.

Like the career development model, person-centered planning is a longitudinal, ongoing process. Person-centered planning is also similar to the career development approach with its broad, lifestyle improvement focus and its emphasis on assessing an individual's strengths, preferences, and interests. Finally, both the person-centered and the career development approaches to assessment use data to develop plans that are outcome oriented and personally satisfying to an individual with a disability.

The Adult Lifestyles Planning Cycle. One example of a person-centered approach to assessment is the Adult Lifestyles Planning Cycle developed by Garcia and Menchetti (2003), designed to help individuals with severe disabilities plan the services and supports they need to attain a personally satisfying adult life. Thus, it may also be used to facilitate the transition planning process. The Adult Lifestyles Planning Cycle begins with an assessment of quality of life using a model developed by Felce and Perry (1995).

After conducting an extensive review of the literature, Felce and Perry (1995) identified five quality-of-life domains: (a) physical well-being; (b) material well-being; (c) social well-being; (d) personal growth, development, and activity; and (e) emotional well-being. Felce and Perry stressed that any assessment of quality of life must consider internal or personal factors such as health, personal values, aspirations, and feelings. In addition, external factors such as economic, social, residential, and political issues were also identified as variables that influence the assessment of quality of life. The concept of quality of life as exemplified by the Felce and Perry model provides a framework for identifying assessment areas for longitudinal transition planning.

Person-centered planning is one part of the Adult Lifestyles Planning Cycle and was used by Garcia and Menchetti (2003) to identify relevant quality-of-life domains. Also discussed are the personal and external factors that are influencing a person's overall quality of life. Once quality-of-life issues are identified and prioritized by individuals and their support networks, the cycle uses ecological inventories to plan specific skill and personal development activities. Finally, the Adult Lifestyles Planning Cycle considers the formal and natural supports needed as individuals make progress toward their personal goals. Like all person-centered approaches, the Adult Lifestyles Planning Cycle is applied frequently to allow for continuous planning, evaluation, and revision of services and supports (Garcia & Menchetti, 2003).

Summary of the Longitudinal Approach

A longitudinal approach to transition assessment has been advocated by proponents of both career development and person-centered theoretical frameworks. The longitudinal approach to transition assessment is characterized by:

- assessment practices that begin early and continue over time;
- a broad, lifestyle-improvement focus;
- an emphasis on assessing an individual's strengths, preferences, and interests;
- the active involvement of students throughout the assessment process; and,
- data used to develop plans that are outcome oriented and personally satisfying to the individual with a disability.

The longitudinal model as characterized previously has been shown to improve adult outcomes for students with disabilities (Hasazi et al., 1999; Kohler, 1998). Every effort should be made to use assessment approaches and transition services that help students and families continuously focus on the long-term goals of special education. Most states, however, concentrate their transition efforts at the secondary level (Amos, 2006).

Consequently, most transition assessment takes place only during Grades 8 to 12. The use of a more longitudinal approach to transition assessment is strongly encouraged because of its potential to improve student outcomes.

OTHER ASSESSMENT PRACTICES THAT IMPROVE STUDENT OUTCOMES

Research has suggested there are other assessment issues that must be addressed to ensure that students with disabilities are fully benefiting from appropriate transition assessment and services. For example, Ysseldyke, Thurlow, Kozleski, and Reschly (1998) identified several challenges to full implementation of IDEA assessment provisions. One critical issue was the lack of communitywide consensus regarding desired postschool outcomes for students with disabilities. Other issues identified by Ysseldyke and colleagues included practitioners' lack of knowledge about, and failure to adhere to, professional guidelines for assessment design and administration.

Consensus Regarding Transition Outcome and Assessment Areas

Perhaps the most important question in transition assessment is, what areas should be measured to document that students with disabilities have attained their preferred postschool outcomes? As we have seen in earlier sections of this chapter, transition experts advocate a broad focus on concepts such as "life roles" or "quality of life." In fact, as we have seen earlier, IDEA 2004 required broad, holistic transition services. What has been missing, however, is a process that school districts and communities could use to agree on a model of outcomes and indicators defining the effectiveness of local transition services (Salvia & Ysseldyke, 2004).

The National Center on Educational Outcomes (NCEO) developed a process that allowed stakeholders in the local community to reach consensus on a system of educational outcomes and indicators to guide the assessment process (Salvia & Ysseldyke, 2004). The educational stakeholders engaged by the NCEO agreed that any outcome model should be applied to all students, regardless of their characteristics. That is, outcomes for special education students should be related to those identified for students without disabilities. The consensus-building process used by the NCEO and the outcomes-based accountability system developed by the center should be considered a model for establishing community consensus on the important transition assessment areas for students with disabilities.

NCEO Process for Developing a Conceptual Model of Outcomes. The NCEO convened hundreds of stakeholders over a 2-year period to identify desired outcomes for the educational system (Ysseldyke, Krentz, et al., 1998). In brief, stakeholders indicated that they expected students to complete their education "with a broad set of skills and behaviors that go beyond literacy and academic content knowledge" (Salvia & Ysseldyke, 2004, p. 669).

Using a multiattribute consensus-building process, the stakeholders interviewed by the NCEO reached agreement on several desired educational outcomes (Ysseldyke, Krentz, et al., 1998). These outcomes and corresponding indicators were submitted to an external review and critique from experts and professional groups, and the original findings were revised and consolidated over time (Ysseldyke, Krentz, et al., 1998). The NCEO now recognizes six outcome domains: (a) academic and functional literacy, (b) physical health, (c) responsibility and independence, (d) citizenship, (e) personal and social well-being, and (f) satisfaction (Salvia & Ysseldyke, 2004). Table 8.1 lists the NCEO outcomes and some sample indicators for each domain.

The NCEO conceptual model included specification of indicators at five developmental levels: age 3 years, age 6, Grade 4, Grade 8, and at school completion (Salvia & Ysseldyke, 2004; Ysseldyke, Krentz, et al., 1998). Salvia and Ysseldyke (2004) pointed out that "school personnel will have to engage in a consensus-building process in their own districts to reach agreement about those indicators that are most important in each of the outcome domains" (p. 670).

TABLE 8.1 *NCEO Outcome Domains and Sample Indicators*

Outcome domain	Sample indicators
Academic and functional literacy	- Individuals demonstrate competence in communication
	- Individuals demonstrate competence in problem solving and critical thinking skills
Physical health	- Individuals have access to basic health care
	- Individuals are aware of basic safety, fitness, and health care needs
Responsibility and independence	- Individuals get around in the environment
	- Individuals make choices and exercise self-determination
Citizenship	- Individuals volunteer
	- Individuals vote
Personal and social well-being	- Individuals possess a good self-image
	- Individuals get along with other people
Satisfaction	- Individuals are satisfied with current situation
	- Parents/Guardians are satisfied with current status of the individual

In addition, the NCEO consensus-building process required stakeholders to identify data sources, develop or adapt data collection methods, and decide how information on educational outcomes will be used.

The NCEO consensus-building process should be used by transition stakeholders to reach agreement on important outcome areas and measurement strategies for transition assessment and to develop their own, unique conceptual model of outcomes to guide the transition assessment process. Student outcomes can be improved when communities come together to (a) develop a shared vision of effective transition services, (b) identify data sources, (c) design data collection methods, and (d) decide how information will be used for individual assessment and program evaluation (Hasazi et al., 1999; Kohler, 1998).

Adherence to Professional Guidelines in Design and Selection of Assessment Methods

In another NCEO report, Ysseldyke, Thurlow, Kozleski, and Reschly (1998) identified several areas affecting the extent of implementation of IDEA assessment provisions. According to this report, assessment design and administration represented a significant challenge to implementation of appropriate assessment practices for students with disabilities for two primary reasons. First, practitioners lack knowledge about appropriate assessment practices. Second, practitioners often fail to adhere to recognized professional guidelines for assessment practice. The NCEO recommended that the development of clear definitions and guidelines for assessment practice was one way to address these problems. Fortunately, such guidelines are available for transition assessment.

Transition Assessment Guidelines. Test and colleagues (2006) offered general guidelines to consider when conducting a transition assessment. They suggest that appropriate practice is defined by six characteristics: (a) transition assessment is student centered and self-determined; (b) transition assessment is an ongoing process; (c) transition assessment occurs in a variety of natural environments; (d) transition assessment gathers information from many people, including professionals, the student, family members, friends, employers, and other stakeholders; (e) transition assessment data must be useful and understandable to all people involved; and finally (f) transition assessment must be sensitive to cultural diversity and different values regarding services and outcomes.

It is important to note the similarities between the guidelines offered by Test et al. (2006) and the recommendations of other transition assessment experts (Clark, 1998; Garcia & Menchetti, 2003; Sitlington et al., 1997). These professionals have all stressed the importance of an ongoing and continuous assessment process. The involvement of students in transition assessment through the development of self-determination has been another consistent proposal. Finally, many have called for the collection of data that are useful in the writing of functional transition plans.

The remainder of the Test et al. (2006) guidelines have also been proposed in earlier transition assessment position papers (Sitlington et al., 1997). For example, the suggestion that assessment be conducted in natural environments has been a consistent proposal by transition professionals. Test and colleagues suggested that students be exposed to a variety of community and educational settings, including employment settings, postsecondary programs, and other places that allow students to "make informed choices and refine their desired postschool outcomes" (p. 65). Students' skills, preferences, interests, strengths, and needs could be assessed in these environments. Thus, Sitlington and Clark (2006) emphasized the "need for personnel to move beyond methods that are isolated from actual life contexts (such as psychometric tests) and move toward methods that are conducted within natural or actual employment, postsecondary, or community settings" (p. 143).

In addition to the recommendation to collect assessment information in settings that resemble desired postschool options, Sitlington and colleagues (1997) echoed the call for sensitivity to cultural and linguistic differences. Consideration of diversity is important because there may be a conflict between the mainstream societal values and the values of an individual student's family. Such conflict may require the adjustment of assessment practices to respond to the preferences of the student and his or her family.

The widespread agreement among professionals indicates there is an emerging consensus regarding best practices for transition assessment. However, agreement on a set of principles does not ensure extensive utilization of appropriate practice or specific policy changes that support effective transition assessment. The challenge now is to train teachers and other practitioners to use accepted guidelines when conducting transition assessments. Administrators, policy makers, and other stakeholders must also be involved so that policies can be created that allow for sustained use of transition assessment best practices. The consensus-building process developed by the NCEO (Ysseldyke, Krentz, et al., 1998) may be one strategy to meet the challenge of making transition assessment practice based on accepted professional guidelines.

Selection of Methods. As you have seen throughout this chapter, transition assessment is a complex, multifaceted process requiring multiple approaches and methods to meet students' individual needs (Clark, 1998). Selection of the appropriate methods will depend on a student's desired postschool outcomes and the information necessary to help the student achieve these goals (Test et al., 2006). The remainder of this chapter describes some transition assessment methods that may be used to help identify student transition goals and services.

TRANSITION ASSESSMENT METHODS

Most professionals agree that multiple methods of gathering information are necessary for appropriate transition assessment (Menchetti & Piland, 2001; Repetto, 2001; Sitlington & Clark; 2006; Test et al., 2006). A variety of approaches have roles to play in transition assessment, including (a) formal methods, (b) informal teacher-made and curriculum-based techniques, and (c) newly emerging, alternative person-centered methods.

Clark (1998) differentiated between formal (i.e., standardized, norm-referenced) and informal (i.e., nonstandardized) transition assessment approaches and instruments. He and others (Repetto, 2001) stressed that both formal and informal assessment methods can be useful in a comprehensive transition assessment of students with disabilities.

Formal Methods

Formal methods refer to psychometric instruments found to have acceptable reliability and validity for specific assessment purposes (Salvia & Ysseldyke, 2004). Formal methods have applicability in transition assessment, especially when there is a clear link between the skill areas being measured (e.g., learning and study strategies) and a student's desired transition outcome (e.g., postsecondary education). Repetto (2001) pointed out that formal, psychometric instruments are available to assess the following areas related to attainment of transition outcomes:

- academic achievement;
- adaptive behavior;
- occupational aptitudes;
- communication skills;

- functional capacity;
- learning styles;
- occupational interests;
- personality and social skills;
- employability skills; and
- knowledge of transition and community living skills.

Some professionals have questioned the widespread use of formal methods for transition assessment, especially for students with severe disabilities (Garcia & Menchetti, 2003; Menchetti & Piland, 2001). Sitlington and Clark (2006) have proposed a movement away from psychometric tests toward more naturalistic, informal transition assessment methods.

Informal Methods

Generally, informal assessment methods refer to criterion-referenced tools, teacher-made materials, observations in community settings, self-ratings, reports from family or friends, and interviews with community stakeholders (Salvia & Ysseldyke, 2004). Other types of informal methods used in transition assessment are direct observations of students performing in natural settings (i.e., situational assessments) and curriculum-based assessments. Person-centered planning, as described in an earlier section of this chapter, represents a specific form of informal transition assessment.

Informal transition assessment methods are now the most widely used transition assessment alternative (Test et al., 2006). Informal methods can be used to gather information in many areas including

- occupational interests and preferences;
- employment strengths and needs;
- postsecondary education;
- financial or income support needs;
- community participation;
- self-advocacy;
- leisure and recreation skills;
- transportation;
- social networks and relationships;
- personal management;
- living arrangements;
- medical issues; and
- insurance issues.

Table 8.2 provides an example of how informal methods may be used to guide comprehensive transition assessment. The 13 different planning areas are used to

TABLE 8.2 *Transition Areas and Questions to Consider for Transition Planning*

Transition area assessed	Questions to consider via interviews, checklists, or planning guides
Occupational interests and preferences	Does the student: • have career interest assessment information on file? • have a realistic career goal? • have a plan to reach his/her goal? • have support for his/her career goal?
Employment strengths and needs	Does the student: • demonstrate understanding of the range of employment options (full-time, part-time, competitive, supported, and volunteer)? • demonstrate the skills and behaviors necessary to reach employment goal? • have or need work experience? • need help finding a job? • need help keeping a job?
Postsecondary education	Does the student: • want or need postsecondary education? • demonstrate understanding of the range of postsecondary options (vocational school, community college, 4-year institution)? • need assistance from an adult agency? • need assistance filling out applications or financial aid forms? • need help selecting an institution? • know and meet deadlines for applications? • meet the criteria for admission?
Financial or income support needs	Does the student: • need financial assistance to obtain goals? • receive SSI and understand the various SSI work incentive programs? • know how to file for benefits? • make purchases appropriate for level of income? • know how to open and maintain a checking and savings account?
Community participation	Does the student: • have a list of preferred community activities? • know how to locate and use public utilities, post office, driver's license bureau, etc.? • utilize shopping malls, theaters, library, grocery stores, etc.? • know how to register to vote? • know how to apply for a driver's license? • know how to use public transportation?
Self-advocacy	Does the student: • understand rights (including IDEA rights) and responsibilities? • demonstrate assertiveness with friends and adults? • express opinions and needs effectively? • demonstrate knowledge of effective accommodations? • know how to set goals and make action plans? • evaluate the outcomes of actions and plan revisions accordingly?

	• participate in IEP transition planning?
	• need ongoing advocacy support?
	• need ongoing guardian support?
Leisure and recreation skills	Does the student:
	• have a list of preferred leisure and recreation activities?
	• participate in preferred school activities?
	• participate in preferred community activities?
	• know how to obtain information about leisure and recreation activities?
Transportation	Does the student:
	• have a preferred method of getting around the community?
	• know how to safely use various methods of transportation?
	• know how to find transportation when needed?
	• have a driver's license?
	• need special transportation services arranged on an ongoing basis?
Social networks and relationships	Does the student:
	• have age-appropriate friends?
	• experience different levels of personal relationships (acquaintances, friends, intimacy, etc.)?
	• have friends who do not have a disability?
	• participate in activities with friends?
Personal management	Does the student:
	• demonstrate good personal grooming and hygiene?
	• prepare meals?
	• select and care for own clothes?
	• manage money effectively?
	• perform routine household chores and maintenance?
	• need help with personal care?
Living arrangements	Does the student:
	• desire to live outside the family home?
	• know the range of living arrangements available?
	• know how to get information about living arrangements?
	• have the knowledge and skills necessary to live in preferred arrangement?
	• need ongoing assistance to live in the preferred location?
Medical issues	Does the student:
	• have medical issues that have to be addressed?
	• know how to describe his/her medical history and allergies?
	• have access to appropriate health care?
	• know how to make medical appointments?
	• know how to explain his/her disability to medical personnel?
	• take medications independently or require assistance in this area?
	• need ongoing medical assistance?
Insurance issues	Does the student:
	• understand the purpose and range of insurance options?
	• need auto, dental, or other insurance?
	• know how to file insurance claims?
	• need ongoing assistance in this area?

help in determining a student's interests, preferences, strengths, and needs. The accompanying questions for each area are intended to generate information to help a student develop his or her transition plan.

The information in Table 8–2 may be used to guide student and family interviews. For example, the questions may easily be converted to a comprehensive transition questionnaire or paper checklist sent home to the family prior to the development of a student's transition plan. Many school districts have developed their own versions of transition interviews, questionnaires, or planning checklists based on areas and questions similar to those found in Table 8–2. Also, transition inventories and checklists are commercially available. Many of the commercially available instruments include areas and questions similar to those found in Table 8–2.

Commercially Available Transition Inventories. Clark and Patton (1997) developed the Transition Planning Inventory or TPI. The TPI includes nine areas to assist with transition planning: (a) employment, (b) further education/training, (c) daily living, (d) leisure activities, (e) community participation, (f) health, (g) self-determination, (h) communication, and (i) personal relationships. The TPI consists of different forms that can be rated independently by the student, at home by the parent or guardian, and at school by a teacher or other education personnel. The TPI profile allows the ratings from different sources to be compared to help arrive at the most comprehensive picture of an individual's needs and desires. A form lists recommendations for further assessments. Finally, the TPI includes a resource guide with an extensive list of over 600 transition goals across its nine transition planning areas. In short, the TPI is a highly developed and comprehensive transition planning tool.

Another transition planning tool that yields a comprehensive view of a person's life is the Quality of Life Questionnaire (Schlaock & Keith, 1993). Designed to be used by individuals with cognitive disabilities such as mental retardation, the Quality of Life Questionnaire is organized into four domains: (a) satisfaction, (b) competence/productivity, (c) empowerment/independence, and (d) social belonging/community integration. An interview format can be used to gather information from individuals with typical communication abilities. For those with limited communication, the Quality of Life Questionnaire can be completed by an independent rater such as parent or family member.

PUTTING IT ALL TOGETHER: DEVELOPING AN INDIVIDUALIZED TRANSITION PROFILE

Thoma and Held (2002) stressed the importance of using a multitude of assessment methods and sources of information over time. To organize all the resulting information, the authors suggested the use of a transition portfolio or profile. A transition profile gives a student and his IEP team (or support group) "a systematic way to track the progress he makes toward achieving his goals and to provide a place to collect what is important" (Thoma & Held, 2002, p. 74).

Information included in a transition profile may come from both formal and informal methods of assessment. Thus, it may include test results, assessment reports, samples of student work, interview or inventory data, student self-reports, and any other artifacts that help guide the transition planning process for an individual student. The transition profile can be presented as a notebook, a series of folders, or electronically. According to Thoma and Held (2002), many school districts are moving toward electronic portfolios.

Thoma and Held (2002) designed a transition profile for a student named Jackson. Jackson's portfolio began with a visual representation of his long-term goals created with a person-centered planning process called Planning Alternative Tomorrows with Hope or PATH (Pearpoint, O'Brien, & Forest, 1993). The portfolio sections were organized using the Next S.T.E.P. planning areas (Halpern, et al., 1997). These were (a) personal life, (b) education and training, (c) living on my own, and (d) jobs. IEP goals for each of these sections were also included in Jackson's transition portfolio.

Other planning areas such as those included in Table 8–2 or the areas found in the TPI (Clark & Patton, 1997) may be used to organize a transition portfolio or profile. The student and the IEP team should make the decision about which framework to use to organize the portfolio based on what information is necessary to assist the transition planning process.

Thoma and Held (2002) suggested a three-step process for determining what areas to include in a transition portfolio or profile.

1. Identify desired outcomes for a student. For example, Daniel's preferred outcomes were to get a job, have his own apartment, and remain living in his current neighborhood so he could keep his social contacts intact. These areas would be used to guide the remaining steps of the Thoma and Held decision-making process.

2. Determine acceptable evidence and artifacts to include in the portfolio. Thoma and Held (2002) recommended identifying tasks that provide the IEP team with evidence that a student is making progress toward his or her transition goals. Situational assessments in employment, apartment, and social settings were included in Daniel's portfolio. As tasks are completed by the student, other considerations such as safety and transportation would become apparent at this point in the process. These areas would also need to be assessed and included in the student's portfolio.

3. Use assessment results to plan transition services and learning experiences. IEP goals and objectives were developed, evaluated, and revised based on the areas included in Daniel's portfolio.

This chapter has delineated these values and the resulting guidelines for appropriate transition practice. In conclusion, Thoma and Held (2002) pointed out that the portfolio strategy (and any alternative assessment method) "must adhere to the basic underlying values that ensure wise transition assessment" (p. 83).

Summary

When the guidelines suggested in this chapter are used to shape practice, transition assessment can expand life opportunities for students with disabilities. Information will be gathered to help teachers, students, family members, employers, adult service providers, and other members of the community make important, sometime life-changing decisions. Most important, however, when the assessment guidelines described here are used, students with disabilities will attain socially important and personally satisfying postschool outcomes.

Study Questions

1. What does IDEA mandate about transition assessment?

    IDEA 2004 specified that transition planning in a student's IEP must be based on age-appropriate transition assessments. One purpose of the transition assessments is to gather the information necessary to identify measurable postsecondary goals on a student's IEP. In addition, IDEA 2004 stated that transition assessment must be broadly focused in order to determine the most appropriate array of possible transition services. Transition services should be planned in the first IEP in effect when a student turns 16 years old. Test et al. (2006) recommended beginning transition planning as early as possible; early planning is allowable under IDEA 2004.

2. What are implications of IDEA for specific areas in transition assessment?

    Among the changes in the IDEA 2004 definition of transition service was a focus on improving both the academic and functional achievement of the child with a disability. The dual focus on scholastic and functional skills implies that these broad areas and the many respective component skills comprising them should be included in a comprehensive transition assessment. Prior to 2004, transition services were required to be based on a student's preferences and interests. This requirement moved schools to involve students with disabilities in transition planning as a means of ascertaining their postschool preferences and interests. According to IDEA 2004, transition services must be based on the individual child's needs, taking into account his or her strengths, preferences, and interests. This new requirement suggests that transition assessment should highlight a student's talents, abilities, and accomplishments.

3. What are proposed strategies to reduce fragmentation of services in the elementary and middle school grades?

   Amos (2006) suggested three strategies to reduce fragmentation of services and build a more cohesive education system that values successful postschool outcomes for students with disabilities. These strategies were (a) nurturing the active and continuous involvement of families in the IEP process, (b) promoting early and ongoing collaboration with local and state agencies, and (c) early and continued participation of students in their IEPs.

4. How can assessment of career development be defined?

   Assessment of a student's career development focuses on the ongoing process of developing all life roles, including worker, family member, lifelong learner, participant in social and interpersonal networks, and community citizen (Sitlington & Clark, 2006). The original Division on Career Development defined assessment as a developmental process beginning in the elementary school and continuing through adulthood. Later, the division defined transition assessment as the ongoing process of collecting data on the individual's strengths, needs, preferences, and interests as they relate to the demands of current and future working, educational, living, and personal and social environments.

5. What is meant by person-centered planning?

   Features of person-centered planning include (a) an effort to increase participation of individuals with disabilities in life planning and decision making; (b) a focus on the preferences, interests, strengths, and abilities of the individual with a disability; (c) the development of a vision of a positive future lifestyle for the individual; and (d) a continuous process of meeting, planning, evaluating, and revising actions to move the individual toward his or her vision for the future. Like the career development model, person-centered planning is a longitudinal, ongoing process.

6. What is the concept of quality of life as exemplified by Felce and Perry (1995)?

   Felce and Perry identified five quality-of-life domains: (a) physical well-being; (b) material well-being; (c) social well-being; (d) personal growth, development, and activity; and (e) emotional well-being. Any assessment of quality of life must consider internal or personal factors such as an individual's health, personal values, aspirations, and feelings as well as external factors such as economic, social, residential, and political issues.

7. Which outcomes are of interest in transition assessment?

    Outcomes for special education students should be related to those identified for students without disabilities. The National Center on Educational Outcomes (NCEO) convened hundreds of stakeholders over a 2-year period to identify desired outcomes for the educational system (Ysseldyke, Thurlow, et al., 1998). The NCEO now recognizes six outcome domains: (a) academic and functional literacy, (b) physical health, (c) responsibility and independence, (d) citizenship, (e) personal and social well-being, and (f) satisfaction.

8. What are recommended professional guidelines for assessment practice?

    Test and colleagues (2006) offered general guidelines to consider when conducting a transition assessment: (a) transition assessment is student centered and self-determined; (b) transition assessment is an ongoing process; (c) transition assessment occurs in a variety of natural environments; (d) transition assessment gathers information from many people including professionals, the student, family members, friends, employers, and other stakeholders; (e) transition assessment data must be useful and understandable to all people involved; and finally, (f) transition assessment must be sensitive to cultural diversity and different values regarding services and outcomes.

9. What are examples of areas related to attainment of transition outcomes that can be assessed by formal, psychometric instruments?

    Formal assessment focuses on such areas as academic achievement, adaptive behavior, occupational aptitudes, communication skills, functional capacity, learning styles, occupational interests, personality and social skills, employability skills, and knowledge of transition and community living skills.

10. What are examples of areas related to attainment of transition outcomes that can be assessed by informal methods?

    Informal methods can be used to gather information in areas such as occupational interests and preferences, employment strengths and needs, postsecondary education, financial or income support needs, community participation, self-advocacy, leisure and recreation skills, transportation, social networks and relationships, personal management, living arrangements, medical issues, and insurance issues.

Recommended Reading

Felce, D., & Perry, J. (1995). Quality of life: Its definition and measurement. *Research in Developmental Disabilities, 16,* 51–74.

Hasazi, S. B., Furney, K. S., & DeStefano, L. (1999). Implementing the IDEA transition mandates. *Exceptional Children, 65,* 555–566.

Menchetti, B. M., & Piland, V. C. (2001). Transition assessment and evaluation: Current methods and emerging alternatives. In S. Alper, D. L. Ryndak, & C. N. Schloss (Eds.), *Alternative assessment of students with disabilities in inclusive settings* (pp. 220–255). Boston: Allyn & Bacon.

Sitlington, P. L., & Clark, G. M. (2006). *Transition education and services for students with disabilities* (4th ed.). Boston: Allyn & Bacon.

Thoma, C. A., & Held, M. (2002). Measuring what's important: Using alternative assessments. In C. L. Sax & C. A. Thoma (Eds.), *Transition assessment: Wise practices for quality lives* (pp. 71–85). Baltimore: Brookes.

Web Resources

Transition Assessment

Council for Exceptional Children (CEC), Division on Career Development and Transition (DCDT)

http://www.dcdt.org/

The mission of DCDT is to promote national and international efforts to improve the quality of and access to career/vocational and transition services, increase the participation of education in career development and transition goals, and to influence policies affecting career development and transition services for persons with disabilities.

Institute on Community Integration: Transition Program Area

http://ici.umn.edu/projectscenters/transition.html

The Transition Services Program Area works to enable schools and community service agencies to better prepare youth with disabilities for life as productive, responsible adults in the community.

National Center on Educational Outcomes (NCEO)

http://education.umn.edu/NCEO/

NCEO provides national leadership in the participation of students with disabilities in national and state assessments, standards-setting efforts, and graduation requirements.

North Central Regional Education Laboratory (NCREL): Approaches to Authentic Assessment

http://www.ncrel.org/sdrs/areas/issues/envrnmnt/stw/swllk8.htm

NCREL was one of 10 federally funded laboratories whose contract to operate ended in 2005. Learning Point Associates conducted the work of NCREL, and many of the resources developed under this contract remain accessible through this Website.

National Post-School Outcomes Center

http://www.psocenter.org/

Its mission is to help state education agencies establish practical and rigorous data collection systems that will measure and profile the postschool experiences of youth with disabilities.

References

Amos, B. (2006). Grades K–8 in the transition process: A critical foundation. In P. L. Sitlington & G. M. Clark (Eds.), *Transition education and services for students with disabilities* (4th ed., pp. 109–126). Boston: Allyn & Bacon.

Clark, G. M. (1998). *Assessment for transitions planning.* Austin, TX: PRO-ED.

Clark, G. M., Carlson, B. C., Fisher, S., Cook, I. D., & D'Alonzo, B. J. (1991). Career development for students with disabilities in elementary schools: A position statement of the Division on Career Development. *Career Development for Exceptional Individuals, 17,* 125–134.

Clark, G. M., & Patton, J. R. (1997). *Transition Planning Inventory.* Austin, TX: PRO-ED.

Felce, D., & Perry, J. (1995). Quality of life: Its definition and measurement. *Research in Developmental Disabilities, 16,* 51–74.

Garcia, L. A., & Menchetti, B. M. (2003). The Adult Lifestyles Planning Cycle: A continual process for planning personally satisfying adult lifestyles. In D. L. Ryndak & S. Alper (Eds.), *Curriculum and instruction for students with significant disabilities in inclusive settings* (2nd ed., pp. 277–306). Boston: Allyn & Bacon.

Halpern, A., Herr, C. M., Wolf, N., Doren, B., Johnson, M., & Lawson, J. (1997). *Next S.T.E.P.: Student transition and educational planning.* Austin, TX: PRO-ED.

Hasazi, S. B., Furney, K. S., & DeStefano, L. (1999). Implementing the IDEA transition mandates. *Exceptional Children, 65,* 555–566.

Individuals with Disabilities Education Improvement Act of 2004, Pub. L. No. 108–446.

Kohler, P. D. (1998). Implementing a transition perspective of education. In F. R. Rusch & J. Chadsey (Eds.), *Beyond high school: Transition from school to work* (pp. 179–205). Belmont, CA: Wadsworth.

Menchetti, B. M., & Piland, V. C. (2001). Transition assessment and evaluation: Current methods and emerging alternatives. In S. Alper, D. L. Ryndak, & C. N. Schloss (Eds.), *Alternative assessment of students with disabilities in inclusive settings* (pp. 220–255). Boston: Allyn & Bacon.

Neubert, D. A. (2006). Legislation and guidelines for secondary and special education and transition services. In P. L. Sitlington & G. M. Clark (Eds.), *Transition education and services for students with disabilities* (4th ed., pp. 35–71). Boston: Allyn & Bacon.

Pearpoint, J., O'Brien, J., & Forest, M. (1993). *PATH: A workbook for planning positive possible futures.* Toronto: Inclusion Press.

Repetto, J. B. (2001). Assessment for transition planning. In J. A. McLoughlin & R. B. Lewis (Eds.), *Assessing students with special needs* (5th ed., pp. 550–582). Upper Saddle River, NJ: Merrill/Prentice Hall.

Repetto, J. B., & Correa, V. I. (1996). Expanding views on transition. *Exceptional Children, 62,* 551–563.

Salvia, J., & Ysseldyke, J. E. (2004). *Assessment in special and inclusive education* (9th ed.). Boston: Houghton Mifflin.

Sax, C. L. (2002). Person-centered planning: More than a strategy. In C. L. Sax & C. A. Thoma (Eds.), *Transition assessment: Wise practices for quality lives* (pp. 13–24). Baltimore: Brookes.

Schlaock, R., & Keith, K. D. (1993). *Quality of Life Questionnaire.* Worthington, OH: IDS Publishing.

Sitlington, P. L., Brolin, D. E., Clark, G. M., & Vacanti, J. M. (1985). Career/vocational assessment in the public school setting: The position of the Division on Career Development. *Career Development for Exceptional Individuals, 8,* 3–6.

Sitlington, P. L., & Clark, G. M. (2006). *Transition education and services for students with disabilities* (4th ed.). Boston: Allyn & Bacon.

Sitlington, P. L., Neubert, D. A., & Leconte, P. J. (1997). Transition assessment: The position of the Division on Career Development and Transition. *Career Development for Exceptional Individuals, 20,* 69–79.

Test, D. W., Aspel, N. P., & Everson, J. M. (2006). *Transition methods for youth with disabilities.* Upper Saddle River, NJ: Merrill/Prentice Hall.

Thoma, C. A., & Held, M. (2002). Measuring what's important: Using alternative assessments. In C. L. Sax & C. A. Thoma (Eds.), *Transition assessment: Wise practices for quality lives* (pp. 71–85). Baltimore: Brookes.

Ysseldyke, J. E., Krentz, J., Elliot, J., Thurlow, M., Thompson, S., & Moore, M. (1998). *NCEO framework for educational accountability: Post-school outcomes.* Minneapolis: University of Minnesota, National Center on Educational Outcomes.

Ysseldyke, J. E., Thurlow, M. L., Kozleski, E., & Reschly, D. (1998). *Accountability for the results of educating students with disabilities: Assessment conference report on the new assessment provisions of the 1997 amendments to the Individuals with Disabilities Education Act.* Minneapolis: University of Minnesota, National Center on Educational Outcomes.

CHAPTER 9

Work-Based Learning: Developing Work Experience Opportunities for Transitioning Students

David Hagner and Dianne Lounsbury
University of New Hampshire

School-sponsored work experiences, in which students are engaged in activities at the workplace, arranged and supported by the school and connected to the rest of the curriculum, have been increasingly recognized as a central component of transition services for youth with disabilities (Agran, Snow, & Swaner, 1999; Johnson, Stodden, Emanuel, Luecking, & Mack, 2002). Perhaps the most powerful and immediately obvious advantage of including work experiences as a part of the secondary curriculum is their impact on postschool employment. Horn and Trach (1998) conducted a follow-up study of students in a demonstration project who worked at community jobs at least 2 hours per day for 120 days as part of their high school program. Two years after graduation, 14 of 18 (77.8%) students interviewed were working in paid employment, for an average of 27 hours per week. Similarly, Fabian, Lent, and Willis (1998) reported the results of a school-to-work program for students with disabilities consisting of 2 weeks of vocational goal setting, 2 weeks of job preparation training, and 12 weeks of paid internship placement with support in a community business. Of 1,725 students completing the program over a 5-year period in seven cities across the United States, 71% entered employment upon graduation. Findings from a National Longitudinal Transition Study (NLTS) (Blackorby & Wagner, 1996) support these reports. Special education students who had a school-sponsored work experience were more likely to hold employment 12 months after leaving school (62.2%) than their counterparts who had not had a school-sponsored work experience (45.2%).

A number of other important educational benefits, for both students with and without disabilities, are associated with school-sponsored work experiences. These include:

- Students experience lower dropout rates and greater commitment to completing their education (Dolainski, 1997; Elliott, Hanser, & Gilroy, 2002). Students report greater engagement in school when they perceive a connection between what they are learning and their future goals (Shernoff & Hoogstra, 2001); participation in a work experience helps make that connection.
- Students gain an awareness of their interests and skills in relation to the requirements of the world of work. Transitioning students with disabilities tend to overestimate their work-related skills (Capella, Roessler, & Hemmerla, 2002) and to possess lower career maturity levels than students without disabilities (Ochs & Roessler, 2001). Work experiences help adjust estimates and expectations in a more realistic direction. In an evaluation of students' perceptions of their work experiences, students with disabilities reported increased motivation to study and work toward a career and increased understanding of skills needed to work with coworkers and supervisors as the most important benefits (Burgstahler, 2001).
- Work experiences provide students with both specific work skills (Dolainski, 1997) and more general skills related to effective citizenship and community

participation (Waxer, 2004). As a result, their wages after leaving school tend to be higher (Cavanaugh, 2004).
- Opportunities for "situated" or "contextual" learning enhance the effectiveness of academic instruction (Bond, 2004). Real-life contexts provide opportunities for learning critical skills that a classroom cannot simulate effectively. For example, work-based instruction often includes learning to identify which skills or facts are relevant in a particular applied context (Sandberg, 2000; Torocco, 1999).
- Employer resources are made available to work experience students. Employers have substantial experience with on-the-job training (Barron, Berger, & Black, 1997; Dolainski, 1997), and they regularly upgrade their equipment and modernize their production processes far beyond what a school district vocational education budget could match. Community work experiences make these resources available to the school and its students.
- Work for pay is a welcome source of income for most students (Rowh, 2003). For those living in poverty, availability of a paid work experience can make a critical difference in the decision to remain in school (Loughead, Liu, & Middleton, 1995).

In this chapter, we provide an overview of the various types of work experiences a school may offer, and outline a set of guidelines for integrating a work experience component into the high school curriculum. We also review some of the considerations involved in the process of developing work experience sites, and discuss the possibilities for using interagency collaboration to maximize the effectiveness of work-based learning.

TYPES OF WORK EXPERIENCES

Student-initiated part-time jobs, outside of school hours and during the summer, can be a valuable source of growth experiences and career development (Rowh, 2003). The potential benefits of any job include such things as better time management skills, interpersonal skills, and experience with particular work tasks. When work experience is connected to the high school curriculum in a meaningful way, as part of the school program, the benefits are multiplied.

School-sponsored work experiences can take a number of forms, ranging from less intensive exposure to the world of work, to more intensive work experiences. These are not mutually exclusive. In fact, they build logically on one another, such that a comprehensive school district commitment to preparing students for life after high school can begin with some types of exposure to work and careers as early as elementary school, and end with perhaps a senior-year internship and a full-time school-sponsored job for students eligible for special education following their fourth year of high school. Table 9.1 summarizes the major types of work experience.

TABLE 9.1 *Common Types of School-Sponsored Work Experience*

Type	Example
Less intensive	
Field trip or tour	Math class visits environmental engineering firm to see practical uses of math in the world of work.
Informational interview	English class assigned to interview an employee and write about his or her career.
Job shadowing	Students matched with an employee in a field of interest to spend two half days observing.
In-school job	Student works one hour per day replacing books on shelves in the school library.
School-based enterprise	School science department contracts with engineering firm for students to conduct monthly tests of local river water quality.
Internship in a community business	Half of senior class spends 3 days per week at work sites in fall semester; second half does the same in spring semester.
More intensive	
School-supported job	School develops and supports community jobs for students during a "postsenior" year, based on their interests and skills.

Work Exposure

Schools and individual teachers can expose students to work contexts in numerous ways. Guest speakers are a common vehicle for introducing students to occupations. Field trips or industry tours conducted in groups by a teacher in connection with a particular course, program of study, or class module provide another form of work exposure. The possibilities for connections between course curricula and the world of work are limitless. One mathematics teacher takes his students to visit an engineering firm that designs amusement rides, and the engineers explain the importance of mathematics in the design of the rides.

Another related type of work experience is a student project that embeds exposure to the workplace within the assignment. In one school, the students in a literature class read their book reviews over a local radio station (Winger, 1995). Perhaps the most common strategies for more in-depth individual exposure of students to work in natural contexts are job shadowing and informational interviewing.

Job shadowing involves visiting a business to observe a job being performed and learn about the work tasks, industrial processes, and workplace of a specific employee (Lozada, 2001). The purpose is primarily to observe a worker and learn about a particular type of work. However, a student may also ask questions of the worker and perhaps nearby workers, and may occasionally assist in performing some minor work tasks. Usually, job shadowing lasts from a half day to 2 days.

The school program should prepare students for their job shadowing experience and provide opportunities to debrief afterward (Lozada, 2001). Some programs provide students with a worksheet for recording their thoughts and impressions about the job, or assign an essay about the job based on the experience.

Informational interviewing involves meeting with an employee for a structured question-and-answer session about a particular job or field of work (Hagner, 2002). The interview usually takes place with someone who is successfully established in a particular job; it may take a half hour to an hour or more. A series of open-ended questions are prepared in advance, and the conversation may be recorded by means of notes or audio recording. When representatives from an occupation of interest to students are unavailable in the local community, interviews can be by phone or e-mail. As with job shadowing, prior preparation and subsequent discussion are an essential part of the experience.

Work Experience

Work experiences go beyond exposure to include students performing work tasks as a central focus of the activity. Work experiences include school-based jobs, school-sponsored enterprises, internships within community businesses, and school-sponsored community jobs.

School-Based Jobs. Students can be assigned to work within the school building as an initial step in experiencing the world of work. This might involve, for example, a job in the school library returning books to the shelves, or doing photocopying and other clerical tasks in the school office. An occasional errand would not constitute a "job," but a regularly scheduled series of tasks that involve taking responsibility, being on time, and completing work that others are counting on can provide a sense of what it is like to work at a job. Horn and Trach (1998) found that school-based jobs alone were not significantly related to postschool employment. Thus, a school-based job is best viewed as a step in a sequence leading to an internship in a community business as high school progresses.

School-Sponsored Enterprises. School-sponsored enterprises are projects within a school that produce goods or services for sale to or use by customers other than the immediate school community (students, faculty, and staff). These experiences involve students in interaction with typical customers and with suppliers and others in the community (Stern, Finkelstein, Stone, Latting, & Dornsife, 1995).

As with other work experiences, the content of school-sponsored enterprises is limited only by the imagination of the individuals involved. For example, many schools operate lunch restaurants open to the public. Ross (2002) described a school store designed and operated by high school students in a marketing education program that generates income to support postsecondary education scholarships. Another school operates a desktop publishing business (Green, 2000). A number of high schools are licensed to operate their own radio stations (Hawkins & Jackson, 1992). Setting up a business is complicated and time-consuming; usually, a school-sponsored enterprise results from the imagination and efforts of a particular faculty member with a strong interest in this type of endeavor.

Internships Within Community Businesses. An internship is a structured, temporary assignment to a job to obtain instruction and practice and gain familiarity with a particular type of work. Internships are generally part-time, and can range from several weeks to a year or more in duration. The most common internship periods are 6 to 15 weeks.

Some schools enter into a partnership with one or more businesses and pre-arrange rotating internship slots for students. Another option is to develop opportunities on an ongoing basis, based on specific student interests. Perhaps the best approach is to treat this as a developmental process, with prearranged internship sites available to students in the early years of high school and development of more individually targeted internships available as student interests and goals begin to crystallize.

Typically, in a weekly student schedule, internship time alternates with in-school time, and the two are integrated into a coherent curriculum. A common scheduling arrangement involves morning classes at the school, and internships scheduled for two, three, or five afternoons per week. An important way of connecting work experience to the rest of the curriculum is to provide a weekly internship seminar at the school, where students discuss what they are learning and experiencing at their work sites. The details of an internship are typically spelled out in a written agreement, indicating the job, the training personnel or method to be used, and the duration of the work experience.

Internships are often known locally by different names, such as "work study placements" or "job try-outs." "Apprenticeship," sometimes used as a synonym for "internship," more properly refers to a sequence of instruction and experiences, usually over a multiyear period, that prepares a trainee for certification or licensure within a specific occupation.

An endpoint review date and, if necessary, a schedule of interim progress reviews should be negotiated in advance with each participating business. At these checkpoints a written evaluation, as well as an informal, conversational assessment of the experience, should be obtained from the site supervisor. The student can be asked to complete an evaluation from his or her perspective as well. Supervisors usually appreciate receiving an evaluation form at the beginning of the internship (Hagner, 2002).

School-Sponsored Community Jobs. Federal eligibility for special education in the United States continues up to at least age 21, and many states have mandated one or more additional years. As a result, many special education students are eligible to spend more than 4 years in high school. But after 4 years, many special education students understandably wish to participate in the same normative graduation-related activities as their nondisabled peers, such as attending the graduation ceremony and the senior prom; and then during the following year or two, either reduce considerably or completely end the daily routine of taking classes within the high school building.

Often the educational planning team agrees with the student that there is little further benefit to be gained from school-based instruction. Yet in the context of a job, or a combination of a part-time job and part-time involvement in other community-based instruction, there is a great deal to be learned during the remaining years of eligibility about such things as adult roles and expectations, age-appropriate relationships (Kamens et al., 2004), money management, and specialized occupational knowledge and skills.

Developing and supporting full-time community immersion opportunities as an alternative to attendance in a school building can be a valuable final step in school-sponsored preparation for adult life, and can set the stage for a smooth transition to adult employment, recreation, and community living.

INTEGRATING WORK EXPERIENCES INTO THE HIGH SCHOOL CURRICULUM

Because work experience is a sound educational practice for all students, a school-sponsored work experience program should be developed as an integral component of the general education program. It is particularly critical that the program be geared toward students who are planning to attend college as well as those who are not (Pauly, 1994). A separate special education work experience program or a separate vocational education work experience program will shortchange all students.

Large-scale system change will require support from general educators, particularly the key faculty in secondary education content areas (science, math, and English). These faculty members must understand how work experience enhances student learning in their particular areas before they buy into the idea. The same sorts of staff resistances and traditional role definitions that inhibit any organizational change make this a complex and sometimes difficult process (Mark & Stoia, 1993).

A comprehensive work experience program cannot be developed in isolation from the other curricular components of a high school program. Just as school-based learning by itself is incomplete, so is work-based learning by itself. One important focus for integration of the two components is to provide work experience students with opportunities for guided reflection and discussion back at school (Polman, 2000). For example, Lozada (2001) emphasized the importance of bringing back information from a job shadowing experience to the classroom for discussion and evaluation. Work experiences should also be integrated with other school-to-career components, such as career planning and job-seeking skills classes.

Two formal academic designs that integrate academic and work experience learning into a comprehensive curriculum are career academies and tech-prep programs. Proponents of these designs emphasize that individuals with disabilities are entitled to equal access to these programs.

A *career academy* is a "school within a school" (Mittelsteadt & Reeves, 2003) that uses a combination of classroom experiences, labs, or other technical instruction, and a sequence of internships or other work experiences focusing on a broad career theme, such as health care or information technology. Usually, the career academy has its own separate admissions process, faculty, student handbook, and so on. In a study of career academies in eight schools across the United States, Elliott et al. (2002) found that career academy students had higher grade point averages, better attendance, and higher graduation rates than students in general academic programs. Career academies have been particularly successful in schools with a more diverse student body (Shorr & Hon, 1999).

Tech-prep is another curricular model, or family of models. A 1995 study found that three fourths of the high schools in the United States participated in some form of tech-prep program (Bragg, 2000). Tech-prep programs consist of a coordinated curriculum for the final 2 years of high school and a planned transition to a postsecondary institution for 2 additional years leading to an associate's degree, usually in a technical or health field. A series of structured work experiences, closely linked to the classroom-based academic component, and increasing progressively from part-time in high school to nearly full-time during the final year in a community college, is typical of most tech-prep programs (Boudria, 2002).

It is not necessary for a work experience program to be affiliated with one of these formal curricular models. In fact, most high schools already offer some form of work experience to at least some of their students. A school's current efforts can form the basis for a more comprehensive program.

In making the switch from a largely school-based and didactic teacher-directed curriculum to a more flexible, context-based curriculum that can include learning opportunities that occur naturally in the community, adequate planning time is essential for success (Parnell, 1999). Planning for a comprehensive work experience program should consider the following structural components.

Adherence to Labor Regulations

As part of its sponsorship of a work experience, a school should ascertain whether the work experience would be considered an "employment relationship" by the U.S. Department of Labor. The Fair Labor Standards Act requires employers to pay for work performed by employees. Field trips and informational interviewing do not involve performing work on the part of the student, but other forms of work experience involve real work. The fact that an individual is a student and the work experience is designed as part of a school program does not automatically exempt a company from the responsibility to pay wages to the worker. Therefore, work experience staff must be familiar with the available options for unpaid and paid work.

Unpaid Work. Anyone can perform volunteer work for a nonprofit, charitable organization. There is no restriction on the length of time an individual may volunteer. However, the person should be working as a volunteer primarily to benefit the organization, because he or she believes in the organization's mission and cause. If the primary—or sole—purpose of the experience is job training, the work experience should be treated as if it were occurring within a for-profit company.

Unpaid work in a for-profit company is allowable only for limited periods of time, and if several other criteria are met (MacDonald, 2000), including:

- The work experience arrangement is written into the IEP (and/or a vocational rehabilitation individual plan of employment or an adult agency service plan) as a strategy for reaching an educational objective.
- The work experience intern does not replace or work instead of a regular employee.
- The additional supervision and training received by the intern, and the fact that the student is learning and has not yet mastered the job, results in a situation where there is not any real net gain to the company from the intern's work.
- The duration of any individual unpaid work experience is limited to 120 hours if the purpose is vocational training, 90 hours if the purpose is assessment, and 5 hours if the purpose is exploration.

If all of these criteria are not met, an employment relationship has been established, and payment of wages in accordance with the Fair Labor Standards Act is required.

Paid Work. Payment of at least the minimum wage is typically required for work performed by employees, and many companies do not hesitate to pay at least the minimum wage to a student intern. However, often the company can rightly point out that the intern is completing only a portion of the work a regular employee would be responsible for. And the need for an internship to fulfill academic requirements may mean that the student is required to participate only partially in the ongoing work, with time built in for observing, accompanying an experienced worker as an "extra" worker, or completing an assignment peripheral to the production process itself. One reasonable strategy is for a school program to establish part-time internships during the first 4 years of high school that are designed to meet all of the requirements for unpaid work, and then develop more extensive periods of work designed as paid jobs for those students registering for additional years of special education.

When a company is approached about hiring for pay, there are times when an individual lacks some of the skills for a position or cannot keep up with the productivity usually required for a position. Requiring payment of the minimum wage in such situations may pose a barrier to setting up the work experience. Two options are available at the federal level.

Section 6(g) of the Fair Labor Standards Act allows employers to pay a lower minimum "youth wage" to students under the age of 20 for the first 90 days. The Wage and Hour Division's Fact Sheet #32 (U.S. Department of Labor, 2004) explains this provision more fully.

Section 14(c) of the Fair Labor Standards Act allows employers to pay a lower minimum "commensurate wage" to individuals who, because of a disability, are limited in their productivity on a particular job. Establishment of a commensurate wage involves analyzing the job to determine productivity standards and then assessing the proportion of the standard represented by the worker's productivity. The worker can then be paid the proportion of the wage ordinarily paid to someone in that position, even if it results in a wage less than the usual minimum. The Wage and Hour Division's Fact Sheet #39 (U.S. Department of Labor, 2004) explains this provision more fully.

In addition to wage and hour standards, school-to-work experience programs must attend to child labor restrictions. For example, minors are restricted from working at several types of hazardous occupations, such as operating machinery, and are limited in the number of hours they can work (MacDonald, 2000).

Finally, many states have their own labor laws and regulations that must be adhered to in addition to the federal requirements. Generally, if a particular situation is governed by both state and federal regulations, the more stringent of the two rules applies. It is also important to note that both state and federal labor regulations are subject to change. Therefore, the coordinator of a work experience program should have ongoing access to up-to-date information.

Provision for Training and Support

Supporting a work experience involves developing a viable partnership between the school and participating businesses. Central to the success of the experience is a clear definition of the role of each party.

All students, including those in special education, should be linked with a specific coworker for day-to-day instruction and mentoring (Thompson, 1995). A written training plan should be developed outlining instructional goals and methods. The personality of the mentor and the chemistry between the mentor and the intern are important factors in the success of the experience. Mentors should volunteer for their role, and the option of switching mentors should be available to both the mentor and the intern. Although seldom necessary, a school might consider paying a small monetary stipend, or perhaps an in-kind benefit like free tuition at an adult education class, to the mentor for dedicating extra time and attention to the internship.

All students, including those in general education, need the availability of school personnel to answer employer questions, help design the work experience job, assist in acclimating to the workplace, and resolve problems. Some employers and some students will require far more support or more specialized support than others. Continual staff presence at a work site should be an available option but used only when needed.

Work-based instruction focuses on two areas: the specific job tasks involved in the production activity at the workplace, and the more general social and work-ethic behaviors involved in the worker role. Once specific job tasks have been identified, each task should be broken down into component steps through tasks analysis (Flexer, Simmons, Luft, & Baer, 2001). The results can be used to guide instruction and to evaluate progress. Direct instruction can be the responsibility of either school staff, an on-site coworker or supervisor mentor with consultation and backup assistance by school staff, or a combination of the two, in which certain tasks or certain days and times are the responsibility of either party.

School personnel should adopt as much as possible the role of a facilitator or consultant who has expertise to share but is not in charge of the activity or the setting. A community business is likely to have a customary "way we do things around here" that should be learned and respected and used to guide the consultation. For example, a company might be picky about one aspect of work quality yet surprisingly (to an outsider) lax about another. Suggestions for how to do a job better or more efficiently may be welcomed or even sought out in one workplace but be perceived as invading someone's turf at another.

It is also important to keep in mind that workplaces are social environments involving important behaviors in addition to performing the job tasks themselves. Important types of behaviors that may need instructional attention include handling social situations, adapting to task variations and disruptions, and achieving a normative degree of independence from close supervision. For example, the ability to complete an assignment without frequent prompting, or to ask for assistance if one is experiencing a problem, is extremely important at most work sites. A work experience is often the first opportunity a student has to experience this type of adult role expectation, and that is what makes the experience so valuable. Some students may be accustomed to having information, answers to questions, and so on handed to them effortlessly in other aspects of their lives. The workplace is an ideal environment for teaching how and when to ask for help, as well as the associated behaviors of showing appreciation and reciprocating.

The traditional role of school personnel is that of direct student instruction; therefore, it is easy for school staff to fall into the role of taking responsibility for conducting all of the training a student requires at a community work site. But it is important to look for opportunities to transfer at least some training to the host business whenever possible, while remaining available to share responsibilities, keeping open the option of taking over the training if determined necessary for the success of an individual student.

Ohtake and Chadsey (2004) have identified six facilitation strategies used by staff at work sites to support individuals with disabilities. These include (a) autonomous support by the coworker without school or disability staff assistance, (b) support from a coworker with staff offering suggestions, (c) support from a coworker implementing a procedure developed by staff, (d) support from a coworker following coworker training by staff, (e) support provided by a coworker and some support provided by a staff person, and (f) full support provided by the staff person.

Work experience staff must be able to make ongoing decisions about which level of support is appropriate in individual situations. Support to the business should also include periodically scheduled debriefing sessions to review progress and resolve any difficulties, and rapid response to any questions or concerns. Rogan and Held (1999) noted that because such a wide array of fairly sophisticated skills and judgments are required of staff, schools must make a serious investment in orientation and training to ensure personnel assigned to a work experience program are knowledgeable.

Another opportunity for developing student independence of staff prompts and support is the use of assistive technology. A range of types of solutions is available for increasing an employee's performance and responsiveness to environmental cues (Langton & Ramseur, 2001). These can include (a) commercially available products, such as timers or nonstick coverings; (b) specialized products for individuals with disabilities, such as adapted tools or speech-recognition software; (c) modifications of existing products, such as raising an indicator light to eye level; or (d) fabrication of new devices for a specialized need. Each state has an assistive technology center that can provide assistance and product information.

Administrative Logistics

Off-site activities of any kind impose several logistical demands on a school district, and administrative support is required to deal with the issues involved. The most basic policy requirement for a work experience program is to have a definition of "school attendance" that is expansive enough to encompass attendance at school-sponsored work experience sites. Insurance and liability issues must also be resolved in connection with the program, and procedures for obtaining parent or guardian permission for students under age 18 (or over 18 with a legal guardian) must be in place.

Transportation to and from work experience sites can be problematic. Many programs require students to arrange their own transportation, but not all work sites are accessible by public transportation and not all students can travel safely on their own. In addition, if community work experience is specified in a special education student's IEP, eligibility for education extends to eligibility for school-provided transportation to the instructional site. School buses project a childish image, and should be used only for transportation to a work site as a last resort.

Staff scheduling must take into account the need to support both the school-based and work-based components of the educational program. When a classroom teacher accompanies a student or visits a work site, one fewer teacher is available for instruction in the school. In addition, school personnel contracts may reference daily and weekly schedules and preestablished grading periods and break schedules. These may or may not match the schedules of community businesses. Thus, coordinating schedules can be difficult (Kamens et al., 2004). Thus, the need for scheduling flexibility may have an impact on school personnel employment contracts.

Availability of Academic Credit

Although work experiences can and should be written into a student's IEP, the work experience program as a whole should not be limited to special education, but be regularly accessed by all students. Stern and Rahn (1995) cautioned that unless work experience is clearly linked to nonvocational subjects and to a course of study that prepares students to enter college, the program is doomed to "second-class status" within the school.

Work-based activities can be linked to academic credit through the simple mechanism of establishing a work experience or community internship course title as an elective course. Work experience opportunities can also be woven more deeply into the academic curriculum by tying individual work-based tasks and instruction to the content areas of required courses using instructional "rubrics."

A rubric is in essence a two-dimensional matrix that lists the learning objectives or criteria for mastery to be attained through an experience on one dimension (the columns) and the tasks or activities to be undertaken to reach those objectives or criteria on the other dimension (the rows). Teachers can fill in the resulting cells with specific activities or assignments geared toward completion of the academic content, and grade the resulting work. The rubric may also be used for employer evaluation or student self-evaluation of a work experience (Bernier, 2004).

The possibilities for connecting real-world activities to academic content are endless. A volunteer at city hall, for example, can be assigned to interview the employees and write an essay about how the city has changed over the years for American history credit. An intern at an automotive mechanic shop can be assigned to calculate customer parts and labor charges as a mathematics assignment. Academic departments within a school should have an established mechanism and at least one faculty liaison experienced in linking a description of the tasks available at a particular community placement opportunity to the credit-bearing courses within the department. At times this will call for flexibility and creativity on the part of the department, and sometimes negotiation with the employer as well, to ensure, for example, that sufficient rigor and task variety are embedded in an experience.

Work experience practices have much in common with other innovative secondary education practices, such as cooperative learning, project-based learning, and portfolio assessment of progress (Armstrong & Savage, 1990). Proponents of these other creative practices are natural allies in the development of a work experience program.

DEVELOPING INTERNSHIPS IN COMMUNITY BUSINESSES

Perhaps the central task in implementing a work experience program is to contact local employers and arrange work experience sites for students. This not only involves an investment in time, but is not something school personnel are typically trained to do or view as part of their job. A school can either employ somebody whose function is to do outreach to the business community or provide release time or summer salary for teachers and other staff to make employer contacts and arrange visits. Alternatively, a school could contract for job development services from another organization. This type of interagency collaboration is discussed in the following section.

In developing work experience sites, the role of personal network contacts is critical. Through networking, large numbers of businesses can be identified and contacted at little expense. In addition, businesses are more likely to respond favorably to a request made directly or indirectly by a personal network contact (Hagner, 2003). Christ (1995) suggests that a social networking approach be used systematically, with each member of the school community—teachers, students, administrators, support staff—exploring his or her own connections to businesses and occupations through parents, spouses, and friends.

Sometimes it is advisable to start small and develop relationships with community businesses in stages. For example, an employer might first be asked to speak to a class, agree to have a job shadow, or conduct a mock interview with a student in a job-seeking skills class. These experiences build a connection that can lead to more opportunities over time.

Businesses listen to other businesses, so many work experience programs call on their current business contacts to take the lead in reaching out to other businesses (Luecking, Fabian, & Tilson, 2004). Some communities have organizations such as a business association or chamber of commerce that can be enlisted for this purpose (Pauly, 1994). Some schools are even fortunate enough to have the business community approach them (Waxer, 2004).

A school can develop marketing materials such as a brochure or portfolio with letters of recommendation to assist in its marketing efforts to local businesses. An advertising department or a printing company may be persuaded to provide assistance as a donation to the school. In preparing these materials, it is important to ask businesses to provide opportunities to transitioning students—not students with disabilities or special needs. Students are not interested in work-based learning opportunities because they have disabilities, but because they want to prepare for adulthood. If a work experience program serves students with and without disabilities as recommended, this is not an issue.

A business advisory committee is a useful tool in the development of a work experience program. The committee can become involved in marketing the program to new employers and can help shape and guide the direction of the work experience effort. The committee can also take on additional initiatives to forge linkages between business and education. For example, participating businesses could review curricula for relevance to the changing demands of the workplace, or sponsor a career day for students.

Schools can provide recognition and positive publicity to participating employers in a number of ways. Employer recognition on "awards night" or through publicity in the school district newsletter can be extremely meaningful.

In addition, school staff and families can be encouraged to make a special effort to patronize businesses that participate in the school's work experience program.

It is important to use care in selecting businesses that have ample opportunities for types of work that will have value to students and that are well managed and have a reputation for being supportive of their employees. To examine the types of work available, a job analysis form such as the form shown in Figure 10.1 of Chapter 10 is useful. Matching the needs of employers in relation to the work tasks that may be required and matching these with the abilities of a graduating student is important. Ensuring that students are placed in companies with a positive, supportive workplace culture is a more subjective process. A company's reputation and the experiences of current and past employees might provide some guidance; also, specific factors can be assessed by means of a visit or conversations with company managers.

Based on a participant-observation study of workplaces employing transitioning students with disabilities, Butterworth, Hagner, Helm, and Whelley (2000) found that transitioning students received more support and better social inclusion at workplaces with four characteristics: (a) employee personal relationships extended beyond work; (b) the workplace had identifiable social customs and opportunities; (c) the management took a personal interest in employees; and (d) jobs were to some degree interdependent, so that employees worked as a team.

INTERAGENCY COLLABORATION

One of the keys to successful transition for youth with disabilities is collaboration across the multiple agencies that have a stake in the transition process. In the transition to employment, these can include the school, the local office of vocational rehabilitation, local or regional developmental and mental health service staff, postsecondary schools and training programs, and employment service provider agencies.

At the simplest level, collaboration can involve awareness of one another's programs, regulations, intake procedures, and so on, along with efforts to refer and accept transitioning students in a timely manner so services are not disrupted when funding shifts from one source to another. For example, a school and vocational rehabilitation office can coordinate services so that a student who has a job in place prior to graduation can continue at the job, with support shifting from the school to vocational rehabilitation following graduation.

Collaborating agencies can also form closer and more creative linkages to effect "seamless transitions" (Certo et al., 2003) for young adults. One such linkage is *a joint contractual relationship* between a high school and an adult service funding agency, and one or more employment service provider agencies. The employment provider agency—sometimes referred to as a community rehabilitation program—can develop and support internships and/or jobs for students in their final years of eligibility for special education on a fee-for-service basis. This has the advantage of allowing for a seamless transition for students being supported in jobs that might potentially be maintained beyond the end of eligibility for special education. Once school funding for the service ends, vocational rehabilitation funding can begin the following workday, with no change in the way the job or the job support is experienced by the employee or the employer, because the same direct service staff remain in place.

Subcontract or vendor relationships between schools and adult service provider agencies require a different way of thinking about providing educational services on the part of a school. Typically, a school district is both the funding agency and the service provider agency for students, whereas in adult services, a distinction between these two types of agencies is commonplace. Subcontracting with another organization for employment supports has advantages to a school in addition to a close compatibility to the way adult services are handled. Adult agencies have in place procedures for job development and support, staff trained in employment services, staff knowledgeable about labor regulations, and existing relationships with community businesses. Contracting with an outside service also has some disadvantages. The school is less in control over the direct instructional support to the student, for example. These advantages and disadvantages are summarized in Table 9.2.

The sequential funding arrangement for employment support just described is only one example of interagency collaboration. Schools can join in developing a wide variety of interagency linkages to benefit transitioning students. For example, a school could contract with an employment service provider for part-time employment for a student in his or her last year of school eligibility and also support the student to take classes at a local college part-time. Or a school could contract with an adult service provider agency to provide training related to employment part-time and recreational or community living goals part-time, and then transition funding for the employment part to vocational rehabilitation and funding for the community living part to the developmental or mental health system, as eligibility for secondary education funding ends. Certo and colleagues (2003) have argued forcefully that it is not a lack of resources or expertise that results in poor transition outcomes, but the lack of a unified, shared effort by all of the parties to transition. They point out further that each of these parties has an

TABLE 9.2 *Advantages of Internal Versus Contracted Employment Services*

Developing internal school capacity to provide job development and support	Contracting with a community rehabilitation program for job development and support
• More control over the process and service quality	• Flexibility to use service as needed
• No additional administrative costs	• Continuous job support parallel beyond graduation
• Existing relationships with students and families	• More "adult" staff orientation and training
	• Familiarity with labor regulations
	• Existing relationships with community businesses

explicit legislative requirement to collaborate. As a result of demonstrating a collaborative model for seamless transition in 14 school districts, Certo et al. found that of 234 students exiting school over a 4-year period, 88% were competitively employed after graduation.

It is important to carefully assess the quality of community rehabilitation program before entering into a service provider relationship. Many programs continue to operate outmoded service models, such as sheltered workshops, group "enclaves," and even nonremunerative "day programs." Gowdy, Carlson, and Rapp (2003) and Rogan, Banks, and Howard (2000) have outlined the quality standards to expect from a community rehabilitation program. It is also a good idea to have relationships with more than one organization, so that students and families can "shop" for the one that fits their needs best, and change providers if they become dissatisfied.

Summary

Work experience should be valued as an integral part of secondary education, not only because it is the preeminent tool for preparing students for success in their careers, but also on nonvocational grounds. Work experiences add relevance, context, meaning, and complexity to the secondary curriculum; provide young people with guided exposure to adult roles and expectations; motivate students to persevere until graduation; and forge closer connections between schools and their communities.

There is even a good argument for switching the usual way in which we think about the relative value of work-based and school-based learning for all students, and for regarding work-based instruction as the more fundamental learning strategy. In *Walden,* Henry David Thoreau (1854/2004) posed an intriguing question:

> Which would have advanced the most at the end of a month—the boy who had made his own jackknife from the ore which he had dug and smelted, reading as much as would be necessary for this—or the boy who had attended the lectures on metallurgy at the Institute in the meanwhile, and had received a penknife from his father? (p. 38)

John Dewey (1916) expanded this view into a powerful philosophy of education, concluding that "education through occupations consequently combines within itself more of the factors conducive to learning than any other method" (p. 309). Dewey argued that "No classification, no selection and arrangement of facts, which is consciously worked out for purely abstract ends, can even compare in solidity or effectiveness with that knit under the stress of an occupation; in comparison, the former sort is formal, superficial, and cold" (p. 310).

Building on the Dewean tradition, Lave and Wenger (1991) maintained a careful distinction between learning and schooling. These authors conceptualized the essence of learning as a process of increasing participation in communities of practice. They noted that in many cases, situated learning, that is, learning connected to real, ongoing community activity, occurs rapidly and efficiently, even when little overt instruction can be observed. By contrast, schooling is a decontextualized, relatively inefficient substitute. We ought not let the fact that the bulk of attempts at education occur within schools to mislead us into concluding that schools are the best or the most important places in which to learn. The interplay among watching, doing, and listening to explanations that characterizes workplace learning represents an extraordinarily effective cognitive development strategy.

Numerous approaches to work experience have been developed and successfully implemented, and most schools have work experience models either in place or readily available. Key components of a successful work experience program include outreach to local employers, linkages with academic content and career guidance, administrative and logistical support, and consultation with participating businesses.

Students with and without disabilities alike benefit from a series of carefully planned school-sponsored work experiences. Specialized or intensive supports may sometimes be required to accommodate for disabilities, to ensure satisfactory social inclusion, or to adapt the job to an individual's capabilities. These support strategies can be linked with and infused into efforts to improve the quality of educational outcomes for all students.

Study Questions

1. What educational benefits are associated with school-sponsored work experiences?

   Perhaps the most powerful and immediately obvious advantage of including work experiences as a part of the secondary curriculum is their impact on postschool employment. Special education students who had a school-sponsored work experience were more likely to hold employment 12 months after leaving school (62.2%) than their counterparts who had not had a school-sponsored work experience (45.2%; Blackorby & Wagner, 1996).

   A number of other important educational benefits, both for students with and without disabilities, are associated with school-sponsored work experiences as well. These include:
   - Students experience lower dropout rates and greater commitment to completing their education.
   - Students gain an awareness of interests and skills in relation to the requirements of the world of work. Work experiences help adjust estimates and expectations in a realistic direction.
   - Work experiences provide students both with specific work skills and more general skills related to effective citizenship and community participation. As a result, their wages after leaving school tend to be higher.

- Opportunities for situated or contextual learning enhance the effectiveness of academic instruction. Real-life contexts provide opportunities for learning critical skills that a classroom cannot simulate effectively.
- Employer resources are made available to work experience students. Employers regularly upgrade their equipment and modernize their production processes far beyond what a school district vocational education budget could match.
- For those living in poverty, availability of a paid work experience can make a critical difference in the decision to remain in school.

2. What does job shadowing mean?

Job shadowing involves visiting a business to observe a job being performed and learn about the work tasks, industrial processes, and workplace of a specific employee (Lozada, 2001). The purpose of job shadowing is primarily to observe a worker and learn about a particular type of work. However, a student may also ask questions of the worker and perhaps nearby workers, and may occasionally assist in performing some minor work tasks. Some programs provide students with a worksheet for recording their thoughts and impressions about the job, or assign an essay about the job based on the experience.

3. What is the difference between work exposure and work experience?

School-sponsored work experiences can take a number of forms, ranging from less intensive exposure to the world of work, to more intensive work experiences. Schools can expose students to work contexts in numerous ways: guest speakers, field trips or industry tours conducted in groups by a teacher, a student project that embeds exposure to the workplace within the assignment, job shadowing, and informational interviewing. Work experiences go beyond exposure, in that the student performs work tasks as a central focus of the activity. Work experiences include school-based jobs, school-sponsored enterprises, internships within community businesses, and school-sponsored community jobs.

4. What are tech-prep programs and what support do they offer?

Tech-prep programs consist of a coordinated curriculum for the final 2 years of high school and a planned transition to a postsecondary institution for 2 additional years, leading to an associate's degree, usually in a technical or health field. A series of structured work experiences, closely linked to the classroom-based academic component, and increasing progressively from part-time in high school to nearly full-time during the final year in a community college, is typical of most tech-prep programs (Boudria, 2002).

5. What is a career academy?

A career academy is a school within a school that uses a combination of classroom experiences, labs, or other technical instruction, and a sequence of internships or other work experiences, focusing on a broad career theme, such as health care or information technology. Usually, the career academy has its own separate admissions process, faculty, student handbook, and so on. Career academies have been particularly successful in schools with a diverse student body (Shorr & Hon, 1999).

6. Do school-sponsored work experiences have to adhere to labor regulations?

As part of its sponsorship of a work experience, a school should ascertain whether the work experience would be considered an employment relationship by the U.S. Department of Labor. The Fair Labor Standards Act requires employers to pay for work performed by employees. Field trips and informational interviewing do not involve performing work on the part of the student, but other forms of work experience do involve real work. The fact that an individual is a student and the work experience is designed as part of a school program does not automatically exempt a company from the responsibility to pay wages to the worker. In addition to wage and hour standards, school work experience programs must attend to child labor restrictions. Work experience staff should be familiar with the available options for unpaid and paid work.

7. What is the focus of work-based instruction?

Work-based instruction focuses on two areas: the specific job tasks involved in the production activity at the workplace and the more general social and work-ethic behaviors involved in the worker role. Workplaces are social environments, involving important behaviors in addition to performing the job tasks themselves. Important types of behaviors that may need instructional attention include handling social situations, adapting to task variations and disruptions, and achieving a normative degree of independence from close supervision. The workplace is an ideal environment for teaching how and when to ask for help, as well as the associated behaviors of showing appreciation and reciprocating. A work experience may be the first opportunity a student has to experience this type of adult role expectation.

8. How can staff support individuals with disabilities in the work experience?

Ohtake and Chadsey (2004) have identified six facilitation strategies used by staff at work sites to support individuals with disabilities. These include (a) autonomous support by the coworker without school or disability staff assistance, (b) support from a coworker with staff offering suggestions, (c) support from a coworker implementing a procedure developed by staff, (d) support from a coworker following coworker training by staff, (e) support provided by a coworker and some support provided by a staff person, and (f) full support provided by the staff person. Work experience staff must be able to make ongoing decisions about which level of support is appropriate in individual situations. Support to the business should include periodically scheduled debriefing sessions to review progress and resolve any difficulties, and rapid response to any questions or concerns.

Another way to develop student independence of staff prompts and support is the use of assistive technology. These can include (a) commercially available products, such as timers or nonstick coverings; (b) specialized products for individuals with disabilities, such as adapted tools or speech-recognition software; (c) modifications of existing products, such as raising an indicator light to eye level; or (d) the fabrication of new devices for a specialized need.

9. How can work experience connect to academic school activities?

The possibilities for connecting real-world activities to academic content are endless. A volunteer at city hall, for example, can be assigned to interview the employees and write an essay about how the city has changed over the years for American history credit. An intern at an automotive mechanic shop can be assigned to calculate customer parts and labor charges as a mathematics assignment. Academic departments within a school should have an established mechanism and at least one faculty liaison experienced in linking a description of the tasks available at a particular community placement opportunity to the credit-bearing courses within the department.

10. How can schools recognize and support participating businesses?

Schools can provide recognition and positive publicity to participating employers in a number of ways. Employer recognition on awards night or through publicity in the school district newsletter can be extremely meaningful. In addition, school staff and families can be encouraged to make a special effort to patronize those businesses participating in the school's work experience program.

Recommended Reading

Blackorby, J., & Wagner, M. (1996). Longitudinal postschool outcomes of youth with disabilities: Findings from the National Longitudinal Transition Study. *Exceptional Children, 62,* 399–413.

Bragg, D. (2000). Tech prep: Winning ideas, challenging practices. *Techniques: Connecting Education and Careers, 75*(4), 14–18.

Butterworth, J., Hagner, D., Helm, D., & Whelley, T. (2000). Workplace culture, social interactions, and supports for transition-age young adults. *Mental Retardation, 3*(4), 342–353.

Christ, G. (1995). Curriculums with real-world connections. *Educational Leadership, 52*(8), 32–35.

Luecking, R., Fabian, E., & Tilson, G. (2004). *Working relationships: Creating career opportunities for job seekers with disabilities through employer partnerships.* Baltimore: Brookes.

Web Resources

Work Experience

Academy for Educational Development: Bridge to Employment

http://www.aed.org/Projects/bte.cfm

The AED uses the Bridge to Employment initiative to foster long-term relationships among businesses, educators, community groups, youth, and parents.

Association for Career and Technical Education (ACTE)

http://www.acteonline.org

ACTE contains a library of career-related lesson plans and a variety of other resources.

The Big Picture

http://www.bigpicture.org/

This for-profit company provides materials and training related to personalizing learning, with a major emphasis on community experiences.

Job Shadowing

http://www.jobshadow.org

The National Job Shadow Coalition sponsors an annual national Job Shadow Day.

National Conference of State Legislatures: Contextual Learning

http://www.ncsl.org/programs/employ/contextlearn.htm

The site promotes contextual learning, with links to successful projects in several states.

Rubistar: Rubrics Creator

http://rubistar.4teachers.org

The website features templates for creating rubrics for assigning academic credit to a work experience.

References

Agran, M., Snow, K., & Swaner, J. (1999). A survey of secondary level teachers, opinions on community-based instruction and inclusive education. *Journal of the Association for Persons with Severe Handicaps, 24*, 58–62.

Armstrong, D., & Savage, T. (1990). *Secondary education: An introduction* (2nd ed.). New York: Macmillan.

Barron, J., Berger, M., & Black, D. (1997). *On the job training*. Kalamazoo, MI: Upjohn Institute.

Bernier, R. (2004). Making yourself indispensable by helping teachers create rubrics. *California School Library Association Journal, 27*(2), 24–26.

Blackorby, J., & Wagner, M. (1996). Longitudinal postschool outcomes of youth with disabilities: Findings from the National Longitudinal Transition Study. *Exceptional Children, 62*, 399–413.

Bond, L. (2004). Using contextual instruction to make abstract learning concrete. *Techniques: Connecting Education and Careers, 79*(1), 30–33.

Boudria, T. (2002). Implementing a project-based technology program for high school women. *Community College Journal of Research and Practice, 26*, 709–722.

Bragg, D. (2000). Tech prep: Winning ideas, challenging practices. *Techniques: Connecting Education and Careers, 75*(4), 14–18.

Burgstahler, S. (2001). A collaborative model to promote career success for students with disabilities. *Journal of Vocational Rehabilitation, 16*, 209–215.

Butterworth, J., Hagner, D., Helm, D., & Whelley, T. (2000). Workplace culture, social interactions, and supports for transition-age young adults. *Mental Retardation, 38*(4), 342–353.

Capella, M., Roessler, R., & Hemmerla, K. (2002). Work-related skills awareness in high-school students with disabilities. *Journal of Applied Rehabilitation Counseling, 33*(2), 17–23.

Cavanaugh, S. (2004). Career programs offer pay boost. *Education Week, 23*(27), 17–20.

Certo, N., Mautz, D., Pumpian, I., Sax, C., Smalley, K., Wade, H., et al. (2003). Review and discussion of a model for seamless transition to adulthood. *Education and Training in Developmental Disabilities, 38,* 3–17.

Christ, G. (1995). Curriculums with real-world connections. *Educational Leadership, 52*(8), 32–35.

Dewey, J. (1916). *Democracy and education: An introduction to the philosophy of education.* New York: Macmillan.

Dolainski, S. (1997). Partnering with the (school) board. *Workforce Management, 76*(5), 28–37.

Elliot, M., Hanser, L., & Gilroy, C. (2002). Career academies: Additional evidence of positive student outcomes. *Journal of Education for Students Placed at Risk, 7,* 71–90.

Fabian, E., Lent, R., & Willis, S. (1998). Predicting work transition outcomes for students with disabilities: Implications for counselors. *Journal of Counseling and Development, 76,* 311–316.

Flexer, R., Simmons, T., Luft, P., & Baer, R. (2001). *Transition planning for secondary students with disabilities.* Upper Saddle River, NJ: Merrill Prentice Hall.

Gowdy, E., Carlson, L., & Rapp, C. (2003). Practices differentiating high-performing from low-performing supported employment programs. *Psychiatric Rehabilitation Journal, 26,* 232–239.

Green, M. (2000). Will I use it in the real world? *NEA Today, 8*(7), 24–26.

Hagner, D. (2002). *Career advancement strategies and tools.* Syracuse, NY: Program Development Associates.

Hagner, D. (2003). Job development and job search assistance. In E. Szymanski & R. Parker (Eds.), *Work and disability: Issues and strategies in career development and job placement* (pp. 343–372). Austin, TX: PRO-ED.

Hawkins, R., & Jackson, S. (1992). Using radio courses in the high school curriculum. *Tech Trends, 37*(4), 27–28.

Horn J., & Trach, J. (1998). Employment outcomes from a collaborative work study program. *Journal of Rehabilitation, 64*(3).

Johnson, D., Stodden, R., Emanuel, E., Luecking, R., & Mack, M. (2002). Current challenges facing secondary education and transition services: What research tells us. *Exceptional Children, 68,* 519–531.

Kamens, M., Dolinyuk, A., Dinard, P., Rockoff, J., Forsyth, J., & Corman, H. (2004). A collaborative approach to enhancing employment and social skills of students with disabilities: Perspectives of the stakeholders. *Preventing School Failure, 48,* 24–39.

Langton, A., & Ramseur, H. (2001). Enhancing employment outcomes through job accommodation and assistive technology resources and services. *Journal of Vocational Rehabilitation, 16,* 27–37.

Lave, J., & Wenger, E. (1991). *Situated learning: Legitimate peripheral participation.* Cambridge, UK: Cambridge University Press.

Loughead, T., Liu, S., & Middleton, E. (1995). Career development for at-risk youth: A program evaluation. *Career Development Quarterly, 43,* 274–284.

Lozada, M. (2001). Job shadowing: Career exploration at work. *Techniques: Connecting Education and Careers, 76*(11), 30–34.

Luecking, R., Fabian, E., & Tilson, G. (2004). *Working relationships: Creating career opportunities for job seekers with disabilities through employer partnerships.* Baltimore: Brookes.

MacDonald, M. (2000, December). School to work programs and the Fair Labor Standards Act. *University of Hartford Rehabilitation Training News.*

Mark, J., & Stoia, J. (1993). Anything that starts with a "C": Combining co-op with career services. *Journal of Cooperative Education, 28*(3), 42–48.

Mittelsteadt, S., & Reeves, D. (2003). Career academies: Cutting-edge reform or passing fad? *Techniques: Connecting Education and Careers, 78,* 38–41.

Ochs, L., & Roessler, R. (2001). Students with disabilities: How ready are they for the 21st century? *Rehabilitation Counseling Bulletin, 44*, 170–176.

Ohtake, Y., & Chadsey, J. (2004). Facilitation strategies used by job coaches in supported employment settings: A preliminary investigation. *Research and Practice for Persons with Severe Disabilities, 28*, 214–227.

Parnell, D. (1999). Making it fly. *Techniques: Connecting Education and Careers, 74*(2), 18–22.

Pauly, E. (1994). Home-grown lessons: There is much to learn from existing school-to-work programs. *Vocational Educational Journal, 69*, 16–18.

Polman, J. (2000). *Designing project-based science: Connecting learners through guided inquiry.* New York: Teachers College Press.

Rogan, P., Banks, B., & Howard, M. (2000). Workplace supports in practice: As little as possible, as much as necessary. *Focus on Autism and Other Developmental Disabilities, 15*(1), 2–11.

Rogan, P., & Held, M. (1999). Paraprofessionals in job coach roles. *Journal of the Association for Persons with Severe Handicaps, 24*, 273–280.

Ross, S. (2002). School-based enterprise: the DECA STORiole. *Techniques: Connecting Education and Careers, 77*, 24–27.

Rowh, M. (2003). Building your future career. *Career World, 32*(2), 17–20.

Sandberg, J. (2000). Understanding human competence at work: An interpretive approach. *Academy of Management Journal, 43*(1), 9–25.

Shernoff, D., & Hoogstra, L. (2001). Continuing motivation beyond the high school classroom. *New Directions for Child and Adolescent Development, 93*, 73–87.

Shorr, A., & Hon, J. (1999). They said it couldn't be done: Implementing a career academy program for a diverse high school. *Journal of Education for Students Placed at Risk, 4*(4), 379–394.

Stern, D., Finkelstein, N., Stone, J., Latting, J., & Dornsife, C. (1995). *School to work: Research on programs in the United States.* London: Falmer.

Stern, D., & Rahn, M. (1995). How health career academies provide work-based learning. *Educational Leadership, 52*(8), 37–40.

Thompson, S. (1995). The community as classroom. *Educational Leadership, 52*(8), 17–20.

Thoreau, H. (1854/2004). *Walden, or a life in the woods* (150th anniversary ed.). New York: Houghton Mifflin.

Torocco, M. (1999). Integrating learning and working: A reconceptualization of workplace learning. *Human Resource Development Quarterly, 16*(3), 249–270.

U.S. Department of Labor. (2004). Topical fact sheets #32 and 39. Retrieved November 22, 2004, from http://www.dol.gov/esa/fact-sheets-index.htm

Waxer, C. (2004). Lesson plan. *Workforce Management, 83*(7), 37–42.

Wheeler, J. (1996). *A way to work.* Syracuse, NY: Program Development Associates.

Winger, M. (1995). Students and radio: Getting the good word out. *Educational Leadership, 52*(8), 36–38.

CHAPTER 10

Job Placement and Job Redesign

Katie E. Hildebrand, Frank R. Rusch, and Balázs Tarnai
Pennsylvania State University
Robert Cimera
Kent State University
and
James E. Martin
University of Oklahoma

It's the beginning of the school year, and Jessica Hoffman will be graduating next June. Jessica is a friendly, kind, and responsible student who enjoys being around other people. Jessica has moderate mental retardation. Jessica's teacher has been encouraging her to use appropriate social skills when communicating with others. The transition coordinator, Mrs. Webster, decides to set up a meeting with Jessica and her parents to discuss her plans once she exits the high school. At the meeting, it is decided by all parties that it is time to locate job placement for Jessica.

Jessica has had several jobs during the summertime when school was not in session. Last summer she worked at a local café for several hours at a time doing custodial tasks (e.g., mopping floors, wiping tables, and washing dishes). Two summers ago, one of Jessica's neighbors who worked full-time needed someone to take her dog for a walk during the day. She asked Jessica to come over twice a day to walk her dog. The neighbor was extremely pleased with Jessica; she mentioned to the local neighbors that Jessica was taking care of her dog, Pepper, while she was at work. Before Jessica knew it, she became the local dog walker for all the neighbors. Jessica loved both of these jobs as she enjoyed interacting with people and animals, not to mention making a few extra dollars.

After meeting with the Hoffman family, Mrs. Webster decides to set up a meeting to discuss job placement options with Jessica. Mrs. Webster has a list, several pages long, of possible job placements within the community that are currently available; she had previously arranged them by contacting numerous employers.

A few weeks later, still early in September, Mrs. Webster and Jessica meet to discuss possible job opportunities and to find out what type of job Jessica is interested in. Knowing that Jessica is friendly and has been working on her social skills, Mrs. Webster determines that it would be a good idea to find a placement where Jessica interacts with people. Mrs. Webster then asks Jessica what her interests are and Jessica expresses a desire to work with people. She also tells Mrs. Webster that she has an interest in working with animals, given her previous summer job. Mrs. Webster examines her list of placements and notices that there is a job opening at a local animal groomer. The job description states that this is a part-time position (i.e., about 20 hours a week) that requires that the individual take care of custodial tasks around the business, enjoys working with people, and enjoys working with animals. Mrs. Webster discusses this placement possibility with Jessica, who is immediately thrilled about this potential opportunity.

Mrs. Webster calls the local animal groomer and finds out that the position is available. Then she sets up a meeting with the owner, Ben, to discuss his expectations in further detail. Ben provides much detail about the job requirements for the position. Tasks include cleaning up after the animals, tidying up the shop, transporting the animals from room to room, among others. He is quite adamant that his *employees arrive to work on time, are respectable, and enjoy working with people and, of course, animals. Mrs. Webster tells Ben that she has a potential job candidate; he is thrilled.*

After her meeting with Ben, Mrs. Webster discusses the job opportunity with Jessica and her parents. Knowing that Jessica has many of the required skills, all parties involved are excited about this potential placement. Mrs. Webster brings Jessica by Ben's shop to meet him, and they set up an interview for the following week. During this time, Mrs. Webster helps Jessica prepare for the interview through role-playing.

The following week Jessica interviews for the job, and Ben offers it to her. Together, they work out a schedule where Jessica comes after school a few days a week and works on the weekends. Ben and Mrs. Webster monitor her progress, and all parties involved are thrilled with the outcome. Ben has increased her responsibilities at the shop and begins training her to groom the animals.

Finding the ideal job for a student with a disability can be a complex undertaking, regardless of the severity of the disability. Long before the actual job placement, potential jobs must be identified and analyzed to ensure that a given position is suitable for the job candidate. However, even when either the perfect or the almost-perfect job is found, it may have to be modified or "redesigned" to ensure the best possible fit. Thus, prior to the actual placement of the student into the job, the transition coordinator must systematically complete several steps to guarantee that the job candidate will be successful. Further, once the student is placed in a position, and the job is redesigned, it is essential to monitor progress in order to help the employee maintain the job. Thus, it is up to the transition coordinator to make certain that the candidate, now the new employee, continues to fulfill the job requirements and that the employer remains content with the work efforts of the employee. Importantly, the student, now employee, needs to remain one of the primary targets of interest and concern. Placing a student in a job because of its availability is not appropriate. The chances are high that the student will tire of the job once the tasks associated with the job are learned and become routine. Constant communication is critical in this process—between the employee and employer as well as the employer and job coordinator—to ensure that all parties are satisfied with the working relationships.

This chapter explores job placement and job redesign. The first section, job placement, outlines nine steps originally discussed by Martin (1986, 1990). The second section explores job redesign, which is a critical component as the job placement process begins. In particular, this section defines and highlights the elements that often go into modifying a job and/or making accommodations so a job candidate can achieve successful outcomes.

Job Placement

Job placement can no longer be considered the endpoint of our efforts to educate students with disabilities. Rather, it is a process that begins as the transition coordinator identifies potential jobs for a candidate and continues as the candidate accepts a job offer to advance in a competitive career, and, as an employee, is successful in the position. (In this context, success is defined as fulfilling all the job requirements outlined in the job description provided by the employer.) Throughout this process, a series of steps should be followed systematically to increase the likelihood that (a) the job position is a suitable placement for a job candidate; (b) the employer communicates his or her expectations before, during, and after the placement; and (c) the job candidate performs successfully in the position.

Historically, vocational rehabilitation, vocational education, and special education have targeted individuals with milder disabilities for competitive employment because they typically possess more skills, and consequently, are believed to need less training, and because persons with less severe disabilities are traditionally thought of as individuals who possessed a higher likelihood of remaining employed. However, in more recent times the focus has shifted to include all individuals with disabilities as these disciplines better understand the complexities and benefits of using the procedures outlined throughout this text.

For any individual—with or without a disability—finding and maintaining a job promotes independence and creates a sense of belonging in the community and the wider world. The job placement process essentially consists of matching the job candidate's abilities and interests to a particular job's requirements. The transition coordinator typically leads the job placement process, being responsible for making connections with businesses, matching students to positions, ensuring that job candidates receive the necessary training, and working with the employer to make modifications if necessary. The ultimate goal is to make sure that the job candidate is successful in a given position. If not, it is essential that the transition coordinator determine what will help promote success and make sure it is implemented. Martin (1990) proposed the following nine steps within the job placement process, conducted in part by the coordinator (see also Table 10.1).

Step 1: **Identifying Community Placement Options**

The first step within the job placement process consists of identifying community placement options, which may entail seeking out entry-level positions within the local area (Rusch & Mithaug, 1980). The transition coordinator can accomplish this task by developing personal networks that help provide the names of business owners and businesses that are likely job prospects, including the families of students, their friends, and a referral network that includes all prior business contacts (Rusch, 1983).

TABLE 10.1 *Overview of the Job Placement Process*

Step	Description of step
Step 1: Identify community placement options	Search for potential job opportunities in the local job market.
Step 2: Undertake a community placement survey	Mail out surveys to employers to identify employers who are interested in hiring a person with a disability. Follow up with a phone call to answer questions.
Step 3: Evaluate employment opportunities	Analyze the job site and tasks required by the position to determine if a given placement is suitable for one of the job candidates.
Step 4: Match candidates and jobs	Match the candidate to a job site based on his or her capabilities and the job requirements.
Step 5: Redesign jobs	Make modifications or accommodations to provide supports for the job candidate to fulfill the job requirements.
Step 6: Develop employer expectations	Meet with the employer to confirm the site as a placement and discuss his or her expectations of the job candidate.
Step 7: Communicate with parents or guardians	Meet with parents or guardians to keep them informed and to secure their input about future endeavors about their child.
Step 8: Interview for the job	The job candidate interviews for the job. Prior to the actual interview, it is a good idea to introduce the job candidate to the working environment.
Step 9: Establish work performance evaluation form	Create and put some type of metric in place to assess the job candidate's performance.

The ideal is for all students with disabilities to seek competitive employment. However, not all job candidates possess the necessary skills. Some will need further development of job-related skills prior to placement in a competitive employment setting, or require accommodations, as discussed further in the second section of this chapter on job redesign.

When seeking out potential positions, it is important to bear in mind that although the job is not completely perfect for a given individual, it should not automatically be ruled out as a potential employment opportunity, as services to develop job-related skills and modifications can be provided prior to the actual attainment of the job. Also it is possible that tasks associated with a job can be "carved" to include only those tasks that can be efficiently performed by the student.

In carrying out this step, the local chamber of commerce can also be contacted to obtain a listing of businesses in the area where the job seeker lives and/or intends to work. Telephone directories usually list contact information for the chamber of commerce in a separate section in the front with other important community contacts (e.g., under a heading such as Guide to Human Services or Consumer Services). Once a listing has been obtained and examined, Step 2 of the job placement process can be undertaken.

Step 2: **Undertaking a Community Placement Survey**

The second step in the job placement process consists of conducting a job community placement survey. This is a straightforward process that can be carried out through a mail survey and follow-up phone calls. Different approaches contacting businesses have been tried, including "cold contacts" (e.g., mail surveys and phone calls) and what has been termed the "referral model" (Nietupski, Verstegen, Reilly, Hutson, & Hamre-Nietupski (1997). Nietupski et al. found that relying on the referral method resulted in almost five times the number of potential employers being willing to consider hiring a student with a disability, a finding also reported by Williams, Petty, and Verstegen (1998).

Briefly, the referral method relies on establishing a network of advocates who can provide the names and phone numbers of potential employers. These potential employers are typically contacted by a member of the network (a family member or a friend) before the school representative contacts them. The potential employer is told of the goals of the school and is asked if they would consider a potential student as an employee.

The alternative approach is to cold contact the potential employer. Although this has been found to be less effective, it has advantages, including the possibility of contacting a lot of employers quickly and disseminating the goals of a high school program. Using this approach, a letter typically is sent to the potential employer to determine if the employer is interested in not only hiring somebody, but hiring somebody with a disability. To increase the chances of receiving a reply, a prestamped response card might be attached to the introductory letter that provides a brief description of the high school transition program.

If no response has been received within a 2-week period, Martin (1990) suggests making a follow-up telephone call. The phone call allows employers who might be hesitant about responding to the letter an opportunity to ask questions. Additionally, it serves as a reminder to employers who might have misplaced the transition coordinator's information or have forgotten to respond. Thus, a follow-up phone call gives the transition coordinator another chance to make a connection with a business in the effort to identify a potential job site.

Step 3: **Evaluating Employment Opportunities**

Evaluating employment opportunities is a critical step within the job placement process. Rusch and Mithaug (1980) highlighted four elements related to an employment setting that must be analyzed to determine if it is suitable for job candidates: (a) work environment, (b) job tasks, (c) conditions of employment, and (d) work requirements. According to Rusch and Mithaug, to appropriately conduct a job analysis, the coordinator should speak with the direct supervisor of the job candidate, converse with the employee currently fulfilling the specific job requirements, and observe the social interactions taking place on the job and the general work environment, essentially fulfilling the duties of the job himself or herself. This will provide insight into whether or not a site is suitable for placement of a given candidate. (Figure 10.1 at the end of this chapter provides a sample Job Placement Analysis Form that has been used extensively over the past 20 years by Rusch and his colleagues.)

For identifying job tasks, job-related activities are task analyzed, resulting in a list of the skills necessary to do a particular job. These skills can then become the topic of discussion when meeting with the employer to identify whether they are indeed important to the job description. Oftentimes, tasks or skills associated with a job are not well identified and, consequently, the actual work demands can become a topic of discussion. For example, the following two jobs (assembling and cleaning) were identified as potential jobs, but after identifying the specific skills required for assembling and cleaning, it was decided that several of the tasks were not really part of the job (see tasks in italics below).

1. Cafeteria job for assembling pizza bagels—job tasks include:
   - *Identifying and locating materials and ingredients*
   - *Having the fine-motor skills necessary to open jars and containers and to cut bagels*
   - Following a pictorial sequence to build a pizza bagel (using the right amounts of ingredients)
   - *Operating an oven*
   - *Arranging bagels according to variety and placing in racks*
   - Cleaning individual work area (for keeping orderliness)
   - *Having the strength or stamina to stand behind the counter for the time of the shift*

2. Cleaning up the utility room at the local community college—job tasks include:
   - Putting office tools and small appliances back in their place on the shelves
   - *Washing the desktops*

- *Cleaning the inside of the microwave oven*
- Checking for spills and cleaning them up in the refrigerator
- Vacuuming the floor
- Emptying and relining trashcans
- Making sure the lights are off when leaving area

The criteria associated with fine-motor skills and stamina for the assembly job did not really exist. Grasping bagels was not seen as a fine-motor function; also, sitting down while sorting the bagels was the accepted practice, not standing up. Cleaning the microwave and the refrigerator were not included in the original list of job skills for the cleaning position. A coworker who did not want to perform these duties anymore added them.

Step 4: **Matching Candidates and Jobs**

Once jobs sites have been identified as suitable placements, the next step is to match candidates to a particular job. The transition coordinator must consider the candidate's abilities and verify that she can fulfill the requirements of the job (Goodall, Wehman, & Cleveland, 1983). In doing so, the coordinator should keep in mind what type(s) of work experience the candidate has had. For example, if the open position is at a local coffee shop fulfilling janitorial duties (e.g., wiping tables, washing floors, and cleaning the bathrooms), and the candidate has had experience with similar tasks in a restaurant, although the setting is different, many of the job tasks remain similar. As a result, it should be deemed as a potential match, provided the job candidate is interested in the position and possesses the necessary experience.

The interest of the candidate in a potential position is crucial and should be given obvious consideration (see Chapters 4 and 5). This will increase the likelihood that the job candidate is successful in a particular position and results in an expression of how much value the high school puts on the student's interests and preferences. If the student is not attracted to the job or is indecisive about it as a possibility, a given placement is not likely to be successful. Thus, considering the candidate's abilities and interests are equally important when finding a job for a candidate.

Chapters 3, 4, and 5 discussed the role and importance of self-determination in the transition process and service/support system for students with disabilities. Foremost, job candidates' experiences should be evaluated to ensure they can make an informed decision when they choose a particular position.

Step 5: **Redesigning Jobs**

Upon matching the job candidate to a specific job (i.e., the student is not yet placed in the job; it is merely still a possibility), it may be necessary to redesign the job in order for the candidate to be successful. For example, a job that requires the employee to work 40 hours per week may be too demanding for a candidate who may be capable of working only 20 hours per week. In such a case, perhaps the coordinator can arrange for the employer to hire two employees, each working 20 hours a week. In another case, the job may require the employee to enter or exit the building by way of a series of steps. If the candidate is in a wheelchair, certain accommodations such as a ramp must be made.

These are only two examples of how a job can be redesigned. Job redesigning is extremely important, and before thinking that a job is not a good match for a candidate, the coordinator must pursue whatever modifications or accommodations can be made before abandoning it. The second section of this chapter provides more examples and details related to job redesign.

Step 6: **Developing Employer Expectations**

After redesigning the job to meet the needs of the job candidate, the transition coordinator and the employer must meet and discuss expectations. Two important pieces of information emerge during this step of the job placement process. First, the coordinator confirms the placement to ensure it is appropriate for the job candidate and that the employer is interested in hiring the job candidate. Second, the coordinator and the employer discuss their expectations of the position as well as how they will gauge the job candidate's performance.

Within this phase of the process, a placement contract is also devised. This is essentially a document that specifies the responsibilities of all individuals involved, including the job candidate (i.e., future employee), employer, job coordinator, and possibly other individuals (coworkers, individuals responsible for transportation). The contract also includes the employer's expectations as well as consequences for either fulfilling or not fulfilling the stated requirements. Additionally, the placement contract should specify how the progress of the job candidate will be monitored, including what data collection procedures will be used by the employer and/or job coordinator.

Performance evaluations are important. Evaluation procedures must be both efficient and effective and provide enough information to all parties, allowing all decisions related to performance to be objective.

For example, decisions such as giving the job candidate more tasks to do if she finishes all that is expected in a given amount of time can be made by systematically reviewing an employee's performance. The contract should also indicate what happens if it is determined that this is not the most ideal job placement for the candidate.

First, the transition coordinator might need to seek out another placement for the candidate. Second, the coordinator might have the option of placing a different candidate in the position. Thus, the contract must be fairly general in nature and not written specifically for just one job candidate. Nonetheless, the outcome of this step is critical. All parties must develop, communicate, and document their expectations, and finally come to an agreement based on the data collected.

Job expectations are important to the overall success of remaining employed. The coordinator and job supervisor alone cannot be the only ones who understand these expectations. The job candidate must fully understand all job expectations. To help create a match between coordinators' or supervisors' expectations and the job candidate's self-evaluation, an evaluation sheet can be composed and used during training and in the initial and follow-up phases of actual work performance. Table 10.2 shows an example of an evalu-

TABLE 10.2 *Sample Evaluation Form for Supervisor and Employee*

	Supervisor's opinion	Employee's self-evaluation (How did I do?)	Match? (Y/N)
Work			
Employee listens to and uses feedback	3—excellent 2—fair/OK 1—needs to improve	3—excellent 2—fair/OK 1—needs to improve	
Employee follows safety regulations	3—excellent 2—fair/OK 1—needs to improve	3—excellent 2—fair/OK 1—needs to improve	
Social			
Employee interacts appropriately with coworkers	3—excellent 2—fair/OK 1—needs to improve	3—excellent 2—fair/OK 1—needs to improve	
Personal			
Employee practices good hygiene	3—excellent 2—fair/OK 1—needs to improve	3—excellent 2—fair/OK 1—needs to improve	

ation sheet that contains work-related, social, and personal expectations of the employer or supervisor, and evaluation rubrics for both the supervisor and the employee to check.

Step 7: **Communicating with Parents and Guardians**

Upon developing employer expectations and designing a contract, the transition coordinator should also meet with the job candidate's parents or guardians once more to discuss all updated information. Parents or guardians need to be informed for several reasons. First and foremost, parents should constantly be kept abreast of opportunities and ultimate changes related to those opportunities. Because so much additional effort is placed on identifying the job and all that is required on the job, it is necessary to discuss changes and new expectations for their son or daughter. For example, parents or guardians will most likely know the schedule of their son or daughter, or at least know more than any other party involved. Second, parents or guardians must be informed about what the potential job entails, including job requirements, tasks, hours, work schedule, and salary. The positive impacts of a given job for the candidate should also be emphasized to the parents.

Obtaining and sustaining a job allows for further integration of the student into the community. For example, the job candidate will work alongside fellow employees without disabilities and, depending on the type of position, have contact with customers both with and without disabilities. Facilitating or enhancing appropriate social behaviors for employment may promote more successful outcomes. Another major impact for the job candidate is that securing a job may help create a sense of autonomy as he or she earns a paycheck for independently fulfilling the requirements of the position. Third, as Rusch and Mithaug (1980) pointed out, parents can provide information about the status of funding the job candidate currently receives such as Supplemental Security Income (SSI). It is possible that receiving another income will impact other sources of funding. Typically, earned income results in changes in the amount of SSI that is allowable per month.

There are endless reasons to communicate with parents or guardians, but the points already mentioned should be highlighted and discussed in a formal meeting with all individuals involved, including the parents.

Step 8: **Interviewing for the Job**

The interview is an important and usually anxiety-provoking part of the process for the job candidate. Many individuals with disabilities have poor interviewing skills. One way to alleviate stress levels and develop interview skills is to conduct, as Rusch and Mithaug (1980) noted, a "pre-interview." This involves taking the candidate to explore the work site to develop a comfort level. Visiting the job site allows the candidate to meet other employees and perhaps even the employer, become familiar with the setting, and observe potential job responsibilities. The job candidate should already be familiar with the responsibilities and should have reached criterion or mastery on potential job tasks as a result of previous work experiences. The purpose of this visit is to help make the candidate feel more comfortable for the interview. Providing an opportunity to meet people and learn more about a job will make the student more relaxed. As a result he will be better able to understand what might be discussed more fully, as well as being able to ask questions and learn that he plays a valued role in their employment.

As a result of the interview, either the job candidate will be offered the position or she will not. If the job candidate gets the job, she is now referred to as the employee, and the process moves to Step 9, which involves establishing a work performance evaluation form. If, on the other hand, it is determined that the candidate is not a match for the position, the coordinator has the option of identifying a different position for the job candidate and matching a different candidate to the position.

Step 9: **Establishing a Work Performance Evaluation Form**

The final step in the job placement process is to establish a work performance evaluation. A trial period should be specified to decide if the new employee has reached the criterion of fulfilling the job requirements. If matched to the position appropriately, the employee should be able to do so. All parties involved must be part of the evaluation, especially the transition coordinator, employer, and employee herself. The evaluation should be a formal, written evaluation that the transition coordinator and/or employer complete several times during the early period of employment and less often later. For example, the evaluation may occur weekly for a month, monthly for 5 months, and then annually.

Regardless of the manner in which evaluation data are collected, the employee's strengths and needs must be identified. Rusch and Mithaug (1980) recommend that the following domains be included within the evaluation: social, vocational, and special skill areas. The data should be collected and shared with all parties. If necessary, decisions and changes based on the evaluation data should be implemented immediately. This step will help foster constant communication among all parties and hopefully promote job maintenance. Table 10.3 provides an example of a work performance evaluation form.

TABLE 10.3 *Sample Work Performance Evaluation Form for Supervisor and Employee*

	Supervisor's opinion	Employee's self-evaluation (How did I do?)	Match? (Y/N)	Comments
Vocational				
Speed of assigned job task	3—excellent 2—fair/OK 1—needs to improve	3—excellent 2—fair/OK 1—needs to improve		
Performance accuracy of assigned task	3—excellent 2—fair/OK 1—needs to improve	3—excellent 2—fair/OK 1—needs to improve		
Job task completed independently	3—excellent 2—fair/OK 1—needs to improve	3—excellent 2—fair/OK 1—needs to improve		
Social				
(specification of the particular skill being evaluated)	3—excellent 2—fair/OK 1—needs to improve	3—excellent 2—fair/OK 1—needs to improve		
Special skills				
(specification of skill)	3—excellent 2—fair/OK 1—needs to improve	3—excellent 2—fair/OK 1—needs to improve		

JOB REDESIGN

As mentioned in Step 5 of the job placement process, redesigning a job may be necessary at different times as well as multiple times during the job placement process. For example, a job might be redesigned prior to placing the job candidate. If later the job candidate is experiencing difficulties, the transition coordinator can work with the employer, job candidate, and his or her parents to determine what modifications are needed to fulfill the requirements of the job task successfully. The following defines and highlights components of job redesign.

Finding a job that is perfectly suitable for a job candidate can be a challenge. This is why it is important for the transition coordinator to know the abilities, strengths, and limitations of each candidate. If the transition coordinator identifies limitations that may cause the candidate to either not get the job or be unsuccessful once on the job, one option is to contact the employer to explore redesigning particular parts of either individual job tasks or the job itself.

Essentially, job redesigning is a systematic effort to tailor or modify a position so that the needs of both parties—the job candidate and employer—are met.

Basically, the goal in job redesign is to modify or adapt the work environment to break down barriers. These barriers can include, but are not limited to, too long of a working day for the job candidate, tasks that are too demanding (e.g., the candidate must stand for long periods of time), or perhaps parts of the job that are beyond the job candidate's cognitive or physical abilities. To tackle these problems, a combination of the following may be implemented: (a) job site modification, (b) job restructuring, (c) job carving, (d) job sharing, (e) assistive technology, and (f) natural supports. We will look at each of these in more detail.

A case study to illustrate some of the techniques of job redesign follows at the end of the chapter. The case presents the steps undertaken after a position was identified for a student and before he was able to start working under the redesigned job conditions.

Job Site Modification

Job site modification is a means of removing the physical barriers that hinder an employee's ability to access or perform a job. For example, if the employee experiences mobility barriers, gross-motor, and/or motor problems, adaptations can be made fairly easily. Furthermore, these modifications are typically inexpensive and beneficial to all employees (Bowe, 2000; Cimera, 2002). If the job candidate has a physical disability and uses a wheelchair for mobility purposes, accommodations must be made in order for him to be able to enter, exit, and access all relevant areas in the work site. This might mean that furniture has to be rearranged or job tasks relocated.

Similarly, if a job candidate has cerebral palsy and has difficulty grasping doorknobs, the doorknobs could be replaced with levers that are more manageable to grab and turn, or the manual doors themselves could be replaced with doors that are automatic or removed altogether.

The specific modifications that are made depend on the needs of the employee as well as options available to the employer. In some instances, the nature of the facility may limit some of the options for modifying the job site; however, the transition coordinator, in conjunction with the employer and employee, can usually overcome most barriers that hinder the employee's capabilities to fulfill the requirements of a position at little or cost (Virginia Commonwealth University, Rehabilitation Research and Training Center, 2000).

Job Restructuring

Job restructuring occurs when the employee encounters difficulty completing some of the essential tasks she is responsible for fulfilling. Even if the employee can fulfill 9 out of 10 tasks, that one remaining task may be critical to the overall business operation. For example, an employee may be able to make sandwiches during the lunch period of a local eatery; however, she may not be able to operate the cash register to complete the typical client transaction that starts with placing the order. A second employee may be identified to complete this step.

In job restructuring, the transition coordinator negotiates with the employer to rearrange some of the job duties for a particular job candidate. In some instances, it may be sufficient to reassign some of the job duties to a coworker, such as in the previous example. In exchange, the new employee may be given an additional task that she can more easily complete (e.g., taking more sandwich orders).

In the second example, if a candidate with mild mental retardation is hired to work at a bank but is unable to answer the phones when the receptionist goes to lunch, one solution might be to rearrange the duties so that during the lunch hour the employee with a disability does some filing and the person who typically does the filing switches places and answers the phones. This would solve the problem as all the job tasks are successfully completed.

Another example of job restructuring could involve combining employees to jointly complete a task. Suppose that two employees are working at a restaurant cooking hamburgers. Each employee is expected to cook hamburgers, prepare buns, wrap the final product, and then put them in a warming bin. Rather than having both workers attempt to complete all these tasks in isolation, the job could be restructured so that one employee cooks the hamburgers while the other prepares the buns, wraps, and sets the food in the bin. Such an assembly-line approach can be very beneficial when one employee is particularly good at several steps of the process but not others.

In job restructuring, the job requirements of each individual involved are altered. As long as everyone is flexible in what they are willing to do, this process is fairly simple. It is essential that the transition coordinator works in tandem with the employer to alleviate any possible concerns.

Job Carving

The examples already noted as part of job restructuring are also examples of job carving. Job carving can be one solution to restructuring a job, making it more suitable for a given individual. Job carving is essentially the process of rearranging job duties so that a coworker accomplishes tasks that are difficult for the original employee to complete. Together, the transition coordinator and the employer review the job descriptions of several positions to determine alternate possibilities.

An example of job carving could involve helping a job candidate who does not have the strength to lift a heavy garbage bag and bring it to the dumpster. One solution might be to have a coworker fulfill that job task while the job candidate takes on the coworker's responsibilities, such as restocking a shelf. Now all of the job tasks are fulfilled. The only difference is that the individual originally assigned to each task has changed.

Job Sharing

Job sharing is another example of job redesign. Although similar to job carving, job sharing incorporates more than one person getting hired. Thus, in job sharing, the transition coordinator suggests to the employer that two job candidates be hired as a team. The two can potentially either work together to complete a single task or each can take on a different set of responsibilities, or complete responsibilities over a designated period of time that is split in half. One employee may work the morning shift with a second employee working an afternoon shift. Employers are often willing to be flexible as long as the tasks are completed and are completed well.

Whenever redesigning jobs, it is important to make sure that other coworkers are not being forced to do something that they do not want to do, as this could create resentment toward the job candidate.

Assistive Technology

Assistive technology is another type of accommodation that may assist the job candidate in fulfilling the responsibilities of the job. Assistive technology is a general term for devices that help an individual overcome a disabling condition (Bender, 2004). There are many different types of assistive technology, ranging from high-tech, such as computerized communication devices or optical scanning equipment, to something more low-tech, such as providing the candidate with a ruler to help draw straight lines.

Natural Supports

Natural supports refer to objects, people, or strategies within an environment that can be used to enhance the success of workers with and without disabilities (Flexer, Simmons, Luft, & Baer, 2005; Nisbet & Hagner, 1988; Rusch & Hughes, 1996; Test & Wood, 1996). For example, natural supports can include coworkers who work alongside job candidates and provide assistance that allows the candidates to operate effectively in the work environment. A coworker might cue the new employee to go to lunch because the employee cannot tell time.

Several studies of the effects of using natural supports on employment outcomes have found that the use of natural supports is associated with higher wages, longer job retention, and friendship formation (Cimera, 2001; Mank, Cioffi, & Yovanoff, 1997; Rusch, Wilson, Hughes, & Heal, 1994; Zivolich, Shueman, & Weiner, 1997). In other words, redesigning a job so that natural supports can be utilized may increase how much money the job candidate can make. Furthermore, it may increase job retention, which is a benefit not only to the job candidate but also to the employer who won't have to keep replacing workers. And, natural supports may lead to coworker relations that benefit all parties. Natural supports are further detailed in Chapter 12.

Benefits of Job Redesign

There are numerous benefits for employers and businesses as a whole when they agree to job redesign. First, and important to all businesses, results of recent studies have suggested that making these types of accommodations is inexpensive

(Cimera, 2002; Rhodes, Sandow, Mank, Buckley, & Albin, 1991). According to Roessler and Sumner (1997), of more than 100,000 accommodations studied, 20% were made at no cost to the employer. Fifty-one percent cost between $1 and $501. Only 25% of the cases cost more than $501. These figures are comparable to those provided by the Job Accommodation Network (JAN) and other studies (Griffin & Sherron, 2001). Roessler and Sumner (1997) surveyed employers and found that the majority of those surveyed indicated that $500 to $5,000 was an "acceptable" range to spend for a single accommodation.

Most accommodations, job modifications, and assistive devices improve the efficiency of all workers involved, not only the job candidate with a disability (Fabian, Luecking, & Tilson, 1996). For example, if the job candidate is pursuing a career in culinary arts and is responsible for some of the cooking, one simple accommodation would be to move all the necessary ingredients so that spices and other seasonings used most frequently are closer. Not only might this improve the job candidate's efficiency, but such an accommodation would make sense for all employees.

Last, and perhaps most important, employers alter job duties, make accommodations, and purchase assistive devices routinely. Drawing attention to these potential job accommodations should never be highlighted as necessary because they are being done to accommodate an individual with a disability; accommodations are important because they make the job easier or more efficient.

Summary

Job placement is fairly straightforward and should be carried out systematically. This process is the first step of promoting successful outcomes for the job candidate—ideally, later the employee. As illustrated, this is a group process encompassing the transition coordinator, job candidates, employers of local businesses, parents and/or guardians, and other relevant parties. It requires much organization and preparation by this group to ascertain if the position is appropriate. Once the job candidate secures the position, further skills usually need to be developed for the employee to successfully maintain the job; this will be discussed in detail in Chapter 12. In some cases, parts of the job may have to be redesigned.

Job redesign is a process that results in removing barriers that promote an acceptable job match for a job candidate. Transition coordinators must systematically examine barriers that are impeding the job candidate's success. To ensure long-term success, in addition to a proper match between job and candidate and careful evaluation and observation to determine if redesign is necessary, steps must be taken to monitor the job candidate's progress. Additionally, constant communication between all parties is essential. Strategies to facilitate long-term success, such as job retention and maintenance, are further elaborated on in Chapter 12.

FIGURE 10.1 Job Placement Analysis Form

Job Analysis Survey—Agency Overview
Agency and Position

Name of agency _____

Address _____

Type of industry _____

Name and title of person interviewed _____

Total number of people employed _____

Employees in position _____

Stability of job (seasonal, temporary, permanent) _____

New Work Environment

Importance of speed _____
_____

Number of coworkers student will work with directly _____

Supervision available (coworker training, supervision training) _____
_____

General social environment (positive, unfriendly) _____
_____

Physical appearance (dress code) _____
_____
_____

Physical conditions (comfortable, hot, noisy) _____
_____
_____
_____

Job Analysis Survey—Job Task Analysis

Approximate times	**Task performed**
1. _____	1. _____
2. _____	2. _____
3. _____	3. _____
4. _____	4. _____

5. _____	5. _____
6. _____	6. _____
7. _____	7. _____
8. _____	8. _____
9. _____	9. _____
10. _____	10. _____
11. _____	11. _____
12. _____	12. _____
13. _____	13. _____
14. _____	14. _____
15. _____	15. _____
16. _____	16. _____
17. _____	17. _____
18. _____	18. _____
19. _____	19. _____
20. _____	20. _____

Comments:
_____
_____

Job Analysis Survey—Conditions of Employment

Work hours per day _____

Per week _____

Shift _____

Pay scale _____
_____

Bonuses/Overtime pay _____
_____

Union operating
   Name _____
   Address _____
_____

Union representative
  Name _____
  Phone number _____

Criteria for promotion _____
_____
_____

Insurance and other benefits _____

Job Analysis Survey—Worker Requirements

Education requirements _____
_____
_____

Previous experience _____
_____

Licenses/Certificates _____
_____

Special skills required _____
_____
_____
_____

Reasons for previous firings/abandonments _____
_____
_____

Contact person
  Name _____
  Address _____
  Phone _____

Don, a student graduating from high school, wants to work competitively in the community. He loves working with people and likes to be actively doing something, preferably using his hands. Don has autism and severe mental retardation, and his mobility and endurance are limited.

A hospital near Don's home needs somebody to walk from exam room to exam room picking up files of patients who have been seen. The person is then supposed to bring the files to the records office and put them away on the appropriate shelf. The hospital is a quiet environment, which Don needs. The nurses are friendly and tolerant; they are willing to work with Don, and he really enjoys being around them. But Don gets tired very quickly and would not be able to walk around for more than a few minutes. He certainly couldn't last an entire 5-hour shift. Furthermore, some of the patients' files weigh several pounds and he would have difficulty carrying even one, let alone several dozen at a time. His ability to navigate around the hospital without getting lost is also of concern, and so is the fact that he wouldn't be able to put the files in any sort of order, as that would be beyond his cognitive ability.

Analyzing his situation, his support team decided to carve out and share the parts of the job that Don couldn't do. In the end, he was hired to go around the hospital and retrieve patient files. As Don collected the files from each examining room, another high school student sat in the records office and put them away. Don was also given a little cart to push around with the files in it; this allowed him to support himself at the same time. The hospital had colored lines on the floor to guide patients to the areas where they had to go. Using these natural supports, Don was taught to follow the lines that went by the examination rooms. In the center of each floor, there was a nurses' station. Dan loved the nurses. Whenever they said hello, he would grin and giggle. A nurse on every floor looked for Don at certain times, and whenever he passed their station, they would cheer him on, "Good job, Don, keep going!"—and Don would. There were no more worries about him getting lost. With these natural supports, the job became a perfect match.

Study Questions

1. What is job placement?

    Job placement is matching the job candidate's abilities and interests to a particular job's requirements. The process begins as the transition coordinator identifies potential jobs for the candidate and continues as the candidate accepts a job offer to advance in a competitive career. It does not end until the job candidate, now an employee, is successful in the position. Success can be defined as fulfilling all the job requirements outlined in the job description provided by the employer.

2. What is meant by job redesign?

The job redesign process defines and highlights elements involved in modifying a job and/or making accommodations for a job candidate to reach successful outcomes. These adaptations, large or small, help the job candidate adjust to the demands of the position.

3. Provide an example of a cold contact method of conducting a survey of potential jobs?

This is a straightforward process that can be done through a mail survey and follow-up phone calls. After ensuring that the business is still operating and on obtaining a contact name, a letter is sent to determine if the employer is interested in not only hiring somebody, but hiring somebody with a disability. Attached to the formal letter should be a prestamped response card asking the employer to indicate if he or she is interested in filling open positions with an individual with a disability. A follow-up telephone call is appropriate.

4. How can it be decided if a certain job is appropriate for a given candidate?

Rusch and Mithaug (1980) highlighted four critical elements to analyze when deciding if an employment setting is suitable for job candidates: (a) work environment, (b) job tasks, (c) conditions of employment, and (d) work requirements. Furthermore, according to Rusch and Mithaug, to appropriately conduct a job analysis, the transition coordinator should speak with the direct supervisor of the potential job candidate, converse with the employee currently fulfilling the job, observe the social interactions and the work environment, and essentially fulfill the duties of the job himself or herself. Learning about all aspects of the job will help the transition coordinator make informed decisions about student–job matches.

5. What is specified in a placement contract?

A placement contract is a document that indicates the responsibilities of everybody involved, including the job candidate (i.e., future employee), employer, job coordinator, and possibly others. The contract includes the employer's expectations as well as consequences for either fulfilling or not fulfilling the requirements. Additionally, the placement contract should outline how the progress of the job candidate will be monitored. Finally, it should indicate what happens if it is determined that a job placement is not suitable for a candidate.

6. What are some ways to help a candidate prepare for the job interview?

   One way to alleviate stress levels and develop interview skills is to have a pre-interview. This involves the job coordinator physically taking the job candidate to explore the site himself or herself in order to develop a comfort level. Visiting the job site allows the candidate to meet other employees and perhaps even the employer, become familiar with the setting, and observe his or her potential job responsibilities.

7. When should job redesign ideally occur?

   Job redesign can occur at various points during the job placement process, sometimes multiple times. A job might be redesigned prior to even placing the job candidate. Furthermore, if the job candidate is experiencing difficulties, the job coordinator can work with the employer, job candidate, and the job candidate's parents to determine what modifications are necessary.

8. What does job carving mean?

   Job carving is essentially the process of rearranging job duties so that difficult tasks are assigned to a coworker. The transition coordinator and the employer can review the job descriptions of several positions to determine alternate assignment possibilities. For instance, if a job candidate does not have the strength to lift a heavy garbage bag and bring it to the dumpster, one solution might be to have a coworker fulfill that job task while the job candidate takes on the coworker's responsibilities.

9. How does job sharing differ from job carving?

   Job sharing is similar to job carving, but incorporates more than one student getting hired. The transition coordinator can suggest hiring two job candidates as a team. If two students are hired, they can potentially either work together to complete a single task or each can take on a different set of responsibilities. Employers are often flexible as long as the tasks are completed and are completed well.

10. What are natural supports?

    Natural supports are essentially objects, people, or strategies within an environment that can be used to enhance the success of workers with and without disabilities. Natural supports can include having coworkers work alongside job candidates and using naturally occurring cues that remind the job candidate of what needs to be done next.

Recommended Reading

Brown, S. D., & Lent, R. W. (Eds.). (2005). *Career development and counseling: Putting theory and research to work.* Hoboken, NJ: John Wiley.

Niles, S. G. (Ed.). (2002). *Adult career development: Concepts, issues and practices* (3rd ed.). Columbus, OH: National Career Development Association.

Parker, R. M., Szymanski, E. M., & Patterson, J. B. (Eds.). (2005). *Rehabilitation counseling: Basics and beyond* (4th ed.). Austin, TX: PRO-ED.

Smith, K., Wilson, C., Webber, L., & Graffam, J. (2004). Employment and intellectual disability: Achieving successful employment outcomes. In L. M. Glidden (Ed.), *International review of research in mental retardation* (Vol. 29, pp. 261–289). San Diego, CA: Elsevier Academic Press.

Szymanski, E. M., & Parker, R. M. (Eds.). (2003). *Work and disability: Issues and strategies in career development and job placement* (2nd ed.). Austin, TX: PRO-ED.

Web Resources

Job Placement and Job Redesign

America's Job Bank

http://www.ajb.org/

America's Job Bank is the nation's largest online labor exchange. Businesses post job listings, create customized job orders, and search resumes. Job seekers post resumes and search for jobs that fit their career goals.

CareerOneStop

http://www.careeronestop.org/

CareerOneStop, sponsored by the U.S. Department of Labor, is an integrated suite of national websites that help businesses, job seekers, students, and workforce professionals find employment and career resources.

Job Accommodation Network

http://www.jan.wvu.edu/

JAN is a free consulting service designed to increase the employability of people with disabilities by (a) providing individualized work site accommodations solutions, (b) providing technical assistance regarding the ADA and other disability-related legislation, and (c) educating callers about self-employment options.

JobWeb

http://www.jobweb.com/

JobWeb, a website of career development and job-search information for college students and new college graduates, is owned and sponsored by the National Association of Colleges and Employers (NACE).

Ticket to Work

http://www.socialsecurity.gov/work/Ticket/ticketinfo.html

The site contains information on the Ticket to Work and Work Incentives Improvement Act of 1999 (P.L. 106-170), and the Ticket to Work Program.

Training Resource Network, Inc.

http://www.trninc.com/

This site offers resources on the full inclusion of persons with disabilities in their communities.

Worksupport.com

http://www.worksupport.com/

Worksupport.com is the website for Virginia Commonwealth University's Rehabilitation Research and Training Center on Workplace Supports and Job Retention. The purpose of the VCU-RRTC is to study those supports that are most effective for assisting individuals with disabilities maintain employment and advance their careers.

References

Bender, W. N. (2004). *Disabilities: Characteristics, identification, and teaching strategies*. Boston: Pearson.

Bowe, F. (2000). *Physical, sensory, and health disabilities: An introduction*. Upper Saddle River, NJ: Merrill/Prentice Hall.

Cimera, R. E. (2001). Utilizing co-workers as "natural supports": Evidence on cost efficiency, job retention, and other employment outcomes. *Journal of Disability Policy Studies, 11,* 194–201.

Cimera, R. E. (2002). The monetary benefits and costs of hiring supported employees: A primer. *Journal of Vocational Rehabilitation, 17,* 23–32.

Fabian, E. S., Luecking, R. G., & Tilson, G. P. (1996). *A working relationship: The job development specialist's guide to successful partnerships with business*. Baltimore: Brookes.

Flexer, R. W., Simmons, T. J., Luft, P., & Baer, R. M. (2005). *Transition planning for secondary students with disabilities*. Upper Saddle River, NJ: Merrill/Prentice Hall.

Goodall, P. A., Wehman, P., & Cleveland, P. (1983). Job placement for mentally retarded individuals. *Education and Training of the Mentally Retarded, 18,* 271–278.

Griffin, C., & Sherron, P. (2001). Finding jobs for young people with disabilities. In P. Wehman (Ed.), *Life beyond the classroom: Transition strategies for young people with disabilities* (3rd ed., pp. 171–209). Baltimore: Brookes.

Mank, D., Cioffi, A., & Yovanoff, P. (1997). An analysis of the typicalness of supported employment jobs, natural supports, and wage and integration outcomes. *Mental Retardation, 35,* 185–197.

Martin, J. E. (1986). Identifying potential jobs. In F. R. Rusch (Ed.), *Competitive employment issues and strategies* (pp. 165–174). Baltimore: Brookes.

Martin, J. E. (1990). Consumer-directed placement. In F. R. Rusch (Ed.), *Supported employment: Models, methods, and issues* (pp. 87–110). Sycamore, IL: Sycamore Publishing.

Nietupski, J., Verstegen, D., Reilly, J., Hutson, J., & Hamre-Neitupski, S. (1997). A pilot investigation into the effectiveness of cold call and referral job development models in supported employment. *Journal of Vocational Rehabilitation, 8,* 89–98.

Nisbet, J., & Hagner, D. (1988). Natural supports in the workplace: A reexamination of supported employment. *Journal of the Association for Persons with Severe Handicaps, 13,* 260–267.

Rhodes, L., Sandow, D., Mank, D., Buckley, J., & Albin, J. (1991). Expanding the role of employers in supported employment. *Journal of the Association for Persons with Severe Handicaps, 16,* 213–217.

Roessler, R., & Sumner, G. (1997). Employer opinions about accommodating employers with chronic illnesses. *Journal of Applied Rehabilitation Counseling, 28,* 29–34.

Rusch, F. R. (1983). Competitive vocational training. In M. E. Snell (Ed.), *Systematic instruction of the moderately and severely handicapped* (2nd ed., pp. 503–523). Columbus, OH: Charles E. Merrill.

Rusch, F. R., & Hughes, C. (1996). Natural supports: Who benefits—"we" or "they?" *Journal of the Association for Persons with Severe Handicaps, 21,* 185–188.

Rusch, F. R., & Mithaug, D. E. (1980). *Vocational training for mentally retarded adults: A behavior analytic approach*. Champaign, IL: Research Press.

Rusch, F. R., Wilson, P. G., Hughes, C., & Heal, L. (1994). A matched-pairs analysis of co-worker interactions in relation to opportunity, type of job, and placement approach. *Mental Retardation, 32,* 113–122.

Test, D. W., & Wood, W. M. (1996). Natural supports in the workplace: The jury is still out. *Journal of the Association for Persons with Severe Handicaps, 21,* 155–173.

Virginia Commonwealth University, Rehabilitation Research and Training Center. (2000). *Fast facts on reasonable accommodations and the Americans with Disabilities Act.* Richmond, VA: Author.

Williams, I. J., Petty, D. M., & Verstegen, D. (1998). The business approach to job development. *Journal of Vocational Rehabilitation, 10,* 23–29.

Zivolich, S., Shueman, S. A., & Weiner, J. S. (1997). An exploratory cost–benefit analysis of natural support strategies in the employment of people with severe disabilities. *Journal of Vocational Rehabilitation, 8,* 211–221.

CHAPTER 11

Natural Supports in the Workplace and Beyond

John S. Trach
University of Illinois at Urbana–Champaign

Our attempt to integrate high school services into the mainstream of community activity has necessitated a focus on individuals apart from school personnel who can provide supports to students. There is a long tradition of providing apprentice opportunities, for example, to students choosing careers. In the very recent past, as we have seen more opportunities become available for students with disabilities in the larger communities in which they reside, new methods and rubrics have been introduced to define support that is found in work environments apart from paid staff and service providers. These emerging supports are referred to as "natural" because they are not provided by a paid service provider. A more general term might be "workplace supports," which would include natural supports.

This chapter describes the process for providing support that resides with the individual or in the environment and does not rely on the provision of support from an employment specialist, job coach, teacher, or some other person not typically found in the employment environment. This discussion of natural supports proceeds from a context that recognizes that this process is different from the training and supports that are traditionally provided. The concept of natural supports looks to support provided by nontraditional means (i.e., not the employment specialist or teacher). Rather, the source would be similar to anyone who might need that particular support but did not have some additional service entity such as the teacher. To accomplish this type of support, this process requires a new framework for conceptualizing services. Table 11.1 provides a comparison of traditional services and supports-based service. The focus on the individual as providing direction and identifying supports as the critical element of service suggests a significant contrast to traditional service for program participation.

Trach and Shelden (1997, 1999) described the theoretical basis for the field-generated model *systematic planning for natural supports (SPANS),* as documenting successful practices, identifying issues for consideration, and providing a menu of options for supports development. More specifically this description provides practices that target resources and individuals to assist with planning employment, determining support needs, and implementing natural supports for individuals with disabilities. The training program promotes a systematic process for determining and implementing natural supports for these individuals, targeting a higher level of integration, acceptance, and satisfaction for them. The SPANS model contains an operational definition of natural supports with six primary component activities: (a) consumer-driven planning, (b) ecological assessment of individual needs, (c) environmental assessment of natural supports, (d) identification of natural supports in multiple environments, (e) matching of natural supports to individual needs, and (f) development of individual natural supports plans. The SPANS training project enhances participants' capacity to develop, implement, and evaluate effective systematic models of natural supports (Trach & Mayhall, 1997).

TABLE 11.1 *Traditional and Supports-Based Perspectives for Employment*

Traditional model	Supports-based model
Context: Consumer-driven planning School and agency staff meet with consumer to ask what he wants to do and then tell him what he has to do	Student determines whom to invite to planning meeting and directs meeting informing the group of interests, desires, and skills directly or through participants
Step 1: Identification of support needs List strengths and weaknesses through traditional evaluation and observation in agency programs	List skills and support needs as identified by the meeting participants and observations in real-world environments
Step 2: Identification of available or potential supports List the capacity of the school, service agency, teacher, and job coach to provide necessary supports Develop training plans and systems to monitor work productivity	List all supports that are or can be made available to the individual and that may come from the individual herself, may be identified by the participants, or may exist in a setting (e.g., preparation to engage the work environment, and transitions between environments before and after work)
Step 3: Matching of appropriate supports to specific support needs Direct the teacher, job coach, or agency to complete all aspects of the job by providing support or performing the job	List all activities and corresponding support to address each identified support need with consideration for impact, availability, accessibility, sustainability, and variety
Step 4: Development of individual natural supports plan IEP, ITP, Individualized Program Plan, Individualized Habilitation Plan, Individualized Program of Education	Identify every activity the supported employee will need to be successful, with at least one corresponding support needed to complete an activity and negotiate the provision of support
Step 5: Ongoing evaluation of the support network Job tenure and hours worked per week Sixty- or 90-day stability for successful case closure	Evaluate (a) employee, employer, coworker, and other stakeholder satisfaction; (b) current level of support for every activity in which the supported employee engages; and (c) the percentage of support provided by someone or something other than the job coach or service agency

NATURAL SUPPORTS DEFINED

The operational definition delineates natural supports as "human or technical resources that are available or can be developed in a setting to facilitate integration, acceptance, and satisfaction, and to promote the goals and interests of all individuals in the setting" (Trach & Mayhall, 1997, p. 44). Natural supports are further organized into seven categories: (a) organizational supports, (b) physical supports, (c) social supports, (d) training supports, (e) social service supports, (f) community supports, and (g) family and personal supports to assist service providers to consider all possibilities for support, to expand support beyond the school program. The definition and categories provide a comprehensive perspective for employment support.

WHY HAVE PROCESSES FOR NATURAL SUPPORTS

The premise for a more comprehensive understanding of natural supports evolved from a lack of consensus in the field surrounding the definition of natural supports and a dearth of "best practice" knowledge about their implementation and maintenance in work settings. When Nisbet and Hagner (1988) introduced the concept they began a discussion in the field around the status and potential of natural supports. There was some discussion concerning what natural supports looked like (Callahan, 1992; Nisbet, 1992), how services might be delivered (Hagner, Rogan, & Murphy, 1992; Rogan, Hagner, & Murphy, 1993), and how natural supports might be defined through practice (Murphy & Rogan, 1994). To add to the ambiguity, when the federal government reauthorized the Rehabilitation Act Amendments of 1992, it adopted regulations that suggested natural supports could be used with supported employment, but provided no definition. Test and Wood (1996) reviewed practices provided in the name of natural supports and, once again, noted that natural supports lacked the definitional clarity and consensus enjoyed by traditional models of supported employment. The lack of definition and agreed-on standards was confounded by limited empirical research and evaluation in this area.

Research has proposed that job development should reflect what is more typical in a work environment (Mank, Cioffi, & Yovanoff, 1997) and use resources (e.g., mentors) that currently exist in employment settings (Lee, Storey, Anderson, Goetz, & Zivolich, 1997). The results of these studies indicated that supported employees had higher wages, more typical social participation, and increased social interactions. Recommendations included that negotiations and development for jobs reflect what coworkers recognize as employment in their settings, and that supports development within a setting must begin with job development.

Even without consensus, there is evidence that natural supports are effective. In parallel efforts that focused on employers rather than disability, and on mutually beneficial partnerships, natural supports were found to exist without carrying that label. Truly innovative practices were defined in models that concentrated on job development and business consultation (Bissonnette, 1994; Fabian & Luecking, 1991; Fabian, Luecking, & Tilson, 1994; Luecking, Fabian, & Tilson, 2004). Trach (1995) described job development as the key to any successful employment situation and found that effective job development involves all relevant parties, fully considers the needs of both the employer and the employee, and results in continuing opportunities, shared benefits, and lasting relationships.

TABLE 11.2 *Traditional and Revised Employer Contact Scripts*

Traditional Script

Hello, my name is John Doe. I'm a marketing specialist for Helpme Employment Services. Have you heard of our company? We assist persons with disabilities in finding employment. Since 1986, we have placed over 300 persons in community jobs. The unique feature of our program is that we can provide on-the-job training. This means that we are available to work with the person to assist in his or her training until he or she is able to do the job to the employer's satisfaction. Would it be possible for me to arrange a time to meet with you to discuss our services in more detail?

Revised Script

Hello, my name is Joan Dee. I'm a community relations consultant for University Employment Services. Have you heard of our company? We assist employers in their efforts to recruit persons with disabilities to fill their hiring needs. Since 1986, local businesses have hired over 300 individuals from our pool of applicants. With the implementation of the Americans with Disabilities Act, we are consulting with employers on accessibility guidelines, training their management/supervisory staff in disabilities awareness, and providing input on reasonable accommodations. I am really interested in learning what your specific needs are in this area. Would it be possible to arrange a time to meet with you so that we might discuss those concerns in greater detail?

The SPANS process proposes three basic principles. First, service providers do not create or provide opportunities for employment; instead employers support employees and determine the continued success of any individual in that setting. Second, employment settings have supports that service providers should use to designate ownership and responsibility for a given job to the employer and the setting. And third, the more employment looks like existing jobs and the more the work setting assumes responsibility for success, the more one can expect the outcomes to resemble coworker outcomes in terms of wages, benefits, and integration. In other words, it is important to minimize job coach responsibility by describing the position and responsibilities of a job coach instead as a consultant to business. This change in perspective for the school and community rehabilitation agency typifies an attitudinal adjustment that significantly redefines employment support activities. Table 11.2 provides an example of this paradigm shift in employment services by one community rehabilitation provider.

How to Develop Natural Supports

The SPANS procedure focuses on identifying the support needs of an individual in relation to employment possibilities and then matching those needs to supports other than those provided by the placement agency (e.g., the school). This does not preclude the use of traditional school- or agency-sponsored supports, but identification of activities that must be systematically transferred to some other source before employees can be independent of the school or agency and reliant on the environments in which they function. The process begins with a planning meeting to determine interests and potential support needs that includes the individual and others invited by him or her. The process proceeds through the six component activities listed previously, within the context of potential employment opportunities. The quintessence of the process is to identify employment opportunities, characterize the unique nature of the situation, describe the support needs and sources, and evaluate progress through employer satisfaction (Trach & Shelden, 1992, 1993, 1997, 1999).

Outcomes of Natural Supports Use

The natural supports process has described how demonstrated successful employment of persons with severe disabilities with minimal use of job coach services could be attained. For example, Trach and Mayhall (1997) reported that when instructed, less than 22% of all supports were training supports, and less than half of those supports were provided by a job coach. This is in contrast to all supports provided by a job coach (e.g., transportation, lunch routine, work productivity). Also, the participation of the employee was enhanced considerably to address previous concerns of limited input (Dwyre & Trach, 1996, 1997). Trach, Beatty, and Shelden (1998) found that the development of supports is limited only by what has been done in the past and an expectation that employers will not participate, when in reality, employers had a more accommodating perception of support than either workshop staff or even inservice participants in the SPANS training. Table 11.2 exemplifies an alternative approach to job development that did not rely on past practices as a foundation for current direction, but rather imagined a new process, a new customer, and a shift from the glass half empty to half full. This represents a paradigm shift.

The context for these types of activities must be one in which the consumer drives the job development, from initiating the search to determining what supports are needed, and one in which the employer is empowered to hire rather than an agency searching for an opportunity to place someone in employment. These activities require that service providers acknowledge that access, development, and maintenance of supports must be the primary focus of their employment efforts. Providers must do this in a systematic fashion (i.e., utilizing a more businesslike approach), be prepared to provide documentation and description of what they intend (i.e., examples of current supports and activities in that employment setting and in others that operate to provide success for employees), and conduct evaluations of support efforts to determine feasibility (i.e., successfully providing support and the necessary adjustments for continued success).

The overarching premise for the process is that if 100% of the support is provided by a job coach or teacher, that same amount must be "faded" or transferred in order for the individual to be independent of a service agency, and for the employer and setting to assume ownership of the employment situation.

Consequently, any percentage lower reverses that process proportionally. In all cases, the service agency should take more of a consultant role to the business. Our experience has shown that employers often take a lead in the development of supports, can quickly come to rely on their own resources, and continue to build their capacity to provide support for all their employees.

This review of the literature on natural supports, job development, and consultative approaches to placement is not exhaustive. More research needs to be conducted to provide the evidence that natural supports work and do not put the supported employee at risk. Rather, the process will enhance outcomes. Considerable attention has been paid to the focus on consumer involvement, self-determination, and choice in the employment process. This then provides the context for the identification, development, and evaluation of supports for employment settings. Finally, programmatic efforts and practice describe the theoretical basis for the field-generated model of natural supports, document successful practices, identify issues for consideration, and provide a menu of options for the development of supports (Trach & Shelden, 1997, 1999; Trach, Crudele, & Shelden, 2001).

The charge is clear: For natural supports to be successful, programs must target resources and individuals to assist with planning employment, determining support needs, and implementing natural supports for individuals with disabilities. The employment program must be a systematic process for determining and implementing natural supports for these individuals and targeting a higher level of integration, acceptance, and satisfaction for them. Furthermore, the employment program must develop, implement, and evaluate effective, systematic models of natural supports. The focus must be on purposeful planning and not the haphazard development of work experience settings and placement without job seeker consideration.

These practices will take more time and effort. For those not accustomed to including the consumer and developing supports, the task may seem overwhelming when considering the caseloads that many employment providers maintain. Starting with only a few job seekers to determine what will be the most effective and efficient practices for the provider should reduce some of the frustration of beginning a new system of service delivery. Everyone will access and implement the system in a way that will reflect their personal characteristics. The use of teams for placements could facilitate the process. This is a perfect opportunity for teachers and community rehabilitation providers to collaborate and become more informed of each other. With some practice and success, expect everyone to get more proficient (i.e., competent), efficient (i.e., expeditious), and effective (i.e., productive) in the use of this system. In other words, this process will take less time to complete as service providers become more familiar with the system through practice.

In a larger sense, this philosophy for a system of natural supports is one that suggests that any support that an individual might need exists (or can be created), that it is our job as supported employment service providers to provide it.

THE ONGOING DISCUSSION

Whereas *natural supports* is a popular term used by those involved in supported employment, the meaning of the term continues to spur discussion. Previously stated, Test and Wood (1996) examined literature related to natural supports and found no consistent definition for the term. In responses to Test and Wood findings, Hagner (1996), Mank (1996), Rogan (1996), and Rusch and Hughes (1996) argued that the lack of an agreed-on definition of natural supports is acceptable and that the lack of such a definition may actually lead to more creativity and innovation in the field. Currently, there still exists an interest in this method of employment support by service providers.

Rogan's response, however, did highlight some commonalities among many of the definitions of natural supports, including that natural supports (a) involve both process and outcome, (b) include assistance that is provided spontaneously or through facilitation, (c) reflect the typicalness of a particular work setting or culture, and (d) are used to help people get and keep employment and achieve goals in other life areas. These commonalities are the essence of what is proposed in this chapter and the target for employment efforts. This is qualitatively different from existing efforts.

NATURAL SUPPORTS—AND THE SPANS MODEL

Both the definition of natural supports and the model for developing natural supports suggested by the SPANS model reflect these common characteristics outlined by Rogan (1996). In this discussion, the breadth of resources that might fall under that umbrella and the process for developing those supports exist in the SPANS process, which has been refined and modified by seven cohorts of SPANS Training Project participants from 1993 to 1999. In this definition, "natural" does not refer to whether a support naturally occurs or is preexisting within an environment. In fact, many natural supports will require extensive planning, development, and negotiation. In the SPANS model, "natural" refers to the outcomes that are expected to be achieved. In other words, it refers to the expected impact of the support. The definition refers to several anticipated outcomes: integration, acceptance, and satisfaction and the promotion of the goals and interests of all individuals in the setting. Hence, a support is evaluated to some extent based on not only whether it addresses a specific support need, but also on whether it facilitates these outcomes.

Although a long-term continuous job coach may fulfill several support needs such as learning the job and staying on task, the presence of that job coach may inhibit integration, acceptance, and satisfaction. In this situation, the support would not be considered a "natural" support. More important than the classification of the support as natural or not, this type of support may actually be detrimental to the goals of the supported employee. In this case, the focus must be on what the support need is and the multiple ways to address the need. The provider must not confuse "support need" with a "support." For example, transportation may be a support need; the employment specialist, a support, may be only one way to address the need. One could imagine a multitude of means to address this need. In a setting, there must be more than one way to address all support needs that will promote the independence of the individual from the support agency and provide management to the employment setting as they do with all other employees. The reliance on the employment specialist to provide the majority of support constructs a dependence that is not easily undone. Program developers may find employers to be an incredible resource for developing supports. In most cases the employer may have already experienced that support need and facilitated that support. For example, transportation issues have existed and been addressed.

The question of "what is natural" cannot be answered with a yes–no response. First, what is natural changes from context to context. Thus, a support that facilitates these outcomes in one setting may inhibit them in another setting. The utility of the support will depend, to a great extent, on the culture of the setting and the people in that setting. Second, often the best solution to a support need is not the ideal solution. For example, although team members may be concerned that having a personal assistant come into work regularly to assist an employee with using the bathroom will seem "different" and inhibit integration, the team may feel it is less of an inhibitor than having a coworker assist the employee with the bathroom. Supports may be viewed as residing in a spectrum of naturalness that is different in each context. Thus, the role of the team is to select supports that are more natural than unnatural and to develop a support network that is predominantly natural. The focus should be on what is expected, typical, and the current norm.

What Types of Resources Are Natural Supports?

Any support that assists a supported employee in obtaining and maintaining a job as well as facilitating the outcomes identified in the definition may be considered a natural support. Several categories of supports are identified in the SPANS model, as a tool to assist in identifying possible supports. The intent of the categories is to demonstrate the breadth of supports that might be used and to move people to consider new avenues of support. These categories are one way to conceptualize the variety of supports; readers may have other ways to accomplish this. The intent should be to expand, recognize, and create a variety of support strategies. Remember, the objective is not to categorize supports but rather to think across categories to develop, identify, and construct supports. The following provides a description of each category.

Organizational Supports

Organizational supports are those supports that involve the preparation and organization of activities in the job setting, including, but not limited to, scheduling, order of tasks, and location of materials. Supported employment professionals may feel uneasy requesting such supports from employers, but the reality is that employers provide similar accommodations regularly to employees without disabilities. Flextime and part-time work schedules are common in today's work world. Examples of organizational supports include:

- All necessary supplies are moved to a storage area accessible to the supported employee.
- The supervisor adjusts the supported employee's schedule to accommodate the public bus schedule. For example, Brad needs wheelchair-accessible transportation to get to and from work. The paratransit system is unreliable on the weekends, so his supervisor excuses him from weekend shifts.
- The supervisor works with the employment consultant to carve out job responsibilities that will be most appropriate for the supported employee.
- The employer assists with child care services.

Physical Supports

Physical supports are those supports that involve the design and function of physical objects and equipment in a job setting, whether technical or nontechnical. These supports can range from the simplest jig to specialized computer equipment. Examples of physical supports include:

- The employer has ramps installed to increase accessibility of the workplace.
- Greg's boss purchased mail pouches, which he attaches to Greg's wheelchair every morning. Greg collects recyclables in the pouches.
- The employment consultant designs a jig for the supported employee and coworkers to use that increases efficiency.
- The supported employee purchases an augmentative communication device through vocational rehabilitation.
- The supervisor gives the supported employee a daily picture schedule.

Social Supports

Social supports are those supports that involve interactions with other individuals in an environment. Whereas social supports often include individuals in the work environment, they can involve individuals from any environment that impacts the supported employee's outcomes at work. Examples of social supports include:

- A coworker provides training to the supported employee.
- The supported employee requests that a coworker help him or her with lunch. For example, with help from the supervisor, John's employment

consultant identified a coworker who has similar interests with John and requested that the coworker take breaks with John occasionally.
- A neighbor gives the supported employee a ride to and from work.
- The supported employee's roommate makes sure that the supported employee is dressed and groomed properly before going to work.
- The employment consultant requests that several coworkers include the supported employee in their after-work social activities.

Training Supports

Training supports are those supports that involve the extension of personal competence and skill through direct training and instruction. The most common training support used in supported employment is direct training by a job coach and probably the most difficult to imagine doing differently. As stated previously, of the supports identified in the final reports of SPANS training participants, Trach & Mayhall (1997) found training supports to be the most commonly used supports; however, only half of the identified training supports consisted of direct training provided by a job coach. Examples of other training supports include:

- A coworker receives consultation from an employment specialist on suggested training activities and then provides training to the supported employee. For example, rather than have a job coach train Mary directly, her employment consultant taught several coworkers the basics on systematic instruction. Coworkers designed and made Mary's picture schedules and checklists.
- An employment consultant assists a supervisor in adopting the formal training materials (e.g., manual for operating equipment) to meet the needs of the supported employee.
- A supported employee job shadows a coworker performing the job that he or she is to perform.
- A supported employee uses picture checklists to monitor completion of his or her work.

Social Service Supports

Social service supports are those supports that involve accessing professional and nonprofessional disability-related services. Many resources are available specifically for individuals with disabilities and can be utilized in a way that facilitates employment success and the outcomes identified in the natural supports definition. Examples of social service supports include:

- The supported employee uses Social Security Plan for Achieving Self Sufficiency (PASS) to pay for transportation to and from work. For example, Reggie's case manager helped him develop a PASS plan to pay for transportation to and from work.

- The supported employee hires a personal assistant to come to work on a regular schedule and assist with going to the bathroom.
- A residential service provider assists the supported employee in finding an apartment near a bus line.

Community Supports

Community supports are those supports that involve accessing community agencies and services that are available to all individuals. Such supports include resources that are accessed on a regular basis by many community members. Examples of community supports include:

- The supported employee gets occasional rides from a local church van service. For example, Karen's city does not have public transportation. She gets rides to and from work through a local church's transportation assistance program.
- The supported employee uses public transportation to get to and from work.
- The supported employee takes adult education courses to upgrade his skills.

Personal and Family Supports

Personal and family supports are those supports that involve accessing family and personal resources. These supports often fall into another category, but the category itself is important as a reminder that often a supported employee and his or her family or personal network hold the answers to addressing many of the support needs that are identified. Examples of personal and family supports include:

- With help from his job developer, Rod shaped his unique clown skills into his own business, performing at children's parties.
- The supported employee joins a self-advocacy group to learn to better advocate for herself at work.
- Family members provide employment referrals to the job seeker and the job developer.
- Family members provide transportation to and from work.
- The supported employee learns to monitor his own progress at work on a daily basis.

By taking the time to brainstorm several support possibilities, teams often come up with very creative solutions to typical support needs. The following is one such example of a unique solution to a support need and an inspiration to creativity. Charlotte's support needs included getting to and from work. Several options were considered, including agency transportation. The most creative solution, and the one utilized during warm weather, was for Charlotte to catch a ride with her supervisor on his tandem bicycle (Trach et al., 2001).

As can be seen in the previous examples, there is overlap among the categories. One support might fall into several categories. Once again, the category itself is not important. Rather, the category structure should be used to promote creative thinking. A team can use the categories to consider support options beyond the first idea that comes to mind. During support planning, this facilitates consideration of several support possibilities. The category structure should be seen as a tool to facilitate drawing support from many different resources.

Summary

This chapter provided a definition of natural supports, a relatively new and not very well understood concept that has emerged over the very recent past. Seven different categories of supports were overviewed as well as traditional procedures for identifying the supports that students might need when using a more traditional approach versus an approach that is supports based. Almost any resource might be identified as a natural support. Whether it is in place or needs to be developed, whether it comes from a social service provider or an employer or family member, as long as the support facilitates positive workplace outcomes, it is a natural support.

Study Questions

1. What are natural supports as defined in this chapter?

    Natural supports are supports that reside with the individual or in the environment and do not rely on the provision of support from an employment specialist, a job coach, a teacher, or some other person not typically found in the employment environment.

2. List the seven categories of natural supports and provide an example of each.

    The seven categories of natural supports include: (a) organizational supports, (b) physical supports, (c) social supports, (d) training supports, (e) social service supports, (f) community supports, and (g) family and personal supports to assist service providers to consider all possibilities for support, and to expand support beyond the school program.

3. List 10 ways you could access a store in a particular shopping mall.

    Access methods include (1) use a main entrance to the mall, (2) use a separate entrance to the particular store only, (3) use a wheelchair ramp, (4) use an elevator or escalator that leads to the store, (5) have somebody assist you in finding the store or leading you to it, (6) have a map assist you, (7) use a catalog to shop from home through the mail, (8) use online shopping, (9) order items on the phone, and (10) have a sales representative visit your home.

4. Pick a task and describe three different ways to complete it.

   To cut down a tree, you could (1) do it yourself, using your own tools; (2) ask friends or neighbors for assistance or their tools and work as a team; or (3) hire and pay a professional.

5. Explain what 100% in 100% out means in relation to employment support.

   If 100% of the support is provided by a job coach or teacher, that same amount must be faded or transferred in order for the individual to be independent of a service agency, and for the employer and setting to assume ownership of the employment situation. Consequently, any percentage lower reverses that process proportionally.

6. Describe the difference between fading and systematic transfer of support and why this is an issue for employment support.

   Fading simply implies the gradual reduction of support over time. Transfer of support, on the other hand, implies the involvement of others in the support system to take over responsibilities, in order to best serve a client in the most natural and typical ways possible.

7. Describe the difference between weaknesses and support needs.

   "Weakness" carries a negative connotation and implies that some deficit is innate to the individual. "Support need" is a relative term, referring to a particular situation. Different needs can emerge or be fulfilled flexibly at any time, changing over time, for any individual in his or her relation to the social and physical environment.

8. Explain the role of consultant in employment support rather than job coach.

   The role of a job coach is to assume the position of a consultant to business.

9. Why would it be important for an employer to hire someone rather than a program place someone in employment?

   This represents a paradigm shift. The context for these types of activities must be one in which the consumer drives the job development from initiating the search to determining what supports are needed. The employer is empowered to hire rather than an agency searching for an opportunity to place someone in employment. These activities require that service providers acknowledge that access, development, and maintenance of supports must be the primary focus of their employment efforts.

10. List five differences in the scripts provided in Table 11.2.

    Differences may include (1) name of the contact person; (2) name of the company/service; (3) focus on job needs of persons with disabilities versus hiring needs of businesses; (4) offer their own services to work with the client versus inquiry about specific needs and generally offering support in accommodating them; (5) offer only one type of support (on-the-job training) versus a continuum of potential ways of individual support.

Recommended Reading

Bissonnette, D. (1994). *Beyond traditional job development: The art of creating opportunity*. Chatsworth, CA: Milt Wright & Associates.

Callahan, M., & Garner, J. B. (1997). *Keys to the workplace: Skills and supports for people with disabilities*. Baltimore: Brookes.

Luecking, R. G., Fabian, E. S., & Tilson, G. P. (2004). *Working relationships: Creating career opportunities for job seekers with disabilities through employer partnerships*. Baltimore: Brookes.

Web Resources

Natural Supports

How to Develop Natural Supports

http://www.dds.ca.gov/publications/PDF/Natural Supports.pdf

A document by the Department of Developmental Services, Sacramento.

Natural Supports and the Job Coach: An Unnecessary Dichotomy

www.vcu.edu/rrtcweb/overview/support.html

Article from the *RRTC Newsletter*, Fall 1994.

The Role Of Natural Supports in Behavioral Health Treatment

http://www.dpw.state.pa.us/Child/BehavHealth ServChildren/ChildAdolescentGuidelines/003670804.htm

Description of the role of natural supports in behavioral health treatment for children and adolescents by the Pennsylvania Department of Public Welfare.

Analysis of the Types of Natural Supports Utilized During Job Placement and Development

www.findarticles.com/p/articles/mi m0825/is 2 63/ai 56175562

Article from the *Journal of Rehabilitation* by John S. Trach and Camille D. Mayhall, April-June 1997.

References

Bissonnette, D. (1994). *Beyond traditional job development: The art of creating opportunity*. Chatsworth, CA: Milt Wright & Associates.

Callahan, M. (1992). Job site training and natural supports. In J. Nisbet (Ed.), *Natural supports in school, at work, and in the community for people with severe disabilities* (pp. 257–276). Baltimore: Brookes.

Dwyre, A. E., & Trach, J. S. (1996). Consumer choice for people with cognitive disabilities: Who makes the choices in the job search process? *Journal of Applied Rehabilitation Counseling, 27*(3), 42–47.

Dwyre, A. E., & Trach, J. S. (1997). *Perceptions of the supported employment job search process: Who makes the choices?* Unpublished manuscript.

Fabian, E. S., & Luecking, R. G. (1991). Doing it the company way: Using internal company supports in the workplace. *Journal of Applied Rehabilitation Counseling, 22*(2), 32–35.

Fabian, E. S., Luecking, R. G., & Tilson, G. P., Jr. (1994). *A working relationship: The job development specialist's guide to successful partnerships with business*. Baltimore: Brookes.

Hagner, D. C. (1996). "Natural supports" on trial: Day 2799? *Journal of the Association for Persons with Severe Handicaps, 21*(4), 181–184.

Hagner, D., Rogan, P., & Murphy, S. (1992). Facilitating natural supports in the workplace: Strategies for support consultants. *Journal of Rehabilitation, 58*(1), 29–34.

Lee, M., Storey, K., Anderson, J. L., Goetz, L., & Zivolich, S. (1997). The effect of mentoring versus job coach instruction on integration in supported employment settings. *Journal of the Association for Persons with Severe Handicaps, 22,* 151–158.

Luecking, R. G., Fabian, E. S., & Tilson, G. P. (2004). *Working relationships: Creating career opportunities for job seekers with disabilities through employer partnerships.* Baltimore: Brookes.

Mank, D. (1996). Natural support in employment for people with disabilities: What do we know and when did we know it? *Journal of the Association for Persons with Severe Handicaps, 21*(4), 174–177.

Mank, D., Cioffi, A., & Yovanoff, P. (1997). Analysis of the typicalness of supported employment jobs, natural supports, and wage and integration outcomes. *Mental retardation, 35*(3), 185–197.

Murphy, S. T., & Rogan, P. M. (1994). *Developing natural supports in the workplace: A practitioner's guide.* St. Augustine, FL: Training Resource Network.

Nisbet, J. (1992). *Natural supports in school, at work, and in the community for people with severe disabilities.* Baltimore: Brookes.

Nisbet, J., & Hagner, D. (1988). Natural supports in the workplace: A reexamination of supported employment. *Journal of the Association for Persons with Severe Handicaps, 13,* 260–267.

Rogan, P. (1996). Natural supports in the workplace: No need for a trial. *Journal of the Association for Persons with Severe Handicaps, 21*(4), 178–180.

Rogan, P., Hagner, D., & Murphy, S. (1993). Natural supports: Reconceptualizing job coach roles. *Journal of the Association for Persons with Severe Handicaps, 18,* 275–281.

Rusch, F. R., & Hughes, C. (1996). Natural supports: Who benefits—"we" or "they?" *Journal of the Association for Persons with Severe Handicaps, 21*(4), 185–188.

Test, D. W., & Wood, W. M. (1996). Natural supports in the workplace: The jury is still out. *Journal of the Association for Persons with Severe Handicaps, 21,* 155–173.

Trach, J. S. (1995). [Review of the book *A working relationship: The job development specialist's guide to successful partnerships with business.* Journal of the Association for Persons with Severe Handicaps, 20,* 165–167.

Trach, J. S., Beatty, S. E., & Shelden, D. L. (1998). Employers' and service providers' perspectives regarding natural supports in the work environment. *Rehabilitation Counseling Bulletin, 41,* 293–312.

Trach, J. S., Crudele, K. S., & Shelden, D. L. (2001). *Systematic plan for achieving natural supports and collaboration: Illustrations from an inservice natural supports training.* Champaign: University of Illinois at Urbana–Champaign, Transition Research Institute.

Trach, J. S., & Mayhall, C. D. (1997). Analysis of the types of natural supports utilized during job placement and development. *Journal of Rehabilitation, 63*(2), 43–48.

Trach, J. S., & Shelden, D. L. (1992). *A competency-based training program to promote, implement, and evaluate a systematic plan for achieving natural supports: Executive summary.* Champaign: University of Illinois at Urbana–Champaign, Division for Rehabilitation Education Services.

Trach, J. S., & Shelden, D. L. (1993). *SPANS model: Definition and categories of natural supports (revised).* Champaign: University of Illinois at Urbana–Champaign, Division for Rehabilitation Education Services.

Trach, J. S., & Shelden, D. L. (1999). Natural supports: A foundation for employment. *Innovations, 16.* Washington, DC: AAMR Monograph Series.

Trach, J. S., & Shelden, D. L. (Eds.). (1997). *Systematic plan for achieving natural supports: Evaluation of an inservice training program.* Champaign: University of Illinois at Urbana–Champaign, Transition Research Institute.

CHAPTER 12

Supporting Students in the Transition from School to Adult Life

Carolyn Hughes, Barbara H. Washington, and Gaylan L. Brown
Vanderbilt University

Josie Redlands arrived at the bus stop at Gateway Road and 18th Avenue at 8:37 a.m.—too late to make the 8:15 bus downtown. Now she would have to wait for the 8:45 bus and she would be late for her 8:30 job interview in the human resources department of the Southern Hills Assisted Living Center. That probably wasn't going to help her get the nurse's aide job she was applying for, she figured. But at least she wasn't sitting at the bus stop when the school bus came by taking everyone else to Centennial High. Since she dropped out of school last year when she was a sophomore, Josie didn't like being seen by anyone from school, especially when she was sitting on the bench at the city bus stop. Yeah, they'd all be thinking what a loser I am, Josie figured—no job, no car, still living at home, nothing to show for a year and a half out of school.

Josie thought back to those days before she quit going to school entirely. Everything was becoming too overwhelming. She was failing history, algebra, and English and hadn't even started on her semester-long biology project, which had been due the week before. She had overslept and missed her college entrance exam on Saturday, and she knew she had too many absences to get credit for the semester anyway. She skipped her first period class on the days she was at school to avoid seeing Ms. Browning, her special ed teacher. How she hated being called "seriously emotionally disturbed" and being seen in that class! The guidance counselor had called her down to the office at least five times that semester, but Josie had used this as an opportunity to disappear down the hall and leave the school building. Finally, she just quit going altogether. Her mother, who was never up in the morning anyway after her all-night job, didn't even know.

But now, looking back, Josie wished she had done something else—maybe asked for help or actually gone to see the guidance counselor. Then maybe she wouldn't be sitting at the bus stop now hoping no one would see her. Maybe someone could have helped her "get her act together." She knew she had something called an IEP and it had goals for her life that she had helped develop, like taking the classes she needed to become a child care worker and maybe even going to college. At the time, those goals seemed so far away. Now she wished she hadn't given up on them. But there never was anyone to help her, she thought. She always felt like she was all on her own. Whom could she have turned to for support?

Unfortunately, outcomes like Josie's are all too common among students with disabilities as they leave high school. Postschool outcomes for these students include unacceptably high rates of unemployment, incarceration, and financial dependence concurrent with strikingly low rates of enrollment in college or other postsecondary education or training. Slightly over half of students with disabilities graduate high school with a standard diploma, whereas approximately one third drop out before graduation (U.S. Department of Education, 2002). One fifth of youth with disabilities either have been suspended or expelled from school, fired from a job, or arrested (Wagner, Cameto, & Newman, 2003), whereas only 40% are employed or 30% attending postsecondary school after leaving high school (Wagner, Newman, Cameto, Garza, & Levine, 2005). In addition, only 32% of adults with disabilities work full- or part-time compared to 81% of adults without disabilities, resulting in severely elevated poverty rates for these individuals (National Organization on Disability, 2004).

Postschool outcomes are particularly bleak for the increasing numbers of minority students with disabilities who are from high-poverty backgrounds. For example, 37% of African American students with disabilities drop out of school versus 26% of their White counterparts (U.S. Department of Education, 2002). Youth from families in the lowest 20% of the income distribution are six times as likely to drop out of school as are youth from families in the top 20% (Swanson, 2003). The employment rate for African American youth with disabilities averages 16% less than that of White youth, which is exacerbated for those who drop out of school (Wagner et al., 2005). Furthermore, weekly earnings of high school dropouts in 2003 averaged $396 compared to $554 for high school graduates and $900 for college graduates (U.S. Department of Labor, 2004).

These unfavorable postschool outcomes are particularly disturbing in light of over 20 years of legislative effort aimed at increasing services and enhancing outcomes for secondary-age youth. The importance of providing support to students as they make the transition from school to adult life has been advocated since the mid-1980s (e.g., Halpern, 1985, 1992; Rusch & Phelps, 1987; Will, 1984). Support models that have received attention in the literature include Will's "bridges" model of school to employment proposed by the Office of Special Education and Rehabilitation Services (OSERS); Halpern's (1985) model of school to "community adjustment;" the Individuals with Disabilities Act (IDEA) of 1990 (P.L. 101-476) and Amendments of 1997 (P.L. 105-17) and 2004 (P.L. 108-446); and the 1994 School-to-Work Opportunities Act (P.L. 103-239), which addressed employment among all youth. Further, the No Child Left Behind (NCLB) Act of 2001 (P.L. 107-110) requires states and school districts to address and document the school performance, academic outcomes, and graduation rates of subgroups of students, including English language learners, members of minority groups, students with disabilities, and students from high-poverty backgrounds. Other support models include the concept of "protective factors," such as caring adults and nurturing schools or communities, which theoretically promote a student's resilience in the face of adverse conditions, such as exposure to violence, poverty, or substance abuse (Murray, 2003).

Although the scope of these models differs, all are designed to promote comprehensive services and support to improve the public school experiences and outcomes for all students, including those from diverse multicultural and economic backgrounds (Johnson, Stodden, Emanuel, Luecking, & Mack, 2002). Further, the models are based on the assumption that students need varying amounts of support to fully participate in general education and the community during their transition from school to adult life (Baer et al., 2003; Hughes & Carter, 2000). For example, support strategies might include providing opportunities for a student to sample a range of community jobs or enlarging a bus schedule for a student with visual disabilities. For discussion purposes, we adopt the definition of support proposed by Thompson et al. (2002) for people with disabilities:

> Resources and strategies that promote the interests and welfare of individuals and that result in enhanced personal independence and productivity, greater participation in an interdependent society, increased community integration, and/or improved quality of life. (p. 390)

The empirical literature provides examples of effective practices that relate to successful student outcomes. These practices include (a) community-based instruction (Gaumer, Morningstar, & Clark, 2004); (b) career-related, paid work experience (Benz, Lindstrom, & Yovanoff, 2000); (c) participation in transition planning (Test et al., 2004); (d) parent involvement (Cooney, 2002); (e) access to continuing education (Benz et al.); (f) participation in vocational education (Baer et al., 2003); (g) instruction in self-determination skills (Palmer, Wehmeyer, Gipson, & Agran, 2004); and (h) follow-up support services (Certo et al., 2003). For example, Palmer et al. increased students' access to general education curricular activities by teaching problem solving and related self-determination skills.

The growing evidence of exemplary secondary transition practices is promising. Nevertheless, postschool outcomes for students with disabilities (e.g., rates of employment, enrollment in postsecondary education, community involvement) persistently lag behind those of students without disabilities (e.g., Benz et al., 2000; Rusch & Braddock, 2004). As schools and adult service programs are asked to compete more and more with other community programs for public dollars, it is critical that secondary educators find cost-effective transition support strategies that are both evidenced based and acceptable to and likely to be adopted by practitioners.

In this chapter, we describe a model of support for the transition from school to adult life that is both empirically sound *and* practitioner tested. First, we overview the development of the model. Next, we describe the components of the model, providing examples of its application among high school students with disabilities. Using a case study approach, we illustrate the model in practice with a high school student in need of support. We conclude with recommendations for high school teachers and related personnel interested in applying the model in their own school situations.

DEVELOPING A MODEL OF TRANSITION SUPPORT: BRIDGING RESEARCH TO PRACTICE

In developing a model of transition support, we first identified components and strategies that secondary personnel could introduce while students are still in high school, maximizing students' potential in the classroom and community by applying the principles of support characteristic of supported employment and supported living arrangements (Wehman, 2000). Wehman argued that "creating an array of person-driven supports [during high school] to catapult the student into the world of adulthood is a much more broad-based approach to helping people reach their potential" (p. xiv). Second, we included strategies that teachers and colleagues could implement at the student or small-group (proximal) level of interaction, such as teaching self-determination skills, rather than on the organizational or community (distal) level, such as developing entrepreneurial opportunities in the community (Bronfenbrenner, 1977). Although coordination with adult service and community agencies is critical to supporting students in the long term (Johnson, 2004; Rusch & Braddock, 2004), our focus in this chapter is the sphere of influence an individual teacher has (see Chapter 7 for a discussion of interagency coordination). Emphasis is placed on skills that can be taught and supports that can be developed while students are still in school, which can be transferred to and maintained during students' adult lives (e.g., learning to navigate a city's bus system).

In addition to addressing high school students' support needs, we sought to respond to a critical area of need in secondary transition: the gap between what has been learned from research and what actually is practiced in the field (Blalock et al., 2003). For example, evidence-based recommended practices, such as community-based instruction, are reported to be inconsistently applied in secondary transition programs (Hasazi, Furney, & DeStefano, 1999). Recommended research findings must be packaged in formats that are accessible to teachers, parents, and colleagues (Hughes & Carter, 2000). If effective transition programming is to be integrated into practice, researchers must present products that are acceptable to high school personnel and that take into account local school and community conditions, attitudes, and values (Lieberman, 1995). An effective means to integrate research and practice in secondary transition is to involve teachers as interactive, contributing partners in model development (Malouf & Schiller, 1995). This interactive approach to model development requires continual feedback from practitioners that is incorporated into program planning, implementation, and evaluation.

The transition support model we propose is unique because it was developed through an interactive 5-year collaboration between teachers and researchers. The process ensures that strategies that comprise the model are research based, field-tested, and acceptable to teachers. In the rest of this section, we briefly describe the interactive research-to-practice process that resulted in the transition support model (Hughes & Carter, 2000; Hughes, Hwang, et al., 1997; Hughes, Kim, et al., 1997).

From an extensive review of the transition literature (i.e., 113 empirical studies), we derived a list of secondary transition support strategies that met a preestablished criterion of at least two empirical demonstrations of effectiveness. We then conducted a national survey among 54 applied researchers in the area of transition to determine the acceptability of the candidate support strategies by the research community (Hughes, Hwang, et al., 1997). Practitioners judged the proposed transition strategies as critical to supporting the transition process and feasible for implementation.

Next, we rank-ordered the strategies according to researchers' responses and combined them into a preliminary model, which we subsequently incorporated into a questionnaire and field-tested among transition teachers from a large metropolitan school district. Teachers' feedback was used to refine and package the model to make it more acceptable, accessible, and useful to practitioners.

We mailed the revised questionnaire to all secondary transition teachers identified in the state of Tennessee (Hughes, Kim, et al., 1997). These teachers ($N = 121$) represented all rural and urban geographic areas of the state, and their students represented all categories of disabilities identified in IDEA 1997. Teachers' responses (response rate = 63%) indicated that they judged the support strategies and model to be both extremely important to the transition process and acceptable to practitioners in the field. Teachers also provided 592 ways in which they implemented the support strategies in their transition programs.

Finally, we combined the teacher-identified support strategies into the transition support model framework (Hughes & Carter, 2000). Our interactive process resulted in a model that (a) is empirically based, field-tested by practitioners, and judged as acceptable to both researchers and teachers; and (b) incorporates input from the field.

THE TRANSITION SUPPORT MODEL: AN OVERVIEW

As we read through the teacher-generated strategies that comprised the model, we were impressed with their quality, soundness, creativity, and practicality and believed that they were important enough to share with the field. Consequently, we compiled them into *The Transition Handbook* (Hughes & Carter, 2000), grouping them into categories and subcategories of strategies with accompanying examples, case studies, reproducible forms, and legislative and research support. In this section, we provide an overview of the model with illustrative examples of each component. Table 12.1 provides a definition and brief example of each component of the transition support model. As shown, the model is composed of two overarching goals: (a) developing support in the environment and (b) increasing students' competence.

Developing Support in the Environment

The first goal reflects a monumental change in the field of disabilities. The traditional deficit model of disability, in which a student must be "fixed" in response to environmental demands, is no longer accepted in education (Thompson et al., 2002). Instead it is being replaced by a more ecological approach in which the environment is modified and naturally occurring support is maximized in response to the full array of an individual's needs, preferences, and choices (Hughes & Carter, 2000). Our research shows that much support is available in

TABLE 12.1 Transition Support Model Components

Strategy	Definition	Example
Developing support in the environment		
Promoting social acceptance	Communicating an attitude of acceptance, providing diversity awareness experiences, teaching skills that promote social acceptance, increasing students' participation in social activities	A job coach points out to a supervisor of a laundry that a young man is completing his work on time even if he hums to himself and walks unsteadily.
Increasing environmental support	Conducting environmental surveys and observations, communicating environmental support needs, developing environmental support plans, gaining access to existing environmental support, modifying the environment	A teacher observes that a young man in a wheelchair cannot reach the wastebaskets while cleaning offices at work. Wastebaskets are then kept next to office doors to make it easier for him to empty them from his wheelchair.
Increasing social support	Conducting site visits and observations, communicating social support needs, developing social support plans, gaining access to existing social support	A young woman with a visual impairment is helped by her brother to find her bus pass. She then walks to the bus stop with a classmate who lives nearby. At her community job in a legal office, she confides in a coworker at break about the frustrations she is having with her boyfriend. As she leaves for the day, her supervisor says, "See you tonight at the party."
Increasing students' competence		
Identifying and promoting students' strengths	Observing performance and collecting data, assessing students' strengths and needs, communicating students' strengths and needs, teaching skills that need strengthening	A teacher asks a student and the supervisor at a greenhouse where the student works to identify skills that the student is and is not performing independently. The teacher also observes the student while performing her job tasks. A coworker assists in teaching skills the student is not performing by herself.
Increasing students' self-determination	Promoting students' self-determination, teaching self-management and self-determination skills, incorporating self-determination into daily living	A student and her teacher role-play having the student introduce members of her IEP team and stating her educational goals at her IEP meeting. When the actual meeting occurs, the student is able to perform these skills independently.
Increasing students' choice and decision making	Identifying students' opportunities for choice and decision making, collaborating to increase students' choice and decision making, teaching and increasing students' choice and decision making	A high school sophomore with an emotional disorder is provided with opportunities to sample many jobs and to discuss his job preferences.
Promoting students' social interaction	Increasing students' social interactions, promoting peer involvement, increasing opportunities for social interaction, teaching social interaction skills	General education peers prompt a student with a speech impairment to engage in conversations at lunch and between classes.

Source: From "Practitioner-Validated Secondary Transition Support Strategies," by C. Hughes, J. Kim, B. Hwang, D. J. Killian, G. M. Fischer, M. L. Brock, J. C. Godshall, and B. Houser, 1997, *Education and Training in Mental Retardation and Developmental Disabilities, 32,* pp. 204–205. Copyright 1997 by the Council on Exceptional Children. Adapted with permission of the author.

most environments and that teachers can learn to tap into and maximize support and acceptance of individual differences across the settings in which students spend their day.

Three major categories of strategies comprise Goal 1: (a) promoting social acceptance, (b) increasing environmental support, and (c) increasing social support. Each is described further below.

Promoting Social Acceptance. Social inclusion in the mainstream of life is a primary goal of the transition movement. The IDEA Amendments of 2004 affirm that all students should participate in the general education curriculum to the maximum extent possible to ensure access to all social and academic opportunities in school as well as successful employment and daily living outcomes after graduation. By participating fully in the interactions within an environment, individuals gain access to myriad benefits, such as friendships, opportunities to learn, and personal satisfaction.

Not only is it critical that transition programming occurs across all settings in which students ultimately will live their lives (e.g., community, home, work), it is equally important that students are socially accepted into these environments as full participants. Physical proximity—merely being present in an environment—does not ensure that one is an active and equal participant in that setting. Teachers and others must actively promote acceptance of students as equal members at the work site, in general education classrooms, and in the community.

Promoting social acceptance in an environment includes strategies related to (a) communicating an attitude of acceptance, (b) providing diversity awareness experiences, (c) teaching skills that promote social acceptance, and (d) increasing students' participation in social activities. For example, Levison and St. Onge (2001) recommend discussing myths and facts regarding disability with general education students as well as providing them accurate information to read. Teachers also can model an attitude of acceptance and demonstrate through their own behavior acceptance of individual differences, such as when a person with a missing limb enters the class or work site. General education students also have been taught to reinforce expected social behavior of their peers with disabilities while participating in leisure activities or lunch at school (Morrison, Kamps, Garcia, & Parker, 2001).

Increasing Environmental Support. For many students, the success of their transition to adult life and their independence depends on the amount of environmental support they receive. When teachers, job coaches, and associates learn to identify available support, they can match it to the needs of individual students, such as a buzzer that signals break time for a student with visual impairments. The first step in identifying environmental support is to visit a site and conduct an environmental survey of naturally occurring supports. Additional information can be gained through interviews with important others and included in a support plan for a student. Teachers may also need to identify ways to modify the environment to increase support, such as propping open a door for a student who uses a wheelchair or providing shoes that do not require tying for a student with limited fine-motor coordination. Environmental support also may be promoted by increasing community awareness and interagency collaboration and by increasing access to services and resources.

Strategies in the transition support model designed to increase environmental support relate to (a) conducting environmental surveys and observations, (b) communicating environmental support needs, (c) developing environmental support plans, (d) gaining access to existing environmental support, and (e) modifying the environment. For example, Renzaglia and Hutchins (1995) recommend conducting a job analysis survey (e.g., Hughes & Carter, 2000) to identify the environmental, task, and social characteristics of a work site (e.g., production rate requirements and customer or coworker presence) and the naturally occurring support within the setting that can promote an employee's success. The Americans with Disabilities Act (ADA) of 1990 (P.L. 101-336) and the Job Accommodation Network (JAN) provide guidelines for environmental modifications that can be used to support an employee's independence and acceptance on the job, such as a jig or counting box when packaging items such as cereal boxes or compact discs.

Increasing Social Support. As students advance through high school and approach graduation, opportunities increase for finding jobs, participating in community events, living away from home, and forming new relationships. As students approach these new transitions and challenges, the amount of social support they receive can influence the degree of success and satisfaction they experience. Social support is manifested in a variety of ways. For example, students may need assistance learning a new job or hobby, obtaining transportation, meeting new people, managing time, finding housing, or solving personal or social problems. In addition, the intensity of social support needed differs from person to person, from task to task, and over time (Thompson et al., 2002). Sometimes a person needs only an occasional reminder and, on other occasions, ongoing assistance or encouragement.

Strategies that teachers can use to identify social support in a setting and match it to a student's needs are similar to those used to identify environmental support. First, it is necessary to visit, observe, and analyze the social demands and available social supports within an environment as well as communicate a student's needs for support and collaborate with important others. Social support may come from a variety of sources, such as a store clerk or someone who waits at the same bus stop to go to work. Sometimes students must learn skills to gain access to social support that exists in an environment; at other times, peers or coworkers must learn to communicate with or offer assistance to a student. Types of strategies teachers can use to increase social support include (a) conducting site visits and observations, (b) communicating social support needs, (c) developing social support plans, and (d) gaining access to existing social support. When support needs are identified and a support plan has been developed, "natural supports," such as coworkers on the job or classmates at school (see Chapter 11), can assist students in a variety of ways (e.g., befriending, advocating, instructing). For example, students with intellectual disabilities increased their engagement in recreational activities in their physical education classes when they interacted with their general education classmates (Hughes et al., 2004). Similarly, the social interactions of employees with disabilities increased at their work site when coworkers taught them new job tasks (Storey & Garff, 1999).

Increasing Students' Competence

The second main goal of the transition support model is increasing students' competence. Although is it critical to modify environments to make them more supportive, it is equally important to increase students' individual competence. When people are viewed as competent, they are more readily accepted into an environment. Being competent also allows people to access a range of benefits, such as job advancement, educational opportunities, and social activities. Competence is judged within the context of an environment and must be promoted, supported, and accepted within that environment (Hughes & Carter, 2000).

Strategies that comprise Goal 2 of our model address students' competence within their everyday environments and skills needed to support and maintain that competence. These strategies are arranged in four major categories: (a) identifying and promoting students' strengths, (b) increasing students' self-determination, (c) increasing students' choice and decision making, and (d) promoting students' social interaction. Each of these categories are further discussed below.

Identifying and Promoting Students' Strengths. Everyone has strengths in various areas: academics, sports, leadership, social relationships, or job performance. The 2004 IDEA Amendments stress that students' individualized education programs (IEPs) emphasize their strengths rather than weaknesses. The move from deficit-based educational programming reflects the belief that all students can and should be maximally included in school, work, and community environments. As active participants in inclusive environments and provided with social and environmental supports, students gain opportunities to expand their competence.

A first step in building students' competence is to identify their individual strengths and the areas in which they need support. Teachers start by observing students' involvement in a variety of activities and settings and systematically recording and evaluating their observations. It is critical to observe students across many different settings because strengths and needs vary according to environmental demands. Teachers also can collaborate with family members, community members, peers, and coworkers, or use assessments other than direct observation to gain additional information on students' strengths and needs. These skills then can be targeted for instructional support.

Types of strategies teachers can use to promote students' strengths include (a) observing performance and collecting data, (b) assessing students' strengths and needs, (c) communicating students' strengths and needs, and (d) teaching skills that need strengthening. For example, Taber, Alberto, Hughes, and Seltzer (2002) observed that students receiving community-based instruction were unable to seek assistance when they could not find their way in the community. Subsequently, the students were taught to use cell phones to call their teachers if lost, thereby increasing the students' independence outside their classroom settings. Similarly, McDonnell, Johnson, Polychronis, and Riesen (2002) taught students with limited sight word recognition to read words aloud that were used frequently in their general education classes.

Increasing Students' Self-Determination. The current focus on self-determination dates to the normalization movement of the 1970s (Nirje, 1972), which argues that important others must promote, respect, and take into account a person's choices, preferences, and aspirations. Skills that promote self-determination include self-management, self-advocacy, choice making, problem solving, decision making, and goal setting.

The 2004 IDEA Amendments and Rehabilitation Act Amendments of 1992 (P.L. 102-569) require that self-determination and individual choice and preference be incorporated into educational and rehabilitation programs. Self-determination requires a change in the thinking and behavior of teachers and others who serve students with disabilities. In the past, teachers often were taught to speak and make major life decisions for students. However, numerous studies have shown that even students with severe disabilities can learn to make decisions, solve problems, and advocate for themselves (e.g., Hughes, Hugo, & Blatt, 1996; Test et al., 2004; Wehmeyer & Palmer, 2003). Teachers and colleagues are learning to provide support so that students can manage their daily lives, be responsible for their own behavior, make decisions, and act on these decisions.

Types of strategies that can be used to increase students' self-determination skills include (a) promoting students' self-determination, (b) teaching self-management and self-determination skills, and (c) incorporating self-determination into daily living. For example, Gilbert, Agran, Hughes, and Wehmeyer (2001) taught students with intellectual disabilities to use self-monitoring to improve their performance of classroom survival skills in their general education classes. Mason, McGahee-Kovac, Johnson, and Stillerman (2002) taught students to increase their involvement in their IEP meetings and to state the purpose of their IEP and their disability rights.

Increasing Students' Choice and Decision Making. The IDEA Amendments of 2004 require that students' preferences, choices, and interests as well as considerations of their cultural diversity be incorporated into their IEPs. However, transition-age students often have little opportunity to make choices and decisions for themselves (Hughes, Pitkin, & Lorden, 1998; Wehmeyer, Agran, & Hughes, 2000). For example, students may have limited opportunity to provide input into developing their own educational goals or they may be placed in a career track that is not of their own choosing. Unfortunately, limited opportunity to choose often continues into adulthood. Too often, choices about everyday living, such as what to wear or eat, how to spend free time, or where to live or work are made by parents, teachers, or service providers, especially for students with more severe disabilities. Learning to make good choices and wise decisions takes practice, sometimes by learning from one's mistakes. Without opportunities to make choices and decisions throughout the day, students may not learn choice and decision-making skills.

Not only is including choice and decision making in a student's educational program a legislative mandate, it also has the potential benefit of expanding students' experiences, learning opportunities, and skill repertoires in their everyday lives. For example, a student may choose to take a Spanish class in order to learn a new language or learn to ride the bus so she can go downtown by herself. Teachers can learn to expand students' opportunities to choose and make decisions throughout the school day.

Effective strategies for increasing students' choice and decision making include (a) identifying students' opportunities for choice and decision making, (b) collaborating with others to increase students' choice and decision making, and (c) teaching and increasing students' choice- and decision-making skills. For example, Parsons, Reid, Reynolds, and Bumgarner (1990) taught individuals with intellectual disabilities to choose job tasks by pointing to tasks materials or stating the task. Similarly, Bambara and Ager (1992) taught adults with developmental disabilities to "self-schedule" by choosing the order in which they engaged in leisure activities throughout the day in their home and community settings.

Promoting Students' Social Interaction. We live in a social world—most activities we engage in involve interacting with others. Part of having satisfying social interactions depends on the social skills a student brings to a situation. If students are perceived as lacking social skills, they may be less accepted by their peers at school, on the job, or in the community. Because so much importance is placed on social skills, failure to meet social expectations within an environment may lead to isolation and feelings of loneliness for a student. When students perform expected social skills, however, such as greeting others or starting conversations about topics of common interest, they are more likely to be accepted by their peers and others in an environment.

Sometimes, students with diverse abilities have had little opportunity to interact with their peers either in or out of school. Teachers can collaborate with others to increase opportunities for social interaction, such as suggesting that a student ride home from work with a coworker. Or teachers can modify a setting or curriculum to promote social interaction, such as having students work in small cooperative learning groups. "Peer buddies" or coworkers can help support students to fit in socially—such as learning to share a snack or conversation at break or lunch—as they begin to increase their involvement with their peers. Teachers also can teach social interactions skills directly through such activities as role playing, problem solving, and peer involvement.

Strategies to promoting students' social interaction include (a) increasing students' social interactions in general education classes and activities, (b) promoting peer involvement, (c) increasing opportunities for social interaction, and (d) teaching social interaction skills. For example, Hughes and Carter (2006) and colleagues developed a districtwide peer buddy program in which general education peers receive class credit for interacting with and supporting their special education peers in inclusive settings. Peer buddies also have taught students with intellectual disabilities to use communication booklets to increase their conversational turn taking with general education classmates (Hughes et al., 2000).

APPLICATION OF THE TRANSITION SUPPORT MODEL

With a Little Help from My Friends

Jerome Baxter had been looking forward to his support team meeting all week. This was his sophomore year at McClintock High, and already he had had three support team meetings just this year. What Jerome really liked about the meetings was that he was the one who got to do a lot of the talking. Mr. Blackstone, his special education teacher, and Jerome had been practicing what he was going to say. First, he would introduce himself and the members of his support team—even his mom and dad. Because he couldn't say all their names (or remember them, for that matter), each team member would sit where his or her name tag was displayed at the table. Then, when Jerome pointed to the members, they would hold up their name tag (with their picture and their name) and say their name. Jerome would even hold up his own name tag to introduce himself. Next, Jerome would present the support goals that he and the team had developed and had been working on this quarter (see Jerome's Transition Support Plan in Table 12.2). Jerome and Mr. Blackstone had been looking at each one, deciding if it had been met or needed to be adjusted. When Jerome presented the goals at the meeting, he would hold up a card describing each goal in words and pictures. First, he would talk about his progress toward the goal, and then he would give everyone else a turn to give their input.

The goal Jerome was really excited to talk about was "Jerome will develop friendships in his classes and at work." When Jerome first started going into general education classes and to his community job sites last year, it was true that he didn't feel like he had any friends. Those were not very happy days for Jerome—he felt like all he would do was sit by himself while everyone around him seemed to be talking to each other and having a good time. But now, Adam, Scott, and Ricardo helped him get from class to class, helped him do his work when they were in the same class, hung out with him in class and around school, and introduced him to their friends. Sometimes, they even did things after

TABLE 12.2 *Jerome's Transition Support Plan*

Support strategy	Goal	Action steps
Develop support in the environment		
Promote social acceptance	Jerome will be accepted as an equal participant in school and the community.	• Mr. Blackstone will observe and assess the extent to which Jerome is accepted in his classes and other school settings as well as in his community placements. • Mr. Blackstone will model including Jerome as an equal participant, as needed. • Mr. Blackstone will provide disability awareness information as needed.
Increase environmental support	Jerome will learn to use exit signs and other markers to find his way.	• Adam, Scott, and Ricardo (Jerome's peer buddies) will help Jerome use signs and markers to find his way around school and the community. • The peer buddies will fade their assistance as Jerome learns to find his way independently across different settings.
Increase social support	Jerome will develop friendships in his classes and at work.	• Adam, Scott, and Ricardo will help Jerome get to his classes, do his work in class, and will befriend him in class. They also will attend school, extracurricular, and outside school events together. • Mr. Owens will help Jerome set up and clean tables at Marcino's Ice Cream Parlor. He will also take Jerome to the break room at break time and help him get to know and interact with his coworkers.
Increase student's competence		
Identify and promote student's strengths	Jerome will learn to ride the city bus downtown to shop by himself.	• Mr. Blackstone will provide Jerome with a color-coded bus schedule and a map with pictures of destinations and transfer stations. • Jerome's brother Matt will accompany Jerome on his bus routes, decreasing his instructional assistance until Jerome can ride independently without getting lost.
Increase student's self-determination	Jerome will identify and communicate his support goals.	• Jerome will complete a goal-setting and evaluation sheet with his parents and Mr. Blackstone on a quarterly basis throughout the school year. • Jerome will role-play communicating his support goals with Mr. Blackstone using picture cards to present his goals at his support team meetings.
Increase student's choice and decision making	Jerome will sample 3–5 different jobs during his sophomore year and express his preferences.	• Mr. Blackstone will arrange a variety of community jobs for Jerome during the year that require different job skills. • Using a pictorial job preference assessment, Mr. Blackstone will assist Jerome in evaluating his job experiences and expressing his preferences.
Promote student's social interaction	Jerome will increase his social interaction skills.	• Jerome will interact socially with his peer buddies Adam, Scott, and Ricardo on a daily basis. They will introduce Jerome to their friends and promote interactions among them. • Jerome's peer buddies will assist him in using his communication book in his classes, the lunchroom, and during extracurricular activities. The peer buddies will also help Jerome learn to say new words.

school or on the weekends together—like going to the mall or the movies, watching McClintock's basketball games, or playing soccer. Last time, Jerome got to play goalkeeper and even made a "save" by catching the ball before it went through the goal posts. At his community job site at Marcino's Ice Cream Parlor, Mr. Owens was helping Jerome set up and clean the tables. He even took Jerome to the break room when it was time, where they liked to sit around and joke with the other employees. Jerome also had been working on the goal "Jerome will sample 3–5 different jobs during his sophomore year and express his preferences," and together he and Mr. Blackstone had decided that he would switch to an office job next semester. Jerome would miss Marcino's, but he liked trying different jobs so that he could decide which one he liked best by the time he was ready to leave high school.

Jerome had been practicing communicating all his other support goals too, and he knew he could do a good job at his support team meeting. He was excited about sharing his progress and hearing what the team members had to say. Jerome was also looking forward to presenting a new goal that he and Mr. Blackstone had been developing together: "Taking the bus downtown alone." Getting a ride with Mom was OK, but Jerome really thought he was ready to go on his own. He loved going to Escapade Music to look for used CDs and posters, but going with his mom just wasn't that "cool." Learning to transfer buses all by himself was Jerome's next big support goal. For a while he would have to go with his older brother to learn the route, but Jerome knew that, with a little support in the beginning, he would be ready to go to Escapade all on his own really soon.

As shown above, a transition support plan is developed as a team consisting of a student's teachers, parents, important others, and the student himself or herself. Even a student with limited verbal skills like Jerome should play an active role in developing the support plan and participating in and conducting a support team meeting. Prior to the actual meeting, students should have ample opportunity to rehearse, with corrective feedback, their participatory role. Support team meetings should be called as frequently as needed on a case-by-case basis to adequately address students' ever-changing needs, preferences, and interests. Progress on the student's support goals should be evaluated at the meeting and goals should be adjusted, dropped, or added, as needed. Support personnel and resources should be specified. If desired, a means of evaluating progress on support goals and a target date for goal achievement can be included. Finally, support goals and strategies included in a transition support plan should address the two overarching goals of the model: (a) developing support in the environment and (b) increasing students' competence.

Summary

Our interactive research-to-practice process produced a model of transition support that emphasizes supportive environments, social acceptance, social support, individual competence, self-determination, and choice and decision making.

The model is consistent with the 2004 IDEA Amendments and their requirement for transition services and supports that (a) are results oriented; (b) address inclusion in everyday life and access to general education and the community; and (c) take into account an individual student's strengths, preferences, and interests. The strategies that comprise the model are evidence based, practitioner approved, and teacher tested. Further, they address the student and small-group level of social engagement and interaction—the sphere over which an individual teacher has the most influence—as opposed to the larger group or community level (Bronfenbrenner, 1977). An array of almost 600 applications of empirically sound strategies that transition teachers actually use comprise the model and are available in a user-friendly fashion in *The Transition Handbook* (Hughes & Carter, 2000). This teacher resource represents the culmination of the research-to-practice model by making shared, empirically sound, and practitioner-validated information readily available to the practice community, as suggested by Malouf and Schiller (1995).

Finally, the recommended support strategies and practices can be applied with students on an individual basis based on their strengths, needs, interests, and preferences. For example, a student's "problem" may be that, although she is performing well in her general education classes, she is not accepted socially by her classmates because she speaks in a high-pitched tone and repeats topics frequently. To address this a teacher can consult strategies that specifically address "promoting social acceptance" in the transition support model, such as stressing students' strengths or providing disability-specific information, and apply them. In addition, the student and her support team may decide that the student can benefit from learning new social interaction skills, which may increase her acceptability among her classmates. In this case, the teacher can consult strategies that address "teaching social interaction skills," such as role-playing or having peers teach social skills, and apply them with the student.

By using the transition support model and the *Handbook*, teachers can be assured that the practices they are applying are not only evidence based but also have been used by actual transition teachers in their own classrooms and community-based settings to improve their students' transition from school to adult life. Widespread application of proven transition support practices, such as recommended in this model, in conjunction with adult and community services, should result in improved postschool outcomes for students with disabilities.

Study Questions

1. Identify the four critical components of promoting social acceptance for a student with a disability and provide an example of each.

    The four critical components include communicating an attitude of social acceptance, providing diversity awareness experiences, teaching skills that promote acceptance, and increasing the student's participation in social activities.

2. When developing an IEP, what strategies could be used to increase the environmental support for a student with disabilities? Identify those who would implement these strategies.

   Strategies would include conducting environmental surveys and observations (conducted by the teacher, job coach, peer, family member, coworker, and important others); communicating environmental support needs (by the student, teacher, job coach, peer, family member, and important others); developing environmental support plans (by the student, teacher, transition support team); gaining access to existing environmental support (by the student, those who share the environment with the student); and modifying the environment (by the job coach, teacher, coworker, and others who share the environment).

3. What strategies should be considered when developing an action plan for a student with a disability to increase social support in the community?

   Conduct site visits and observations, communicate social support needs, develop a social support plan, and gain access to existing social support in order to increase the student's social support in the community.

4. Discuss ways a teacher could identify and promote a student's strengths.

   The teacher should observe performance and collect data, assess the student's strengths and needs, communicate student's strengths and needs, and teach skills that need strengthening.

5. Why is it important for students to increase their self-determination as part of their transition?

   Increasing their self-determination helps students manage their daily lives, be responsible for their own behavior, make (and act on) their decisions, learn from their mistakes, and advocate for themselves.

6. What are ways in which a teacher could use the environment to increase student choices and decision making?

   The teacher could identify opportunities for a student to make choices and decisions, identify opportunities to collaborate with others to increase choice-making opportunities, and teach decision-making skills in the environment in which they will be used.

7. What factors should be considered in formulating goal statements to promote students' social interaction in their environment?

   Goal statements should address factors increasing social interaction, promoting peer involvement, increasing opportunities for interaction, and teaching social interaction skills.

8. Identify and explain the two overarching goals that comprise the transition support model.

   The first overarching goal is to provide support in the environment, which includes strategies such as communicating an attitude of acceptance, providing diversity awareness experiences, teaching skills that promote social acceptance, increasing students' participation in social activities, conducting environmental surveys and observations, communicating environmental support needs, developing environmental support plans, gaining access to existing environmental support, modifying the environment, conducting site visits and observations, communicating social support needs, developing social support plans, and gaining access to existing social support.

   The second goal is to increase student competence, which includes strategies such as observing performance and collecting data, assessing students' strengths and needs, communicating students' strengths and needs, teaching skills that need strengthening, promoting students' self-determination, teaching self-management and self-determination skills, incorporating self-determination into daily living, identifying students' opportunities for choice and decision making, collaborating to increase students' choice and decision making, teaching and increasing students' choice and decision making, increasing students' social interactions, promoting peer involvement, increasing opportunities for social interaction, and teaching social interaction skills.

9. Explain the benefits students can acquire from learning to participate equally in their environment.

   Through equal participation, students can find opportunities to increase overall skills, make new friendships, attain personal satisfaction and social acceptance, and have an improved quality of life.

10. Identify effective practices that promote students' success in their transition from school to adult life.

    Effective practices include community-based instruction (CBI), career-related experiences, students' participation in IEP development and planning, parent involvement, access to postsecondary education opportunities, participation in vocational education, promoting of self-determination skills, and community follow-up services.

Recommended Reading

Bauer, A. M., & Brown, G. M. (2001). *Adolescents and inclusion: Transforming secondary schools.* Baltimore: Brookes.

Hughes, C., & Carter, E. W. (2000). *The transition handbook: Strategies high school teachers use that work!* Baltimore: Brookes.

Hughes, C., & Carter, E. W. (2006). *Success for all students: Promoting inclusion in secondary schools through peer buddy programs*. Boston: Allyn & Bacon.

Janney, R., & Snell, M. (2000). *Modifying schoolwork*. Baltimore: Brookes.

Wehmeyer, M. L., Agran, M., & Hughes, C. (1998). *Teaching self-determination to students with disabilities: Basic skills for successful transition*. Baltimore: Brookes.

Web Resources

Supporting Students in the Transition from School to Adult Life

American Association on Intellectual and Development Disabilities (AAIDD)

http://www.aamr.org

AAIDD (formerly the American Association on Mental Retardation [AAMR]) promotes progressive policies, sound research, effective practices, and universal human rights for people with intellectual and developmental disabilities.

Association for Supervision and Curriculum Development (ASCD)

http://www.ascd.org

ASCD is a community of educators advocating sound policies and sharing best practices to achieve the success of each learner.

Best Buddies

http://www.bestbuddies.org

Best Buddies is a nonprofit 501(c)(3) organization dedicated to enhancing the lives of people with intellectual disabilities by providing opportunities for one-to-one friendships and integrated employment.

National Center on Secondary Education and Transition (NCSET)

http://www.ncset.org

NCSET coordinates national resources, offers technical assistance, and disseminates information related to secondary education and transition for youth with disabilities in order to create opportunities for youth to achieve successful futures.

The Association for Persons with Severe Handicaps (TASH)

http://www.tash.org

TASH believes that no one with a disability should be forced to live, work, or learn in a segregated setting; that all individuals deserve the right to direct their own lives. TASH's mission is to eliminate physical and social obstacles that prevent equity, diversity, and quality of life.

References

Americans with Disabilities Act (ADA) of 1990, Pub. L. No. 101-336, 42 U.S.C. §§ 12101 et seq.

Baer, R. M., Flexer, R. W., Beck, S., Amstutz, N., Hoffman, L., Brothers, J., et al. (2003). Collaborative followup study on transition service utilization and post-school outcomes. *Career Development for Exceptional Individuals, 26,* 5–27.

Bambara, L. M., & Ager, C. (1992). Using self-scheduling to promote self-directed leisure activity in home and community settings. *Journal of the Association for Persons with Severe Handicaps, 17,* 67–76.

Benz, M. R., Lindstrom, L., & Yovanoff, P. (2000). Improving graduation and employment outcomes of students with disabilities: Predictive factors and student perspectives. *Exceptional Children, 66,* 509–529.

Blalock, G., Kochhar-Bryant, C. A., Test, D. W., Kohler, P., White, W., Lehmann, J., et al. (2003).

The need for comprehensive personnel preparation in transition and career development: A position statement of the division and career development and transition. *Career Development for Exceptional Individuals, 26,* 207–226.

Bronfenbrenner, U. (1977). Toward an experimental ecology of human development. *American Psychologist, 32,* 513–531.

Certo, N. J., Mautz, D., Pumpian, I., Caren, S., Smalley, K., Wade, H. A., et al. (2003). Review and discussion of a model for seamless transition to adulthood. *Education and Training in Developmental Disabilities, 38,* 3–17.

Cooney, B. F. (2002). Exploring perspectives on transition of youth with disabilities: Voices of young adults, parents, and professionals. *Mental Retardation, 6,* 425–435.

Gaumer, A. S., Morningstar, M. E., & Clark, G. M. (2004). Status of community-based transition programs: A national database. *Career Development for Exceptional Individuals, 27,* 131–149.

Gilbert, G. H., Agran, M., Hughes, C., & Wehmeyer, M. (2001). The effects of peer delivered self-monitoring strategies on the participation of students with severe disabilities in general education classrooms. *Journal of the Association for Persons with Severe Handicaps, 26,* 25–36.

Halpern, A. (1985). Transition: A look at the foundations. *Exceptional Children, 57,* 479–486.

Halpern, A. (1992). Transition: Old wine in new bottles. *Exceptional Children, 58,* 202–211.

Hasazi, S. B., Furney, K. S., & DeStefano, L. (1999). Implementing the IDEA transition mandates. *Exceptional Children, 65,* 555–566.

Hughes, C., & Carter, E. W. (2000). *The transition handbook: Strategies high school teachers use that work!* Baltimore: Brookes.

Hughes, C., & Carter, E. W. (2006). *Success for all students: Promoting inclusion in secondary schools through peer buddy programs.* Boston: Allyn & Bacon.

Hughes, C., Fowler, S. E., Copeland, S. R., Agran, M., Wehmeyer, M. L., & Church-Pupke, P. P. (2004). Supporting high school students to engage in recreational activities with peers. *Behavior Modification, 28,* 3–27.

Hughes, C., Hugo, K., & Blatt, J. (1996). A self-instructional model for teaching generalized problem solving within a functional task sequence. *American Journal on Mental Retardation, 100,* 565–579.

Hughes, C., Hwang, B., Kim, J., Killian, D. J., Harmer, M. L., & Alcantara, P. R. (1997). A preliminary validation of strategies that support the transition from school to adult life. *Career Development for Exceptional Individuals, 20,* 1–14.

Hughes, C., Kim, J., Hwang, B., Killian, D. J., Fisher, G. M., Brock, M. L., et al. (1997). Practitioner-validated secondary transition support strategies. *Education and Training in Mental Retardation and Development Disabilities, 32,* 201–212.

Hughes, C., Pitkin, S. E., & Lorden, S. W. (1998). Assessing preferences and choices of persons with severe and profound mental retardation. *Education and Training in Mental Retardation and Development Disabilities, 33,* 299–316.

Hughes, C., Rung, L. L., Wehmeyer, M. L., Agran, M., Copeland, S. R., & Hwang, B. (2000). Self-prompted communication book use to increase social interaction among high school students. *Journal of the Association for Persons with Severe Handicaps, 25,* 153–166.

Individuals with Disabilities Education Act (IDEA) Amendments of 1997, Pub. L. No. 105-17, 20 U.S.C. §§ 1400 *et seq.*

Individuals with Disabilities Education Act (IDEA) of 1990, Pub. L. No. 101-476, 20 U.S.C. §§ 1400 *et seq.*

Individuals with Disabilities Education Improvement Act (IDEA) of 2004, Pub. L. No. 108-446, 20 U.S.C. §§ 1400 *et seq.*

Johnson, D. R. (2004). Supported employment trends: Implications for transition-age youth. *Research and Practice for Persons with Severe Disabilities, 29,* 243–247.

Johnson, D. R., Stodden, R. A., Emanuel, E. J., Luecking, R., & Mack, M. (2002). Current challenges facing secondary education and transition services: What research tells us. *Exceptional Children, 68,* 519–531.

Levison, L., & St. Onge, I. (2001). *Disability awareness in the classroom: A resource tool for teachers and students.* Springfield, IL: Charles C Thomas.

Lieberman, A. (1995). Practices that support teacher development: Transforming conceptions of professional learning. *Phi Delta Kappan, 76,* 591–596.

Malouf, D. B., & Schiller, E. P. (1995). Practice and research in special education. *Exceptional Children, 61,* 414–424.

Mason, C., McGahee-Kovac, M., Johnson, L., & Stillerman, S. (2002). Implementing student-led IEPs: Student participation and student and teacher reactions. *Career Development for Exceptional Individuals, 25,* 171–192.

McDonnell, J., Johnson, J. W., Polychronis, S., & Riesen, T. (2002). Effects of embedded instruction on students with moderate disabilities enrolled in general education classes. *Education and Training in Mental Retardation and Development Disabilities, 37,* 363–377.

Morrison, L., Kamps, D., Garcia, J., & Parker, D. (2001). Peer mediation and monitoring strategies to improve initiations and social skills for students with autism. *Journal of Positive Behavior Interventions, 3,* 237–250.

Murray, C. (2003). Risk factors, protective factors, vulnerability, and resilience: A framework for understanding and supporting the adult transitions of youth with high incidence disabilities. *Remedial and Special Education, 24,* 16–26.

National Organization on Disability. (2004). *2004 N.O.D./Harris survey of Americans with disabilities.* Washington, DC: Louis Harris & Associates.

Nirje, B. (1972). The right to self-determination. In W. Wolfensberger (Ed.), *Normalization: The principle of normalization* (pp. 176–200). Toronto, Ontario, Canada: National Institute on Mental Retardation.

No Child Left Behind Act of 2001, Pub. L. No. 107-110, 115 Stat. 1425 (2002).

Palmer, S. B., Wehmeyer, M. L., Gipson, K., & Agran, M. (2004). Promoting access to the general curriculum by teaching self-determination skills. *Exceptional Children, 70,* 427–439.

Parsons, M. B., Reid, D. H., Reynolds, J., & Bumgarner, M. (1990). Effects of chosen versus assigned on the work performance of persons with severe handicaps. *Journal of Applied Behavior Analysis, 23,* 253–258.

Rehabilitation Act Amendments of 1992, Pub. L. No. 102-569, 29 U.S.C. §§ 701 *et seq.*

Renzaglia, A., & Hutchins, M. (1995). Materials developed for *A model for longitudinal vocational programming for students with moderate and severe disabilities.* Washington DC: U.S. Department of Education, Office of Special Education and Rehabilitation Services.

Rusch, F. R., & Braddock, D. (2004). Adult day programs versus supported employment (1988–2002): Spending and service practices of mental retardation and developmental disabilities state agencies. *Research and Practice for Persons with Severe Disabilities, 29,* 237–242.

Rusch, F. R., & Phelps, L. A. (1987). Secondary special education and transition from school to work: A national priority. *Exceptional Children, 53,* 487–492.

School-to-Work Opportunities Act of 1994, Pub. L. No. 103-239, 20 U.S.C. §§ 6101 *et seq.*

Storey, K., & Garff, J. T. (1999). The effect of coworker instruction on the integration of youth in transition in competitive employment. *Career Development for Exceptional Individuals, 22,* 69–84.

Swanson, C. B. (2003). *Who graduates? Who doesn't? A statistical portrait of public high school graduation, class of 2001.* Washington, DC: The Urban Institute.

Taber, T. A., Alberto, P. A., Hughes, M., & Seltzer, A. (2002). A strategy for students with moderate disabilities when lost in the community. *Research and Practice for Persons with Severe Disabilities, 27,* 141–152.

Test, D. W., Mason, C., Hughes, C., Konrad, M., Neale, M., & Wood, W. M. (2004). Student involvement in individualized education program meetings. *Exceptional Children, 70,* 391–412.

Thompson, J. R., Hughes, C., Schalock, R. L., Silverman, W., Tasse, M. J., Bryant, B., et al. (2002). Integrating supports in assessment and planning. *Mental Retardation, 40,* 390–405.

U.S. Department of Education. (2002). *Twenty-fourth annual report to Congress on the implementation of the Individuals with Disabilities Education Act.* Washington, DC: Author.

U.S. Department of Labor. (2004). *Education pays.* Retrieved June 13, 2005, from http://www.bls.gov/emp/emptab7.htm

Wagner, M., Cameto, R., & Newman, L. (2003). *Youth with disabilities: A changing population: A report of findings from the National Longitudinal Transition Study (NLTS) and the National Longitudinal Study–2 (NLTS2).* Menlo Park, CA: SRI International.

Wagner, M., Newman, L., Cameto, R., Garza, N., & Levine, P. (2005). *After high school: A first look at the postschool experiences of youth with disabilities. A report from the National Longitudinal Study–2 (NLTS2).* Menlo Park, CA: SRI International.

Wehman, P. (2000). Foreword. In C. Hughes & E. W. Carter, *The transition handbook: Strategies high school teachers use that work!* (pp. xiii–xv). Baltimore: Brookes.

Wehmeyer, M., & Palmer, S. B. (2003). Adult outcomes for students with cognitive disabilities three years after high school: The impact of self-determination. *Education and Training in Developmental Disabilities, 38,* 131–144.

Wehmeyer, M. L., Agran, M., & Hughes, C. (2000). A national survey of teachers' promotion of self-determination and student-directed learning. *Journal of Special Education, 34,* 58–68.

Will, M. (1984). *Bridges from school to working life: OSERS programming for the transition of youth with disabilities.* Washington, DC: U.S. Department of Education, Office of Special Education and Rehabilitative Services.

CHAPTER 13

Dropout Prevention: Using Self-Determination to Achieve Desired Postschool Outcomes

Thomas Holub
Edgewood College
and
Frank R. Rusch
Pennsylvania State University

Ensuring the successful achievement of all students as they progress through the education system from early childhood into adulthood is a challenge. Statistics show that this task becomes even harder when working with children and youth with disabilities (Good & Weinstein, 1986). The efforts of multiple participants must be aligned with the specialized needs of these students as they move from one educational level to another, working toward the ultimate goals of succeeding in the workplace and becoming independent adults. In order to achieve these goals, educators must strengthen collaborative structures at each stage of the learning process, at all educational levels.

As mentioned in Chapter 1, fewer students with disabilities graduate from high school than students without disabilities. Often the problem is even more significant in our nation's larger cities. Consistently defining "who" the dropout population is has been a struggle. There is no common definition of the term and the data gathered cannot be effectively aggregated because different methods are typically used to report separating from high school. This chapter provides a brief review of statistics related to dropping out of high school and the consequences typically associated with dropping out. The primary focus of this chapter is to introduce the pathways to self-determination model—a five-phase model that addresses youth retention in the early teens, before the majority of youth with disabilities separate from high school.

Current labor market data reveal continued rising concern for youth with disabilities involved in the transition process (Wagner, 1990; Wagner & Blackorby, 1996). Transition from school to work is hindered by barriers associated with disability and access to the world beyond high school (DeBettencourt, Zigmond, & Thornton, 1989; Mithaug, Horiuchi, & Fanning, 1985; Neel, Meadows, Levine, & Edgar, 1988; Wagner, 1990, 2001). These youth continue to experience high rates of unemployment or underemployment, too often fail to receive a high school diploma, have difficulties in independent living, and lack the social and vocational skills needed to hold jobs (Chadsey-Rusch, Rusch, & O'Reilly, 1991). Compared to same-age youths without disabilities, school leavers with disabilities have higher levels of unemployment and significantly lower than average high school completion rates (Sitlington & Frank, 1990; Thornton & Zigmond, 1988). In addition, youth with disabilities are generally employed in low-skilled occupations and industries that provide limited social status and quality-of-life satisfaction (White, 1992). Whereas 56% of similar-age students without disabilities go on to postsecondary educational institutions, only 15% of youth with disabilities attend postsecondary institutions (Wagner, 1990; White, 1992).

Dropping Out of High School

Research on dropouts has primarily focused on the general education student population. Studies of the high school completion rates of students with disabilities are scarce, but it is clear that the special education dropout problem is significant compared with the overall general population dropout rate (see chapter 1). Additionally, there is research to suggest that the rate of dropping out is higher for certain categories of students with disabilities than for the general student population (Blackorby & Wagner, 1996; Jay & Padilla, 1987; MacMillan, 1991; Zigmond & Thornton, 1995). There is evidence to suggest that the negative consequences (e.g., unemployment, loss of opportunity for postsecondary schooling, and lack of engagement in productive activities after high school) of dropping out of high school may be more significant for youth with disabilities (Padilla & Jay, 1990).

The dropout rate among high school youth in the general population is about 25%. By comparison, the dropout rate for students with disabilities is about 32% (Wagner, 1990). These rates are higher for both groups when counting only youth between the ages of 15 and 20. In this age range, youth in the general population drop out at a rate of 32%, whereas youth with disabilities drop out at a rate of 43% (Wagner, 1990).

According to the U.S. Department of Education's Office of Special Education Programs (OSEP), 229,368 students with disabilities exited high school during the 1991–1992 school year. Of these, 100,742 (43.9%) graduated with a diploma, 30,839 (13.5%) received a certificate, and 4,337 (1.9%) reached maximum age for staying in school (Grayson, 1998). It is important to note that OSEP requests states to report only students who formally withdraw from school without completing their educational program to be counted as dropouts. This is a reporting problem that has plagued statisticians for decades, in that many more youth are known to "stop out" without formally withdrawing. This means that a student who simply stops attending school but fails to formally withdraw is not counted as a dropout. Such students are counted by OSEP in the "status unknown" category, which simply means the student left school for other reasons. It is relatively safe to assume that many of these students are dropouts who did not inform anyone in the school district that they were dropping out.

During the 1991–1992 school year 51,489 students (22.4%) dropped out of school. An additional 41,961 (18.3%) exited school for other unknown reasons. Given these rates, and recalling that research tells us that the unemployment rate for individuals with disabilities is somewhere between 50 and 75% (Wehman & Revell, 1996), most of those unemployed individuals are likely the same individuals who have dropped out of school.

Other research suggests even higher special education dropout rates than those reported by OSEP, Holsch, Karen, and Franzinin (1992) and MacMillan and First (1990) reported dropout rates between 25 and 35%; Kortering and Braziel (1992) found the dropout rate to be somewhere between 30 and 40%; and the National

Longitudinal Transition Study (NLTS) of Special Education Students noted that 32% of students with disabilities exit school by dropping out (Wagner, 1990).

MacMillan (1991) found evidence suggesting higher dropout rates for students with mild disabilities, particularly for students with learning disabilities and emotional disturbance. Jay and Padilla (1987) found that students with specific learning disabilities had a higher dropout rate (75% of individuals with specific learning disabilities dropped out of school) than students classified as severely emotionally disturbed, mentally retarded, or multiply disabled, each of whom had a dropout rate of 12%. Wagner (1990) found that students with severe emotional disturbances were significantly more likely to drop out of school than students with other disabilities. In a more pessimistic report, Wagner reported a much higher incidence of incarceration among people who were emotionally disabled. These studies reinforce MacMillan's findings that students from two disability groups (i.e., learning disabilities and emotional disturbances) have a much higher probability of dropping out of school.

Students with singular sensory disabilities are another group who tend to drop out of school at higher rates and who frequently fall through the cracks in transition planning. For example, Allen, Rawlings, and Schildroth (1989) found that about 52% of deaf youth graduated with high school diplomas, whereas 29% dropped out of school. Of these dropouts, none had documented transition plans. Wehman and Revell (1996) surmised that these results are typical and can be anticipated also for students who are blind or have visual impairments.

Dropouts experience higher unemployment rates than their graduating counterparts, and are much more likely to be assigned lower paying jobs in adulthood (Thurlow, Elliott, Ysseldyke, & Erickson, 1996). Numerous secondary transition studies provide data supporting the importance of all stakeholders having a clear understanding of IDEA transition requirements that lead to school success and completion. Promoting student self-determination, which was described in earlier chapters (see Chapters 3 and 4), is regarded as one of the most effective strategies for improving postschool outcomes for students with disabilities (Agran, Blanchard, Wehmeyer, & Hughes, 2001; Hasazi, Furney, & DeStefano, 1999; Johnson, 2000; Williams & O'Leary, 2001). Additional strategies leading to improved chances for high school completion provide the basis for the development of dropout prevention.

Consequences of Not Completing High School

A society of well-educated citizens has always been a national priority. One artifact of such a citizen is the high school diploma. Not holding such a diploma weakens the individual's chances of success in the workplace, access to postsecondary education, and overall life satisfaction.

The Institute for Educational Leadership reported that our society as a whole loses approximately $200 billion each year in lost revenue, welfare, unemployment, and crime prevention due to the lack of high school completion (Thurlow et al., 1996).

Pathways to Self-Determination

Pathways to self-determination is based on a five-phase interactive format, in which the student is the key player. The model encourages student ownership and full participation in all decisions and discussions of transition-related outcomes, and infuses an ecological and comprehensive student assessment process that allows the student to become more self-aware and to apply self-knowledge to achieve desired outcomes, including and focusing on high school completion. The five phases of the model are (a) focus, (b) synthesis, (c) exploration, (d) connection, and (e) evaluation. Together, these phases extend from the time the student first begins to consider transition-related outcomes (e.g., 9th grade or earlier) until the student has exited high school.

The focus of all efforts has been to provide a framework based on empirically driven theoretical work upon which instructional models and strategies may be implemented and curricula, assessment, and environmental modifications may be developed that would promote self-determination. Pathways to self-determination is based on a definitional and theoretical framework foundation that acknowledges the importance of self-determination. Promoting pathways to self-determination will have the dual benefits of enabling students to transition from school to adult life more successfully and ensuring that they will be able to assume the responsibilities of controlling their lives.

Each of the five phases of the pathways model is described in more detail in the following sections.

Focus. During the focus phase students work in small groups or individually with a transition specialist or staff person, concentrating on their aspirations and potential contextual learning opportunities while enrolled in the eighth grade. These lessons help students focus on issues of self-awareness, individual learning styles, individual support networks, and future planning. Students are also involved in student-directed classroom activities that focus on work issues. Additionally, focus phase activities include parent conferences with the transition team, course scheduling for the upcoming school year, visits to the high school campuses, peer mentoring with older high school students, and general information sessions about academic and social high school survival skills.

Synthesis. During the synthesis phase, which occurs while students are enrolled in the 9th and 10th grades, students work independently or on a one-to-one basis with a school staff person to organize information that will help them throughout the transition process. During this phase, students gather and synthesize information about the types of postsecondary education programs in which they might be interested, employment options and various instructional and learning needs they might have in relation to postsecondary education, employment, and community living. A key aspect of the synthesis phase is that each student completes a comprehensive vocational assessment. This assessment, discussed in more detail by

Menchetti (Chapter 8) provides formal and informal indicators of leisure and career interests, work behaviors, medical conditions, functional skills, basic academic skills and needs, life skills, learning styles, social skills, and values clarification. Students receive extensive feedback from school staff regarding the mesh between their goals and their current level of functioning in each of the areas listed. At the end of the synthesis phase each student and his or her parents are provided with a description of the student's strengths and areas needing attention as well as strategies to remove potential barriers. Goals to eliminate these barriers are then developed and implemented. In the synthesis phase of the process, the student is the key figure in goal-setting and decision-making activities.

Exploration. In the exploration phase, students pursue areas of interest identified during the previous phases. The exploration phase takes place while students are enrolled in 9th, 10th, and 11th grades and encompasses a wide array of activities, including checking credits obtained for graduation, scheduling appointments with guidance counselors and in the career/college center in the high school, contacting postsecondary schools of interest, exploring possible living arrangements outside the family home, exploring financial-aid options, considering job shadowing and work-based learning experiences, and so forth. The exploration phase is developed individually for each student based on his or her identified areas of interest.

Connection. In the connection phase, which takes place when students are in the 11th and 12th grades, students are assisted in making formal connections with various postschool institutions and organizations, including scheduling apprenticeship interviews with trade union representatives, attending admissions conferences with community college or university admissions officers, and investigating acceptance criteria to postsecondary vocational education programs. Students involved in the pathways model develop a portfolio before they leave high school containing information on educational assessment data, vocational assessment information, vocational experiences, postsecondary planning, and contact information for community resources and postsecondary education programs. The portfolio becomes a traveling resource guide for students that has practical value after they exit the secondary setting.

Evaluation. The evaluation phase of the program centers around follow-along activities with each student in order to track their successes and emergent concerns. Telephone contacts from the school to program graduates at regular intervals the first 2 years after graduation allow transition specialists from the high school to remain involved with former students and enable them to provide additional information or resources. Table 13.1 provides a list of sample activities that can be used to evaluate the pathways to self-determination model. Each of the sponsored activities can be used to evaluate whether the pathways program was actually implemented.

TABLE 13.1 *Sample Activities for the Five Phases of the Pathways to Self-Determination Model*

Phase	Approximate grade level	Sample activities
Focus	7th and 8th	• high school scheduling • survival skills training • learning styles inventory • academic skills inventory
Synthesis	9th and 10th	• discussions on postsecondary education • discussions of potential employment options • vocational assessment
Exploration	9th through 11th	• credit checks for graduation • job shadowing • visits to postsecondary institutions • contacting apprenticeship programs
Connection	11th and 12th	• apprenticeship interviews • admissions conferences with colleges • conferences with military recruiters • graduation from high school
Evaluation	Post–high school	• telephone contact with student • telephone contact with home • telephone contact with university • face-to-face contact with employer

Illustration of the Pathways Model—Mark

Mark is a bright first-year student in college with a mild learning disability. A year ago when Mark's high school education was coming to an end, his parents were worried whether he would be successful at the postsecondary level. Fortunately, Mark and his parents had been involved in the pathways program since Mark was in the eighth grade and had developed a positive working relationship with the transition specialist. The following chronological case study illustrates how the pathways program was implemented for Mark based on his interests, abilities, needs, and goals for the future.

Focusing on the Future. During the eighth grade, the transition specialist interviewed Mark at his middle school. The initial interview was followed by a series of informal small-group meetings with some of Mark's peers who had similar interests and concerns about high school programs and beyond. The small group generated a list of potential postsecondary goals and plans to reach those goals. Mark's parents were integrally involved in assisting Mark with the decisions he needed to make regarding his high school education. During the middle of Mark's eighth grade year, he selected a high school and made course selections for ninth grade. The remainder of eighth grade was spent preparing Mark and his parents for the academic challenges presented in high school.

Synthesizing Information. During the 9th and 10th grades, Mark and his parents participated in numerous formal and informal vocational assessment strategies. Because Mark had no definite postsecondary plans, it was important that he be provided with assessment activities that would allow him to explore potential options and discuss the positive and negative features of each of those options. Some of the assessment activities selected by Mark and his parents included a situational assessment of learning style, a community-based volunteer job shadowing experience, numerous formal and informal interest inventories, and the State of Wisconsin Gateway Vocational Assessment.

Mark enjoyed his work in the technology education courses he elected to take; however, he also enjoyed writing and wanted to pursue a career in journalism. Based on these two areas of interest, Mark, along with the transition specialist, gathered information about careers in both journalism and technology. By the end of 10th grade, Mark had decided to work toward a career in journalism and to maintain his interest in technology as a hobby.

Exploring and Connecting. In the 11th grade, Mark explored the specifics of several postsecondary schools. Mark determined how far away from home he was willing to move, the admissions requirements of a number of schools, the cost of attending college, including financial-aid possibilities, and the student support services available to students with learning disabilities. Mark and the transition specialist visited four postsecondary schools within Wisconsin, Mark's home state. Mark applied to three of the four schools and was accepted to two.

During 12th grade, Mark chose to attend one of the institutions where he was accepted and worked with the transition specialist and a student support services representative from that campus on developing a list of competencies he would need in order to be successful in college. Mark spent a large part of his senior year learning and refining notetaking, study skills, and testing-taking strategies that would help him be successful in college. He worked with the transition specialist and resource teacher on implementing these strategies in his general education classes.

Evaluating. During the fall and spring semesters of Mark's first year in college, the transition specialist remained in contact with Mark, his parents, and the student support services facilitator at the college through quarterly telephone contracts. Although Mark did not need additional direct services from the transition specialist, ongoing communication was maintained to monitor his progress and provide support. Both Mark and his parents appreciated the involvement and encouragement of the transition specialist.

Mark recently completed his first year at college. He earned a B average and wrote a few short articles for the school paper. Both Mark and his parents realize that there will be problems that will need to be addressed as Mark progresses through college; however, they are all satisfied with his current progress.

Illustration of the Pathways Model—Melissa

Melissa is a student on the 10th-grade Pathways team. She is a friendly, outgoing, and caring young woman. She loves sports and is a member of the volleyball team and an avid skier. She has both a hearing impairment and a learning disability. She started 10th grade very anxious about her academic performance and ability to succeed in high school. She enrolled in two classes that were required for graduation. Her anxiety level escalated and she started talking about dropping out of high school. Her parents felt that she needed the more intense experience of the self-determination class to explore her disabilities as well as her strengths to help her gain more self-confidence in conjunction with an academic environment that would foster her self-advocacy skills and consider her learning needs. Her mom explained it like this: "As Melissa's parents we had been encouraging her to be more assertive about her needs and her beliefs. We felt that a class that would give her time to discuss and reflect on the importance of taking the lead for herself would be an important opportunity for Melissa." Her parents maintained that the main reason she was thinking about dropping out was that she knew she would fail classes, yet did not know how to advocate for herself around disability needs. Eventually she did enroll in the self-determination class and she, her parents, and the staff saw success. Like all of the students, Melissa wrote her self-advocacy plan.

> Dear Teachers,
>
> I have a severe hearing loss. I wear two hearing aids but my hearing is still not normal with them. Almost always I use lip-reading. If I can't see you, I probably won't understand what you are saying. Sometimes I hear the words but I don't know what they mean. My vocabulary is around the fifth-grade level. The vocabulary words are usually the hardest part for me. People need to face me and not cover their mouth when they talk. Also, I can lip-read only one person at a time. Large groups are hard for me. When people talk quickly I miss everything they say.
>
> I must have closed-captioned videos and TV because hearing-impaired persons can't lip-read TV. If you write on the overhead during class that really helps. The closer a person is to me the easier it is for me to lip-read, hear, and understand. If I work in small groups, I like my group to work in a quieter room or a hallway without distractions. Lip-reading and trying to listen and understand takes a lot of concentration. Sometimes I get confused and after a while I don't understand the topic.

Tests are difficult for me, especially essay. It's easier for me when I can tell the person the answer and he or she writes it down for me. I have a hard time putting my thoughts in writing. I seem to do better with multiple-choice tests because I usually recognize the answer. I have trouble memorizing. I also have trouble remembering things that I studied. I can learn something the night before a test, but I may have a hard time calling it back up for the test. I can't take notes, listen, and lip-read a teacher at the same time. I work with a teacher's aide, but feel uncomfortable when she hovers over me. I don't want to look different from the other kids. When I use her, she helps me understand a lot of what I miss during class. I do better on projects and reports than on written tests. I like to learn new things and I'm looking forward to learning in your class. I'm a hard worker and I try my best.

When I gave serious thought to dropping out of high school, it was not because I didn't like school. It was because I did not want to fail in front of my friends. Please help me succeed.

Sincerely,

Melissa

After sharing the plan with her teachers Melissa reported, "The teachers told me my plan was very helpful. It gave them a better idea of how to help me. It helped them learn about hearing impairments." One teacher even said that she never would have guessed that Melissa would consider dropping out of school. "Melissa was such a good girl, never a problem at all. She is the last person I would have listed as in danger of not completing high school," the teacher stated. At the end of the year Melissa summed up her 10th-grade experience this way: "All of my classes helped me believe in myself and what I can do. They helped me stick up for myself."

Melissa's parents played an active role in her educational experience. They wrote a letter to her teachers expressing their perspective on how they might think about their daughter's learning. An excerpt from their letter follows:

Melissa has a desire to learn. It seems that it would be helpful to use the metaphor of a racecar driver and the pit crew. In this story Melissa is the racecar driver and we are all the pit crew. Our racecar driver is determined to make it around the track. Granted, there was one time when she considered pulling off the track, but we, as a team, helped her avoid that devastating swerve. How can we as the pit crew work together with the precision necessary to have our driver reach her goal and cross the finish line not once, but over and over—not so much to be the winner of the race but to finish and finish with pride? The pit crew shares in the driver's victory by having provided every opportunity within reason to contribute to the driver's success. We are proud to have you on Melissa's team.

In the fall of her junior year, Melissa was hired to monitor and maintain the women's locker room at a local athletic club. She was able to transfer her self-determination skills into the work setting. "When the members of the club mumbled and talked softly, I asked them to speak louder. The second time, I told them I had a hearing impairment and would they please speak up." After nearly a year's experience at the job, Melissa has a new goal:

> I really believe that in my job I can learn to work at the front desk. It will be hard because there are a lot of things happening—the phone, people at the desk, messages. I will need to have more training time than other people. The work of self-determination helped me be strong enough to take on the challenge of learning new things. I am ready to try another job.

Summary

The life of a high school dropout typically includes numerous negative postschool outcomes. These outcomes can vary from loneliness to lower earnings. Historically, dropping out of high school has been associated with youth without disabilities; however, youth with disabilities are dropping out of school at rates much higher than the general population. The problems are many and the reasons for dropping out are not very well understood. In this chapter we introduced the pathways to self-determination model that capitalizes on engaging the student at a very early age. The model first focuses on what the student wants in the 7th and 8th grades, then synthesizes skill training and academic engagement through more directed discussions during the 9th and 10th grades. These phases are followed by exploration, connection, and evaluation. Each step requires that the student actually participate in job shadowing, visits to postsecondary institutions, apprenticeship interviews, and eventually post–high school contacts with the student, the family, employers, and university personnel to evaluate overall effectiveness.

Study Questions

1. List and describe some of the characteristics of youth who drop out of high school.

    Reasons typically include, but are not limited to, poverty, race, ethnicity, language, educational attainment (years of schooling completed/highest grade level or degree completed).

2. Comment on some special populations of individuals who may encounter disproportionately negative high school completion rates.

   Two disability groups—those with learning disabilities and those with emotional disturbances—have a much higher probability of dropping out of school. Students with singular sensory disabilities are another group who tend to drop out of school at higher rates and who frequently fall through the cracks in transition planning.

3. Cite some of the reform initiatives and efforts that have been attempted with this disenfranchised population.

   Student self-determination is regarded as the most effective strategy for improving postschool outcomes for students with disabilities.

4. What role does the school-to-work transition process play in promoting high school completion?

   There is evidence to suggest that the negative consequences (e.g., unemployment, loss of opportunity for postsecondary schooling, and lack of engagement in productive activities after high school) of dropping out of high school may be as significant for youth with disabilities as for other youth.

5. Who are the collaborators who should work toward high school completion?

   Family involvement has significant impact on youth outcomes. Reform aimed at self-determination would distribute the responsibility for learning and performance as shared among teachers, parents, and the student, with primary control remaining with the student.

6. Define self-determination.

   Models have been piloted and crafted to enable students to become self-determined, and thus assume greater responsibility for and control over their lives, including successful high school graduation.

7. Why is it important to complete high school?

   Completion of high school is the first step in the transition process from adolescence to adulthood. Without taking this first step, the next steps of finding a job, cultivating relationships, and choosing to raise a family may seem unlikely as the students transition to adult life.

8. What lessons can be gleaned from follow-up and follow-along studies?

   Promoting student-directed approaches clearly leads to greater postschool outcomes, which include but are not limited to employment and access to postsecondary education.

9. What are the five phases of the pathways to self-determination model? Briefly describe them.

Focus: During the *focus* phase students work in small groups or individually with a transition specialist or staff, concentrating on their aspirations and potential contextual learning opportunities while enrolled in the eighth grade.

Synthesis: During the *synthesis* phase, which occurs while students are enrolled in the 9th and 10th grades, students work independently or on a one-to-one basis with a school staff person to organize information that will help them throughout the transition process. During this phase, students gather and synthesize information about the types of postsecondary education programs in which they might be interested, employment options and various instructional and learning needs they might have in relation to postsecondary education, employment, and community living.

Exploration: In the *exploration* phase, students pursue areas of interest identified during the previous phases. The exploration phase takes place while students are enrolled in 9th, 10th, and 11th grades and encompasses a wide array of activities, including checking credits obtained for graduation, scheduling appointments with guidance counselors and in the career/college center in the high school, contacting postsecondary schools of interest, exploring possible living arrangements outside the family home, exploring financial-aid options, considering job shadowing and work-based learning experiences, and so forth. The exploration phase is developed individually for each student based on his or her identified areas of interest.

Connection: In the *connection* phase, which takes place when students are in the 11th and 12th grades, students are assisted in making formal connections with various postschool institutions and organizations, including scheduling apprenticeship interviews with trade union representatives, attending admissions conferences with community college or university admissions officers, and investigating acceptance criteria to postsecondary vocational education programs. Students involved in the pathways model develop a portfolio before they leave high school containing information on educational assessment data, vocational assessment information, vocational experiences, postsecondary planning, and contact information for community resources and postsecondary education programs. The portfolio becomes a traveling resource guide for students that has practical value after they exit the secondary setting.

Evaluation: The *evaluation* phase of the program centers around follow-along activities with each student in order to track their successes and emergent concerns. Telephone contacts from the school to program graduates at regular intervals the first 2 years after graduation allow transition specialists from the high school to remain involved with former students and enable them to provide additional information or resources.

10. What are some activities that schools can employ to promote each of the five phases of the pathways to self-determination?

See sample activities located in Table 13.1.

Recommended Reading

Blackorby, J., & Wagner, M. (1996). Longitudinal post-school outcomes of youth with disabilities: Findings from the National Longitudinal Transition Study. *Exceptional Children, 62,* 399–414.

Catterall, J. S. (1985). *On the social costs of dropping out of school.* Stanford, CA: Center for Educational Research at Stanford.

Eckstrom, R. B., Goertz, M. E., Pollack, J. M., & Rock, D. A. (1986). Who drops out of high school and why? Findings from a national study. *Teachers College Record, 87*(3), 3 56–373.

Grayson, T. (1998). Dropout prevention and special services. In F. Rusch & J. Chadsey (Eds.), *Beyond high school: Transition from school to work.* Belmont, CA: Wadsworth.

Padilla, C. L., & Jay, E. D. (1990). Dropping out: A look at the problem in special education. *Readings on Equal Education, 10,* 193–225.

Web Resources

Dropout Prevention

Educational Attainment in the United States: U.S. Census Bureau

http://www.census.gov/

A versatile site with access to information and search programs.

National Center for Educational Statistics (NCES)

http://nces.ed.gov/das/library/

The Tables Library contains tables that focus on various topics in postsecondary education. These topics include access to postsecondary education, persistence and attainment of a degree, financial aid, student demographics, and institutional characteristics.

National Center on Educational Outcomes (NCEO)

http://education.umn.edu/nceo/

NCEO provides national leadership in the participation of students with disabilities in national and state assessments, standards-setting efforts, and graduation requirements.

U.S. Census Bureau: American FactFinder

http://factfinder.census.gov

Source for population, housing, economic, and geographic data.

References

Agran, M., Blanchard, C., Wehmeyer, M., & Hughes, C. (2001). Teaching students to self-regulate their behavior: The differential effects of student- vs. teacher-delivered reinforcement. *Research in Developmental Disabilities, 4*, 319–332.

Allen, T. E., Rawlings, B. W., & Schildroth, A. (1989). *Deaf students and the school-to-work transition.* Baltimore: Brookes.

Blackorby, J., & Wagner, M. (1996). Longitudinal post-school outcomes of youth with disabilities: Findings from the National Longitudinal Transition Study. *Exceptional Children, 62*, 399–414.

Chadsey-Rusch, J., Rusch, F. R., & O'Reilly, M. (1991). A review of research on transitioning youth from school to integrated communities. *Regular and Special Education, 12*, 23–33.

DeBettencourt, L. U., Zigmond, N., & Thornton, H. (1989). Follow-up of postsecondary-age rural learning disabled graduates and dropouts. *Exceptional Children, 56*, 40–49.

Good, T. L., & Weinstein, R. S. (1986). Schools make a difference. *American Psychologist, 10*, 1090–1097.

Grayson, T. (1998). Dropout prevention and special services. In F. Rusch & J. Chadsey (Eds.), *Beyond high school: Transition from school to work.* Belmont, CA: Wadsworth.

Hasazi, S. B., Furney, K. S., & DeStefano, L. (1999). Implementing the IDEA transition mandates. *Exceptional Children, 4*, 555–566.

Holsch, S. A., Karen, R. L., & Franzinin, L. R. (1992). Two-year follow-up of the competitive employment status of graduates with developmental disabilities. *Career Development for Exceptional Individuals, 15*(2), 149–155.

Jay, E. D., & Padilla, C. L. (1987). *Special education dropouts: The incidence of and reasons for dropping out of special education in California.* Menlo Park, CA: SRI International.

Johnson, S. T. (2000). The live creature and its expectations for the future. The 2000 Charles H. Thompson Lecture—Colloquium Presentation. *Journal of Negro Education, 69*(1–2), 150–158.

Kortering, L. J., & Braziel, P. M. (1992). *School dropouts among rural youth with and without learning disabilities.* Unpublished manuscript, Appalachian State University, Boone, NC.

MacMillan, B., & First, C. (1990). *The progressive/collaborative high school: A model program.* (ERIC Document Reproduction Service No. ED321478)

MacMillan, T. F. (1991). An assessment of educational benefits: A response by 1990–91 (Mendocino College Graduates Research Report 91-8). Ukiah, CA: Mendocino College.

Mithaug, D. E., Horiuchi, C. H., & Fanning, P. N. (1985). *Exceptional Children, 51*, 397–404.

Neel, R. S., Meadows, N., Levine, P., & Edgar, E. B. (1988). What happens after special education: A statewide follow-up study of secondary students who have behavioral disorders. *Behavioral Disorders, 13*, 209–216.

Sitlington, P. L., & Frank, A. R. (1990). Are adolescents with learning disabilities successfully crossing the bridge into adult life? *Learning Disability Quarterly, 13*, 97–111.

Thornton, H., & Zigmond, N. (1988). Secondary vocational training for LD students and its relationship to school completion status and post school outcomes. *Illinois Schools Journal, 67*, 37–54.

Thurlow, M., Elliott, J., Ysseldyke, J., & Erickson, R. (1996). *Questions and answers: Tough questions about accountability systems and students with disabilities.* (Synthesis Report 24). Minneapolis: University of Minnesota, National Center on Educational Outcomes.

Wagner, M. (1990). *Highlights of the National Longitudinal Transition Study of special education students.* Menlo Park, CA: SRI.

Wagner, M., & Blackorby, J. (1996). Transition from high school to work or college: How special education students fare. *The Future of Children: Special Education for Students with Disabilities, 6*(1), 103–120.

Wehman, P., & Revell, G. W. (1996). Supported employment from 1986 to 1993: A national program that works. *Focus on Autism and Other Developmental Disabilities, 11,* 235–242.

White, W. J. (1992). The postschool adjustment of persons with disabilities: Current status and future projections. *Journal of Learning Disabilities, 25,* 448–456.

Williams, J., & O'Leary, J. (Eds.). (2001). What we've learned and where we go from here. *Career Development for Exceptional Individuals, 24,* 51–71.

Zigmond, N., & Thorton, H. (1995). Follow-up of postsecondary age LD graduates and dropouts. *Learning Disabilities Research, 1,* 50–55.

CHAPTER 14

Evaluation Practices for Transition Planning

Judy Elliott
Long Beach Unified School District
and
Martha Thurlow and Erin Reid
University of Minnesota

Student assessment and program evaluation are critical for all instructional programs, including those for students with disabilities. In fact, these components make up the cornerstone of No Child Left Behind (2001) and the Individuals with Disabilities Education Act (2004). Typically, assessment and students with disabilities refers to assessments conducted for eligibility of special education services. Although there are many ways to assess the effectiveness of student transition plans via the individualized education program (IEP) process also known as the individualized transition plan (ITP), little has been written on evaluation of transition programs.

The focus of this chapter is on assessment and evaluation of transition services and programs. Using a well-established outcome-based framework, we outline some general outcomes and indicators to describe several approaches to assessment and program evaluation of transition services.

After defining the terms *assessment* and *evaluation* within the context of the different purposes of assessment that may be used during the transition years, we examine (a) factors to be considered when assessing the success of individual transition services, (b) elements to consider when identifying potential employers to establish work-based learning experiences, and (c) challenges and strategies for setting students and work-based learning programs up for success.

WHAT DO WE KNOW ABOUT THE TRANSITION PLANNING PROCESS?

Historically, poor outcomes for students exiting from special education have served as a backdrop for federal initiatives to improve transition planning for youth with disabilities (Grigal, Test, Beattie, & Wood, 1997; Johnson & Rusch, 1993). Research findings and federally funded model demonstration efforts have confirmed the importance of the transition provision required under IDEA 2004 as well as identified strategies for promoting successful transitions. Some of these strategies and practices include (a) student involvement in transition planning (Powers et al., 2001); (b) student participation in general education, including extracurricular activities (Halpern, Yovanoff, Doren, & Benz, 1991; Sands, Bassett, Lehmann, & Spencer, 1998); (c) support for student participation in postsecondary education (HEATH Resource Center, 1993; U.S. Department of Education, 2002); (d) student-centered career planning and community work experience in career areas chosen by the student (Mank, 1994; Sowers, McAllister, & Cotton, 1996); (e) attention to multicultural issues in transition (Chesapeake Institute, 1994; Geenen, Powers, Lopez-Vasquez, & Bersani, 2003); (f) access to instruction that included teaching skills in the areas of self-advocacy, independent living, and self-determination (Powers et al., 2001; Wehmeyer & Schwartz, 1997); (g) mentorship experiences (Campbell-Whatley, 2001; McLearn, Colasanto, Schoen, & Shapiro, 1999); (h) support for family involvement in transition planning and preparation (Halpern et al., 1991; Morningstar, Turnbull, & Turnbull, 1995; Powers, Turner,

Matuszewski, Wilson, & Loesch, 1999); and (i) interagency collaboration (Hasazi, Furney, & DeStefano, 1999).

Although there appears to be a plethora of studies to confirm the essential provisions of transition services mandated under IDEA, little to no research addresses assessment and program evaluation of transition programs.

Students with disabilities who receive special education services are assessed frequently during their school careers. The purposes of the assessments vary, as do the consequences of the students' participation in the assessments. Most educators agree that the initial assessment to determine eligibility for special education services is the most critical of all assessments of students with disabilities. Second in importance is the use of accountability assessments or large-scale assessment that school districts and states mandate to assess how students are performing in standards-based curriculum throughout their K–12 school career. The third critical area of assessment is transition assessments. Given the current national landscape of accountability and assessment, it is amazing how little has been written about formalized assessment in relation to transition planning and program evaluation for students with disabilities.

It is important to clarify the context of transition on which this chapter is based. Transition can mean the movement of students from grade level to grade level. For example, preschoolers moving into kindergarten, or fifth graders moving into sixth grade (in most places this means a student transitioning from elementary to middle school), eighth-grade students moving into ninth grade (middle school into high school), and finally high school–age students (ages 18–22) transitioning into job-related vocational programs. In this chapter we focus on students who are of high school age moving into career and vocational programs.

The new changes in IDEA 2004 as they relate to transition services (see Box 14.1), both in definition and IEP requirements, emphasize the critical nature of assessment and evaluation of transition services for students with disabilities. Thus, transition services have now become more visible in terms of accountability for student outcomes. The new emphasis on transition assessments, and specifically written IEP goals that address transition, makes clear the importance of the efforts to provide successful programs and services in this area.

When we speak of transition services here, we include all students with disabilities. It is not uncommon to think about students with more significant disabilities or those with "visible" disabilities as the only students who need traditional transition or vocational opportunities. However, now more than ever, transition opportunities and programs are relevant for the wide spectrum of students with disabilities receiving special education in today's schools. Increased implementation and use of high-stakes graduation exams as a condition for receiving a high school diploma (at the printing of this book, 28 states use high-stakes graduation exams) has greatly raised the concerns about and attention to students with disabilities who may not pass them.

As the stakes continue to rise in this area, the more unanticipated outcomes will continue to surface. In some states, students with disabilities are allowed to

> **BOX 14.1 IDEA 2004 Changes Related to Transition Services**
>
> "Transition services" means a coordinated set of activities for a child with a disability that
>
> (a) is designed to be within a results-oriented process that is focused on improving the academic and functional achievement of the child with a disability to facilitate the child's movement from school to post-school activities, including post-secondary education, vocational education, integrated employment (including supported employment), continuing and adult education, adult services, independent living, or community participation;
>
> (b) is based on the individual child's needs, taking into account the child's strengths, preferences, and interests; and
>
> (c) includes instruction, related services, community experiences, the development of employment and other post-school adult living objectives, and when appropriate, acquisition of daily living skills and functional vocational evaluation.
>
> *Source*: IDEA 2004 (602(34)(B)).

use any accommodation that appears in their IEPs for these tests without restriction. That is, there is no limitation or disallowed accommodations. As a result, referrals for special education eligibility has increased in hopes that students will qualify and thereby be allowed to use accommodations to help them pass the graduation test. In other states, waivers and appeals are sought and granted for students with disabilities who are viewed as disadvantaged to take such tests. The real question is whether these students have been exposed to the curriculum and effective instruction allowing them the same opportunities to learn the content and give them a fair chance at passing the test. Although an important discussion, this is not the focus of this chapter. Rather, these points bring into clear view the need to expand transition opportunities and think about transition programs to include the wider spectrum of students with disabilities.

DEFINITIONS

The terms *assessment* and *evaluation* are sometimes defined very specifically; at other times they are used interchangeably. Consistent with Salvia and Ysseldyke (2004), we use *assessment* to mean the collection of data to make decisions. Salvia and Ysseldyke define 13 types of decisions that can be made, ranging from eligibility decisions to decisions about program effectiveness. The decisions may be made in relation to individual students (what are the student's strengths, what instructional procedures does the student need, is the program meeting the student's needs? etc.) or to programs (e.g., are the overall goals of the program being achieved?).

Evaluation professionals (cf. Worthen & Sanders, 1987), although recognizing the many alternative evaluation approaches, generally define *evaluation* to mean the procedures used to determine the worth of something. For example, program evaluation usually refers to the process of holding a program up to a set of standards to determine where the standards are or are not met.

In this chapter, we talk about data collection that covers both assessment and evaluation. When we talk about assessment, we are referring to the collection of data on students to make decisions about them. In turn, when we talk about evaluation we are referring to the collection of data to make decisions about programs. We believe it is not the specific term that is important, but the act of collecting data to make decisions.

Why Assessment and Program Evaluation Are Important During Transition

Transition through school or out of school occurs regardless of whether there is good assessment-based planning in place or not. For a long time, educators were not required to document a plan for students' movement through school to a postschool environment of work, postsecondary education, or other activity. Without a plan, there was nothing against which success could be measured. In fact, it is the poor postschool outcomes of students with disabilities, the lack of planning for the transition of these students, and the failure to define the important outcomes of education for these students that probably best explain why assessment and evaluation are so important during transition.

Poor Postschool Outcomes

For some time, questions have been raised about the efficacy of schooling for students graduating from American schools (see International Association for the Evaluation of Educational Achievement, 1987; National Longitudinal Transition Study–2 [NLTS2], 2003; Secretary's Commission on Achieving Necessary Skills [SCANS], 1991). These concerns have also been raised for students with disabilities, who in adulthood have been found to be unemployed or underemployed, dependent on others, and dissatisfied with their social lives (Chadsey-Rusch & Heal, 1995; Chadsey-Rusch, Rusch, & O'Reilly, 1991; Wagner, 1995; Wagner, D'Amico, Marder, Newman, & Blackorby, 1992; Wagner et al., 1991). Fortunately, some of these outcomes seem to have been improving in recent years (Wagner, Newman, Cameto, & Levine, 2005; Wagner, Newman, Cameto, Garza, & Levine, 2005).

Lack of Planning

Before 1990, when transition plans were first required for all students with disabilities, transition was discussed almost exclusively in relation to students with low-incidence disabilities (e.g., severe cognitive delays, multiple disabilities). However, findings of poor postschool outcomes made it evident that students with less severe or invisible disabilities also were having difficulties after completing school, with few graduates finding adequate employment or assuming adult responsibilities (Rusch & Phelps, 1987; Wehman, Kregel, & Seyfarth, 1985). In fact, these students were among the most likely to leave school before graduating, joining the ranks of the dropouts (Wagner et al., 1991; Wolman, Bruininks, & Thurlow, 1989). Thus, the appropriateness of secondary programs for students with less significant disabilities was also called into question (Edgar, 1987). Despite some improvement, these issues (Wagner, Newman, Cameto, & Levine, 2005; Wagner, Newman, Cameto, Garza, et al., 2005) still remain for certain subsets of students with disabilities, such as students with emotional or behavioral disabilities.

Failure to Define Educational Outcomes

Regardless of label or type of disability, it is clear that the traditional curriculum of basic skill remediation, although perhaps necessary, is not sufficient to prepare students to meet the challenges of today's society. Secondary programs have been shown to be heavily academic oriented, and too often focusing on basic skill remediation for students with disabilities (Edgar, 1987). Why so many students' schooling was unrelated to their postschool success has been attributed, to some degree, to a failure to define the important outcomes of their education and an associated lack of information about how students were progressing toward those outcomes (DeStefano & Wagner, 1992). Recent evidence indicates that student coursework is focused more than ever on core academics and that there is an overall decrease in the number of students taking vocational education courses (Wagner, Newman, & Cameto, 2004).

A recent report (Achieve, Inc., 2004) revealed that few of the nation's high schools prepare or expose students to the knowledge and skills they need to successfully transition out into postsecondary school experiences or the workforce. One clear and important explanation for this phenomenon is that no state requires its graduates to take courses that reflect the real-world demands of work and postsecondary education. Thus, little emphasis or attention is given to the ultimate skill set needed to prepare students for success post–high school. Hence, the issues surrounding the need for better evaluation of student knowledge and skills related to transition is much broader than special education.

Special education programs have been greatly influenced by several relatively recent federal and state reforms, including the School-to-Work Opportunities Act of 1994, Goals 2000: Educate America Act of 1994, No Child Left Behind Act of 2001, and the Individuals with Disabilities Education Improvement Act of 2004.

This legislation has promoted comprehensive strategies for improving public school programs for all students, including students with disabilities. Briefly, these reforms (a) stress high academic and occupational standards; (b) promote the use of state and local standards-based accountability systems; (c) point to the need to improve professional development; and (d) call for broad-based partnerships between schools, employers, postsecondary institutions, parents, and others.

Ultimately, assessment and evaluation for transition are about not only accountability but also program effectiveness. Is the student prepared for the ultimate transition—entering the postsecondary community? Is the individual student planning and transition program doing what it was intended to do? Is the program working? How do we know? It is not enough to assess, plan, and write transition IEP goals and review them annually. If the ultimate goal of transition planning is to ready students with disabilities for postsecondary life, we need to evaluate whether students are, in fact, successful in postsecondary life. The notion of conducting an evaluation of the planning process may seem monumental, but so was the idea of transition when it was initially introduced in federal law in 1990. Despite the need for evaluation, especially in the transition planning process, such program evaluations have not been carried out—or if they have, it has most likely been in response to requests or legal mandates.

If we do not have solid program evaluation in place, how do we decide which transition programs to continue because they are successful and which to discontinue because they are not? Because we are required by law to assess and plan for students with disabilities, which in turn involves multiple stakeholders, it only makes sense to check whether we are on the right track.

There are many pragmatic reasons to initiate and conduct evaluations of the transition planning process. Such evaluation provides information that can be used to document needs and support requests for additional resources. More important, evaluation of the transition planning process as well as the overall programs can provide information about what is effective, what is not, and what can be done to improve the process that directly impacts planning and the ultimate program success for individual students.

Program evaluation must be practical and designed to answer questions about the progress of planning, programming, and respective effectiveness. For example, if we want to know whether community-based instruction and mobility training lead to productive employment and on-time arrival at the job site or other setting, we must gather information about how to define "productive employment" and how to measure it. We must evaluate whether instruction is producing the outcomes we said it would for the individual student.

Evaluation of the process can help determine the effectiveness of individual transition plans as well as the overall program. It can help identify areas of the process that need reorganizing or restructuring and those that are effective as is. Evaluation of the transition planning process can help determine the direct relationship between the secondary curriculum or student preparation and student success in postsecondary settings. Is there a correlation between the student's transition IEP plan and success in the targeted setting? If not, why not? For example, does the self-esteem or social skills program really help the student learn socially acceptable behaviors and generalize them to postschool settings? If not, why not? One discovery might be that certain skills need to be taught and retaught throughout a student's career, either independently or within the context of a work site.

Framework for a Comprehensive Transition Assessment and Program Evaluation

IDEA refers to a variety of postschool activities that could be targeted when thinking about transition assessment and evaluation. Some say that the essential components of successful transition are employment, independent living, and community integration. Others go into much more detail about what the important components are. Regardless, there is agreement that, as indicated in IDEA, the focus must be on the outcomes of the process rather than the process itself.

Outcomes of Education

In 1990, the National Center on Educational Outcomes (NCEO), a federally funded technical assistance center, was charged with the task of working with states and federal agencies to develop a conceptual model of educational outcomes for students with disabilities. The result was a conceptual model that encompassed outcomes and indicators for students at age 3, age 6, Grade 4, Grade 8, school completion, and postschool.

The basic model of outcomes developed through the work of NCEO (see Figure 14.1) encompasses general areas that should be assessed and evaluated for effectiveness or robustness in helping students plan and complete successful transition programs. These domains include:

- **Presence and Participation**—opportunities for physical presence as well as active and meaningful participation in school and the community by all individuals.
- **Accommodation and Adaptation**—extent to which students have and use adjustments, adaptive technologies, or compensatory strategies that are necessary for individuals to achieve outcomes.
- **Physical Health**—extent to which the individual demonstrates or receives support to engage in healthy behavior, attitudes, and knowledge related to physical well-being.
- **Responsibility and Independence**—extent to which the individual's behavior reflects the ability to function, with appropriate guidance or support, independently or interdependently, and to assume responsibility for oneself.

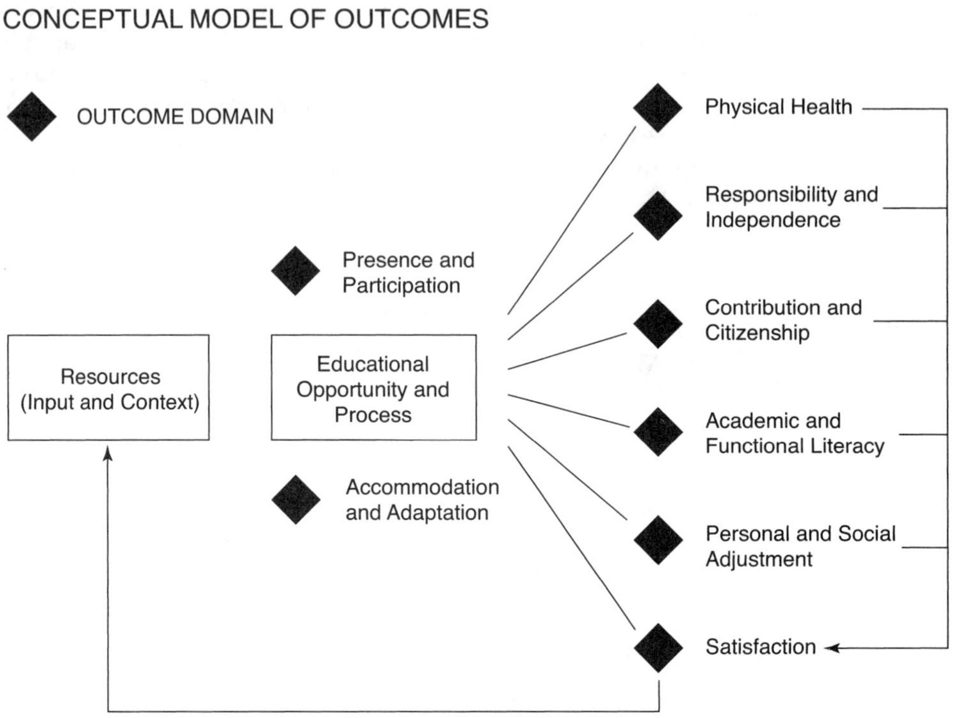

CONCEPTUAL MODEL OF OUTCOMES

FIGURE 14.1 NCEO Model of Outcomes
Source: Ysseldyke, Thurlow and Gilman (1993b). Reprinted by permission.

- **Contribution and Citizenship**—extent to which the individual gives something back to society or participates as a citizen in society.
- **Academic and Functional Literacy**—use of information to function in society, to achieve goals, and to develop knowledge.
- **Personal and Social Adjustment**—extent to which the individual demonstrates socially acceptable and healthy behaviors, attitudes, and knowledge regarding mental well-being, either alone or with guidance and support.
- **Satisfaction**—extent to which a favorable attitude is held toward education.

Table 14.1 highlights the specific outcomes for the three levels directly relevant for transition planning (Grade 8, school completion, and postschool). These reflect the real-world demands of work and postsecondary education. The NCEO model provides a continuum of outcomes that target specific skill sets that can be assessed for and in turn drive instruction.

The NCEO model, on one hand, provides a framework for evaluating how well transition programs are meeting students' needs starting at Grade 8 and moving through postsecondary settings. This provides several years of planning

TABLE 14.1 *Outcomes in NCEO Model at Grade 8, End of School, and Postschool*

Domain	Grade 8	School completion	Postschool
Presence and Participation	A1. Is present is school A2. Participates	A1. Is present in school A2. Participates A3. Completes school	A1. Is in community A2. Participates in community A3. Is employed
Accommodation and Adaptation	B1. Uses enrichments, adaptations, accommodations, or compensations necessary to achieve outcomes in each of the major domains B2. Demonstrates the presence of family	B1. Makes adaptations, accommodations, or compensations necessary to achieve outcomes in each of the major domains B2. Demonstrates family support and coping skills	(No outcomes were identified for this domain at the postschool level.)
Physical Health	C1. Makes healthy lifestyle choices C2. Is aware of basic safety, fitness, and health care needs C3. Is physically fit	C1. Makes healthy lifestyle choices C2. Is aware of basic safety, fitness, and health care needs C3. Is physically fit	C1. Makes healthy lifestyle choices C2. Is aware of basic safety, fitness, and health care needs C3. Is physically fit
Responsibility and Independence	D1. Demonstrates age-appropriate independence D2. Gets about in the environment D3. Is responsible for self	D1. Gets about in the environment D2. Is responsible for self	D1. Gets about in the environment D2. Is responsible for self D3. Functions independently
Contribution and Citizenship	E1. Complies with school and community rules E2. Knows the significance of voting E3. Volunteers	E1. Complies with school and community rules E2. Knows the significance of voting and procedures necessary to register to vote E3. Volunteers	E1. Complies with school and community rules E2. Votes E3. Volunteers E4. Pays taxes
Academic and Functional Literacy	F1. Demonstrates competence in communication F2. Demonstrates competence in problem-solving strategies and critical thinking skills F3. Demonstrates competence in math, reading, and writing skills F4. Demonstrates competence in other academic and nonacademic areas F5. Demonstrates competence in using technology	F1. Demonstrates competence in communication F2. Demonstrates competence in problem-solving strategies and critical thinking skills F3. Demonstrates competence in math, reading, and writing skills F4. Demonstrates competence in other academic and nonacademic areas F5. Demonstrates competence in using technology	F1. Demonstrates competence in communication F2. Demonstrates competence in problem-solving strategies and critical thinking skills F3. Demonstrates competence in math, reading, and writing skills used in daily life F4. Demonstrates competence in other academic and nonacademic areas F5. Demonstrates competence in using technology
Personal and Social Adjustment	G1. Copes effectively with personal challenges, frustrations, and stressors G2. Has a good self-image	G1. Copes effectively with personal challenges, frustrations, and stressors G2. Has a good self-image	G1. Copes effectively with personal challenges, frustrations, and stressors G2. Has a good self-image

(continued)

TABLE 14.1 (*continued*)

	G3. Respects cultural and individual differences	G3. Respects cultural and individual differences	G3. Respects cultural and individual differences
	G4. Gets along with other people	G4. Gets along with other people	G4. Gets along with other people
Satisfaction	H1. Student satisfaction with school experience	H1. Student satisfaction with high school experience	H1. Individual's satisfaction with current status
	H2. Parent/guardian satisfaction with education that student is receiving	H2. Parent/guardian satisfaction with the education that student received	H2. Parent/guardian satisfaction with current status of individual
	H3. Community satisfaction with education that student is receiving	H3. Community satisfaction with the education that student received	H3. Community satisfaction with current status of individual

Sources: Grade 8: From Ysseldyke, Thurlow, and Erickson (1994a). School Completion: From Ysseldyke, Thurlow, and Gilman (1993b). Postschool: From Ysseldyke, Thurlow, and Gilman (1993a).

opportunities as well as evaluation of outcomes. On the other hand, the model also can provide a framework for thinking about the assessment of students for transition planning. For example, it helps focus on and identify the skills a student needs in order to be successful in the responsibility and independence level at the school completion and postschool levels.

There is no shortage of guides, pamphlets, and books on transition planning. However, the field still lacks a systematic approach to evaluating transition programs. The NCEO model is one systematic approach to developing good assessment and program evaluation methodologies for transition services.

Another valuable aspect of the NCEO framework is that it also identifies indicators for each outcome, the elements and sources that can lead to valid data, which are a vital aspect of program evaluation. For example, within the Responsibility and Independence domain for the outcome "Gets about in the environment," four indicators were identified at the school completion level:

D1a. Percent of students who can get to and from a variety of destinations

D1b. Percent of students who know how to access community services (rehabilitation, counseling, employment, health, etc.)

D1c. Percent of students who complete transactions (shopping, banking, drycleaning, etc.) in the community

D1d. Percent of students with a driver's license

Although these indicators are designed for programs, they can easily be applied to individual students according to need (e.g., "student can get to and from a variety of destinations"). The model provides domains, outcomes, and indicators, all of which can be used to plan specific instruction for individual students and/or groups of students, as well as transition programs that reflect a standards-based comprehensive program. (Additional documents prepared by the NCEO identify possible sources of data for each of the indicators identified within its model (e.g., Ysseldyke, Thurlow, & Erickson, 1994b; Ysseldyke, Thurlow, & Erickson, 1995; Ysseldyke, Thurlow, & Vanderwood, 1994.)

The NCEO model is not the only model that could be adopted to evaluate transition services and programs. However, it is the only model that outlines outcomes, indicators and data requirements that promotes assessment of student progress against a set of standards. The NCEO argues that it is critical to include local programs and their constituents in defining the important outcomes, and strongly recommends that a consensus-building process be used to develop outcomes to target during transition planning, assessment, and program evaluation for students (Vanderwood, Ysseldyke, & Thurlow, 1993; Ysseldyke & Thurlow, 1993). In doing so, a personalized model can be developed and used to help design an assessment plan that complements the requirements identified in law and that meets the needs of individual students. It is critical to identify what stakeholders consider to be the important outcomes, then to design assessments to address those domains.

Recommended Practices

In the sections that follow, we explore how to assess the transition planning process and program evaluation. In addition, we look at challenges and strategies for setting up programs for success. Because the process of transition takes place over several years and is student specific, it is imperative for school personnel to proactively plan and establish partnerships with potential businesses and organization that can provide work-based learning opportunities for students as they move through their transition years.

Using Assessment and Evaluation During the Transition Process

Status of Transition Assessment and Program Evaluation. Over the past two decades, since federal transition requirements have been in place, researchers have explored implementation of those mandates by examining transition planning processes, including analyses of student IEPs or ITPs.

One of the first studies (Lawson & Everson, 1993) simply looked at IEP team members' familiarity with IDEA's mandates and/or purpose of transition planning. The findings are not surprising. Two to 3 years after transition plans were mandated, many IEP team members needed training in how to develop effective and inclusive transition plans. Another study analyzed 100 transition plans (deFur, Getzel, & Kregel, 1994). Findings in this study showed that representatives of community agencies rarely participated in IEP transition meetings and that fewer than half of the students attended their own transition planning IEP.

Another study that evaluated the IEPs of high school students (Grigal et al., 1997) found that poor post–high school outcomes could be relegated to, in part, the lack of quality transition planning meetings. These authors concluded that statements of student outcomes and activities, responsible personnel, and timelines were absent from or vaguely written in student IEPs, therefore indirectly or directly setting the student and the student's work-based experiences up for failure or poor results. These results were consistently found across all disability groups (e.g., those with learning disabilities, mentally retardation, deafness).

Hasazi and colleagues (1999) investigated the implementation of IDEA mandates across nine states, five of their considered model sites. These sites had participated in a federal transition systems change project and had national reputations in the area of transition planning and implementation. The study found that the model sites had more supporting and fewer preventing elements. The supporting elements included (a) leadership from all levels within the district, (b) interagency collaboration, (c) effective professional development, and (d) integrated transition services within general education initiatives. Challenges included the need to expand transition services and opportunities to a wider range of youth with disabilities. These sites indicated that adequate services and financial support for 18- to 21-year-old youth were lacking and the pressure to choose between academic and vocational curricula was often overwhelming for students and their families.

Two additional studies highlight the impact of transition planning in terms of setting students and programs up for success and failure. An analysis of 68 student IEPs revealed that student transition plans lacked clarity regarding postsecondary education, employment goals, and residences (Shearin, Roessler, & Schriner, 1999). Additionally, important skill areas such as safety, personal care, self-advocacy, and family planning were overlooked and not addressed. Similar findings were revealed in an analysis of 329 transition plans (Everson, Zhang, & Guillory, 2001).

Finally, a recent study (Powers et al., 2005) analyzed 399 IEPs and a total of 1,747 goals. Overall, approximately 63% of the goals provided minimal or no detail on what was to be achieved during transition. Only 6.4% made reference to accommodations and supports needed by students to achieve their transition goals. Whereas school personnel and family members were designated as one of the parties responsible for implementing an action step leading to goal completion (41% and 42%, respectively), students were responsible for carrying out action steps 77% of the time. And, in 14% of these cases, the student was not present or did not sign his or her IEP indicating agreement with the responsibility. Less than 1% of the student IEP transition goals indicated that vocational rehabilitative staff was the designee for implementing action steps toward goal completion. Similar findings were established for other community agencies (12%). Among other things, researchers found that students expected to receive a standard diploma were significantly more likely to have one or more goals related to postsecondary school (74%) than students expected to graduate with a modified diploma or some alternative document (12%). Less than 7% of the goals reflected any type of self-determination education or self-advocacy education. This is particularly disappointing given research findings indicating that self-determination skills support both immediate and postschool outcomes (Benz, Lindstrom, & Yovanoff, 2000; Martin et al., 2003).

These and other recent research efforts have helped focus the field on the important elements of a good ITP and the transition planning process. However, a focus on academics is still missing. Indeed, crafting an ITP with important transition components is critical for setting students up for postsecondary success. But what academic standards and content areas are these students accessing? Many students with ITPs go on to postsecondary school settings (e.g., community colleges, universities). Transition planning for these students will necessarily involve similar transition planning components; however, the focus on successful course completion and the identification of needed accommodations for both instruction and assessment is critical, as is the need to develop self-advocacy and self-determination skills. In fact, self-advocacy and self-determination skills are important skills for all students, including those with disabilities, regardless of their career path. However, most of what has been written and researched on transition programs and planning processes has emphasized readying students who will not be attending postsecondary learning institutions. Both types of transition students need similar planning considerations that include access to academics and standards-based instruction, identification of needed accommodations, and development of self-advocacy and self-determination skills.

The next sections discuss the importance of considering important elements of transition planning. Although there may not be a systematically developed program evaluation process for each work-based setting or program of study, we know that proactively building a complete transition program that encompasses research-based components will allow us to start the planning process with where we want the student to be and build a roadmap to get him or her there.

Evaluating a Program: Where to Begin

Research suggests that it is the IEP planning process that is most important in setting students up for success in career and vocational settings. Transition planning is relatively uncomplicated to do via a step-by-step IEP process. However, the outcome of the process is the biggest concern. That is, one can be compliant with mandates (e.g., write a legally defensible IEP) and still produce poor student outcomes. Therefore, well-written student-focused IEPs that meet federal mandates must be implemented with integrity and monitored for program and instructional effectiveness.

One of the most difficult steps in program evaluation is deciding where to begin. If a program is based on a framework like the NCEO model identified earlier in the chapter, that framework can be used to direct the evaluation. If a framework has not been used to guide transition planning, one should be developed for its evaluation. Several principles must be kept in mind when beginning to plan for an evaluation of the transition planning process (Vallecorsa, deBettencourt, & Garriss, 1992).

1. Evaluate only a few indicators at a time. Do not attempt to simultaneously evaluate every aspect of the process. Carefully pick your targets.
2. Select a data collection method that will capture the outcomes you are measuring. Avoid complex, jargon-filled designs or those that create the perception of extra work.
3. Collect information from everyone involved; that is, all stakeholders, from students to teachers and administrators. Consumer satisfaction, perceptions, and achieved outcomes are all vital to the process of such an evaluation.
4. Gather information that will identify strengths and weaknesses of the process while focusing on how this information may guide actions for improvement. Gather specific information that can be operationalized into action plans.

Because transition planning is a process that occurs over several years, both formative assessment and summative evaluations should be considered. Some formative areas could include:

1. What do the student's parents/guardians or other significant family members think about the transition process and progress? Do they perceive the transition planning process to be on the right track? What are the bases for these perceptions? What are their expectations and goals of the program?
2. What suggestions do parents/guardians and/or teachers have about the process and progress the student is making toward the targeted outcomes?
3. What does the student think? How is the plan working for him or her? Is it helping? How? Is it providing the student with necessary learning experiences? What suggestions does the student have?

For students who age out, leave, or graduate, summative questions must be asked of the students, parents, and other stakeholders. For example,

1. How did the planning process help? If indication is given otherwise, find out what suggestions or changes would have been helpful in the process. To avoid after-the-fact information, evaluate early and in an ongoing manner. Document what has worked well and areas in need of change.
2. How did students adjust to their targeted postsecondary school settings? What are the indicators of success? What areas and indicators are problematic?

3. How and what are students doing 1 year after they enter the postsecondary school settings? How are they doing 5 years later?

Evaluation questions are endless. Although we recognize the nature and scope of individual students' needs vary dramatically, evaluation of the overall transition planning process and programs is the key. Collaboration, assessment, planning, and writing of transition goals for any student's IEP will take on a similar format. That format or framework is what must be evaluated. Is it effective? Does it allow for the best planning possible for each student?

Impacting Program Evaluation: Proactive Planning for Success

Employers have operational and economic stakes in the success of programs that connect them with youth with disabilities. Employers must consider both the costs and the benefits associated with having youth with disabilities in their workplaces. Thus, it is essential for educators, transition specialists, workforce development professionals, family members, and youth to understand employers' needs, circumstances, and perspectives as work experiences are established.

Effective work-based learning experiences have been found to have a positive impact on school achievement and student outcomes (Colley & Jamison, 1998). For example, youth who participate in work-based learning show an increase in completion of related coursework as well as increased attendance and graduation. And, work-based learning experiences provided during secondary school have been shown to lead to higher rates of adult employment and success for all categories of disability (Luecking & Fabian, 2000).

To set students, and potential employers, up for success, school-based transition personnel should take into consideration the following critical steps when contacting potential employers to establish work-based learning experiences. These steps help identify the skills students need to have to enter and be successful in work programs.

Transition specialists must be able to:

1. Identify and discuss the nature of a potential company's or organization's business.
2. Identify and help facilitate discussion about the benefits for companies of bringing youth with disabilities into their workplace.
3. Identify and develop multiple partners.
4. Identify and plan for perceived and real challenges.
5. Celebrate successes!
6. Use these experiences as testimony to other employers and programs that serve youth with disabilities or those with which a work-based setting is being fostered.

These elements are important to setting up successful external partnerships or work experiences, but much of the hard work begins when students enter high school (and, in many places, middle school). Research has demonstrated that the work-based learning is one of the best ways to improve outcomes for students with disabilities in secondary education (Hughes, Moore, & Bailey, 1999). Secondary students who participate in such experiences have the opportunity to receive more individual guidance and support that will prepare them for successful adult employment.

There are a multitude of challenges and strategies to consider when setting programs (and individual students) up for success. Many of these challenges also apply to students without disabilities. The important piece is how schools and educational programs plan to address them to ensure the best student outcomes possible. Below we outline some challenges and respective strategies to consider.

Challenge. There is a perceived lack of connection between what students are learning in school and work-related expectations.

Strategy. Schools must provide students and parents the chance to make the connection between work experiences, expected work behavior, and school-based behavior and learning. Making the connection between school-based learning and work-based learning is critical. Work-based learning or hands-on experiences in real-life settings should include a broad range of opportunities to include introductory activities such as job shadowing, informational interviews with people already employed in the targeted field, workplace tours, as well as more long-term and intensive training. Examples of long-term and intensive training include workplace mentoring, apprenticeships, volunteer and paid employment, service learning, and activities on school campuses.

Challenge. Students lack the skill set necessary for gainful employment and career success.

Strategy. Starting career and vocational awareness and opportunities early is critical to building crucial job-keeping or "soft skills" necessary for success. Box 14.2 provides a partial list of soft skills that employers expect and look for in their employees. Most businesses and employers want employees who are ready and eager to work and learn what they need to in order to be productive in the work environment. They also want workers who show respect and take job commitment seriously. Whereas basic academic skills (reading, writing, mathematics and technology) and problem-solving skills are desired and often required, it is the soft skills that have been said to make a difference in whether a student is hired or fired from a job (Bremer & Madzar, 1995). Specifically, employers look for employees who display positive social skills, a strong work ethic, self-discipline, self-respect, and a friendly demeanor (Bremer & Madzar, 1995).

BOX 14.2 Soft Skills and Employer Expectations of Student Workers

The student worker should:

- come to work on time
- be a team player
- be positive
- ask for help when needed
- be courteous and friendly
- use office equipment for work-related tasks only
- when voicing concerns, be constructive, not accusatory
- complete all work neatly and accurately
- show respect for self and others
- keep personal telephone calls to a minimum
- take personal responsibility
- stay on task and complete all work in a timely manner
- come to work appropriately dressed
- keep personal visits to a minimum
- be reliable and follow through
- ask for more work when tasks are complete
- use good personal hygiene
- keep absences to a minimum and call in when sick (in a timely manner)
- work hard

Source: From Bremer and Madzar (1995).

These soft skills can be taught and worked on in the secondary setting. Indeed, they are what makes students successful in school. Therefore, it is critical that IEP goals address the development of these job-keeping skills. IEP teams can set students up for success by developing work-based learning goals that bring students to proficiency in these soft skills.

Challenge. Students' IEP goals do not clearly define or address work-based learning opportunities.

Strategy. Developing self-advocacy competency is critical. IEP goals that address self-advocacy and leadership are one of the keys to students learning responsible and successful career and vocational success. For example, teaching students how to ask for needed accommodations for instruction, classroom learning, or a work-based setting is an important skill to develop. Such skills should be taught, learned, and practiced in both secondary settings as well as work-based learning experiences.

Challenge. Families fail to understand or get involved in work-based learning as a part of individual transition planning.

Strategy. Parental involvement is much greater in the early years of schooling and then significantly drops off in the student's secondary years. To remedy such situations it is often a good idea to start by providing family members individualized support, resources, and assistance to heighten their awareness of and ability to become actively involved in their student's career and vocational experiences. It is not uncommon for families to feel a disconnect related to how work-based learning is a part of the school experience. Empower parents to look within their own networks, neighborhoods, and friends for work-based learning opportunities for their students. Be *sure* to include parents as equal planning partners in the IEP transition planning process. Encourage them to take a leadership role in the process, including exploring work-based learning experiences on the IEP.

Challenge. Many families fear that student employment will result in the loss of Supplemental Security Income (SSI) and Social Security Disability Insurance (SSDI).

Strategy. All IEP team members, including the student, must have accurate information about SSI and SSDI work incentive programs and the impact of wages on benefits. A good approach to this is to connect with the nearest Social Security office. Providing information helps students and families with make informed choices about work-based learning and employment. Some states have benefit analysis organizations that can calculate the impact of student wages on benefits for the student and family. It is a good idea to bring this up at IEP meetings, as needed.

ESSENTIAL COMPONENTS FOR CREATING SUCCESSFUL WORK-BASED LEARNING OPPORTUNITIES

Setting Up Host Employers

Another important element of setting programs and students up for success is making sure that schools that approach potential employers know the factors that can make or break the success of students in these placements. A study was conducted with 11 business employers to explore what motivates an employer to host youth with disabilities in work-based learning environments (Luecking, 2004). Employers were identified through a national search, and nominations were solicited from programs and colleagues who had such contacts. They were selected for three reasons. First, they were all satisfied with the experience of having youth with disabilities in their workplaces. Second, they represented a diverse range of industries, geographical locations, sizes, and private- and public-sector entities. Finally, they provided a variety of work-based experiences that included job shadowing, mentoring, volunteering, internships, apprenticeships, and paid employment.

Several factors influence employers' participation in work-based transition programs. These factors ranged from chance encounters or events with school-based personnel to proactive, selective, and sophisticated efforts to recruit employers as well as eligible students. These efforts resulted in a good match between the employer and student.

Employers involved in this study also indicated that more than just one factor influenced their willingness to participate in youth transition and work-based program development. Some of them were as follows:

1. Meeting a perceived need of the community
2. Meeting an ongoing need of the industry
3. Meeting a company-specific need
4. Encountering individual students who had a lasting impression on the prospective employer

Some general guidelines offered in this study lend insight into critical elements to consider when setting up successful programs and, in turn, create valid good program evaluation. Common themes of the employers included considering the following:

- The need to work with competent professionals to ensure appropriate matches (and follow-up) between youth and job assignments, including accommodations where necessary.
- Work experience options that can be expanded when employers and youth programs share resources and sometimes costs.
- Disability awareness and training for youth coworkers as a vital component of success for most work experiences.
- The use of standard human resource procedures when bringing youth with disabilities into the workplace, but also a willingness to make and provide extensive accommodations or adaptations with assistance from competent disability professionals.

This study shows the importance of school-based professionals' ongoing need to seek out and listen to the voices of potential employers. With a targeted focus on employers' needs, there is good reason to expect improved participation and program success, in providing youth with meaningful work-based opportunities, leading to successful experiences and good program outcomes. It is essential to transition program success and, in turn, program evaluation that school personnel understand and address the circumstances of employers who might provide youth these opportunities.

Work experience for youth with disabilities is one of the most critical factors for their postsecondary employment success. Both research and practice show that youth benefit from frequent and continuous exposure to real-work environments throughout the secondary school years and beyond. However, these experiences occur only when employers are available, willing, and prepared. Proactive planning and familiarity about what research tells us with what has been missing from ITPs and the planning process is critical when setting up successful work-based opportunities for schools and potential host employers.

Summary

School personnel, as required under federal law, are responsible for monitoring and evaluating the quality of instructional programs and service delivery in their schools, districts, and states. Evaluation goes well beyond the issue of legal compliance. It is a moral and ethical obligation. Therefore, evaluation of the transition planning process should be thought of as more than an externally mandated activity. We need to continually evaluate whether transition planning meets the needs of students, and provide students with the support necessary to achieve their intended outcomes.

Johnson, Stodden, Emanuel, Luecking, and Mack (2002) identified five major challenges impacting secondary education and transition services: (a) ensuring that students with disabilities have access to the full range of learning experiences and options offered within the general education curriculum; (b) making sure that high school graduation decisions are based on meaningful indicators of students' learning and skills as well as clarifying the implications of different diploma options for youth with disabilities; (c) ensuring students access to and full participation in postsecondary education, employment, and independent living options; (d) supporting student and family participation in the transition planning process; and (e) improving collaboration and system linkages at all levels. It is imperative that each of these areas is assessed and evaluated within the context of student achievement and postsecondary success.

Throughout this chapter we have highlighted the complexity of assessing student success during transition services, and ways to evaluate whether or not they are working. Not only is transition planning very individualized, but there are many proactive ways in which school-based personnel can set up successful work-based learning opportunities and thereby influence program success. It is essential that students' ITPs be outcome based with steps or indicators along the way that allow data to be collected to show whether the program and the ITP is focused on the correct targets for individual students.

We must become proficient in identifying students' skills, the characteristics of the desired future environments, the skills needed to be successful in those future environments, and the necessary for potential employers or work-based learning opportunities. We must devise the plans to assist the student in moving from current skills to skills needed in the identified future environments, and then keep track of progress toward the desired skills. Finally, we must be able to evaluate the overall effectiveness of these transition programs and work-based opportunities. As we do all this, there are certain things we need to remember.

Need for Individualization

Transition planning is not a canned curriculum. Likewise, assessment for transition must be tailored to students. The need for student assessment and program evaluation is paramount in the area of transition planning. However, along with the need for individual student ITPs is the recognition that certain elements that factor into successful transition programs, including the skill set a student has and needs to further develop and the business needs of the work site or work-based setting. Consideration and planning for these will help ensure success in current and future postsecondary settings.

Need for Comprehensiveness and Knowledge of Future Environments

In order to contribute to effective and efficient transition services and program evaluation, planning must be comprehensive. There is a need to define a framework within which student assessment and evaluation is planned and conducted. NCEO's framework can be used as individual student and/or program evaluation.

Interconnected with the need to be comprehensive is the need for the transition planners and the assessment developers to be knowledgeable about the characteristics of the future environments and the elements or factors that lead to an employer's motivation to host youth with disabilities in work experiences. Furthermore, it is important to know about the skills that are required to be successful in that future environment, so that it is possible to design instructional programs that will help the student move from his or her current skill level to that needed in the future environments.

Need for Evaluation of the Transition Planning Process and Programs

Students receiving special education services have IEPs. Within the IEP is an ITP component. All IEPs are reviewed annually, but what about the time in between? It is critical not only to evaluate the essence of an ITP at least annually, but also to ensure that the overall transition program or work-based learning experience be regularly evaluated as to its relevance and effectiveness in helping develop the skills and abilities that will allow students to successfully move into postsecondary life.

This case study highlights the transition planning process for a student with mild to moderate learning disabilities. It illustrates the assessment and planning process over the middle school and high school years.

Joshua is a seventh-grade student with disabilities. He attends a middle school in a large urban school district and receives resource room services through a study skills support class. Joshua was originally diagnosed with learning disabilities in reading comprehension and expressive writing in Grade 4. At the conclusion of Grade 7, Joshua and his guardian met with his resource room teacher to complete a transition assessment. As a result of this screening, Joshua's initial career interests and immediate transition needs were identified. Joshua indicated he would "like to work on computers and help people use them better." Relevant areas in need of further development included developing general independence, task perseverance, and a greater awareness of what is required of someone planning to attend a postsecondary school. Although Joshua was interested in this career, his guardian wondered how realistic it was given Joshua's disabilities. It was felt that by having Joshua "look into" the career, he might gain a better perspective on whether he was "capable" of pursuing it.

As a result of the assessment and meeting, transition goals for Joshua's IEP included increasing his independence in the school setting; exploring the career of computer consultant by reading and gathering information; increasing task perseverance and completion of independent assignments, homework, and projects; and developing the ability to make his needs known and access support for them.

The resource room teacher created an academic goal that integrated Joshua's interest in becoming a computer consultant, the need to increase independence and task perseverance, and the continued need to remediate and instruct expressive writing skills. The IEP goal stated: "Joshua will gather information and respective requirements about his career interest (computer consultant) and share that information through a written medium."

In addition, discussion ensued around the need to begin exploring the accommodations Joshua may need to be successful in his work with computers. For example, he may need a word processor with a spell check or grammar check to address his expressive writing skill needs. Also, it was deemed necessary to determine whether his need to work on task perseverance relate to skill deficits or the need for extended time to complete assigned tasks. Although it was decided that Joshua currently did not need these accommodations, this discussion was noted in the IEP minutes in order to monitor these potential accommodation needs over the next school years.

Three years later, when he was a 10th grader, Joshua's transition goals were reviewed as part of an annual process. Information gathered from his current progress reports, report cards, and stakeholders were used to inform transition planning, including postsecondary school opportunity for Joshua. During his IEP meeting, specific needs were identified that would provide Joshua a smooth transition into a local university to start his path of schooling to gain a degree in computer technology. At this IEP, with both Joshua and his guardian in attendance, the guardian indicated that he could not believe how the time had flown by. The guardian reflected on the initial transition meeting at which time Joshua had announced that he wanted to be a computer consultant, noting that now 3 years later, they were actually planning for that career. "I really thought he would have changed his mind several times. Even though he did think of other careers he always came back to this one."

In reviewing the accommodations stated on Joshua's IEP, it was clear that the need for a reader, a person who could clarify directions, and extended time for written assignments continued and had to be integrated into his postsecondary schooling. As a result of this meeting and assessment, Joshua's transition goals were written as follows:

> Joshua will go to the career center and begin to identify geographic locations and schools with computer degrees. Upon locating a school of choice, Joshua, with the assistance of his school counselor, will contact the admissions office to obtain an application and gather more specific information about the school and available supports for students with special needs.

As an 11th grader, Joshua's last high school IEP was developed. It was anticipated that he would graduate from high school as a 12th grader at age 17. Transition goals for Joshua's IEP included:

> Joshua will independently enroll in and complete a preparation course for the SAT offered by the school district.
>
> Joshua will, with assistance from his school counselor, sign up for and take the SAT until he has achieved a passing score.
>
> Joshua will actively participate in the application process to schools of choice by completing and submitting at least five applications.
>
> Joshua will access at least three postsecondary education support services at the school of acceptance.

Joshua successfully completed his transition IEP goals, was accepted into a program, and is currently completing his second year of postsecondary schooling. With the coordinated support of the campus services for students with special needs, Joshua *has been able to maintain the level of support and assistance necessary to be successful in his program.*

CASE STUDY 2

This case study highlights the transition planning process of a student with a significant developmental disability. It illustrates the assessment and planning process through her middle school years. Donelle is an eighth-grade student with Down syndrome. She attends a middle school in a large urban school district. Donelle has received special education services through a self-contained special day class since kindergarten. At the conclusion of Grade 8, Donelle and her mother met with her IEP team to complete a transition assessment. Discussed were also the results of an interest inventory, and Donelle's initial career interests and immediate transition needs were identified. She indicated that she would like to "help kids." Discussion of Donelle's present levels of academic and functional performance consisted of classroom observation checklists and input from IEP team members, including Sara and her family members, regarding Donelle's learning characteristics and interests. As a result, the team determined that the following are relevant areas or domains of need:

Academic and Functional Literacy—Donelle must develop critical thinking skills to demonstrate problem-solving ability.

Responsibility and Independence—Donelle must demonstrate skills in interacting and decision making in social situations as well as making appropriate choices. Donelle needs to improve how she advocates for herself and must be able to get to and from a variety of common destinations.

Although Donelle is interested in working with children, her mother shared concerns about how realistic it was given Donelle's disabilities. It was determined that Donelle would, with the help of her teacher, investigate various employment options with children. In addition, instruction would continue to focus on the domain areas in which Donelle exhibited skill deficits. This combined approach would allow the team to gain a broader picture of the opportunities available to Donelle as well as information to inform transition planning that would provide the most appropriate work-based learning opportunities.

As a result of the IEP meeting, transition goals for Donelle's IEP consisted of increasing her independence inside and outside the school setting, increasing task completion, including following multiple-step directions and developing the ability to make her needs known and access support for them. The special day class teacher created a goal that integrated Donelle's interest in working with others and the need to increase independence and task completion. Her IEP goals stated:

> *When given multiple-step directions, Donelle will independently complete the task assigned to her and communicate its completion with the person who assigned the task four out of five times.*
>
> *Using public transportation, Donelle will independently go to and from a set location (supported employment site, leisure activity, etc.) by following the bus schedule and riding the bus appropriately 100% of the time.*
>
> *Donelle and her teacher would investigate appropriate opportunities that could be available to her that included working with children. Upon investigation they concluded the following settings would allow Donelle to participate in developing skills needed to fulfill her desire to help kids:*

After-school clubs	*Early childhood programs*
Breakfast clubs	*Libraries*
Day camp assistant	*Nursery schools/preschools*
Day care assistant	*Summer play activities (e.g., playgrounds, parks)*
Community programs (e.g., Boy/Girl Scouts)	*Toy companies*

As Donelle enters high school, she will continue to investigate employment options as well as focus on improving skills in her deficit areas such as independence and problem solving per her IEP. In addition, she will volunteer as an assistant worker in one of the identified settings to begin to develop the skills she may need to fulfill her overall desire to work with kids.

Study Questions

1. What are some identified strategies for promoting successful transition?

   Strategies for promoting successful transition include (a) student involvement in transition planning; (b) student participation in general education, including extracurricular activities; (c) support for student participation in postsecondary education; (d) student-centered career planning and community work experience in career areas chosen by the student; (e) attention to multicultural issues; (f) access to instruction that included teaching skills in the areas of self-advocacy, independent living, and self-determination; (g) mentorship experiences; (h) support for family involvement in transition planning and preparation; and (i) interagency collaboration.

2. What types of youth with disabilities need transition planning?

   Transition planning and programs are imperative for a wide spectrum of students with disabilities receiving special education in today's schools. This includes students with significant disabilities or those with "visible" disabilities as well as students with learning disabilities who are considered diploma-bound.

3. What is the difference between assessment and evaluation?

   Assessment is defined as the collection of data to make decisions. Researchers define 13 types of decisions, ranging from eligibility decisions to decisions about program effectiveness. The decisions can be made regarding individual students (what are the student's strengths, what instructional procedures does the student need, is the program meeting the student's needs? etc.) or programs (are the overall goals of the program being achieved?).

   Evaluation refers to the procedures used to determine the worth of something. Program evaluation usually refers to the process of holding a program up to a set of standards to determine where the standards are met and where they are not met.

4. Why is assessment and program evaluation important during transition?

   Three reasons why assessment and evaluation are so important during transition are poor postschool outcomes of students with disabilities, lack of planning for the transition of these students, and failure to define what the important outcomes of education for these students are.

5. Why is it important to use an outcomes framework to organize transition planning and program evaluation?

   An outcomes-based framework requires a system to look at the bigger picture as well as long-term goals versus only short-term goals that are often insignificant in the bigger scheme of things. It is important to be able to look at a process or system as whole. Such evaluation provides information that can be used to provide evidence of needs and support requests for additional resources. Evaluation of the outcomes of the transition planning process can provide information about what is effective and what is not, and what can be done to improve the process that directly impacts planning and the ultimate program success for individual students.

6. What has research shown in terms of what is missing from or impacting successful transition planning process?

   Existing research has shown that the following are missing from or impacting successful transition planning process:

- Effective training to develop effective transition plans
- Attendance and participation by representatives of community agencies at IEP transition meetings
- Student attendance at their own transition planning IEP
- Quality transition planning meetings
- Statements of student outcomes and activities, responsible personnel, and timelines (absent from or vaguely written) in student IEPs across all disability groups
- Program elements or components focusing on supporting prevention rather than
- Adequate services and financial support for youth
- Pressure to choose between academic and vocational curricula (often overwhelming for students and families)
- Clarity of transition plans regarding student postsecondary education, employment goals, and residences
- Important skills such as safety, personal care, self-advocacy, and family planning
- Minimal or no detail on what was to be achieved during transition
- Goals referencing accommodations and supports needed by students to achieve their transition goals
- Student responsibility for carrying out action steps most of the time
- Student IEP transition goals indicating vocational rehabilitative staff and other community agencies as the designees for implementing action steps toward goal completion
- Goals related to postsecondary schooling for students expected to graduate with a modified diploma or some alternative document
- Goals reflecting any type of self-determination education or self-advocacy education

7. What are things to keep in mind when beginning to design program evaluation for transition programs?

   Several principles should be kept in mind when beginning to design an evaluation of the transition planning process:
   - Evaluate only a few indicators at a time.
   - Select an appropriate data collection method.
   - Collect information from everyone involved.
   - Gather information that will identify the strengths and weaknesses of the process.

8. What are some challenges and respective strategies to consider in proactive planning for successful transition programs?

   Important challenges and strategies to consider when planning for successful transition programs include:

Challenge	Strategy
There is a perceived lack of connection between what students are learning in school and work-related expectations.	Use a broad range of opportunities to connect school to work opportunities, to include introductory and long-term and intensive training for work-based learning or hands-on experiences in real-life settings.
Students lack the skill set necessary for gainful employment and career success.	Teach and provide students opportunities to practice soft skills in the secondary setting to enhance program and student success in the workplace.
Students' IEP goals do not clearly define and/or address work-based learning opportunities.	Develop IEP goals that address self-advocacy and leadership as crucial to students' learning.
Families fail to understand and/or be involved in work-based learning as part of individual transition planning.	Provide family members individualized support, resources, and assistance to heighten their awareness of and ability to become actively involved in their student's career and vocational experiences.
Many families fear that student employment will result in the loss of Supplemental Security Income (SSI) and Social Security Disability Insurance (SSDI).	Connect with the nearest Social Security office to retrieve information for all IEP team members, including the student. The IEP team must have accurate information regarding SSI and SSDI work incentive programs and the impact of student wages on benefits.

9. What are some components to consider in setting up successful work-based learning opportunities?

   Components to consider when setting up successful work-based learning opportunities are:
   A. The need to work with competent professionals to ensure appropriate matches between youth and job assignments.
   B. Work experience options that can often be expanded when employers and youth programs share resources and sometimes costs.
   C. Disability awareness and training for youth coworkers as a vital component of success for most work experiences.
   D. The use of standard human resource procedures when bringing in youth with disabilities into the workplace, but are willing to make and provide extensive accommodations or adaptations when they have assistance from competent disability professionals.

10. What are the five majors challenges impacting secondary youth and transition services?

According to Johnson and colleagues (2002) five major challenges impact secondary youth and transition services:
A. Ensuring that students with disabilities have access to the full range of learning experiences and options offered within the general education curriculum
B. Making sure that high school graduation decisions are based on meaningful indicators of students' learning and skills as well as clarifying the implications of different diploma options for youth with disabilities
C. Ensuring students access to and full participation in postsecondary education, employment, and independent living options
D. Supporting student and family participation in the transition planning process
E. Improving collaboration and system linkages at all levels

Recommended Reading

Chelimsky, E., & Shadish, W. R. (1997). *Evaluation for the 21st century: A handbook.* Thousand Oaks, CA: Sage.

Martin, L. L., & Kettner, P. M. (1996). *Measuring the performance of human service programs.* Thousand Oaks, CA: Sage.

Salvia, J., & Ysseldyke, J. E. (2006). *Assessment* (8th ed.). Boston: Houghton Mifflin.

Schalock, R. L. (2001). *Outcome-based evaluation* (2nd ed.). New York: Plenum.

Tucker, M. S., & Codding, J. B. (1998). *Standards for our schools: How to set them, measure them, and reach them.* San Francisco: Jossey-Bass.

Web Resources

Evaluation Practices for Transition Planning

Assessing Students with Disabilities: Transition Planning for the IEP

http://old.transitioncoalition.org/assessing/index.htm

The purpose of this website is to provide information and resources to persons wanting to do assessment for transition planning. Good assessment is the basis for meaningful planning for students, families, and schools as they consider transition needs and needed transition services in the IEP process.

National Center for Work Based Learning Partnerships

http://www.mdx.ac.uk/www/ncwblp

Work Based Learning is a modern way of creating university-level learning in the workplace. Its special work-linked features enable learning to take place at, through, and be centered on the working environment. By using an actual work role and an organization's objectives as the focus for academic inquiry, Work Based Learning is uniquely structured to benefit both the individual employee and the employing organizations.

National Center on Secondary Education and Transition (NCSET)

http://www.ncset.org

NCSET coordinates national resources, offers technical assistance, and disseminates information related to secondary education and transition for youth with disabilities in order to create opportunities for youth to achieve successful futures.

Vocational and Educational Services for Individuals with Disabilities: Lifelong Services Network (LSN)

http://www.vesid.nysed.gov/lsn/transition.htm

LSN is a gateway to technical assistance, information, and referral services for children and adults with disabilities and professional development provided by the Office of Vocational and Educational Services for Individuals with Disabilities (VESID).

References

Achieve, Inc. (2004). *The expectations gap: A 50-state review of high school graduation requirements.* Washington, DC: Author.

Benz, M. R., Lindstrom, L., & Yovanoff, P. (2000). Improving graduation and employment outcomes of students with disabilities: Predictive factors and student perspectives. *Exceptional Children, 66*(4), 509–529.

Bremer, C. D., & Madzar, S. (1995). Encouraging employer involvement in youth apprenticeships and other work-based learning experiences for high school youth. *Journal of Vocational and Technical Education, 12*(1), 15–26.

Campbell-Whatley, G. (2001). Mentoring students with mild disabilities: The "nuts and bolts" of program development. *Intervention in School and Clinic, 36,* 211–216.

Chadsey-Rusch, J., & Heal, L. (1995). Building consensus from transition experts on social integration outcomes and interventions. *Exceptional Children, 62*(2), 165–186.

Chadsey-Rusch, J., Rusch, F. R., & O'Reilly, M. F. (1991). Transition from school to integrated communities. *Remedial and Special Education, 12*(6), 22–33.

Chesapeake Institute. (1994). *A report for the U.S. Department of Education, Office of Special Education and Rehabilitative Services. National agenda for achieving better results for children and youth with serious emotional disturbance.* Washington, DC: Author.

Clark, G. M., & Patton, J. R. (1998). *The Transition Planning Inventory (TPI).* Austin, TX: PRO-ED.

Colley, D. A., & Jamison, D. (1998). Post school results for youth with disabilities: Key indicators and policy implications. *Career Development for Exceptional Individuals, 21,* 145–160.

DeFur, S., Getzel, E. E., & Kregel, J. (1994). Individual transition plans: A work in progress. *Journal of Vocational Rehabilitation, 4*(2), 139–145.

DeStefano, L., & Wagner, M., (1992). Outcome assessment in special education: What lessons have we learned? In F. R. Rusch, L. DeStefano, J. Chadsey-Rusch, L. A. Phelps, & E. Szymanski (Eds.), *Transition from school to life* (pp. 173–207). Sycamore, IL: Sycamore.

Edgar, E. (1987). Secondary programs in special education: Are many of them justifiable? *Exceptional Children, 53,* 555–561.

Everson, J. M., Zhang, D., & Guillory, J. D. (2001). A statewide investigation of individualized transition plans in Louisiana. *Career Development for Exceptional Individuals, 24*(1), 37–49.

Geenen, S., Powers, L. E., Lopez-Vasquez, A., & Bersani, H. (2003). Understanding and supporting the transition of minority youth. *Career Development for Exceptional Individuals, 26,* 27–46.

Grigal, M., Test, D. W., Beattie, J., & Wood, W. M. (1997). An evaluation of transition components of individualized education programs. *Exceptional Children, 63*(3), 357–372.

Halpern, A. S., Yovanoff, P., Doren, B., & Benz, M. R. (1991). Predicting participation in postsecondary education for school leavers with disabilities. *Exceptional Children, 62*(2), 151–164.

Hasazi, S., Furney, K. S., & DeStefano, L. (1999). Implementing the IDEA transition mandates. *Exceptional Children, 65*(4), 555–566.

HEATH Resource Center, Association on Higher Education and Disability, & Educational Testing Service. (1993). Study spreads the word about successful practices for students with disabilities. Washington, DC: Author.

Hughes, K. L., Moore, D. T., & Bailey, T. R. (1999). *Work-based learning and academic skills.* Retrieved from http://www.teacherscollege.edu/iee/BRIEFS/Brief27.htm

Individuals with Disabilities Education Improvement Act of 2004, Pub. L. No. 108-446.

International Association for the Evaluation of Educational Achievement. (1987). *The underachieving curriculum. Assessing U.S. school mathematics from an international perspective.* Champaign, IL: Stipes.

Johnson, D. R., Stodden, R. A., Emanuel, E. J., Luecking, R., & Mack, M. (2002). Current challenges facing secondary education and transition services: What research tells us. *Exceptional Children, 68*(4), 519–531.

Johnson, J. R., & Rusch, F. R. (1993). Secondary special education and transition services: Identification and recommendations for future research and demonstration. *Career Development for Exceptional Individuals, 16*, 1–18.

Lawson, S., & Everson, J. (1993). *A national review of statements of transition services for students who are deaf-blind.* Sands Point, NY: Helen Keller National Center/Technical Assistance Center.

Luecking, R. (2004). *Employer perspectives on youth with disabilities in the workplace.* Minneapolis: University of Minnesota, Institute on Community Integration, National Center on Secondary Education and Transition.

Luecking, R. G., & Fabian, E. S. (2000). Paid internships and employment success for youth in transition. *Career Development for Exceptional Individuals, 23*, 205–222.

Mank, D. (1994). The underachievement of supported employment: A call for reinvestment. *Journal of Disability Policy Studies, 5*(2), 1–24.

Martin, J. E., Mithaug, D. E., Cox, P., Peterson, L. Y., Van Dycke, J. L., & Cash, M. E. (2003). Increasing self-determination: Teaching students to plan, work, evaluate, and adjust. *Exceptional Children, 69*(4), 431–448.

McLearn, K. T., Colasanto, D., Schoen, C., & Shaprio, M. Y. (1999). Mentoring matters: A national survey of adults mentoring young people. In J. B. Grossman (Ed.), *Contemporary issues in mentoring.* Retrieved from http://www.ppv.org/content/reports/issuesinmentoring_pdf.htm

Morningstar, M. E., Turnbull, A. P., & Turnbull, H. R. (1995). What do students with disabilities tell us about the importance of family involvement in the transition from school to adult life? *Exceptional Children, 62*(3), 249–260.

National Longitudinal Transition Study–2. (2003). Menlo Park, CA: SRI International.

Powers, K., Gil-Kashiwabara, E., Powers, L., Geenen, S., Balandran, J., & Palmer, C. (2005). Mandates and effective transition planning practices reflected in IEPs. *Career Development for Exceptional Individuals, 28*(1), 47–59.

Powers, L. E., Turner, A., Matuszewski, J., Wilson, R., & Loesch, C. (1999). A qualitative analysis of student involvement in transition planning. *Journal for Vocational Special Needs Education, 21*(3), 18–26.

Powers, L. E., Turner, A., Westwood, D., Matuszewski, J., Wilson, R., & Phillips, A. (2001, Spring). Take charge for the future: A controlled field-test of a model to promote student involvement in transition planning. *Career Development for Exceptional Individuals, 24*(1), 89–104.

Rusch, F. R., & Phelps, L. A. (1987). Secondary special education and transition from school to work: A national priority. *Exceptional Children, 53*, 487–492.

Salvia, J., & Ysseldyke, J. E. (2004). *Assessment* (7th ed.). Boston: Houghton Mifflin.

Sands, D. J., Bassett, D. S., Lehmann, J., & Spencer, K. C. (1998). Factors contributing to and implications for student involvement in transition-related planning, decision making, and instruction. In M. L. Wehmeyer & D. J. Sands (Eds.), *Making it happen: Student involvement in education, planning, decision making, and instruction* (pp. 25–44). Baltimore: Brookes.

Secretary's Commission on Achieving Necessary Skills, U.S. Department of Labor. (1991). *What work requires of school: A SCANS report for America 2000*. Washington, DC: Author.

Shearin, A., Roessler, R., & Schriner, K. (1999). Evaluating the transition component in IEPs of secondary students with disabilities. *Rural Special Education Quarterly, 18*(2), 22–25.

Sowers, J., McAllister, R., & Cotton, P. (1996). Strategies to enhance the control of the employment process by individuals with severe disabilities. In L. E. Powers, G. H. S. Singer, & J. Sowers (Eds.), *On the road to autonomy: Promoting self-competence for children and youth with disabilities* (pp. 325–346). Baltimore: Brookes.

U.S. Department of Education. (2002). *No Child Left Behind: A desktop reference*. Washington, DC: Office of Elementary and Secondary Education. Available at http://www.ed.gov/NCLB

Vallecorsa, A. L., deBettencourt, L. U., & Garriss, E. (1992). *Special education programs: A guide to evaluation*. Newbury Park, CA: Crown Press.

Vanderwood, M., Ysseldyke, J., & Thurlow, M. (1993). *Consensus building: A process for selecting educational outcomes and indicators* (Outcomes and Indicators Report Number 2). Minneapolis: University of Minnesota, National Center on Educational Outcomes.

Wagner, M., Newman, L., Cameto, R., & Levine, P. (2005). *Changes over time in the early postschool outcomes for youth with disabilities. A report from the National Longitudinal Transition Study–2 (NLTS2)*. Menlo Park, CA: SRI International.

Wagner, M., Newman, L., Cameto, R., Garza, N., & Levine, P. (2005). *After high school: A first look at the postschool experiences of youth with disabilities. A report from the National Longitudinal Transition Study–2 (NLTS2)*. Menlo Park, CA: SRI International.

Wagner, M., Newman, L., & Cameto, R. (2004). *Changes over time in the secondary school experiences of students with disabilities. A special topic report of findings for the National Longitudinal Transition Study–2 (NLTS2)*. Menlo Park, CA: SRI International.

Wagner, M. M. (1995). Outcomes for youths with serious emotional disturbance in secondary school and early adulthood. *The Future of Children: Critical Issues for Children and Youths, 5*(2), 90–112.

Wagner, M., D'Amico, R., Marder, C., Newman, L., & Blackorby, J. (1992). *What happens next? Trends in postschool outcomes of youth with disabilities*. Menlo Park, CA: SRI International.

Wagner, M., Newman, L., D'Amico, R., Jay, E. D., Butler-Nalin, P., Marder, C., et al. (1991). *Youth with disabilities: How are they doing?* Menlo Park, CA: SRI International.

Wehman, P., Kregel, J., & Seyfarth, J. (1985). Employment outlook for adults with mental retardation. *Rehabilitation Counseling Bulletin, 29*, 90–99.

Wehmeyer, M. L., & Schwartz, M. (1997). Self-determination and positive adult outcomes: A follow-up study of youth with mental retardation or learning disabilities. *Exceptional Children, 63*, 245–255.

Wolman, C., Bruininks, R. H., & Thurlow, M. L. (1989). Dropouts and dropout programs: Implications for special education. *Remedial and Special Education, 10*(5), 6–20.

Worthen, B. R., & Sanders, J. R. (1987). *Educational evaluation: Alternative approaches and practical guidelines*. New York: Longman.

Ysseldyke, J. E., & Thurlow, M. L. (1993). *Self-study guide to the development of educational outcomes and indicators*. Minneapolis: University of Minnesota, National Center on Educational Outcomes.

Ysseldyke, J. E., Thurlow, M. L., & Erickson, R. N. (1994a). *Educational outcomes and indicators for grade 8*. Minneapolis: University of Minnesota, National Center on Educational Outcomes.

Ysseldyke, J. E., Thurlow, M. L., & Erickson, R. N. (1994b). *Possible sources of data for post-school level indicators*. Minneapolis: University of Minnesota, National Center on Educational Outcomes.

Ysseldyke, J. E., Thurlow, M. L., & Erickson, R. N. (1995). *Possible sources of data for grade 8 indicators*. Minneapolis: University of Minnesota, National Center on Educational Outcomes.

Ysseldyke, J. E., Thurlow, M. L., & Gilman, C. J. (1993a). *Educational outcomes and indicators for individuals at the post-school level*. Minneapolis: University of Minnesota, National Center on Educational Outcomes.

Ysseldyke, J. E., Thurlow, M. L., & Gilman, C. J. (1993b). *Educational outcomes and indicators for students completing school*. Minneapolis: University of Minnesota, National Center on Educational Outcomes.

Ysseldyke, J. E., Thurlow, M. L., & Vanderwood, M. L. (1994). *Possible sources of data for school completion indicators*. Minneapolis: University of Minnesota, National Center on Educational Outcomes.

AUTHOR INDEX

Abery, B., 58, 77
Achieve, Inc., 309, 334
Ager, C., 277, 284
Agosta, J., 113, 132
Agran, M., 56, 57, 58, 60, 61, 62, 64, 65,
    66, 67, 69, 70, 71, 75, 76, 77, 201,
    221, 269, 275, 276, 278, 285, 286,
    287, 291, 302
Alberto, P. A., 276, 286
Albin, J., 113, 130, 240, 248
Alcantara, P. R., 270, 285
Allen, S. K., 61, 75
Allen, T. E., 291, 302
Americans with Disabilities Act
    of 1990, 32, 35, 40, 51, 274, 284
Amos, B., 181, 184, 195, 198
Amstutz, N., 269, 284
Anderson, J. L., 253, 265
Archer, J., 102, 108
Armstrong, D., 212, 221
Arnett, J., 3, 21
Aspel, N. P., 14, 22, 180, 187, 199

Baer, R. M., 14, 21, 210, 222, 239, 248,
    269, 284
Bailey, T. R., 320, 335
Baker, S. R., 65, 77
Balandran, J., 316, 335
Ballinger, R., 108
Bambara, L. M., 277, 284
Banks, B., 216, 223
Barcus, M., 113, 131
Barron, J., 202, 221
Bassett, D. S., 305, 336
Beattie, J., 305, 316, 334
Beatty, S. E., 255, 265
Beck, S., 269, 284
Bellamy, G., 113, 130
Bender, W. N., 239, 248
Benet-Martinez, V., 103, 109

Benz, M. R., 7, 21, 27, 51, 61, 75, 269,
    284, 305, 317, 334, 335
Berger, M., 202, 221
Bernier, R., 212, 221
Bersani, H., 305, 334
Bingham, R. P., 102, 109
Bissonnette, D., 253, 264
Blacher, J., 113, 130, 131
Black, D., 202, 221
Black, R. S., 79, 80, 102, 103, 104, 105,
    107, 108, 109
Blackmountain, L., 103, 108
Blackorby, J., 4, 22, 27, 53, 201, 217,
    221, 289, 290, 302, 308, 336
Blalock, G., 270, 284
Blanchard, C., 62, 67, 75, 291, 302
Blatt, J., 276, 285
Bohm, D., 163, 174
Bond, L., 202, 221
Boudria, T., 207, 218, 221
Bowe, F., 237, 248
Braddock, D., 5, 22, 113, 132, 269,
    270, 286
Bragg, D., 207, 221
Braziel, P. M., 290, 302
Bremer, C. D., 320, 321, 334
Brock, M. L., 270, 272, 285
Brolin, D. E., 30, 51, 182, 198
Bronfenbrenner, U., 270, 281, 285
Brooke, V., 113, 131
Brothers, J., 269, 284
Brown, G. L., 266
Bruininks, R. H., 309, 336
Bryant, B., 269, 287
Buber, M., 163
Buckley, J., 240, 248
Bumgarner, M., 277, 286
Burgstahler, S., 201, 221
Butler-Nalin, P., 308, 336
Butterworth, J., 214, 221

Cai, X., 76
Callahan, M., 114, 131, 252, 264
Cameto, R., 4, 10, 12, 21, 22, 102, 109,
    114, 131, 268, 287, 308, 336
Campbell-Whatley, G., 305, 334
Capella, M., 201, 222
Caplan, J., 113, 131
Caren, S., 285
Carl D. Perkins Vocational Education
    Act of 1984, 31, 32, 51
Carlson, B. C., 198
Carlson, L., 216, 222
Carol, K., 113, 131
Carter, E. W., 60, 65, 76, 113, 114, 131,
    269, 270, 271, 274, 275, 278,
    281, 285
Carter, S., 113, 131
Cash, M. E., 317, 335
Cavanaugh, S., 202, 222
Cavin, M., 62, 76
Centers for Medicare and Medicaid
    Services (CMS), 43, 51
Certo, N. J., 114, 127, 131, 132, 164,
    174, 175, 214, 215, 216, 222, 285
Chadsey, J., 14, 22, 210, 219, 223
Chadsey-Rusch, J., 114, 132, 289, 302,
    308, 334
Chambers, C. R., 113, 131
Chang, K. B. T., 40, 52
Chapman, S., 113, 131
Chesapeake Institute, 305, 334
Christ, G., 213, 222
Church-Pupke, P. P., 275, 285
Cimera, R. E., 224, 237, 239, 240, 248
Cioffi, A., 239, 248, 253, 265
Clark, G. M., 30, 51, 181, 182, 187,
    188, 189, 192, 193, 195, 198,
    269, 285, 334
Cleveland, P., 231, 248
Colasanto, D., 305, 335

Coleman, H. L., 103, 109
Coleman, J. C., 139, 159
Colley, D. A., 319, 334
Comprehensive Employment and Training Act (CETA) of 1973, 30, 32, 51
Cook, I. D., 181, 198
Cooney, B. F., 113, 131, 269, 285
Copeland, S. R., 62, 65, 66, 75, 76, 275, 278, 285
Corman, H., 206, 222
Correa, V. I., 181, 198
Cotton, P., 305, 336
Covert, S., 113, 132
Cox, P., 317, 335
Coy, D. R., 6, 23
Crudele, K. S., 256, 261, 265

D'Alonzo, B. J., 181, 198
D'Amico, R., 308, 336
Darrow, C., 3, 22
DeBettencourt, L. U., 289, 302, 318, 336
DeFur, S. H., 112, 113, 131, 315, 334
DeStefano, L., 114, 132, 181, 184, 186, 198, 270, 285, 291, 302, 306, 309, 316, 334, 335
Dewey, J., 216, 222
Dinard, P., 206, 222
Dolainski, S., 201, 202, 222
Dolinyuk, A., 206, 222
Doren, B., 193, 198, 305, 335
Dornbush, S. M., 12, 22
Dornsife, C., 204, 223
Dwyre, A. E., 255, 264

Edgar, E. B., 289, 302, 309, 334
Education for All Handicapped Children Act of 1975, 30, 31, 51
Education of the Handicapped Act Amendments of 1983, 31, 51
Elementary and Secondary Education Act (No Child Left Behind) 2001, 35, 38, 39–40, 52
Elliot, D., 12, 22
Elliot, J., 185, 199, 291, 302, 304
Elliot, M., 201, 222
Emanuel, E., 201, 222, 268, 285, 324, 333, 335
Erickson, R., 291, 302, 314, 315, 336, 337
Erwin, E., 113, 132
Everson, J. E., 14, 22

Everson, J. M., 115, 123, 131, 136, 139, 140, 146, 147, 150, 156, 157, 159, 180, 187, 199, 315, 316, 334, 335
Ewalt, P. L., 103, 105, 107, 108

Fabian, E. S., 201, 213, 222, 240, 248, 253, 264, 265, 319, 335
Family Perspectives on Inclusion and Transition, 113, 131
Fanning, P. N., 289, 302
Felce, D., 183, 196, 198
Feldman, R., 110
Feldstein, L. M., 138, 139, 159
Field, S., 27, 52, 61, 76
Finkelstein, N., 204, 223
Finley, M., 159
First, C., 290, 302
Fisher, D., 164, 174, 181
Fisher, G. M., 270, 272, 285
Fisher, S., 198
Fleming, R., 113, 131
Flexer, R. W., 14, 21, 210, 222, 239, 248, 269, 284
Florida, R., 159
Flowers, C., 61, 75
Forest, M., 193, 198
Forsyth, J., 206, 222
Fowler, S. E., 62, 75, 275, 285
Frank, A. R., 289, 302
Frankland, H. C., 103, 108
Franzinin, L. R., 290, 302
Frazier, E. S., 79, 99, 109
Fujiura, G., 113, 132
Furney, K. S., 181, 184, 186, 198, 270, 285, 291, 302, 306, 316, 335

Garcia, J., 273, 286
Garcia, L. A., 182, 183, 184, 187, 189, 198
Gardugue, L., 12, 22
Garff, J. T., 275, 286
Garner, N., 66, 77
Garriss, E., 318, 336
Garza, N., 268, 287, 308, 336
Gaumer, A. S., 269, 285
Geenen, S., 305, 316, 334
General Accounting Office, 115, 131
Gerton, J., 103, 109
Getzel, E. E., 72, 77, 113, 131, 315, 334
Gil-Kashiwabara, E., 316, 335
Gilbert, G. H., 62, 67, 76, 276, 285
Gilman, C. J., 312, 314, 337

Gilroy, C., 201, 222
Gipson, K., 269, 286
Godshall, J. C., 272
Goetz, L., 253, 265
Good, T. L., 289, 302
Goodall, P. A., 231, 248
Gosling, S. D., 103, 109
Gossage, D., 110
Gove, P. B., 58, 76
Gowdy, E., 216, 222
Grack, A., 79, 106, 108
Grayson, T., 290, 302
Green, M., 204, 222
Greenberger, E., 6, 12, 21, 22
Griffin, C., 240, 248
Grigal, M., 305, 316, 334
Guillory, J. D., 139, 140, 146, 147, 150, 156, 157, 159, 316, 334

Hagner, D., 200, 205, 213, 214, 221, 222, 239, 248, 253, 257, 265
Hall, G., 113, 131
Halpern, A., 193, 198, 268, 285, 305, 335
Hamre-Neitupski, S., 229, 248
Hanser, L., 201, 222
Harmer, M. L., 270, 285
Harris, L., 57, 76
Harry, B., 104, 108, 109
Hart, D., 27, 52
Hasazi, S. B., 181, 186, 198, 270, 285, 291, 302, 306, 316, 335
Hawkins, R., 204, 222
Heal, L., 7, 21, 22, 239, 248, 308, 334
HEATH Resource Center, 305, 335
Held, M., 193, 194, 199, 211, 223
Helm, D., 214, 221
Hemmerla, K., 201, 222
Henderson, A., 112, 113, 131
Herman, A. M., 12, 21
Herr, C. M., 193, 198
Hershenson, D., 6, 21
Hildebrand, K. E., 224
Hoffman, A., 27, 52
Hoffman, L., 269, 284
Hogan, D. P., 7, 23
Holburn, C. S., 63, 77
Holburn, S., 62, 76
Holland, J. L., 6, 21
Holsch, S. A., 290, 302
Holub, T., 288
Hon, J., 207, 219, 223

AUTHOR INDEX

Hoogstra, L., 201, 223
Horiuchi, C. H., 289, 302
Horn, J., 201, 204, 222
Houser, B., 272
Howard, M., 216, 223
Hoyt, K. B., 29, 52
Hughes, C., 7, 22, 57, 60, 62, 64, 65, 66, 68, 70, 75, 76, 77, 113, 114, 131, 239, 248, 257, 265, 266, 269, 270, 271, 272, 274, 275, 276, 278, 281, 285, 286, 287, 291, 302
Hughes, K. L., 320, 335
Hughes, M., 276, 286
Hugo, K., 276, 285
Husch, J. V., 79, 99, 109
Hutchins, M., 274, 286
Hutson, J., 229, 248
Hwang, B., 76, 270, 272, 278, 285

Ianni, F. A. J., 12, 21
Individuals with Disabilities Education Act (IDEA) Amendments of 1997, 36, 37, 38, 39, 52, 60, 76, 161, 174, 179, 285
Individuals with Disabilities Education Act (IDEA) of 1990, 5, 22, 30, 32, 35, 36, 37, 40, 52, 179, 268, 285
Individuals with Disabilities Education Improvement Act of 2004, 37, 38–39, 52, 109, 161, 179, 198, 273, 275, 276, 281, 285, 307, 335
Inge, K., 113, 131
International Association for the Evaluation of Educational Achievement, 308, 335
Ivester, J., 136, 139, 159

Jackson, S., 204, 222
Jacobson, J. W., 63, 77
Jamieson, D. W., 159
Jamison, D., 319, 334
Jay, E. D., 290, 291, 302, 308, 336
Jerman, P. A., 84, 109
Job Training Partnership Act of 1982, 30, 32, 52
Job Training Reform Act of 1993, 32, 42, 52
Johnson, D. R., 79, 106, 109, 201, 222, 268, 270, 285, 324, 333, 335

Johnson, J., 112, 127, 131
Johnson, J. R., 305, 335
Johnson, J. W., 276, 286
Johnson, L., 61, 76, 276, 286
Johnson, M., 193, 198
Johnson, R. D., 61, 76
Johnson, S. T., 291, 302
Jones, M., 110
Jones, M. A., 40, 52
Justice, T., 159

Kalyanpur, M., 104, 108, 109
Kamens, M., 206, 211, 222
Kamps, D., 273, 286
Karen, R. L., 290, 302
Katsiyannis, A., 61, 77
Keith, K. D., 192, 198
Kennedy, J. F., 28, 52
Killian, D. J., 270, 272, 285
Kim, J., 270, 272, 285
Kim, K., 113, 131
King-Sears, M. E., 65, 75
Klein, E., 3, 22
Kleinhammer-Tramill, J., 115, 132
Knowlton, H. E., 64, 77
Kochhar-Bryant, C. A., 270, 284
Kohler, P. D., 14, 22, 29, 52, 113, 131, 181, 184, 186, 270, 284
Konrad, M., 61, 76, 269, 286
Kortering, L. J., 290, 302
Kozleski, E. B., 64, 77, 184, 186, 199
Kraemer, B. R., 113, 131
Kregel, J., 113, 133, 309, 315, 334, 336
Krentz, J., 185, 188, 199
Kretzman, J. P., 139, 159

LaFollette Act of 1943, 28, 32, 52
LaFromboise, T., 103, 109
Lagomarcino, T. R., 68, 76
Langton, A., 211, 222
Lankard, B. A., 115, 132
Latting, J., 204, 223
Lave, J., 216, 222
Lawson, J., 193, 198
Lawson, S., 315, 335
Leake, D., 79, 80, 102, 103, 104, 105, 107, 109
Leconte, P. J., 182, 187, 198
Lee, M., 253, 265
Lehmann, J., 270, 284, 305, 336
Lent, R., 201, 222
Lerner, R., 3, 22

Levine, P., 102, 109, 268, 287, 289, 302, 308, 336
Levinson, D., 3, 22
Levinson, M., 3, 22
Levison, L., 273, 286
Lieberman, A., 270, 286
Lindstrom, B. D., 27, 52
Lindstrom, L., 7, 21, 27, 51, 61, 75, 269, 284, 317, 334
Liu, S., 202, 222
Loesch, C., 306, 335
Lopez-Vasquez, A., 305, 334
Lorden, S. W., 276, 285
Loughead, T., 202, 222
Louis Harris Poll, 114, 132
Lounsbury, D., 200
Lozada, M., 22, 203, 204, 206, 218
Lubin, S., 113, 131
Luecking, R. G., 114, 132, 202, 213, 222, 240, 248, 253, 264, 265, 268, 285, 319, 322, 324, 333, 335
Luft, P., 14, 21, 210, 222, 239, 248

MacDonald, M., 208, 209, 222
Mack, M., 201, 222, 268, 285, 324, 333, 335
MacMillan, B., 290, 302
MacMillan, T. F., 290, 291, 302
Madzar, S., 320, 321, 334
Malott, R. W., 67, 68, 76
Malouf, D. B., 270, 281, 286
Mank, D., 113, 130, 239, 240, 248, 253, 257, 265, 305, 335
Manning, W. D., 12, 22
Mapp, K. L., 112, 113, 131
Marder, C., 4, 12, 22, 308, 336
Mark, J., 206, 222
Marshall, L. H., 61, 76, 79, 84, 85, 87, 89, 92, 109
Martin, J. E., 61, 70, 71, 75, 76, 77, 78, 79, 84, 94, 95, 96, 97, 99, 101, 102, 103, 109, 224, 226, 227, 229, 248, 317, 335
Mason, C., 61, 65, 76, 269, 276, 286
Matuszewski, J., 61, 77, 305, 306, 335
Mautz, D., 127, 131, 174, 214, 222, 285
Maxson, L. L., 84, 109
Mayhall, C. D., 251, 252, 255, 260, 265
McAllister, R., 305, 336
McDonnell, J., 276, 286
McGahee-Kovac, M., 61, 76, 276, 286
McGlashing-Johnson, J., 62, 76

McKee, B., 3, 22
McLearn, K. T., 305, 335
McMorris, B., 6, 22
McNight, J., 139, 159
McNulty, K., 115, 123, 131
Meadows, N., 289, 302
Menchetti, B. M., 63, 76, 178, 182, 183, 184, 187, 188, 189, 198, 293
Middleton, E., 202, 222
Mihalic, S. W., 12, 22
Millar, D., 14, 22
Mithaug, D. E., 58, 64, 70, 71, 76, 77, 79, 99, 109, 227, 230, 234, 235, 245, 248, 289, 302, 317, 335
Mittelsteadt, S., 206, 222
Mokuau, N., 103, 105, 107, 108
Moore, D. T., 320, 335
Moore, M., 185, 199
Moore, S., 69, 75
Morningstar, M. E., 113, 115, 131, 132, 269, 285, 305, 335
Morrison, L., 273, 286
Morse, S. W., 138, 139, 159
Mrasek, K. D., 108
Murphy, S., 253, 265
Murray, C., 268, 286

Nathanson, R., 65, 77
National Alliance for Secondary Education and Transition, 112, 113, 132
National Center on Secondary Education and Transition, 41, 52, 113, 123, 132
National Council on Disability, 114, 115, 132, 162, 163, 174
National Longitudinal Transition Study-2, 308, 335
National Organization on Disability, 268, 286
National Parent Teacher Association, 112, 132
National Research Council, 10, 22
National Service Trust Act of 1994, 32, 42, 52
Neale, M., 269, 286
Neel, R. S., 289, 302
Neubert, D. A., 180, 182, 187, 198
New Freedom Initiative Report Delivering on the Promise, 43, 52
Newman, L., 4, 22, 102, 109, 268, 287, 308, 336

Nietupski, J., 229, 248
Nirje, B., 276, 286
Nisbet, J., 113, 132, 239, 248, 253, 265
No Child Left Behind Act of 2001, 52, 268, 286
Noyes, D., 160, 161, 164, 175

O'Brien, J., 109, 193, 198
Ochs, L., 201, 223
Office of Disability Employment Policy, 113, 114, 132
Ohtake, Y., 210, 219, 223
O'Leary, J., 291, 303
Oliphint, J. H., 99, 109
Olvey, G., 109
Olympus Research Corporation, 29, 52
O'Reilly, M., 289, 302, 308, 334

PACER Center, 113, 123, 132
Padilla, C. L., 290, 291, 302
Palmer, C., 216, 335
Palmer, S. B., 60, 70, 77, 269, 276, 286, 287
Parent, W., 110, 113, 133
Parker, D., 273, 286
Parnell, D., 207, 223
Parsons, M. B., 277, 286
Patton, J. R., 192, 193, 198, 334
Pauly, E., 213, 223
Pearpoint, J., 193, 198
Pennebaker, J. W., 103, 109
Perry, J., 183, 196, 198
Peterson, L. Y., 317, 335
Petty, D. M., 229, 249
Phelps, L. A., 13, 22, 114, 132, 268, 286, 309, 335
Phillips, A., 61, 77, 305, 335
Piland, V. C., 76, 182, 188, 189, 198
Pitkin, S. E., 276, 285
Polman, J., 206, 223
Polychronis, S., 276, 286
Porché-Burke, L., 102, 109
Potter, J. P., 103, 109
Powers, K., 316, 335
Powers, L. E., 61, 77, 305, 316, 334, 335
Pumpian, I., 127, 131, 164, 174, 175, 214, 222, 285
Putnam, R. D., 138, 139, 159

Rahn, M., 212, 223
Ramirez-Esparza, N., 103, 109

Ramseur, H., 211, 222
Rapp, C., 216, 222
Rawlings, B. W., 291, 302
Reeves, D., 206, 222
Rehabilitation Act Amendments of 1992, 32, 40, 52, 286
Rehabilitation Act Amendments of 1998, 161, 175
Rehabilitation Act of 1973, 29, 32, 52
Reid, D. H., 277, 286
Reid, E., 304
Reilly, J., 229, 248
Renzaglia, A., 274, 286
Repetto, J. B., 181, 188, 198
Reschly, D., 86, 184, 199
Revell, G. W., 290, 291, 302
Revell, W. G., 127, 133
Reynolds, J., 277, 286
Rhodes, L., 113, 130, 240, 248
Riesen, T., 276, 286
Robbins, H., 159
Roberts, K. D., 24, 102, 109
Rockoff, J., 206, 222
Roessler, R., 201, 222, 223, 240, 248, 316, 336
Rogan, P., 114, 131, 211, 216, 223, 253, 257, 265
Ross, M., 204, 223
Rowh, M., 202, 223
Rueda, R., 104, 108
Ruggiero, M., 12, 22
Rung, L. L., 278, 285
Rusch, F. R., 2, 5, 7, 13, 14, 21, 22, 29, 52, 68, 71, 76, 113, 114, 115, 132, 224, 227, 230, 234, 235, 239, 245, 248, 257, 265, 268, 269, 270, 286, 288, 289, 302, 305, 308, 309, 334, 335

Sage, H., 6, 23
Sale, P., 113, 133
Salvia, J., 180, 185, 188, 189, 198, 307, 336
Sandberg, J., 202, 223
Sandefur, G. D., 7, 23
Sanders, J. R., 308, 336
Sandow, D., 240, 248
Sands, D. J., 60, 64, 65, 77, 305, 336
Sarkees-Wincenski, M., 29, 52
Savage, T., 212, 221
Sawilowsky, S., 61, 76

AUTHOR INDEX

Sax, C. L., 127, 131, 160, 161, 164, 174, 175, 198, 214, 222
Schalock, R. L., 269, 287
Schildroth, A., 291, 302
Schiller, E. P., 270, 281, 286
Schlaock, R., 192, 198
Schoen, C., 305, 335
School-to-Work Opportunities Act of 1994, 268, 286
Schorr, L. B., 138, 159
Schriner, K., 316, 336
Schuh, M., 113, 132
Schwartz, A., 63, 77
Schwartz, M., 60, 64, 72, 77, 305, 336
Scott, J. L., 29, 52
Secretary's Commission on Achieving Necessary Skills, U.S. Department of Labor, 308, 336
Seltzer, A., 276, 286
Senge, P., 163
Seyfarth, M., 309, 336
Shapiro, E. S., 61, 77
Shaprio, M. Y., 305, 335
Sharpe, N. M., 61, 76
Shearin, A., 316, 336
Shelden, D. L., 251, 255, 256, 261, 265
Shernoff, D., 201, 223
Sherron, P., 240, 248
Shorr, A., 207, 219, 223
Shueman, S. A., 239, 249
Silverman, W., 269, 287
Simmons, T. J., 14, 21, 210, 222, 239, 248
Singer, G., 113, 132
Sirolli, E., 159
Sitlington, P. L., 62, 76, 182, 187, 188, 189, 195, 198, 289, 302
Skinner, M. E., 27, 52
Smalley, K., 127, 131, 164, 174, 214, 222, 285
Smith, A. C., 61, 75
Smith-Fess Act of 1920, 28, 32, 52
Smith-Hughes Act of 1917, 28, 32, 52
Smith, M., 61, 75
Smith-Sears Act or Soldiers Rehabilitation Act of 1918, 28, 32, 52
Snow, K., 64, 75, 201, 221
Snyder, E. P., 61, 77
Social Security Administration, 162, 174
Solomon (2005), 122

Soodak, L., 113, 132
Sowers, J., 305, 336
Spencer, K. C., 305, 336
SRI International, 113, 132
St. Onge, I., 273, 286
Stancliff, R. J., 58, 77
Steinberg, L. D., 3, 6, 10, 12, 21, 22
Stern, D., 204, 212, 223
Stillerman, S., 61, 76, 276, 286
Stodden, R. A., 24, 27, 40, 52, 201, 222, 268, 285, 324, 333, 335
Stoia, J., 206, 222
Stone, J., 204, 223
Storey, K., 164, 174, 253, 265, 275, 286
Sue, D. W., 102, 104, 109
Sumi, C., 12, 22
Sumner, G., 240, 248
Super, D. E., 6, 22
Swaner, J., 64, 75, 201, 221
Swanson, C. B., 268, 286
Sylvester, L., 78, 97, 98, 109
Szymanski, E. M., 6, 21, 114, 132

Taber, T. A., 276, 286
Tamura, R., 65, 77
Tarnai, Balázs, 224
Tasse, M. J., 269, 287
Technology-Related Assistance for Individuals with Disabilities Act of 1988, 42 43, 52
Technology-Related Assistance for Individuals with Disabilities Act (Tech Act) of 2004, 42 43, 52
Test, D. W., 14, 22, 61, 75, 76, 180, 187, 188, 189, 194, 199, 239, 248, 253, 257, 265, 269, 270, 276, 284, 286, 305, 316, 334
Thoma, C. A., 65, 72, 77, 193, 194, 199
Thompson, J. R., 269, 271, 274, 287
Thompson, S., 185, 199, 209, 223
Thoreau, H., 216, 223
Thornton, H., 289, 290, 302, 303
Thurlow, M., 184, 185, 186, 196, 199, 291, 302, 304, 309, 312, 314, 315, 336, 337
Ticket to Work and Work Incentives Improvement Act of 1999, 41–42, 52
Tilson, G. P., 114, 132, 213, 222, 240, 248, 253, 264, 265
Tindall, L. W., 29, 53
Tinsley, C., 138, 159

Todd-Allen, M., 113, 131
Torocco, M., 202, 223
Trach, J. S., 201, 204, 222, 250, 251, 252, 253, 255, 256, 260, 261, 264, 265
Trainor, A. T., 102, 103, 104, 109
Tuckman, D. W., 140, 156, 159
Turnbull, A. P., 103, 108, 113, 131, 132, 305, 335
Turnbull, H. R., 113, 132, 305, 335
Turnbull, R., 113, 132
Turner, A., 61, 77, 305, 335
Turner, P., 110

Uggen, C., 6, 22
U.S. Department of Education, 8, 9, 268, 287, 290, 305, 336
U.S. Department of Labor, 12, 22, 208, 209, 219, 223, 268, 287

Vacanti, J. M., 182, 198
Valenzuela, R. L., 79, 103, 109
Vallecorsa, A. L., 318, 336
Van Dycke, J. L., 317, 335
Vanderwood, M., 315, 336, 337
Vasquez, M., 102, 109
Vaux, A., 12, 22
Verstegen, D., 229, 248, 249
Virginia Commonwealth University, 237, 249
Vocational Education Act Amendments of 1976, 30, 32, 53
Vocational Education Act of 1963, 28, 31, 32, 53
Vocational Rehabilitation Amendments of 1954, 28, 32, 53
Vocational Rehabilitation Amendments of 1967, 29, 32, 53
Vocational Rehabilitation Amendments of 1968, 29, 32, 53

Wachter, M. I., 138, 159
Wade, H., 127, 131, 174, 214, 222, 285
Wagner, M., 4, 12, 18, 22, 27, 53, 201, 217, 221, 268, 287, 289, 290, 291, 302, 308, 334, 336
Wagner, W., 102, 107, 109
Wakefield, S. M., 6, 23
Walker, C., 110
Washington, B. H., 266
Waxer, C., 202, 213, 223

AUTHOR INDEX

Wehman, P., 57, 77, 113, 114, 127, 133, 231, 248, 270, 287, 290, 291, 302, 309, 336
Wehmeyer, M. L., 56, 57, 58, 59, 60, 62, 63, 64, 65, 66, 67, 68, 70, 72, 75, 76, 77, 103, 108, 269, 275, 276, 278, 285, 286, 287, 291, 302, 305, 336
Weiner, J. S., 239, 249
Weinstein, R. S., 289, 302
Weisenstein, G. R., 29, 53
Wells, L., 109
Wells, T., 7, 23
Wenger, E., 216, 222
WESTAT, 113, 133
Westwood, D., 205, 335
Wheeler, J., 223
Whelley, T. A., 27, 52, 214, 221
White, W. J., 270, 284, 289, 303

Whitman, T. L., 69, 77
Will, M., 32, 33, 53, 268, 287
Williams, I. J., 229, 249
Williams, J., 291, 303
Willis, S., 201, 222
Wilson, P. G., 7, 22, 239, 248
Wilson, R., 61, 77, 305, 306, 335
Winger, M., 203, 223
Wolf, N., 193, 198
Wolman, C., 309, 336
Wood, W. M., 61, 75, 239, 248, 253, 257, 265, 269, 286, 305, 316, 334
Woods, L. L., 78, 97, 109
Workforce Development Act of 1995, 42, 53
Workforce Investment Act (WIA) of 1998, 41, 53
Worthen, B. R., 308, 336

Wray, D., 109
Wright (2004), 161

Yankelovich, D., 163, 166, 172, 175
Yeager, D., 66, 77
Yovanoff, P., 7, 21, 27, 51, 61, 75, 239, 248, 253, 265, 269, 284, 305, 317, 334, 335
Ysseldyke, J. E., 180, 184, 185, 186, 188, 189, 196, 198, 199, 291, 302, 307, 312, 314, 315, 336, 337

Zafft, C., 27, 52
Zhang, D., 61, 77, 103, 104, 109, 316, 334
Zhang, J., 61, 77
Zigmond, N., 289, 290, 302, 303
Zimbrich, K., 27, 52
Zivolich, S., 239, 249, 253, 265

SUBJECT INDEX

Academic and functional literacy in the National Center on Educational Outcomes (NCEO) model, 311
Academic credit for work experiences, 212
Access and accommodations, 29–30
Accommodation and adaptation in the National Center on Educational Outcomes (NCEO) model, 311
ACT EXPLORE assessment, 83, 93
Action plans (work plans), 145
Active student involvement, 60–61, 184
ACT's Educational Planning and Assessment System (EPAS), 83, 93
Adequate yearly progress (AYP), 39
Adolescence
  definition of, 3
  early, middle, and late, 3
  transition to adult roles, 2–23
  See also Students with disabilities; Students without disabilities
Adult Lifestyles Planning Cycle, 183–184
Adult roles. *See* Transition to adult roles
Adult services, 16
  eligibility for, 5
Advocacy, 137
  self-advocacy, 58, 61
  in supported employment, 114
Advocacy groups, 35
African American students with disabilities, 268
Agent, defined, 59
American with Disabilities Act (ADA) of 1990, 32, 35, 40–41

America's Career Infonet, 83
Andersonville County (case study), 146–153
Antecedent cue regulation (picture cues), 69–70
Apprenticeships, 205, 251, 323
Arrest rates, 5
Assessment. *See* Transition assessment
Assistive technology (AT), 43, 162
  in job redesign, 239
  and supported employment, 114
AYP (adequate yearly progress), 39

Behavioral training techniques, 114
Business groups, 138

Capacity-enhancement approach in student-directed transition planning, 63–64
Career academies, 206–207
Career development models, 182
Career development theories, 6, 182
Career education, 29
Career options, 6
Career planning. *See* Person-centered career planning
Career technology school, 93
Carl D. Perkins Vocational and Technical Act (1984), 31, 32
Case management services, 138
Case studies
  Andersonville County, 146–153
  Christopher, 81–82, 93–102
  in dialogue, 166–170
  evaluation practices for transition planning, 326–329
  in interagency and interdisciplinary teams, 146–153
  Jenkins Parish, 146–153
  job placement, 225–226, 244

Julie, 80–81, 83–93
  in person-centered career planning, 57, 72–73
  in preparing students for adult roles, 3, 17
  teams and interagency coordination, 168–170
  in transition legislation and policy, 25–26, 45–47
  transition support (Josie and Jerome), 267, 278–280
  in working with parents, 111–112
Casey Life Skills, 83, 84
Causal agents, defined, 59
Centers for Medicare and Medicaid Services (CMS), 43
CETA (Comprehensive Employment and Training Act of 1973), 30, 32
Chambers of commerce, 213, 229
Change Grants for Community Living, Real Choice Systems, 43
Child labor restrictions, 209
Choose and Take Action software, 94–98
Choosing Employment Goals, 84–87
Christopher (case study), 81–82, 93–102
Citizenship and community participation, 201–202
Civic engagement, 138
Civic groups, 138
Civil rights law (ADA), 40
CMS. *See* Centers for Medicare and Medicaid Services
Cofacilitation, 164–165
Collaboration
  in interagency and interdisciplinary teams, 161–163, 181
  in work-based learning, 214–216

345

Collectivism, 103
College preparatory courses, 4
Commercial transition inventories, 192–193
Communication, in interagency and interdisciplinary teams, 161, 163
Communication skills, 61
Community-based job settings, 95
Community connections, 122, 138
Community development, 137–140
  core elements of, 143–145
Community-level teamwork, 140–143
Community needs and demographics, 146
Community participation, 15, 16, 201–202
Community placement options, 227–229
Community placement survey, 229
Community rehabilitation programs, 216
Community supports, 261
Community transitions, 125
Compensatory strategies, 114
Competitive employment, 114
Comprehensive Employment and Training Act (1973), 30, 32
Connection in pathways to self-determination model, 293, 294
Contextual learning, 202, 217
Contribution and citizenship in the National Center on Educational Outcomes (NCEO) model, 311
Council for Exceptional Children (CEC), Division on Career Development, 182
Cultural frame-switching, 103
Culturally and linguistically diverse (CLD) students, 102–105
Cultural reciprocity, 103–105
Customized employment, 114

Day programs, 114, 216
Departments of rehabilitation (DRs), 164, 168
Determinism, philosophical doctrine of, 58
Developmental levels, 185, 311
Development disability systems (DDSs), 164

Dewean tradition, 216–217
Dialogue, 163–166
  versus debate, 172
Disabilities
  training and rehabilitation for persons with, 28–29
  types of, 7, 291, 309
  veterans with, 28
  See also Students with disabilities
Discrimination, in employment, 40
Diversity awareness, 273
Diversity in community connections, 138
Dream Job Shadowing Worksheet, 87–92
Dropout prevention, 288–303
  background and statistics, 4, 201, 268, 289–291
  consequences of not completing high school, 291
  definition of "dropout," 289
  illustrations of the pathways model, 294–298
  pathways to self-determination, 292–298

Early adolescence, 3
Education, transition legislation and policy, 35–40
Education for All Handicapped Children Act (1975), 30, 31
Education of the Handicapped Act Amendments (1983), 31
Education-related services, 5
  mandatory, 5
Elementary and Secondary Education Act (ESEA), 35, 38, 39–40. *See also* No Child Left Behind (NCLB)
Elementary schools
  career and work studies, 202
  transition services in, 181
Employers, 61
  expectations of, 232–234, 320–321
  resources of, 202
  wants and needs of, 113
Employment
  benefits versus costs, 13
  competitive, 114
  customized, 114
  discrimination in, 40
  internal versus contracted services, 215

  opportunities for, 230–231
  of people with disabilities, 6–7, 57, 114
  as primary goal, 113
  rates of, 5
  specialized training in, 3, 4
  supported, 113–114, 138
  transition legislation and policy, 40–42
  See also Person-centered career planning
Employment programs, 30
Employment vision, 78–109
  ACT EXPLORE assessment, 83, 93
  ACT's Educational Planning and Assessment System (EPAS), 83, 93
  America's Career Infonet, 83
  career technology school, 93
  Casey Life Skills, 83, 84
  Choose and Take Action software, 94–98
  Choosing Employment Goals, 84–87
  Christopher (case study), 81–82, 93–102
  community-based job settings, 95
  cultural frame-switching, 103
  culturally and linguistically diverse (CLD) students, 102–105
  cultural reciprocity, 103–105
  Dream Job Shadowing Worksheet, 87–92
  Employment Vision Circle, 97–98
  family-centered or collectivist decision-making process, 79–80, 94, 102–105
  family cultural values, 79
  four-stage career awareness, exploration, and placement model, 93–94
  high school exploration and preparation, 84–93, 98–101
  IEP team meetings, 84, 97, 100
  individualism and collectivism, 103
  interest inventory, 93
  interests, 79
  job options, 79
  job site self-evaluation assessment, 101
  job site visits, 84, 87
  Julie (case study), 80–81, 83–93

SUBJECT INDEX

life skills program, 94
limits, 79
middle school career exploration, 83–84, 93–98
online assessments, 83
on-the-job supports, 100
parental outreach program, 94
self-determination, 94, 103, 104
Self-Directed Employment handbook, 99, 100
skills, 79
"take your child to work day," 83
transition class, 84
updates, 93
U.S. Department of Labor, Bureau of Labor Statistics' Occupational Handbook website, 83
vocational assessment portfolio, 99, 100
vocational interest portfolio, 97
vocational preference instructional and assessment process, 79
Employment Vision Circle, 97–98
English language learners, 268
Entry-level occupations, 12
Evaluation in pathways to self-determination model, 293, 294
Evaluation practices for transition planning, 304–337
challenges and strategies, 320–322, 332
definitions of assessment and evaluation, 307–308
failure to define educational outcomes, 309–311
formative assessment, 318
host employers, 322–323
IEP process, 317
importance of, 308–311
lack of planning, 309
National Center on Educational Outcomes (NCEO) model, 185–186, 311–315
need for comprehensiveness and knowledge of future environments, 325
need for evaluation of the transition planning process and programs, 325–326
need for individualization, 325
poor postschool outcomes, 308

proactive planning for success, 319–322
recommended practices, 315–322
soft skills and employer expectations, 320–321
studies of, 315–317
summative evaluation, 318
work-based learning opportunity components, 322–324
See also Transition assessment; Transition planning
Evidence-based practice, 27
Exploration in pathways to self-determination model, 293, 294

Facilitator's Handbook, The (Justice and Jamieson), 143
Fair Labor Standards Act, 12, 108–109, 207
Faith-based groups, 138
Families. *See* Parents
Family-centered or collectivist decision-making process, 79–80, 94, 102–105
Family cultural values, 79
FAPE. *See* Free and appropriate public education
Field trips or industry tours, 203
Financial dependence, 267
Focus in pathways to self-determination model, 292, 294
Formal methods of transition assessment, 188–189
Formative assessment, 318. *See also* Evaluation practices for transition planning, 318
Forming stage in teams, 146–147
Four-stage career awareness, exploration, and placement model, 93–94
Free and appropriate public education (FAPE), 5

General education courses, 4
Group enclaves, 216

Habitat for Humanity, 138
Halpern's model of school to community adjustment, 268
Handicapped, 30
Hazardous occupations, 209

High schools, 3
basic curricula, 4
diplomas earned by students with disabilities, 268, 290, 291
enrollments, graduation, and dropouts, 8–11
exploration and preparation for employment, 84–93, 98–101
integrating work experience into the high school curriculum, 206–207
internal versus contracted employment services, 215
real-life work and community experiences, 162
services for students with disabilities, 6
transition services in, 181
Host employers, 322–323

IDEA. *See* Individuals with Disabilities Education Act
IEP. *See* Individualized education program
Incarceration, 267, 291
Inclusion principle, 35
Independence-interdependence continuum, 64
Individualism and collectivism, 103
Individualized education program (IEP), 30, 305
and culturally and linguistically diverse (CLD) students, 102, 104
defined, 36, 38, 39
documents for, 79
employment vision, 84, 97, 100
student participation in, 60, 61, 64
in transition assessment, 179, 180, 325
Individualized transition plan (ITP), 161, 305, 317
Individualized transition profile (portfolio), 193–194
Individuals with Disabilities Education Act (1975), 30, 32, 37
Individuals with Disabilities Education Act (1983), 32, 37
Individuals with Disabilities Education Act (1990), 32, 35–37, 179, 268
Individuals with Disabilities Education Act (1997), 36–38, 60, 161, 179, 268

SUBJECT INDEX

Individuals with Disabilities Education Act (2004), 37, 38–39, 79, 161, 179, 180, 305, 306–307
Individuals with Disabilities Education Act (IDEA), 5, 27, 33–40
Informal methods of transition assessment, 189–192
Informational interviewing, 204
Institution for Educational Leadership, 291
Interagency and interdisciplinary teams, 136–175
   case studies in dialogue, 166–170
   case study overviews, 146–153
   civic engagement, 138
   cofacilitation, 164–165
   collaboration, 161–163, 181
   communication, 161, 163
   community connections, 138
   community development, 137–140
   community-level teamwork, 140–143
   community needs and demographics, 146
   core elements of community development, 143–145
   defined, 139, 140
   dialogue, 163–166
   dialogue versus debate, 172
   Facilitator's Handbook, The (Justice and Jamieson), 143
   forming stage, 146–147
   norming stage, 150–153
   planning, 16
   social capital, 139
   storming stage, 147–150
   team leaders, 143
   teamwork concepts, 137, 139–140
   teamwork stages and milestones, 140–143
   University Centers for Excellence in Developmental Disabilities Education, Research, and Service (UCEDDERS), 140–153
   work plans (action plans), 145
Interdisciplinary research, 13. *See also* Interagency and interdisciplinary teams
Interest inventories, 93
Intergenerational status of students with disabilities, 7

International Association for the Evaluation of Educational Achievement, 308
Internships within community businesses, 205, 212–214, 323
ITP. *See* Individualized transition plan

Jenkins Parish (case study), 146–153
Job Accommodation Network (JAN), 274
Job carving, 238
Job coaches, 113–114
Job Corps Centers, 42
Job interviews, 234–235
Job modifications, 114
Job options, 79
Job placement, 226–236
   analysis survey, 241–243
   defined, 227
   overview of, 228
   sample evaluation form for supervisor and employee, 233
   sample work performance form for supervisor and employee, 236
Job placement steps, 227–235
   Step 1) identifying community placement options, 227–229
   Step 2) undertaking a community placement survey, 229
   Step 3) evaluating employment opportunities, 230–231
   Step 4) matching candidates and jobs, 231
   Step 5) redesigning jobs, 232
   Step 6) developing employer expectations, 232–234
   Step 7) communicating with parents and guardians, 234
   Step 8) interviewing for the job, 234–235
   Step 9) establishing a work performance evaluation form, 235
Job redesign, 232, 236–240
   assistive technology, 239
   benefits of, 239–240
   defined, 236–237
   job carving, 238
   job restructuring, 237–238
   job sharing, 238–239
   job site modification, 237
   natural supports, 239

Job restructuring, 237–238
Job shadowing, 203–204, 323
Job sharing, 114, 238–239
Job site modification, 237
Job site self-evaluation assessment, 101
Job site visits, 84, 87
Job training, 39
Job Training Partnership Act (1982), 30, 32
Job Training Reform Act (1993), 32, 42
Job tryouts, 4, 205
Joint contractual relationship, 214–215
Julie (case study), 80–81, 83–93

Kennedy, John F., 28

Labor regulations, 207–209
LaFollette Act, 28, 32
Late adolescence, 3
Laws. *See* Transition legislation and policy
Learning, situated or contextual learning, 202, 217
Legislation. *See* Transition legislation and policy
Leisure activities, harmful, 6
Life decisions, 179
Lifelong learning opportunities, 27
Life skills program, 94
Linguistically diverse students, 102
Living services, supported, 138

Mandatory education-related services, 5, 27
Medicaid, 41–42, 43
Medicare, 41–42, 43
Mental retardation, President's Panel on, 28
Mentoring, 209, 253, 305, 323
Middle adolescence, 3
Middle school career exploration, 83–84, 93–98
Middle schools, 3–4
   transition services in, 181
Minorities, students with disabilities, 268
Mobility barriers, 237
Multicultural issues in transition, 305

SUBJECT INDEX

National Center on Educational
  Outcomes (NCEO) model,
  185–186, 311–315
  conceptual model of outcomes, 312
  domains of, 311–312
  outcomes at grade 8, end of school,
    and postschool, 313–314
National Council on Disability, 162
National Longitudinal Transition
  Study (NLTS) of Special
  Education Students
  (1987–1991), 7, 201, 291, 308
National Longitudinal Transition
  Study-2 (NLTS2), 4, 7, 10, 308
National Service Trust Act (1994),
  32, 42
Native Americans, 102
Natural supports in the workplace,
  184, 239, 250–265
  benefits of, 253–254
  community supports, 261
  defined, 252–253, 257
  developing natural supports,
    254–255
  organizational supports, 259
  outcomes of, 255–257
  personal and family supports, 261
  physical supports, 259
  social service supports, 260–261
  social supports, 259–260
  and the SPANS model, 251, 254,
    255, 257–258
  traditional and revised employer
    contact scripts, 254
  traditional and supports-based
    perspectives for
    employment, 252
  training supports, 260
  types of, 258–262
New Freedom Initiative, 43
Next S.T.E.P., 193
No Child Left Behind (NCLB) Act
  of 2001, 35, 38, 39–40,
  268, 305
Norming stage in teams, 150–153

Occupational Handbook
  website, 83
Office of Career Education, 29
Office of Special Education and
  Rehabilitation Services
  (OSERS), 31–33, 268

Office of Special Education Programs
  (OSEP), U.S. Department of
  Education, 8
Online assessments, 83
On-the-job supports, 100
On-the-job training, 4, 202
Opportunity-enhancement approach
  in person-centered career
  planning, 63–64
Organizational model for transition
  process, 13–16
Organizational supports, 259
OSERS (Office of Special Education
  and Rehabilitation Services),
  31–33
OSERS transition model, 33
Outcomes
  domains in transition assessment,
    185–186
  National Center on Educational
    Outcomes (NCEO) model,
    185–186, 311–315
  of natural supports in the
    workplace, 255–257
  poor postschool outcomes, 308
  postschool for students with
    disabilities, 267–269
  and processes, 35
  Transition-Post School Outcomes
    Team, 162
  of transition process, 179
  See also Evaluation practices for
    transition planning; Transition
    assessment

Paid work, 202, 208–209, 323
Parental outreach program, 94
Parent forums, 119
Parent resource networks, 122
Parents, 110–133, 181
  benefits from involvement of,
    112–113
  college nights, 121
  communicating with parents and
    guardians, 234
  community contacts, 122
  community transitions, 125
  district-level strategies, 123–126
  parent connections and support
    groups, 122–123
  parent forums, 119
  parent resource networks, 122

problems in promoting positive
  outcomes, 115
recommended practices for
  working with, 114–126
resource fairs, 119, 121
roles in transition, 113
school-level strategies, 119–123
and Social Security Income (SSI), 322
student-level strategies, 115–119
transition coalitions, 123–126
transition councils, 121–122
transition tips for parents, 117
transition tips for teachers, 120–121
PASS (Social Security Plan for
  Achieving Self Sufficiency), 260
Pathways to self-determination
  model, 292–298
People-first language, 30
People of color, 102
  culturally and linguistically diverse
    (CLD) students, 102
People with disabilities
  employment of, 6–7, 57, 114
  See also Students with disabilities
Personal and family supports, 261
Personal and social adjustment in the
  National Center on
  Educational Outcomes (NCEO)
  model, 311
Person-centered approaches in
  transition assessment,
  182–184, 193
Person-centered career planning,
  56–77
  active student involvement, 60–61
  antecedent cue regulation (picture
    cues), 69–70
  capacity-enhancement approach,
    63–64
  goal setting, 61, 62,
    65–66
  independence-interdependence
    continuum, 64
  opportunity-enhancement
    approach, 63–64
  person-centered planning, 62–64
  problem solving, 70
  recommended practices, 64–71
  self-determination defined, 58–59
  self-directed learning, 61–62
  self-evaluation, 67–68
  self-instruction, 68–69

Person-centered career planning (cont.)
  self-monitoring, 66–67
  self-reinforcement, 68
  teaching skills for, 64–65
  transition planning, 60–61, 62, 63
  volition in self-determination, 58–59
Philosophical doctrine of determinism, 58
Physical barriers, 237
Physical health in the National Center on Educational Outcomes (NCEO) model, 311
Physical supports, 259
Picture cues (antecedent cue regulation), 69–70
Placement. *See* Job placement
Placement in organizational model for transition, 14–16
Placement services, 115
Planning Alternative Tomorrows with Hope (PATH), 193
Planning in organizational model for transition, 14–15
Policy. *See* Transition legislation and policy
Policy group views on transition legislation and policy, 34–35
Political climate factors in transition legislation and policy, 34
Postsecondary education, 3, 4
  instructors, 61
  part-time while in last year of school eligibility, 215
  students with disabilities in, 27, 267
  students without disabilities entering college, 4, 289
Poverty in students with disabilities, 4, 57, 202, 268
Preparation in organizational model for transition, 14–15
Presence and participation in the National Center on Educational Outcomes (NCEO) model, 311
Problem solving in person-centered career planning, 70
Professional advocacy groups, 35
Professional guidelines for transition assessment, 186–188
Program evaluation. *See* Evaluation practices for transition planning; Transition assessment

Protective factors, 268
Psychometric instruments, 188–189
Public accommodation and services, 40

Quality-of-life domains in transition assessment, 183–184
Quality-of-life in transition legislation and policy, 42–43
Quality-of-Life Questionnaire, 192–193
Quality-of-life satisfaction, 289

Real Choice Systems, Change Grants for Community Living, 43
Real-life work and community experiences, 162
Rehabilitation Act (1973), 29, 32
Rehabilitation Act Amendments (1992), 32, 40
Rehabilitation Act Amendments (1998), 161–162
Rehabilitation engineering, 114
Residential independence, 5
Resource fairs, 119, 121
Responsibility and independence in the National Center on Educational Outcomes (NCEO) model, 311

Satisfaction in the National Center on Educational Outcomes (NCEO) model, 311
School-based jobs, 204
Schools
  individualist school society, 103
  middle, 3–4
  postsecondary, 3, 4
  problems in promoting transition activities, 115
  specialized employment training, 3, 4
  staffing for transition services, 6
  transition services in, 164
  White school culture, 102
  See also Elementary schools; High schools; Middle schools; Postsecondary education; Work-based learning
School-sponsored community jobs, 202, 205–206
School-sponsored enterprises, 204–205

School-to-Work Opportunities Act (1994), 32, 268
Secondary special education, 5, 13–14
Secretary's Commission on Achieving Necessary Skills (SCANS), 308
Self-advocacy, 58, 61, 104
Self-determination, 14, 58
  defined, 58–59
  individualism and collectivism in, 103, 104
  pathways to self-determination model, 292–298
  skills for, 94
  See also Dropout prevention
Self-Directed Employment handbook, 99, 100
Self-directed learning, 61–62
Self-evaluation, 67–68
Self-instruction, 68–69
Self-monitoring, 66–67
Self-reinforcement, 68
Service groups, 138
Sheltered workshops, 114, 216
Situated or contextual learning, 202, 217
Smith-Fess Act (1920), 28, 32
Smith-Hughes Act (1917), 28, 32
Smith-Sears Act (1918), 28, 32
Social adjustment, 5
Social capital, 139
Social change organizations, 138
Social isolation of students with disabilities, 5
Social Security Administration, 162
Social Security Income (SSI), 322
Social Security Insurance (SSI) benefits, 168, 169, 170, 322
Social Security Plan for Achieving Self Sufficiency (PASS), 260
Social service supports, 260–261
Soft skills and employer expectations, 320–321
SPANS model and natural supports in the workplace, 251, 254, 255, 257–258
Special education, 202, 227
  dropout problem in, 290
  eligibility for, 305, 306
  purpose of, 79
  secondary, 5, 13–14
Specialized employment training, 3, 4
Special Olympics, 138

SUBJECT INDEX

Standardized, norm-referenced assessment methods, 188
Storming stage in teams, 147–150
Student initiated jobs, 202
Student involvement, planning, and assessment, 55
Students
  actively participating in transition plans, 27
  culturally and linguistically diverse (CLD) students, 102
  developmental levels, 185
  interests in employment vision, 79
  work-based learning projects, 203
  See also Adolescence
Students with disabilities, 4–6
  arrest rates, 5
  dissatisfaction with life situation, 57
  dropping out of school, 4, 201, 268
  employment-related participation after age 14, 10, 12–13
  high school enrollments, graduation, and dropouts, 8–10
  interests, skills, and limits of, 79
  intergenerational status, 7
  involvement in transition planning, 180, 181, 184
  minority, 268
  postschool outcomes, 267–269
  postsecondary education, 5
  poverty in, 4, 57, 202, 268
  residential independence, 5
  services in high schools, 6
  social isolation, 5
  theories about training, 6–7
  unemployment or underemployment, 5
  work experience of, 6–7
  See also People with disabilities; Person-centered career planning; Transition model
Students without disabilities, 5–6
  entering college, 4, 289
  high school enrollments, graduation, and dropouts, 10, 11
Subcontract or vendor relationships, 215
Substance abuse, 268
Summative evaluation, 318. *See also* Evaluation practices for transition planning
Supported employment, 113–114, 138

Supported living services, 138
Support in organizational model for transition, 15–16
Support networks, 184
Synthesis in pathways to self-determination model, 292–293, 294

"Take your child to work day," 83
Teaching skills for person-centered career planning, 64–65
Team leaders, 143
Teamwork
  concepts of, 137, 139–140
  for effective transition services, 116
  stages and milestones of, 140–143
  and values, 105
  See also Interagency and interdisciplinary teams
Technology-Related Assistance for Individuals With Disabilities (Tech Act) of 1988 and 2004, 42–43
Tech-preps in work-based learning, 207
Telecommunications, 40
Thoreau, Henry David, *Walden*, 216
Ticket to Work and Work Incentives Improvement Act of 1999, 41–42
Traditional and revised employer contact scripts, 254
Traditional and supports-based perspectives for employment, 252
Training supports, 260
Transition assessment, 178–199
  Adult Lifestyles Planning Cycle, 183–184
  career development models, 182
  commercial transition inventories, 192–193
  consensus in, 185–186
  defined, 182
  developmental levels, 185
  formal methods, 188–189
  IDEA 2004, 179, 180–181
  in IEP, 179, 180
  individualized transition profile (portfolio), 193–194
  informal methods, 189–192
  legal requirements for, 179–181
  longitudinal approaches to, 181–184
  methods of, 188–193

National Center on Educational Outcomes (NCEO) model, 185–186
Next S.T.E.P., 193
outcome domains, 185–186
outcomes of transition process, 179
person-centered approaches, 182–184, 193
Planning Alternative Tomorrows with Hope (PATH), 193
professional guidelines, 186–188
quality-of-life domains, 183–184
Quality of Life Questionnaire, 192–193
transition planning, 179, 180, 190–192
Transition Planning Inventory (TPI), 192
See also Evaluation practices for transition planning
Transition legislation and policy, 24–53
  appropriate access and accommodations, 29–30
  civil rights law (ADA), 40
  early legislation, 27–31
  education, 35–40
  emergence of initiatives for youth with disabilities, 31–33
  employment and training, 40–42
  evidence-based practice, 27
  expansion in 1990s and 2000s, 33–43
  funds to develop transition models and practices, 31
  Individuals with Disabilities Education Act (IDEA), 27, 35–40
  legal requirements for assessment, 179–181
  list of legislative acts, 32
  mandated practice, 27
  policy group views, 34–35
  political climate factors, 34
  quality of life, 42–43
  students actively participating in transition plans, 27
  support and training for veterans with disabilities, 28
  training and rehabilitation for persons with disabilities, 28–29
  See also specific legislative acts

Transition planning, 179, 180, 190–192
  definition of transition, 306
  IDEA 2004 changes regarding transition, 306–307
  process of, 305–307
  research findings, 305
  See also Evaluation practices for transition planning
Transition Planning Inventory (TPI), 192
Transition-Post School Outcomes Team, 162
Transition support, 266–287
  background and statistics, 267–269
  case study and application of model, 278–280
  choice and decision making of students, 276–277
  competence of students, 275–278
  environmental support, 271–275
  models for, 268
  overview of model, 271–278
  research to practice development of model, 269–271
  self-determination of students, 276
  social interaction of students, 277–278
  social support, 273, 274–275
  strengths of students, 275–276
  Transition Handbook, The (Hughes and Carter), 271, 281
Transition to adult roles, 2–23
  classes in employment vision, 84
  community transitions, 125
  organizational model, 13–16
  in person-centered career planning, 60–61, 62, 63
  placement services, 115
  problems in promoting transition activities, 115
  services defined in IDEA 1997, 36–38
  services defined in IDEA 1990, 36
  staffing in schools, 6
  tips for parents, 117
  tips for teachers, 120–121
  transition coalitions, 123–126
  transition councils, 121–122
  transition planning, 60–61, 62, 63
  transition services defined, 161–162
Transportation, 40

Underemployment, 5, 308
Unemployment, 5, 267, 289, 290, 291, 308
University Centers for Excellence in Developmental Disabilities Education, Research, and Service (UCEDDERS), 140–153
Unpaid work, 207–208
U.S. Department of Education, Office of Special Education Programs (OSEP), 8
U.S. Department of Labor, Bureau of Labor Statistics' Occupational Handbook website, 83

Vendor relationships, 215
Veterans with disabilities, 28
Violence, 268
Vocational assessment portfolio, 99, 100
Vocational courses, 4
Vocational Education Act (1963), 28, 31, 32
Vocational Education Amendments (1976), 30, 32
Vocational interest portfolio, 97
Vocational preference instructional and assessment process, 79
Vocational rehabilitation, 162, 227
Vocational Rehabilitation Amendments (1954), 28, 32
Vocational Rehabilitation Amendments (1967), 29, 32
Vocational Rehabilitation Amendments (1968), 29, 32
Vocational rehabilitation counselors, 61
Volition in self-determination, 58–59
Volunteerism, 138, 207–208, 323

Wage and hour standards, 209
Walden (Thoreau), 216
White school culture, 102
Will, Madeliene, 31
Will's bridges model, 268
Work
  paid, 202, 208–209, 323
  sheltered, 114
  unpaid, 207–208
Work-based learning, 200–223
  academic credit for work experiences, 212
  administrative logistics, 211
  apprenticeships, 205
  assistive technology, 211
  benefits of, 201–202
  career academies, 206–207
  chambers of commerce, 213
  child labor restrictions, 209
  citizenship and community participation, 201–202
  community rehabilitation programs, 216
  Dewean tradition, 216–217
  employer resources, 202
  facilitation strategies, 210
  Fair Labor Standards Act, 108–109, 207
  field trips or industry tours, 203
  hazardous occupations, 209
  informational interviewing, 204
  instruction in, 209–210
  integrating work experience into the high school curriculum, 206–207
  interagency collaboration, 214–216
  internal versus contracted employment services, 215
  internships within community businesses, 205, 212–214
  job shadowing, 203–204
  job try-outs, 205
  joint contractual relationship, 214–215
  labor regulations, 207–209
  mentoring, 209
  on-the-job training, 202
  opportunity components, 322–324
  paid work, 202, 208–209
  research on school-sponsored work experiences, 201
  school-based jobs, 204
  school-sponsored community jobs, 202, 205–206
  school-sponsored enterprises, 204–205
  situated or contextual learning, 202, 217
  student initiated jobs, 202
  student projects, 203
  subcontract or vendor relationships, 215
  tech-preps, 207

SUBJECT INDEX

training and support provisions, 209–211
types of work experiences, 202–206
unpaid work, 207–208
volunteer work, 207–208
wage and hour standards, 209
work-based instruction, 209–210
work exposure, 203–204
work study placements, 205
written training plans, 209
See also Schools
Work experience history, 6. *See also* Work-based learning
Work experience of students with disabilities, 6–7
Work exposure, 203–204
Workforce Development Act of 1995, 42
Workforce Investment Act (WIA) of 1998, 41
Working with parents. *See* Parents
Work plans (action plans), 145
Work-study opportunities, 12
Work study placements, 205
Written training plans, 209